Bob Jones University
hereby gratefully acknowledges
a gift of $25 from

Miss Pam Hansel

for the building of
the new library addition
dedicated September, 1980,
to the glory of God.

Music Librarianship:
A Practical Guide

second edition

by
E.T. BRYANT

with the assistance of
GUY A. MARCO

The Scarecrow Press, Inc.
Metuchen, N.J., & London
1985

Excerpt from "Qualifications of a Music Librarian," Journal of Education for Librarianship (a publication of the Association for Library and Information Science Education), Vol. 15, No. 1 (Summer 1974): 53-59, reprinted by permission of the Music Library Association and the ALISE. This article also appeared, under the same title, in Fontes artis musicas, XXI (1974):139-43, and in College Music Symposium, XV (1975): 87-93.

Excerpt from Ruth Watanabe's "American Music Libraries and Music Librarianship: An Overview in the Eighties," Notes: The Quarterly Journal of the Music Library Association, Vol. 38, No. 2 (December 1981): 239-256, reprinted by permission of the author and publisher.

The first edition was published by James Clarke & Co., Ltd., London, and Hafner Publishing Co., Inc., New York, 1959.

Library of Congress Cataloging in Publication Data

Bryant, E. T. (Eric Thomas)
  Music librarianship.

  Bibliography: p.
  Includes index.
  1. Music librarianship. 2. Music--Bibliography.
3. Cataloging of music. 4. Classification--Music.
5. Sound recordings libraries. I. Marco, Guy A.
II. Title.
ML111.B83 1985   026'.78   84-27731
ISBN 0-8108-1785-3

FOR K. C. HARRISON, O.B.E., F.L.A.,

Friend and professional colleague for nearly fifty years

CONTENTS

FOREWORD

The second edition of Eric Thomas Bryant's Music Librarianship: A Practical Guide is a most welcome addition to library literature. It includes discussion of the many facets of administration, acquisition and collection development, cataloging and classification, and reference and reader services essential to the maintenance of music materials in libraries. As the author states in his preface, "This book is intended primarily for the non-specialist librarian and for the student of librarianship"; it presupposes a knowledge of the basic principles and tools of the profession for a complete understanding of its contents. Given this prerequisite, the reader will find an extraordinary wealth of information, both practical and theoretical, to put into operation in a real-life situation or to consider philosophically in a scholarly fashion.

The demand for this sort of book has been steadily increasing during the past few decades, as public and academic librarians, in response to popular interest, have incorporated musicalia into their collections or have developed such resources into full-fledged music departments. Many generalists have been obliged to administer a corpus of specialized materials--scores and recordings which are idiosyncratic in both their format and content and which require processes that differ noticeably from those ordinarily employed in the treatment of books and periodicals. The author has wisely placed such matters into their proper perspective in the context of the broader scope of general librarianship.

Although the author addresses his remarks primarily to British public librarians, for it is they who have borne the brunt of the greatest pressure of community demand, he also discusses broad topics of universal concern from which public and academic librarians in both Canada and the United States may also profit. His discussions run the gamut from outlining basic procedures to consideration of such highly technical problems as generating cataloging and classification codes. Thus,

both the non-specialist librarian being initiated into a music
collection and the advanced scholar of library science research-
ing underlying philosophies have, in their divergent ways,
much to gain from this book.

  The initial chapter on Music Library Administration is
practical, all-inclusive, straightforward, and logically presented. The second, on Reference Books and Periodicals,
provides an overview of basic bibliography for a small- to
medium-sized collection, a list of tools useful for selection
and acquisition, and an introduction to reference-work. Most
impressive is Chapter III, in which the author defines cataloging and analyzes and compares a number of cataloging
codes, both national and international, currently used in the
English-speaking countries. Likewise, Chapter IV, on Classification, contains an excellent study of the half-dozen major
classification codes most often found today. The last chapter,
a complete vade mecum on sound recordings, deals with the
introduction, development, maintenance, and administration of
all types of recorded sound. Finally, there is an extensive
bibliography of more than two hundred entries and a key to
references cited in the text.

  The author has accomplished what few others, even
the most intrepid, have dared to attempt by writing a course
of study in music librarianship in one volume. With its careful consideration of North American and British terminologies,
practices, and library governance, and philosophy, Music Librarianship is required reading for all practitioners, as well
as profitable collateral reading for students of librarianship.
Moreover, although the author does not touch upon music in
large university and research collections, even the most experienced and sophisticated specialist is bound to find something of interest and profit. And finally, the author's fluent,
readable style attests to the fact that good library administration is a human activity.

                              Ruth Watanabe
                              June 1985

PREFACE

This book is intended primarily for the non-specialist librarian and for the student of librarianship. It is hoped that
there will also be some material of value for the qualified
and experienced music librarian but, if this is present, it
should be regarded as a bonus. It would be presumptuous
to expect more for, like my British predecessors in this subject area (J. D. Brown and L. R. McColvin), I have always
been basically a generalist--but one with an insatiable interest in music.

The first edition [33] took nine years to prepare; this
one has occupied fifteen. There are three reasons for this
extremely slow process. As work progressed, it became
clear that my original optimistic assumption that only a limited amount of rewriting would be necessary proved completely erroneous. Very little of the original text has remained unaltered; at a guess it is less than 5 percent.
Secondly, the task of writing has been done in the spare
time while holding a full-time post; retirement gave more
time, but a move well away from any major city proved to
be a considerable handicap. The final drawback has been
my continuing inability to put my ideas on paper in a form
that, upon a second reading a few days later, I still find
acceptable. As a result, none of the text has been re-
written fewer than three times--an expensive weakness in
both time and stationery.

There have been few general surveys in this field
since the first edition of 1959. Mention should be made of
the revision of McColvin & Reeves' Music Libraries made by
Jack Dove [129]. The Music Library Association's Manual of
Music Librarianship [23] and the anthology Reader in Music
Librarianship [24] (both works edited by Carol June Bradley) might be regarded, in parts, as textbooks. A useful
gathering of articles appeared in the Encyclopedia of Library
and Information Science [133]. Certain contributions to these

collective works will be cited later in appropriate chapters.
Much more has been published on sound recordings, particularly in periodicals.

Friends have gently suggested that it is no longer possible for one person to write a good book on music librarian-
ship--they claim that it needs a team of specialists. This
could well hold a large element of truth, but it must be
clear I consider a one-author approach to have its virtues,
not least among them, I hope, is a general consistency of
outlook (although I have occasionally changed my views over
the past twenty-five years on specific points), and also a
demonstration that the non-specialist can assimilate appreciably more than a basic knowledge of this field. Again, it
has been suggested to me that some textual points are obvious. This may be true, but it should never be forgotten
that what is self-evident to one reader may be a necessary
explanation to another.

Reviews of the first edition were noticeably generous,
none more so than that by the late Harold Spivacke (then
Chief of the Music Division of the Library of Congress)
[207]. His two main criticisms were "Nowhere is there any
discussion of the work of the reference librarian ..." and
"What is strange is that Bryant does not discuss at all the
problems relating to the assignment of special numbers to
individual items--'cuttering' is the term used in American
library jargon...." It is a matter of personal regret that
Dr. Spivacke is no longer alive to see that his first point
has evoked some response in the pages that follow; a brief
section has been included to rectify, to some degree, the
previous omission. On "cuttering" however, there is still
nothing, since this is an exercise I have never undertaken
nor am I aware of any British library that has!

With a text written and revised over a very long period, trying to keep it updated has been a major problem. In
general, the typescript was completed in the middle of 1977,
but some considerable amendment has been made since that
date up to the middle of 1983. As with the first edition, I
have found it necessary to get in touch with many friends
and colleagues for information, help, and advice. It has
always been readily forthcoming, and I am extremely grate-
ful for the assistance. I am sure that my list of acknowledgements is far from complete, and I offer my apologies to

all those whose names have been inadvertently omitted. I
accept responsibility of all opinions expressed, except those
that are clearly direct or indirect quotations or reflect the
views of others. It is probably inevitable that the occasional mistake or repetition has been overlooked; for these I
must assume any discredit.

ACKNOWLEDGEMENTS

Reviewing the second edition of Donald Jay Grout's A Short
History of Opera, Elaine Brody thought that "Revising an
earlier text is a very ungratifying experience for any author" [29]. This is, perhaps, too pessimistic a claim, yet
it must almost certainly apply to anyone who acts as unpaid
consultant, adviser, and stimulus. I have been extremely
fortunate in that John Bryon (formerly of the Dept. of Library & Information Studies at Liverpool Polytechnic), who
did so much for the first edition of this book, has been almost as helpful with the present revision. His many other
commitments limited the time he could spare, but I continued
to receive a stream of comments, queries, and suggestions
as the various drafts travelled back and forth in regularly
amended versions, and I owe him very considerable thanks.

A major expression of gratitude must also go to my
former colleague at Manchester Polytechnic, John F. Farrow.
He was particularly helpful with the chapters concerning
cataloguing and classification, noticeably improving the text
in a number of places. For good measure, he assisted in
proofreading--but must not be blamed for errors that remain. The chapter on sound recording libraries incorporates a number of helpful ideas and comments from George
Saddington, Deputy Borough Librarian of the London Borough of Havering, a man highly experienced in this aspect
of public library service. Equally expert in a different way,
and just as helpful, has been Ivan March of the Long Playing Record Library Ltd., of Blackpool. H. David Goodwin,
a former colleague and now with Cheshire Libraries & Museums, has made a number of suggestions. He proved particularly helpful in providing appropriate examples from the
world of pop music recordings.

Ursula Birkett (Salford City Libraries) read the first

and last chapters in one of their several drafts and made welcome suggestions for improving some phraseology. Vernon Hyde (Manchester Cultural Services) cheerfully shared his knowledge of periodicals dealing with the more popular end of the musical spectrum, and helpful comments in the same field were made by David Duckett (Lancashire Libraries). Warren McKay, Head of the Music Section, Cataloging Division of the Library of Congress, tried to ensure the factual accuracy of the section on LC music catalogues, while Patrick Mills of the British Library provided similar checks for two of its roles--as a register of deposits and as a user of a classification scheme. These two gentlemen are not responsible, however, for comments and criticisms, which are entirely my own. W. A. Munford supplied authoritative information on the National Library for the Blind.

For photographs promptly supplied upon request some years ago, my thanks are due to Westminster City Libraries, to the London Borough of Bromley Public Libraries, to the City of Manchester Cultural Services (also to permit reproduction of data label) and to the Public Library of Cincinnati and Hamilton County, Ohio, USA.

Some details about the Music Library Association were sent to me by its then President, Dena J. Epstein; types of reference library queries received by the Henry Watson Music Library were discussed with me by Leonard Duck, the Music Librarian there. I also used the library of the Royal Northern College of Music (Librarian: Anthony Hodges), and these Manchester collections were invaluable for checking sources and references. The section on rebinding was read and amended by Mr. K. J. Atkinson of Messrs. Dunn & Wilson Ltd.

My appreciation must be recorded to Jean Snape, who typed much of the copy from which the book has been printed. She was delightfully accurate, and also quick to spot discrepancies, ambiguous statements, and downright errors. I could not have asked for more. Finally, thanks and apologies to those many other persons who have helped in any way, but whose names were not set out above. My appreciation for their efforts remains undimmed.

E. T. Bryant

A NOTE ON THE SECOND EDITION

As a distinct discipline, music librarianship--born of musicology and library science--is fifty-four years old at this writing. (I think of June 22, 1931, as the birthdate, with the establishment on that day of the Music Library Association.) A substantial scholarly and technical literature has emerged in that half-century, including historical studies, cataloging codes, journals, directories, and so on; the typical manifestation of a learned profession at work. What has been strikingly absent is a promulgation of comprehensive manuals of practice: volumes intended for the total guidance of the neophyte or for the reference requirements of the more experienced music librarian. In fact, there seems to be just one example of the genre: E. T. Bryant's Music Librarianship, issued in 1959. An exemplar as well as an example, it has met the needs of the field so well that competitors have not come forth to challenge it. Finally it is Bryant himself who offers us a new manual, one that--like its progenitor--will surely leave music librarians wondering what else could possibly be said about the topics that it illuminates.

I was honored to have a share in the preparation of this second edition, for both the book and its author are old friends. A word about my role seems to be in order. When I first saw the manuscript a couple of years ago, I suggested that it might have even more impact on the profession if it could be somewhat internationalized. North American readers in particular had noted the overriding British coloration of the first edition. So with the consent of author and publisher I did extend the frame of reference to bring in more events and bibliographic citations from the west side of the Atlantic. What I wish to emphasize is that apart from that kind of contribution my function has been purely editorial and supplemental. The intellectual task was Bryant's alone, and he needed no assistance from anyone with that.

Guy A. Marco
Washington, D.C.
April 1985

Chapter I

MUSIC LIBRARY ADMINISTRATION

INTRODUCTION

In 1950, Ralph Vaughan Williams wrote: "I am very glad to
see that in late years the public libraries have woken up to
the importance of music as part of our general culture. Many
libraries have a good collection of music scores, but as you
yourselves know, much remains to be done" [222]. It is the
intention of this book to indicate what that service might be,
or what could be provided. The responsibility then lies with
the individual librarian and committee members. The provision of good music is one of our more rewarding activities
and an adequate collection is an asset in any community.

Throughout the book, reference is sometimes made to
large, medium, small and very small public library authorities. The terms are elastic and are perhaps not used as
consistently as they might be but, generally speaking, the
library serving a population of 150,000 or more in a reasonably compact area is considered here as a large library,
75,000 to 150,000 as medium, from 40,000 to 75,000 as small
and below 40,000 as very small. The 1974 local government
reorganization in England and Wales put all the county authorities and nearly all those of the metropolitan districts
into the large category; in most cases, however, the counties have divided their library administrative areas into divisions or districts, which may well be considered to be the
effective units when considering suggestions and recommendations that are made in this book. Scottish authorities
vary much more widely in size and the thinly populated
areas of both Scotland and Wales present administrative
problems which are possibly more akin to those found in

1

some countries outside Britain where the very small authority is frequently found.

An alternative method of classification, particularly
relevant to academic and college music libraries is by size
of stock. Ruth Watanabe has categorized libraries with a
stock of up to 5,000 volumes of music material as small,
those with between 5,000 and 20,000 volumes as medium,
and those with over 20,000 as large [227].

HISTORY AND GENERAL COMMENTS

"A Catalogue of Standard Music Deposited by Way of Loan in
the Warrington Library and Museum by Mr. Marsh" was printed as an appendix to the catalogue of books published in 1850
[226]. It contained 123 items loaned by John Fitchett Marsh
(1818-1880), Town Clerk of Warrington (then in Lancashire,
since 1974 part of Cheshire), for whom an entry may be
found in The Dictionary of National Biography, where he is
described as an "antiquary." This remarkable man's other
claim to library immortality is that he gave practical evidence
before the Royal Commission of 1849; the report of the Com-
missioners led to the passing of the first Public Libraries
Act (1850) in Britain. Liverpool, some twenty miles away
from Warrington, was the second library to lend music, from
1859; the idea slowly spread to other British libraries. In
the USA, the first public library to collect printed music as
a matter of policy was Boston, which acquired the de Kou-
delka collection in 1858; but Brooklyn appears to have been
the library to initiate circulation of scores, in 1882 [131].
There is evidence that Brooklyn was charging fees to borrowers of music during this period. See [121], in which
there is an illuminating discussion of music rental libraries
in the USA and Europe. Charles Ammi Cutter, at Northampton, Mass., wrote in 1896:

> Following the lead of Brooklyn, several public librar-
> ies have in the last decade put on their shelves works
> of music to be circulated like books. As they have
> reported that this has given their patrons great sat-
> isfaction, I seized upon an opportunity which offered
> itself lately to buy on peculiarly advantageous terms,
> the complete works in Breitkopf & Härtel's well-edited
> and clearly printed editions, of Beethoven, Chopin,

Grétry, Mozart, Palestrina, Schubert, Schumann,
Schütz and Johann Strauss, 312 volumes in all.
Lassus, Mendelssohn and Wagner (both pianoforte
and full score editions) will soon be added. I had
already picked up the Bach Society's edition of
Bach, and the Händel Society's edition of Händel,
in 119 volumes, a few shelves of miscellaneous music, and some of the publications of the Musical Antiquarian Society, and the Plainsong and Medieval
Music Society. You will see that I have chosen for
first purchase the standard composers.... [74]

The population of Northampton, it should be remarked, was
fewer than 30,000.

Although starting some thirty years later, American libraries quickly outstripped British libraries in the size of
stock and the provision of music departments. The penny
rate limitation in Britain for library expenditure meant that
very little money was available for books, and music with its
limited appeal and need for expensive binding suffered in
consequence. Some enterprising advertising agents presented bound volumes of music, interleaved with advertisements, to certain libraries, which must have been both dis-
concerting and infuriating to the performer. In 1893 James
Duff Brown wrote his pamphlet "Guide to the Formation of a
Music Library." This "tract" has four pages of text and
eighteen pages of recommended works, arranged under thirty-
five headings with books and scores in a single sequence. It
is obvious from Brown's comments that many libraries at that
time had no music stocks and the pamphlet was intended as
a spur, while the subject lists were "to rectify ... library
formation on the happy-go-lucky principle of selection by
instinct instead of knowledge ..." [31]. By 1900 there were
87 public libraries in Britain which had some music in stock
[27a, p. 270]. In 1908 Brown was able to say that Music
collections were "in proportion to their extent ... most used
of any class of books, not excepting fiction" [a lecture,
quoted in 131].

From that time, music collections grew fairly steadily
both in number and in size, but the process was a long one.
In the Kenyon Report of 1927 [82], under the heading "Urban library practice" in Table LXXIV--"Special collections"--
has a separate line for Music. From this, it can be seen that

fifty-eight County Boroughs, sixteen Metropolitan Boroughs,
forty-four Municipal Boroughs, thirty-nine Urban Districts
(but no Parish Councils which maintained independent public library services) had scores in stock. The total of 157
would represent less than half of the library authorities then
existing.

It is perhaps worth quoting from the text of the report, since the comments have a timeless ring. On page
140, paragraph 400, we may read:

> There are certain types of library provision which
> present special problems. Among these must be men-
> tioned music scores and sets of plays. Musical and
> dramatic societies experience the same difficulties as
> the adult education movement in obtaining the multi-
> ple copies which represent their particular need, and
> only the largest libraries can hope to supply them
> out of local resources. Music collections naturally
> represent a common feature of local library provision;
> we have a note of 157 urban authorities which main-
> tain collections, and several of the new country li-
> braries are adopting the same policy. Most of these
> are very small in extent and cannot hope to meet
> fully the needs of choral and orchestral societies.
> Others, such as the Henry Watson Music Library at
> Manchester and the John B. Camm Library at Bourne-
> mouth are of great value and importance....
>   A music library naturally offers very special prob-
> lems in regard to classification, cataloguing and bind-
> ing into which we cannot enter. But it is clear that
> very few libraries can maintain adequate music collec-
> tions on their own account, and that every argument
> for co-operation and for some form of central library
> as regards the provision of books applies with equal
> force to the provision of music scores.

Today the provision of multiple copies of scores for
choral and orchestral societies remains a considerable problem, although some improvements have been made in the situation. Music cooperation is no better than partial, although
music may be borrowed through the interlending schemes.
Several of the points raised in the report receive consideration in the course of the following pages.

USERS

The first and largest group of potential users in the public
library is that of instrumentalists, who are usually amateurs.
Although the majority of these are likely to be pianists,
there will almost certainly also be performers on stringed
instruments, such as violin, violoncello, or guitar, and of
wind instruments, particularly recorder, oboe, and clarinet.
Second are the singers, either soloists or members of a
group, such as a choir or choral society--a dwindling section in most southern counties of England though still important in such areas as Wales, Lancashire, and Yorkshire, and
parts of Scotland where the old choral tradition remains
strong. The third group is usually the smallest but has an
influence far out-weighing its numbers; this comprises the
music teachers who will normally have their personal libraries but who should find the public library valuable for its
reference books and periodicals, for scores not in their own
collections, and for recommendations to pupils. Fourth, there
are the learners who present a problem of policy upon which
every librarian must reach a decision; this question is discussed a little later. The listener who, although often the
unwilling recipient of music lessons in childhood does not
necessarily play an instrument, but wishes to borrow a score
for fuller enjoyment of a particular performance is the fifth
important category of user. The novice may be able to do
little more than follow the words--yet it is generally possible
to get some idea of the vocal line being sung from the position of the notes on the stave. Those who have some training as singers or instrumentalists will obviously be able to
follow a score with enhanced pleasure and understanding.

Students have not been included as a separate category since many libraries will see nothing of the budding
composer, conductor, professional instrumentalist, or singer,
unless it be out of term time when embryo professionals may
descend on the library with immediate demands for scores
and textbooks, often quite out of the way and unlikely to be
in the library stock.

In contrast to public libraries, those in the academic
and college field will have their own faculty members and
students to serve, and basic coverage in stock will be guided
by the teaching requirements of the institution, although
this should be no more than a starting point.

Until fairly recently the major handicap considered by
libraries was blindness, and special provision was made for
the registered blind. Now, because of medical advances
since World War II, many physically handicapped children
who would formerly have died in infancy, have a normal life
expectancy and are potential users of both public and academic libraries.

Under the provisions of the Chronic Sick and Disabled
Persons Act of 1970, all new buildings in Britain must allow
access for the disabled to all public service areas, and this
will encourage further use of libraries by the handicapped,
particularly as new ones are erected and older ones are modified to conform to the current standards. The Disabled
Living Foundation of London has undertaken a number of
research projects in this field, and will be pleased to offer
advice and information to the interested librarian. Mention
might be made that the Foundation is prepared to suggest
means of getting in touch with handicapped people, and was
responsible for the report Music and the Physically Handicapped, by Irwyn R. Walters, published in 1969 [225]. Attention should be drawn to the fact that the Foundation has
also published a list of music for one-handed pianists (nearly
all for left-handed players, but with a certain number of
items intended for those who have a right hand only), and
with a proportion of the listed items graded according to difficulty [110].

Blindness is a major handicap, but it is one that is
often most successfully overcome by musicians. The National
Library for the Blind has an extensive collection of braille
music and its holdings are listed in three catalogues, available in both printed and braille form [162]. The first volume, dated 1969, is of organ music, with the last two pages
devoted to "Harmonium or American organ" and to "Piano
accordion"--this last a trifle unexpected in this context.
Coverage shows a wide range from an admirable selection of
Bach and the complete organ sonatas of Rheinberger to works
by such Victorian favourites as Hollins and Wolstenholme.
The Catalogue of Piano Music: Including Music Written for
Virginals, Clavichord, Harpsichord and Spinet was issued in
1972. In addition it contains books about music, a handful
of biographies, tutors, and exercises. The third part is of
vocal music, "including also music for stringed instruments
and books about music" (1975). All works are classified by

the <u>Dewey Decimal Classification</u> (14th ed., adapted). The
NLB usually lends direct to readers, but is willing to supply
books and scores through local public libraries, if so requested. It might be added that the publishing of books and
music in Britain (some items using the "solid dot" method) is
carried out by the Royal National Institute for the Blind, a
completely separate body from the NLB, while the British
Talking Book Service is a joint responsibility of the RNIB
and St. Dunstan's.

Looking outside Britain [47] one reads that "The Public Library in Amsterdam is the only one in Europe which
operates, beside a public music library, a music library for
the blind, whose territory extends all over the Netherlands.
The other ten music libraries for the blind in Europe are
all part of special training institutions for the blind" [230a].
If music is requested that is not already available in braille,
the public library supplies the score to be transcribed. The
article points out that "An experienced copyist still needs
from half an hour (for simple music) to one hour (for more
difficult music) to transcribe one page," and that Braille's
own scheme used for music includes more than 200 symbols.
The library has over 6,000 volumes in stock, and also supplies music cassettes for loan to the blind. There is a certain amount of printed, as against hand copied, braille music but this, understandably, requires a fairly substantial
sale to be economic.

Attention is drawn to the activities of the American
Foundation for Overseas Blind, in New York, which is concerned with blind citizens in other countries, and does not
limit its activities to its nationals--a piece of genuine American altruism. The Foundation has issued the <u>International</u>
<u>Catalogue of Music Publications in Braille</u> (1956) arranged in
classified order and limited to instrumental music, emanating
from twenty braille printers. For vocal music, the librarian
has no alternative but to get in touch with these publishers,
not all of whom produce catalogues with any regularity.

In the USA itself, materials may be obtained on free
loan from the Music Section of the National Library Service
for the Blind and Physically Handicapped at the Library of
Congress, Washington. The stock includes braille music
(mainly classical, but with some popular items) for beginners;
there is more difficult material also to college undergraduate

level. Reasonably enough, provision is related to demand.
The stock, therefore, is strongest on piano and organ music, but is much less comprehensive in other areas.

Books in braille cover a wide spectrum, and should be
found generally satisfactory for all but the advanced specialist. Cassettes are, as might be expected, very popular and
the Library of Congress stock includes teaching courses in
piano, organ, and guitar. It is expected that the really keen
and serious student will learn braille and so be able to continue beyond the level available on cassette. For music books
transcribed into braille, examples in score are recorded so
that the student can hear them (an advantage that many
sighted students would appreciate). In the same way, some
tapes of musical analysis have a recording of a performance
to accompany the instruction. The collection also includes
some large-print music, mainly for voices and piano. Use
here is primarily by young beginners with limited vision and
by older people who have partly lost their sight.

As this section has shown, the librarian has many al-
lies if faced with the problem of providing for the blind or
physically handicapped music lover.

ORGANIZATION

The advantages of a music department to professional musicians, students, and the host of people outside those very
limited numbers who have an interest in good music needs
no stressing, yet it may be justifiably asked why music
should receive preferential treatment in the matter of a subject department. There are at least two good reasons:
first, because music comes in a number of different formats,
with books, scores, vocal and instrumental parts, and sound
recordings, related yet diverse forms which present special
problems of integration; and second, that interest in music
(both in and outside the standard classical field) continues
to grow at an appreciable rate and so provides opportunities
for one of our most valuable activities. On the first point,
it is obviously desirable that the music section should be
treated as a single unit which can take into account the special nature of the problem. On the second, good music may
be ranked with the best literature as a cultural force.
Gramophone, radio, television and other forms of sound

recording have brought classical music within the reach of
an immensely greater audience than was possible at the turn
of the century, when only a few (usually well-to-do) listeners had the chance of regularly hearing good music, properly performed, at first hand.

A separate department normally confines itself (at least
in Britain) to books, scores, periodicals, and sound recordings. There was, for many years, a display of musical instruments of historic interest in the Henry Watson music library in Manchester, but these had to be moved elsewhere
in the city when the space they occupied could no longer be
spared in a busy building with constantly increasing demands
made upon it.

Since the first edition of this book, the provision of
facilities for listening to recordings in the music department
has become less unusual, although still far from general.
The availability of a piano, as recommended over the years
by a number of writers on both sides of the Atlantic, is still
a rarity. A genuinely soundproof room is expensive to con-
struct and may well conflict with the current planning belief
that buildings should be designed to allow for maximum internal flexibility. Problems might also arise with fire regulations. The answer, however, could well be in the provision of a "piano" of the kind built by Wurlitzer which has
the standard type of keyboard, is fitted with a pair of headphones to allow the player to hear what he or she is doing,
but which produce no external sounds except for the click of
the keys as they are played. By this means, music can be
tried over by a potential borrower with minimal annoyance to
other users of the department.

Although there are apparently no published recommendations as to the size of a library or that of the population
served before a separate department is considered desirable
or necessary, some consensus can be found. Wheeler and
Goldhor [23a, p. 339] state: "The latest American Library
Directory shows numerous cities of under 100,000 with at
least one subject department, usually Art and Music...."
Later, they advance the view that "Art and music may not
be matters of first importance in a community. Neither are
they sources of employment for more than a small portion of
the population. Nevertheless, these two subjects, because of
their popularity, comprise the most frequently found subject

departments. Art received more attention in previous years,
whereas today music has taken the lead because of the influ-
ences of radio, TV, and musical recordings.... These subjects can be separated from the general library collections
with less penalty than can any other major subjects" [230,
p. 350]. The art library, as a separate entity or one administered in conjunction with a music collection, is outside
the scope of this present work.

Ernest Savage considered that a stock of between
8,000 and 10,000 [195, p. 32] books and scores and a staff
of at least two members are necessary before a separate department, open for similar hours to the rest of the library,
can be regarded as advisable. Otto Luening, in a notable
study [127], described a model music library, and says:
"It is obviously not a practical goal for communities of less
than 100,000 population. It might, however, be achieved
through library cooperation under a regional unit of service" [p. 55].

A sound recordings or audiovisual library containing
more than a basic stock would make almost compulsory the
need both for specialist staff and for separate accommodation. The matter is considered in some detail in Chapter V,
where it is suggested that one assistant cannot deal comfortably or adequately with more than 150 records daily unless
routine work is to suffer. If the music collection is part of
a larger department, there should be little problem in having
staff available at all times, but it also means that qualified
personnel on duty at any one time could have no specialist
music knowledge, to the disadvantage of the section's users.
There is still much to commend the alcove or separate area
in the general lending library. Such modest provision is
within the scope of a very small library if reasonable floor
space is available. Because so many British libraries are
housed in old, cramped, and totally inadequate buildings
designed to carry bookstocks a fraction of their present
size, floor space is frequently at a tremendous premium--
but this is not the place to argue the need for a much higher rate of building new library premises.

It is worth comment that virtually every new central
library built in England from the late 1940s to early 1970s
had a separate music department incorporated and, as far
as can be discovered, results fully justified this provision.

The problem has now to be faced afresh by many of the new local government authorities created in 1974; it is to be hoped that, when new major public library buildings are planned, a carefully designed music department (with adequate audio-visual facilities) will be incorporated.

THE COLLECTION

Principles

In Britain it has always been assumed that the legal power to buy books, conferred on libraries under the 1855 Public Libraries Act, extended to music, and this view has never been challenged. The intention to provide music is perhaps too vague; the equally important decision must be taken as to the types of music to be provided. There is no set standard for public libraries nor agreement as to what should be included. Even the largest library would probably find it beyond its resources to attempt to provide all things for all users. Even so, some agreed policy should be possible—that librarians themselves should reach a decision as to what they can reasonably be expected to provide in their stocks and what they feel should, if required, be bought by the individual. Provision would increase in both range and depth with increased population; some types of music (such as the utterly ephemeral popular tune) might be considered outside the scope of any library, although there is no universal agreement even on this. Since so many small independent libraries in 1974 and 1975 have become regional or district library headquarters as part of much larger systems, the service in these large authorities should improve, not least because of the opportunity to eliminate wasteful duplication in stock. There may well remain the need to lean upon the resources of the Central Music Library in London and on the stocks of those eight cities which, before reorganization, had populations of over 400,000 and which have remained, in general terms, unaltered by the changes that have been so drastic elsewhere. The new authorities, many of whom have even bigger total populations than these cities, should accept particular responsibilities and contribute to the common pool as well as benefiting from it. Better provision is almost certain to be reflected in greater demand.

The music collection, to be of permanent value, must
be begun, expanded, and maintained in accordance with a
definite plan--modified from time to time in the light of public demand or by a change of personnel. Any collection will
reflect something of the interests of the person in charge
and that is not without advantages. A successor will probably have slightly different interests and another facet of
the music stock may become slightly more prominent as a result. The active-minded librarian will read as many musical
periodicals as possible, partly to keep abreast of current affairs but also to check upon reviews of new books, music,
and recordings. It is almost certain that some of this reading will have to be done in the librarian's own time--the interested and dedicated professional does not automatically
"switch off" when leaving the building, to be motivated again
when upon return to duty. It may be possible to allot responsibility for reading (with particular reference to the reviews) certain periodicals to one or more members of staff.
If the selected periodical(s) can be chosen to coincide with
the interests of a particular staff member, so much the better. Any enhancement of one's knowledge, be it achieved
on or off duty, must surely contribute to the librarian's personal satisfaction as well as to that of the library users.

The competent public librarian will naturally endeavour
to make the maximum provision possible of books and scores,
but some types of work will necessarily be excluded. The
problem of providing, or refusing to provide, tutorial books
and music must be faced; books on harmony, counterpoint,
and musical form are not usually in question, but with instrumental tutors the borrower is likely to require a copy for
several months or even longer, unless interest in the particular instrument is quickly extinguished. This dual approach
has been well expressed by Richard G. Williams:

> A library can offer him much if it is adequately
> stocked, but the amateur musician should not per-
> haps expect the library to provide him with copies
> on long-term loan, any more than should, say, some-
> one learning an instrument expect to borrow for a
> long period instrumental "tutors." With books, a
> library can offer a legitimate substitute for purchase,
> but there comes a time when the reader finds the
> book sufficiently rewarding to try and purchase a
> copy himself. Because of the particular nature of

> music and its transience in the sense that it has to
> be performed to be really experienced, I would sug-
> gest that that point in time comes much earlier with
> music than it does with a book, and that there should
> be more encouragement for individual performers to
> purchase music that interests them rather than rely
> on what the library can offer, in spite of the high
> cost of music [231, p. 15].

One complication is that tutorial books for wind and
brass instruments may include excerpts from half-forgotten
sonatas and concertos that are useful for technical training
when the student has acquired a fair proficiency upon the
chosen instrument. The series of tutors by Otto Langey
(published by Boosey & Hawkes) is of this type. There are
librarians who maintain a very large collection of tutors so
that teachers and pupils can try several and then perhaps
choose the one best suited to their needs. Many smaller libraries do not buy choral works such as the anthem, part-
song, and motet, partly through handling difficulties with
single copies, partly because a choir is likely to require at
least a dozen copies. Another general exclusion in smaller
libraries is orchestral parts. Orchestras, like choirs, usually build up their own libraries; an expensive work unlikely to be played more than once in a period of years may be
hired from the publishers. With many modern works the
parts are not for sale so that the library itself would have
no option but to hire the parts if local orchestras were to
be supplied with music. Orchestras do not normally make
application to the local public library unless it is known that
scores and parts are in stock or can be borrowed through
the library without difficulty. The last general exclusion to
be considered here is that of music for minor instruments
(i.e., those rarely learned by the amateur). Such music is
usually bought when there is expressed demand; the librarian who buys music for the double bass or bassoon will
probably find that it receives very little use though this
may be increased by loan to other libraries upon request.

While these exclusions are fairly general among small
and medium-sized public libraries it is not suggested that
they should be automatic or a fixed policy. The only rigid
line drawn (so far as is possible) should be that of musical
quality and every effort should be made to exclude the
ephemeral work. A small library may receive orchestral

parts and scores from a defunct local orchestra and it will
naturally wish (even if not compelled under the terms of
the donation) to retain these works for possible use by other
orchestras. Similarly sets of anthems may be received as
gifts and put into stock for loan to other choirs in the
neighbourhood. In this case, a system of interloan could
be organized between choirs, all copies being regarded as
part of a central pool and the library acting as headquarters and clearing house. For example, this has been done
most successfully at Burnley.

Although music is written for many instruments and
combinations of instruments as well as for the human voice,
the newly started collection is often severely restricted in
scope, and experience suggests that the limitations described
above are justified. A collection of scores totalling less than
a thousand usually includes vocal scores of operas, musical
plays, oratorios and the like; songs, music for piano (the
largest groups in the collection), organ, violin, and clarinet;
miniature scores and perhaps the parts of a handful of chamber music works. Such a collection is likely to answer the
needs of the great majority of our library users who wish to
borrow music. Instruments that have a lower proportion of
players among musicians, such as the viola or violoncello may
possibly have two or three local performers; for these, a
token selection may have to suffice, to be increased when
local demand justifies and finances permit. This is the sort
of music that cries out for cooperative provision between
neighbouring libraries in order to increase the selection at
no greater cost to any individual library.

For orchestral scores, the dictum of Ernest Savage
may be recalled [195, p. 65]: "I think the following rule is
reasonable: in a small library buy the miniatures of full
scores by the principal composers; and in the medium library
the big scores of these composers, and all the miniatures
available. In the large library, such limitations are not necessary." This might be considered a rather over-generous
approach to full scores for they are normally extremely expensive and often cumbersome. On the other hand, full
scores are available for many works that are not available
in miniature form. Dr. Savage is not, in general, in favour
of the provision of orchestral parts; in his view, the small
library should also omit chamber music parts but moderate
provision should be made by the medium-sized library and
wide coverage by the large library. He continues:

A great part of the collection will consist of vocal
and piano scores or orchestral works, solo-
instrumental and vocal music, and especially chamber
music--quintets, quartets, trios--in which lies the
strength of any music department. Miniature scores
of the most celebrated chamber music are essential.

The provision of too many musical arrangements will
weaken an otherwise good collection. There is so much good
original music for the piano, for instance, that it is unfortunate, to say the least, if the collection of piano scores
proves to consist mainly of orchestral works and operas arranged for the instrument. In the field of piano duets and
organ works, the arranger seems to be even more strongly
in evidence. There are certain instruments, such as the
viola and oboe, which do not have a large repertory of original works and the collection will perforce have to be strengthened by the addition of arrangements but this should be a
later and not the first resort.

The selection should be made as wide as possible by
the inclusion of the lesser-known with the more familiar
works; the contemporary with music written before the age
of Bach. The librarian should remember that a standard of
selection that may be regarded as too high is much preferable to the more common error of too low a standard. Quite
often libraries will provide inferior music while the classics
are missing. Librarians should not need to be told to buy
the best, yet money is often spent on ephemeral music. At
the same time, it is admitted that this view is by no means
universally accepted. Many librarians would argue that it
is their duty to provide what the public wants, and selection of stock will therefore vary according to how far the
librarian agrees or disagrees with this idea. This writer
has argued that piano selections from all but a handful of
films and musical plays are a waste of money, and the counter-
suggestion has been made that these items (if retained) can
provide useful background music at some future date for
helping to give the correct atmosphere for an historical period or even as a way of studying social history. In short,
the standards of selection for a collection of music are as
open to different viewpoints as the choice of fiction, to take
an obvious parallel.

Where a library has no music collection but wishes to
start one, it is most difficult to offer the current cost of

that 350 collection recommended in the first edition since
prices have since risen astronomically. Readers will have
to do their own transposition of both for that 1958 figure and
for the suggestion that Ł150 should be allocated for rebinding
items which require strengthening before being put into circulation. The collection may receive a number of donations
from well-wishers, but these are often far more of a hindrance
than a help, since time will be needed to check through the
material. In too many cases, it will be found that scores are
in poor physical condition. In the USA a number of libraries
have been fortunate to receive financial help from well-wishers
towards the buying of new material; such gifts are virtually
unknown in Britain, except for some major collections which
are now known by their respective donors' names such as
those in the public libraries of Manchester, Burnley, and
Bournemouth.

Development of the Basic Stock

Unfortunately, librarians with little or no musical knowledge
tend to have no settled policy for the music section however
definite their ideas in other fields. With music, as with other
sections of the stock, good supply will often create the demand. The present stock may be fairly large but unless it
provides a wide selection of scores suitable for current demands, kept in good condition, its use will probably be disappointing. A score should not automatically retain its place
on the public shelves until it disintegrates. If it is in some
demand and/or is a standard work, then it should be replaced if its condition is poor; otherwise, it should simply
be withdrawn. Many public libraries carry a reserve stock
of books in limited demand which still deserve retention;
this reserve should certainly include music.

      In fact, the first step towards building up a collection
may well be to remove a generous proportion of the present
stock from the public shelves, some to be replaced by more
modern editions and the rest to be retained in reserve, however makeshift the provision for the latter may be. Generally speaking, the score that has not been borrowed for at
least twelve months should be regarded as a candidate for
withdrawal or reserve. Placing in stack will further reduce
very considerably a score's chances of being borrowed. It
is therefore suggested that, before this step is taken, a

check should be made to separate works which appear to
have no permanent place in musical history, e.g., compositions by some older composers who rate at most a few lines
in Grove, Thompson or similar standard dictionaries, as well
as those who are so minor or obscure as to be omitted entirely. These volumes of music may well be discarded, but
British libraries should offer them to the respective subject
specialising library in their region or to the Central Music
Library in London, to ensure that nothing of real or potential use is thrown away. It is usually fairly safe to dispose
of arrangements (orchestral works edited for performance on
piano or organ, etc.) unless the composer is of the first
rank.   In doubtful cases the safest plan is to retain the work
in reserve stock. In areas that are cultural backwaters, the
librarian may find that even excellent standard works are not
used, and there seems to be no genuine answer to this most
depressing problem--lowering the standard of selection is
certainly not the solution.

When replacements and new editions are considered
there are a number of guides to show the librarian what is
available though such guides will not usually indicate the
suitability of a particular edition for library use. This is
an aspect of music librarianship without a textbook answer;
only with wide musical knowledge and experience can one be
dogmatic about the "best" edition, and even then still invite
the question; "Best for whom?" The general methods of selection of classics for the library shelves, the choice between
available editions of Shakespeare or Jane Austen, are also
applicable to music. When there is a choice, the librarian
will generally tend to adopt a cautious approach and choose
an edition by a well-known publisher, perhaps with an equally well-known editor and certainly one that is well produced.
Reputable publishers with an international standing cannot
afford to produce poor editions and only occasionally would
a particular edition be recommended in preference to rivals
because the standard of alternative versions is almost equal.
The first type of guide as to what is available is provided
by the leaflets and catalogues of music publishers; these will
often indicate works that are new to the catalogue and also
ones which have been brought back into circulation after being out of print. If a library considers it worthwhile to be
on the mailing list of a music publisher, this can usually be
arranged without difficulty; in any case, such brochures
can frequently be obtained through one's normal music sup-

plier. There are some excellent second-hand dealers who
will willingly send their lists to public libraries.

Lists of new music publications with reviews are to be
found in a number of the music periodicals discussed in
Chapter II. Notes [169] is particularly valuable for its long
reviews by music librarians for their colleagues. Not only
is coverage of American publications excellent, but many
items originating outside the USA are considered and the
list of "Music received" is arranged in classified order, quoting publisher and price for each item.

For many years, British music librarians had no major
domestic bibliographical aids in tracing music scores, but the
position has been very much improved since the appearance
of The British Catalogue of Music (BCM) in 1957 [26]. Fuller consideration of this publication is given in Chapter II.
It need only be remarked here that coverage is by no means
comprehensive; in general, new British and some overseas
publications are to be found in its pages (but omitting certain music that the compilers feel to be purely ephemeral).
Reprints are usually excluded from BCM. There have been
no cumulative volumes to date, which is unfortunate; the music librarian is faced with a lengthening file of annual volumes to be searched for the answer to a particular query as
to publisher, etc.

The differences between BCM and the American Catalog
of Copyright Entries [217] are considerable. The latter
makes entry under title (compared with the British publication's subject entry, under its own classification scheme),
but is comprehensive in including all sorts of music, along
with a large amount of unpublished material--a result of the
very different copyright laws in the USA and in Britain.

There is, unfortunately, no example to date of either
a national or international system of individual numbers for
scores, as has grown up in recent years in the world of
books. International Standard Book Numbers were regarded
by many librarians, when the scheme was first introduced,
as yet another unnecessary complication in what should be
the fairly simple matter of ordering books. Nowadays, this
adjunct to correct identification is taken almost for granted,
and it certainly helps to prevent the arrival of a wrong book
or a wrong edition in response to an order.

Recently some useful lists of music "in print" (i.e.,
currently available from publishers) have appeared in the
United States. They cover music for piano [77 and 185],
organ [161], orchestra [66], strings [67], solo voice [160],
and chorus [159]. There may be difficulties for the librarian who wishes to order an out-of-print score for library
stock, or who is anxious to borrow one through an inter-
library loan system. For standard music, written by composers of repute who have been dead sufficiently long for
their music to be in the public domain, the problem is not
too acute. At worst, one can order the music from an established supplier and hope that the copy supplied is from
an equally reputable publisher; but what about contemporary music, or nineteenth-century or earlier items, by composers who are not in that magic circle of "well-known
names"?

If one is aware that the composer is still living or has
died within the last few years, one would normally have re-
course to the volumes of the BCM or the Library of Congress
catalogue, as may be appropriate. If the enquirer has heard
the music on a gramophone record and can produce a copy of
the disc, the British music librarian should be saved any further searching, for the record label of a British company will
show the name of the publisher. This seems to have been an
excellent and unpublicised benefit arising from the passing of
the 1956 Copyright Act.

The larger the library, the more probable it is that it
has better bibliographical resources than its smaller counter-
parts--but it is also probable that it will be faced with a
higher proportion of requests for works that are difficult to
trace. The large public or academic library, particularly in
the USA, is likely to have either or both of the massive G. K.
Hall reprints in volume form of the public libraries' music
catalogues of Boston [20a] and New York [167]. These two
works are invaluable in tracing books and scores, but are
beyond the financial resources of the smaller library and
possibly beyond the available space as well. Another vast
library catalogue is in progress as this is being written:
the Catalogue of Printed Music (CPM) of the British Library
[27]. Finally, mention must be made of the National Union
Catalog, Pre-1956 Imprints [163], in which holdings of North
American libraries are presented. Music scores are entered
by composer, with all editions and arrangements given place.

It is probably true to say that in music selection, more
than in any other section of a public library stock (except
for works by Latin and ancient Greek authors), it is customary to buy a very large proportion of works written by people now dead. Contemporary music represents but a minor
part of the output of most music publishers--the eighteenth-
and nineteenth-century classics provide their "bread and
butter" and an impressive series of back lists. How far this
is desirable is highly debatable. Frank Howes, formerly
chief music critic of The Times of London felt that "The ac-
cumulation of masterpieces from the past is becoming a serious problem to twentieth century music.... Eighteenth-
century composers never contemplated anything more than
current usage for their works and a good deal too much
Bach, Haydn and Mozart has survived" [99, p. 27]. If one
agrees that this preoccupation with older music is unhealthy,
then the librarian should help the contemporary musician in
the most practical way--by buying copies of his music and
doing what he can to get some of it performed, preferably
more than once.

At the same time, works by acknowledged masters
should be replaced as a matter of course when the condition
of a copy deteriorates below the acceptable. It should not
be too readily assumed, however, that to buy a new copy
of the same edition is the best course. Steps should be
taken to discover what editions are currently available and
to decide, within one's knowledge, which one to purchase.
In general, an "Urtext" edition is to be preferred, but one
needs to take into account the reputation of the publisher
and/or the editor, the format and standard of printing and,
by no means least, the price. The "Urtext"--from the
German--means the original text; "usually taken to be an
edition embodying the author's own final thoughts" (Oxford
Companion to Music). Unfortunately, perhaps, and certainly confusingly, some popular major composers are now represented by Urtext editions from rival publishers, and there
are often differences between their versions.

If the librarian has little musical knowledge, the problem of buying works by contemporary composers is one of
very real difficulty, and in general it might be suggested
that no such work should be bought unless the reviews suggest it is likely to be of more than passing interest, and the
librarian has some confidence that library users will borrow

the work. This is particularly necessary where the allowance
for new music is very small, for works covered by the copyright are generally much more expensive than those which
are in the public domain. However much one may desire to
support a struggling composer there seems little point in
buying, for example, a tuba sonata of some complexity when
there is not, so far as the librarian is aware, a single tuba
player for miles around. Though perhaps an extreme example it illustrates the point. In general, the unmusical librarian who is unable or unwilling to have any sort of assistance
would be well advised to limit initial accessions to piano music (mainly solo but with a few duets and some piano concertos, arranged for two-piano playing), solo pieces for violin, for clarinet, violoncello, and organ, some songs (for all
types and ranges of voice) and a number of miniature scores
of the more popular classics. The stock lists in the second
volume of this book are intended to be of assistance here.

It has already been indicated that, in the writer's
view, even the library with a very conservative policy in
selection should still be prepared to buy at least a modest
selection of current works. In larger authorities, with greater funds to be spent, there should be a much wider coverage
of specialist periodicals which will review new music and it
should be a matter of principle to ensure that a minimum sum
is allocated each year to be spent on musical compositions by
living composers.

A systematic approach to selection of works by living
Composers is offered in James Coover's thoughtful essay on
selection policies [42]. His recommendation is that the library establish a list of composers whose works will be collected, and then simply acquire all their new output.

Money can be saved, but it can also be wasted, by
buying second-hand music. This form of accession is not
generally recommended for the library that does not include
a fairly expert music assistant on its staff. There are certain firms which specialize in second-hand music and who
circularize lists of available scores to librarians. Such reputable dealers are reliable, but since they are experts the
prices asked may be regarded as being as high as the market will accept, and one is unlikely to discover any outstanding bargains. On the other hand, the librarian will not normally be asked for more than a fair market price. This

source of supply is most valuable for filling a particular gap when a work is out of print or there are difficulties in obtaining a copy through normal sources. If purchase is made with the idea of increasing the size of the music stock at a reduced cost, a check should be made whenever possible on the current price of a new copy, for second-hand copies may sometimes be quoted at prices little less than that to be paid for new ones when the library discount is taken into account.

In the normal way it is not worth trying to buy music at general auction sales. The physical condition of the music is often poor and a high proportion of it not suitable for public-library use. Those works that are worth adding are all too often the ones which are already represented in the stock. It does sometimes occur, however, that a sale is known to include works that the library would be pleased to have. In such a case it may be possible to secure a real bargain as music usually fetches very low prices in the auction room. This paragraph, it should be clear, refers only to the sales of furniture and effects and not to specialised sales of music. Music may also usefully be bought, on occasion, from private individuals who are local residents.

Second-hand music must be carefully collated; the last sheet would seem to be a frequent casualty and flimsy string parts can easily be lost. The bottom corners of a well-used score tend to become dog-eared, pages are likely to get torn with hasty turning over and fingering and marks of expression may have been indelibly entered on the printed page. Music that has been treated in this way or which has been extensively repaired should be bought only when there is no other apparent possibility of getting the work in better condition. Loose binding is of less importance, for the librarian would automatically send the score for rebinding before placing it on the open shelves and any weakness in the publisher's binding may lower the purchase price. The library user who marks a library copy and who fails to remove the marks neatly before returning the copy is a pest of the first order, and the librarian should try to set a good example to his patrons by ensuring that no music reaches the shelves with pencil marks of this nature.

The foregoing two paragraphs have been reprinted unaltered from the first edition, but it must be admitted that

the number of good dealers in second-hand music seems to
be steadily diminishing and that second-hand prices, in
parallel with those for new music, have risen steeply over
the last few years. The second-hand market is now very
much more the hunting ground of the antiquarian and the
academic librarian than of public librarians who, in most
cases, are primarily interested in items for performance
rather than for musicologists and others working towards
research degrees.

Keeping the Stock Fresh

In a small public library the problem of providing adequate
variety for the music borrower is as difficult as with any
other section of the stock. Limitations of space and shortage of money for new accessions must result in a fairly
small and slowly changing stock; this is a sound reason for
a higher rather than a lower standard of selection. No work
should be bought that cannot be envisaged as a permanent
asset to the stock, be it two years or thirty-two before it
is in sufficiently poor condition to be withdrawn. This may
appear to assume clairvoyant powers in the librarian but is
not really so.

It may be possible as suggested in the previous section to eke out funds by the judicious purchase of some
second-hand items but there is no satisfactory answer to
the problem of maintaining and enlarging a music stock without enough money being available. It has been suggested
that a certain percentage of the book fund should be ear-
marked for music and, where there is a separate music library, an annual allotment, perhaps calculated as a fairly
constant percentage of the total book fund. The smaller
the stock, the more obvious to the regular user are the new
accessions and, if shelf space is very restricted, some attempt should be made to compensate for this, as far as possible, by the provision of a generous amount of shelf space
in the stacks. Limited display room on the open shelves
should not be made the excuse to reduce purchases to the
lowest possible level, neither should the economy of buying
albums of works rather than single items blind the librarian
to the fact that requests will often be for compositions that
are not available in albums but which must be bought singly,
if at all. In brief, the small library authority has a difficult

task in maintaining a good and adequate stock of music that
will constantly attract music-lovers, unless there is a readi-
ness to spend regularly upon the section.

If the space for scores is very limited then the stock
should be changed at intervals to give some of the works in
reserve an occasional spell upon the open shelves. A number
of seasonal works, such as those written for Christmas, Lent,
Easter, etc., may well be removed from the shelves for nine
months each year and their places taken by some of the items
in stock, providing always that the physical condition of the
latter justifies this temporary promotion.

The library system with branches should find it much
less difficult to keep the stock fresh at its different service
points. On balance it is probably better for each branch to
have its own small nucleus stock of works that are in constant popular demand, particularly piano music. There are,
however, good arguments against branches having any permanent music stock but for considering instead all scores as
part of a general pool which serves the whole library system. Unless the branch is a large one it may be difficult
to increase the stock beyond the nucleus, when the position
becomes similar to that which faces the small authority without branch libraries. With no permanent music stock in the
branch or a skeleton selection kept rigorously within definite
limits, music can be loaned from the central library stock or
a central pool for several months at a time. Where each
branch has no permanent stock, all music accessions, including duplicate copies, will be added to central stock or central pool. Where a work is worth duplicating it is often good
policy to buy a different edition for the second copy where
this is possible. There are some cases, of course, where
one edition is much superior to its alternative in which cases
duplication of the original edition is fully justified. Where
songs or song albums are to be duplicated the second copy
should be bought for a different voice range, or in a different translation where the original is in a foreign language.
Duplication should not be carried out automatically and without thought, but the desirability of an alternative edition
should be considered whenever there is such a choice. With
some works it is possible to add four or five different editions and to justify such a variety without difficulty.

For the county library split into regions or divisions,

or for the equivalent in a metropolitan district, the general
approach is normally to make each group of libraries basically self-sufficient in its collection of music scores. To ensure
that stock is regularly exchanged between branches and to
have a plan which provides that even the small collection in
a fairly remote or isolated part of the group will have the
less usual item on its shelves for a time, for the benefit of
the local music lover whose choice of music is a little outside
the common run, it may be thought desirable to create a
number of music "units." The method used in the Coulsdon
& Purley libraries (now part of the London Borough of Croydon) during its days of independence could be used as a
basis. A "unit" consisted of either twenty-five or fifty
scores, and each collection was allocated to a branch library
for a set period (six months proved to be the most convenient length of time, both for users and for staff). In this
way, a music score was to be seen on the shelves of each
library in the group and so had a much better chance of being borrowed than if it had been in the permanent stock of
any one of the libraries.

   With this method, administration should be centred on
one library (not necessarily the central or group headquarters library) and it is probably best, even though a little
cumbersome, for a unit to be returned to that administrative
library at the end of each sojourn at a branch. The responsible librarian can then check the condition of the scores for
withdrawal, rebinding, or repair. Where withdrawals have
taken place, the collection can be brought up to strength
again with new works, replacements of the withdrawn items,
or a mixture of both. There should be, when the scheme is
fully operational, enough units for the smallest library to
have at least two of them; bigger branches will need more.
In this way, as one unit is withdrawn after its accepted period (and it will probably require a month to complete this
process, to allow for the return of items in the hands of library users), so there will always be a second one on the
shelves to ensure that there is some music immediately available for loan, to be reinforced as another unit is received.

   At the regional/district headquarters (or at each library) if a union catalogue of whatever format is maintained,
the item in the unit would have the normal entries but a
clear indication also that a score is part of "Unit $\underline{x}$." Some
system will be needed for both staff and public to know the

current whereabouts of any unit. It is probably better that
each unit consist of a selection of different types of music,
rather than all of one category, such as miniature scores.
On the other hand, there is little point in sending a mixed
unit of fairly standard items to any branch which already
has a good stock of music permanently located there, and
some units could be formed of items of which there is but a
single copy in the group of libraries and such more unusual
or specialist collections could take their respective turns at
all libraries.

The music librarian will do well to try to work out the
cost of running this type of exchange, taking into account
the cost of transport and administration, to see whether it
would be cheaper and more generally satisfactory to try to
build up a good music collection at each service point, if
there is shelf space to do this. Further details of the unit
scheme described here can be found elsewhere [36].

Binding Music

The problems of purchase and selection are closely related
to that of binding. Because of large page size compared
with that of an ordinary book, and taking into account the
usually narrow spine, music rebinding may appear to be
quite expensive although this is not so if one compares it to
the rebinding cost of the average book. Miniature scores
are, naturally enough, much cheaper to bind, yet even here
the cost of rebinding may be noticeably higher than the
price paid for the score itself. As a result of this, there
is an understandable temptation to save money by binding
two or three scores together for the same price that would
be charged for just one of them. This procedure may be
accepted, providing that the scores so combined in one
casing have a near relationship both in format and content.
The first six string quartets of Beethoven, which make up
his opus 18, would provide a convenient basis for one or
two volumes, as would similar groups of chamber works by
such other composers as Haydn or Mozart. The saving is
partly offset by inconvenience, for two patrons each requiring a different, separate work that happen to be bound together cannot both be satisfied at the same time. On the
other hand, a collection of very slim scores, with spines too
narrow to carry easily visible titling is difficult to keep in

order and may well slow down the search for one particular
item. Thicker volumes, be they of longer individual works
or of shorter ones bound together, may provide guideposts
in the quest for a single, slim piece of music on a full shelf.

Some libraries send all music scores, excluding the occasional volumes that are published in stiff covers, for rebinding before they are first put on the shelves ready for
borrowing. Unless there is a loose insert or separate parts
(as with most instrumental works with piano accompaniment,
and other chamber music), it should be possible to allow selected scores to circulate in publishers' casings for a few issues before sending them to be rebound. The original paper
covers may well add a pleasant, if temporary, touch of colour
to the shelves, and this deliberate delay before rebinding
could prove to be a small economy overall, although it must
be admitted that professional binders do not accept the argument; they recommend rebinding before the score is made
available for loan.

For slim items of sheet music, there are several possible methods of treatment. First, the music may be sewn
into a stiff brown paper or similar cover. Scores of eight
or twelve pages, i.e., with two or three folds, can be
treated with ordinary needle and thread. This minimal protection should be sufficient for works retained in vertical
files, arranged in composer, class, or other order. The
scheme is both effective and economical, but suffers from
the defect that many musical browsers are unlikely to be
sufficiently patient to work through a thick file in the hope
of finding something of interest; not all librarians would
consider this to be undesirable. More serious is the limitation that only one person can use a single drawer or, more
probably, a complete cabinet at a time. It also means that
such a file imposes the need for a separate sequence of works
away from other related sources, which is unhelpful to users.

Should the decision be made that scores of this flimsy
nature should be filed in sequence with the rest of the scores,
then rather stronger protection is needed. Binders' thread,
made from a terylene and cotton blend, is extremely strong
and the thickness described as "16-2" is perfectly adequate
for the purpose and can be used with a size 18 needle. Employing these items for sewing scores into manila covers is
not taxing. What may be more difficult is the tracing of

suppliers which sell bookbinding materials, for they are apparently few. (However, British libraries can order from Redbridge Bolton Ltd. in Greater Manchester.) Scores thus strengthened, with the composer, work's title, and classmark shown on the front cover can be easily overlooked, however, since they have virtually no thickness of spine and can be easily misplaced on the shelves.

When a volume is a little more substantial, it may be sent to a library rebinder to be so treated, but with the original cover protected by a durable plastic film. If the music content begins on the reverse of the cover (as is common with much thin sheet music), the first page of the score may be photocopied, the sheet then stiffened with board and the photocopy pasted on the inside of the board. This means that the front cover is appreciably more substantial than before, but the music can still be found on its reverse. However, this form of strengthening may be considered unsuitable or undesirable in some cases. If so, an alternative would be to make the front cover of the binding from a thin, transparent plastic; the final result, very similar to a popular form of periodical or pamphlet binding, allows the front cover to be clearly visible, yet the original score is now protected at both front and back and is altogether more substantial than in its original form. Such treatment is probably best limited to scores that do not exceed sixteen pages. Above this figure, normal cloth binding is advisable.

Quarter- and half-leather binding, standard treatment for many music scores forty and more years ago, is now generally restricted to special (particularly antiquarian) work. This is partly because of the cost which is now likely to be considered beyond the means of most library budgets, and also because regular handling will almost certainly result in the pages' becoming too torn or dirty for the score to be retained in stock, yet the binding itself will probably still be in good condition. If the score is rarely handled, the leather will tend to shrivel and flake as time passes, so that such volumes will require regular brushing once or twice a year with a recognized preservative in order to keep the skin in good condition.

"Perfect" or unsewn binding, which was generally damned when it apparently failed dismally to live up to its earlier promise is, nevertheless, usually quite satisfactory for miniature scores and for works with a large page format but no more than thirty-two pages in thickness. Failure of the adhesive, the usual cause of unsatisfactory results in the 1950s, is now rarely encountered as the technology has immensely improved over the years. The most common reason today for any failure is through the use of this technique with a wrong class of paper. Photocopied scores and those printed on similar hard paper are not suitable, as the adhesive cannot penetrate the surface.

When a work requires parts for more than one performer, as in chamber music, the normal method is to bind the thickest part (if there is one) in the usual way, but with the spine of the binding widened sufficiently in order to provide a pocket inside the back cover to accommodate the other part(s), which are cased in manila or limp cloth; alternatively, all parts may be sewn separately in limp covers and the binding itself consist simply of a case or box to house the individual parts. The "binding" will carry the usual details of composer, title, and classification on the spine and will contain the bookcard, date label, etc. Whichever method is used, a note should always be written or stamped on the date label or bookcard to the effect that there are x parts in the pocket or pockets, since a missing part may render the others useless. Where a work is brief, with a single or double sheet only for the solo instrument with a keyboard accompaniment of little greater thickness, it is often possible to use a manila folder with a rear pocket made by stapling a piece of manila inside the back cover and having the solo part covered with a transparent laminated or sprayed-on plastic, or else protected by a paper or card cover. This is both simple and highly economical.

Ernest Savage suggested many years ago that "the lettering (always in the language of the title) on thin volumes should be made up the spine, but across the spine wide enough to take legible titles: [195]. There would be general agreement among librarians in favour of the last point. The relevant British Standard is no. 1544, originally published in 1949. It is nominally concerned with "Bound account and manuscript books (other than scholastic books)." Five variants were offered in the method of lettering, including a) across the spine, b) with title running up the spine, while e) shows the lettering running horizontally across the front cover of the book. Section 47 of the Standard read: "Method (a) is generally recommended, with either (b) or (e) as preferred alternatives." In the 1973 revision of this same Standard, lettering across the spine and across the front cover are the only two styles listed, which is perhaps unexpected since the great majority of books published today (admittedly not "account and manuscript" ones) have titles running down the spine.

British librarians used to prefer lettering running up the spine (as the Savage quotation above indicates) because, as one's eye moves along a shelf of books from left to right, it is fairly easy to read spine titles as one glances at them, but it is noticeably more awkward to do so when titles run down the spine. Nevertheless, the latter plan is much preferred by booksellers because the spine title is "right way up" when a book is lying flat with its front cover uppermost, and librarians often prefer this scheme for the sake of consistency.

It is in the choice of wording on the spine that one would take issue with Dr. Savage. Where a work's title is one of form, as with symphonies, concertos, preludes, etc., English (or other appropriate language) is much to be preferred. If one simply copies what is on the title page, as is always liable to happen when a volume is sent for rebinding and the librarian's instructions are not crystal clear, then identical works which happen to have title pages in different languages are likely to be separated on the shelves-- a matter which the cataloguer has (one hopes) carefully tried to avoid by means of the filing title device. For individual titles, the original will generally be preferred. The matter is discussed more fully in Chapter IV.

It is the custom in some public libraries (and may be followed elsewhere) to bind works of a particular type in the same colour, e.g., all piano works in brown, all operas in green. This results in large blocks of colour on the shelves which may be useful in the identification of a work, but it is possible that a sufficient variety of colours may not be obtainable to carry out the scheme without limiting the colour classification to very broad categories indeed. Liverpool formerly used but two colours, red and blue, for instrumental and vocal works and made no further sub-division of this type. A colour scheme may fail through use of different

cloths by different binders; even the same company may vary
its colours to some degree because of minor differences in
dyes. A guaranteed repeatable range of colours seems to
offer a decidedly dull selection. We would strongly recommend a variety of colours in binding works of the same
genre, partly for the sake of variety and also to allow
works in publishers' bindings keep a happy anonymity so
that they do not stand out amid a series of volumes of a
single colour. There is a compromise that could be generally acceptable, although it adds to rebinding costs. This
is to affix to each score a small strip or circle of coloured
tape or cloth at a standard height from the base of the
spine. This allows the eye of an assistant to glance quickly along each shelf and discover at once if any score is
mixed with members of another category, gives the same
assistance to patrons that is claimed for a colour scheme of
binding, yet still retains the brightness and attractiveness
of variety.

   Where there is a music librarian on the staff, that
person will be responsible for supervising the listing and
checking of volumes to be sent to the binder. Particular
care must be taken to ensure that correct instructions are
given to the binder and that the details of required lettering are precise. This may seem elementary, yet Otto Kinkeldey has told American librarians, "I could quote you
several instances of otherwise well-ordered libraries in which
you could have found the several instrumental parts of a
chamber composition handsomely and securely bound together" [112, p. 461]. We have seen copies of violin concertos,
in British libraries, with the separate violin part bound in
with the piano accompaniment thus completely defeating the
object of issuing a separate part for the soloist. When two
or more items are bound together in a single volume there
should always be a strong and easily apparent link between
the individual items, e.g., songs should always be by a
single composer and preferably for a particular type of
voice. The spine title should either list the individual
items or, if room is insufficient, be given a generic title
that covers the contents, such as "Songs for soprano,"
"Piano pieces from op. 10 and op. 12." In the first edition
chapters of Part II of that book, indications have been given
of those cases where it seems suitable to bind separate items
into a composite volume. The individual items in such a volume may not all be printed on pages of the same size; the

single volume is of unorthodox appearance, though perfectly
practical, and the binder will need to be warned against
trimming too closely the sheets of the largest item in the volume. A contents list should be stencilled or typewritten (unless there is a member of staff whose handwriting is both
clear and attractive in appearance), and all the items to be
bound together should have the pages numbered consecutive-
ly in manuscript. In this way, a potential borrower can
quickly see what items are to be found in any "made up"
volume and locate a required work without difficulty. If
the composite volume is one prepared by a music publisher,
problems of varying page sizes for separate items and of
contents lists should not arise. Finally, when the volume is
returned from binding it is probably as well, if time can
possibly be found, for the music librarian personally to
check the spine titling to see that the binder has followed
instructions correctly, particularly where these require different wording to that found on the title page of the score.

Cooperation

This is an aspect of library services, both academic and
public, to which lip service is constantly paid, but the practical results have usually been miserably inadequate. Outside Britain, cooperation would seem to be virtually nonexistent insofar as music is concerned. In British public libraries, the creation of large local government units has made a
much higher degree of self-sufficiency possible and desirable.
Yet financial pressures also mean that cooperation is more
necessary than ever, in order to extract the maximum benefit from monies allotted to the music stock.

The North-Western Regional Library System (which
covered the libraries of Lancashire and Cheshire) showed
what could be done by introducing a scheme for the purchase of multiple copies of vocal scores of popular works in
the early 1960s. The plan was very simple--libraries bought
twenty copies of the vocal score of a particular work; these
were lent as a batch on request to another library for use
by a local operatic or choral society. A small subcommittee
decided, on the basis of previous requests through the System, which titles should be bought. Any library could borrow sets; the "entry fee" was an undertaking to buy a set
of works on the system's list of desiderata and to make up

a second set of another work in due course. In this way, for a very modest cost, each library had access to multiple copies of a range of choral works in regular demand, from Annie Get Your Gun to the Fauré Requiem. A decade later, the idea was taken up and developed further in the Greater London area. Not only did libraries there cooperate in the purchase of multiple copies of scores, but orchestral parts were also added to libraries' stocks on a similar basis and, from 1 April 1972, gramophone records were acquired on an agreed plan within certain specified fields, so that every disc within the agreed categories that was commercially available in Britain was bought by at least one library and retained permanently in stock, to form the basis of a constantly growing reference or archive collection.

This scheme (the Greater London Audio Specialist Scheme, with its acronym GLASS) attempted to impose responsibilities as equitably as possible on each authority. The most prolific composers, so far as the production of recordings of their work is concerned, were allocated to individual libraries; slightly less numerically popular composers were allotted in pairs to a second group of libraries while the remainder were divided according to the initial letters of their surnames among the remaining libraries. If a disc contains more than one work and these compositions are by different composers, each library which has responsibility for any of the composers represented is expected to buy the disc. This means a varying amount of duplication, but ensures that no disc slips through the metaphorical net because the librarian assumes that one of the others will be buying it. For jazz, a variety of possible schemes was considered; eventually responsibility was decided upon by the name of the instrumentalist or vocalist, again on the basis of surnames, spread between the thirty-one library authorities.

Yet even cooperative schemes are not 100 percent effective or, it may be argued, necessary. Choirs and orchestras may occasionally require an older work or comparatively obscure composition that is out of print or which would be difficult to justify for purchase, even on a sharing basis, because of the unlikelihood of further demand within the foreseeable future. For this reason alone, many libraries and societies will remain subscribers to the loan schemes operated by such libraries as Liverpool, Manchester, and

Plymouth. Libraries in the London area have access to the
Central Music Library, which combines much of the excellent
collection built up by Westminster public libraries with that
of CML itself, which is nominally an independent collection.
As to requests by individuals, some enquiries for works not
in the stock of an individual library may be answered by
means of the regional library system; where that fails, the
British Library may have the necessary score, but it could
well prove that the enquirer is neither willing nor able to
pay a personal visit, and the cost of a photocopy of a work
running to more than a few pages may be found prohibitive.

        An answer to part of this problem would appear to be
possible both at local and regional levels. When a librarian
is considering the purchase of any out-of-the-way music, it
might be well worth while to check with neighbouring libraries which perhaps already have the work in stock and would
be prepared to lend it. By cooperation in this way a small
local group of libraries can aim at a wider coverage than
would be possible in any one of them. The idea can be carried further with the suggestion that some attempt should be
made at regional level to include music in any subject specialization scheme. There would appear to be two possible
basic methods. A library would agree to collect all works
and editions as published of a particular composer or composers; or, it would agree to buy all scores issued for a
particular instrument or group of instruments. The larger
libraries would need to accept responsibility for the more important or voluminous composers or for the more popular instruments or collections of instruments; the smaller library
would collect the works of a minor master or the music for
an unusual instrument. The publication of a separate cumulation of new music scores in the British Catalogue of Music
has partly removed one of the main problems, that of discovering just what new music or new editions are available
in this country.

Music in the Junior Library

While many children learn music, in one form or another, it
is probably safe to say that the majority do so under protest. Where there is a feeling that practice is a burden,
young musicians are not very likely to use the music scores
provided in the library--but there are always those children

who will. Piano music, together with smaller selections of
violin, violoncello and recorded music and also some vocal
music should be provided. This last will include nursery
rhymes, settings of verses by A. A. Milne, Lewis Carroll,
etc., carols and similar works. Where such a collection is
inadequate for a particular case, the logical course is to
send the child to the adult music section.

Music intended for the use of children should, naturally, be reasonably simple, but simplicity and the third-rate
should not be confused. There are thousands of pieces al-
legedly portraying fairies, elves, gnomes, and the like at
different activities but the greater part of this material has
practically no musical value.

Standards should be as high as in the adult library;
music by recognized composers should be provided and selection should be made by the music librarian, though the
children's librarian ought to be consulted. The reverse
process is not recommended. The greatest composers have
written music within the compass of many children; the music librarian will know suitable pieces while the children's
librarian may be completely unaware of their existence.
Books on music and biographies of composers should also be
chosen in cooperation; the music librarian will know if the
work is factually accurate while the children's librarian can
tell if the book is written and presented in a manner likely
to appeal to children and will also check on the typography,
illustrations, and general layout of the book.

Local Activities and Local Musicians

Music should have its own place in local history. There are
amateur operatic societies, local choral societies, church
choirs, local groups, bands, orchestras, and soloists who
achieve a reputation that may become national or even international. All of these come within the scope of the local
collection and the music librarian may well be the best person to obtain relevant material. Programmes of concerts
held in the area provide useful information about artists and
can give useful background material if any of those mentioned
on the programmes later achieve fame. Such programmes
have their own places in the social history of the area, indicating something of local taste at any given time. The

point is well illustrated by the practice followed in the Free
Library of Philadelphia:

> In every phase of department service, the collecting
> of local material is aggressively emphasized. Since
> 1953 the Music Department has kept a written record
> of every musical and dance event in the Philadelphia
> area. It is probable that these annals may some day
> be of value to a music historian. Clippings, press
> releases, pictures, announcements, and programs are
> carefully preserved whether of local or general in-
> terest [119, pp. 584-585].

In this context, that unexpected adverb "aggressively" is
fully justified.

For the local composer, treatment should be as generous and comprehensive as for the local author; the public
library should collect and retain all available material. The
composer may be a very minor one but if the local library
does not attempt to accumulate as much material as possible
it is tolerably certain that no one else will. Charles Avison
(1710-1770) might be quoted as an example. The finest collection of the works of this little-known British composer and
of material about him is to be found in the public library at
Newcastle upon Tyne, his home town. In the same way, Salford public libraries in Greater Manchester are collecting material relating to Peter Maxwell Davies (who was born in
Swinton, which was incorporated in Salford Metropolitan District in 1974) and obtaining items when they are first published and so easily obtainable.

Detroit makes a special point of collecting music and
books by Michigan composers and authors.

> Quality standards are largely abandoned in favor of
> comprehensive regional representation. A great ef-
> fort has been made to establish current and historical
> lists of Michigan composers. We scrutinize gifts with
> particular care for Michigan Collection items. It is
> surprising how rapidly a local collection can grow if
> its existence is made known and eyes are kept open
> for new publications and old ones which turn up in
> gifts. One or two amateur dealers in sheet music,
> knowing of our interest, have turned up many local

items for us which they have sold to the library at
reasonable prices. We attempt to collect manuscript
as well as published material. Each spring we have
a concert of new works by Michigan composers; this
is an effective way of making obvious our interest in
local music. We also undertake to keep what we call
"Season Books" in which we mount clippings, reviews,
programs and pictures to give an overall picture of
what transpires in the local music world year by
year [156].

Music Periodicals

It is a sensible policy for music periodicals to be displayed
in a music library or department where this is a self-contained
entity, and one assumes this to be the norm. Matters may
be more difficult when the library has a separate reading
room or other location where all periodicals are displayed in
one place, and the music section is part of the general collection or has an area in a Fine Arts, or similar, department. If it can be managed, the specialist nature of music
and audio magazines suggests that these periodicals would be
much better used if displayed as closely adjacent to the music section as is practicable. It is suggested in Chapter II
that librarians should try to select periodicals which have
useful review sections, and these can be an added inducement to providing as varied a range of material in this section as can be afforded. Brief outline descriptions of a few
suitable journals will also be found in the next chapter.

Some Problem Categories

Challenges are presented by certain types of music or physical formats. A volume of Chopin waltzes causes no real difficulty; it is of reasonable bulk, will rebind conveniently
and can be treated almost exactly as a normal book except
that it will require higher and deeper shelf space. Not all
music is so convenient for the librarian and some of the more
usual problems are briefly considered in this section.

Some piano concertos are published in versions arranged
for solo piano. The pianist, in such an arrangement, plays
both the solo and the orchestral accompaniment with the score

adapted for the limitations of two hands. The more usual
and popular version is that for two pianos. One pianist
plays the original solo part; the orchestral score is arranged
for piano and this reduction is played by the second pianist.

Music written for two pianos is a very different matter, though obviously there are certain basic similarities.
Generally, the composer regards the two pianists to be of
equal standing whereas with the concerto the solo part is
normally considered paramount. It is perfectly possible
(with two copies) to play piano duets at two pianos but
quite hopeless to attempt two-piano works as a piano duet,
since both players may be required to use a wide keyboard
range. For this reason the two types of music should be
classified separately (though preferably at adjoining places).

There is generally little point in attempting to play one
part of a two-piano piece without its complement so that the
two parts should be bound separately but housed within the
same cover and automatically issued together. With piano
concertos and similar works for piano and orchestra there
are many people who get enjoyment by playing the solo part
and, when the solo pianist is given a brief rest by the composer, continue to play the accompaniment which is usually
indicated in small notes or is shown in parallel staves below
that of the solo part. When the soloist re-enters, the domestic pianist returns to the accompaniment; the result being
that such a performance will bear some similarity to that
played from a solo piano arrangement of the concerto. It
will be less satisfying to any listener since the pianist using
the two-piano arrangement will probably continue to play the
solo part even when the melody is being given out by the
orchestra; the arranger of a solo piano version would ensure
that the melody was given adequate prominence here. So,
although two copies of a concerto will be needed for performance at two pianos it may be thought best to bind them separately rather than include them in one cover. This would
allow two separate pianists in different localities to enjoy
themselves attempting the solo part. It should also result
in fairly even wear on the two copies; when housed in the
same cover the second copy is likely to receive much less
wear than the first. The disadvantage of the complete separation of the two scores is that the user with two pianos,
and a partner to play the orchestral score arrangement, may
find that only one copy of the work is on the shelves and so
have to wait until the second copy is returned.

Orchestral parts should be kept in pamphlet boxes or manila folders, and it is sensible for each work to be filed separately. The method used in Manchester's Henry Watson library is recommendable. On the inside cover of each container is a combined list of parts and a date label. Thus, the top half shows the contents of the set, starting with the strings and with the other parts listed in appropriate score order. Since it is possible for the lid, or even the whole box, to be lost by a borrower, the back of the set's book card carries a duplicate list (a rubber stamp provides the skeleton to be filled in as necessary). If the original list/ date label is lost or mislaid, the staff can still check the returned parts without difficulty. The list is also useful for conductors, orchestral secretaries, or other officials to see if the number of parts available is adequate for the players at a rehearsal. With orchestral parts, and also with multiple copies of vocal scores and parts, the Henry Watson procedure is to issue an entire set. At one time it was possible to borrow only those scores or parts that one actually needed, but it was found that this was extremely costly to operate if staff time was taken into account, and that it was both much simpler and more effective to issue a collection of such items in its entirety, even though this might mean that some copies of a vocal work or certain of the orchestral parts were not used by the borrowing organization.

It is advisable, before issuing orchestral parts, to reinforce the edges with linen tape or similar material. It is also necessary to check, upon return of the box, that any marks of phrasing, bowing, cuts, etc., which may have been inserted by the conductor, players, or singers have been satisfactorily removed. Although a library's rules are likely to forbid the marking of parts, it seems virtually impossible to prevent this practice. If marks are made in an ink which cannot be erased, the damaged parts should be charged for, or the borrower should be required to replace them by unmarked copies. Because of the different ideas of individual conductors over bowing and phrasing, the Royal Liverpool Philharmonic Orchestra's library includes, for many of the standard repertory items, a set of parts whose use is restricted to the regular conductor of the orchestra. Visiting conductors have an entirely different set provided for their use. The method is clearly expensive in the need for duplicate copies, but economical of the orchestral librarian's time and apparently effective.

HENRY WATSON MUSIC LIBRARY

Please check the contents of this container upon receipt, and return not later than the last date stamped below.

Violin 1	Horn	Tambourine
Violin 2	Trumpet	Glockenspiel
Viola	Trombone	Celesta
Cello	Tuba	
Double bass		Cornet
	Timpani	Saxophone
Flute		
Piccolo	Side drum (tamb.)	Solo instruments
Oboe	Bass drum	
Cor anglais	Cymbals	
Clarinet	Harp	
Bassoon	Triangle	Piano conductor

G337 (6)

Sets of copies of short choral works can be filed similarly to orchestral parts, in boxes or folders. Only one work should be filed in a box; if this is wasteful then there should be some connecting link between works sharing the same folder--the obvious one would be that of composer. For works in small demand the simplest and cheapest filing plan is to pack the set in cardboard and brown paper to exclude dust. A tag should be attached to each parcel showing the composer, title, and number of copies. This method is only economical for a work in request not more than once or twice a year; otherwise more staff time is lost in packing and unpacking than would pay for a box or folder.

While some of these works can be issued as supplied by the publisher, items difficult to replace or likely to receive regular use can have the spine strengthened with linen tape, may be sewn into brown paper covers for added strength, or laminated or sprayed with plastic. One method may be standard in a library, or each item considered on its merits and treated accordingly.

Sheet music, which occupies but a few pages, is sometimes avoided by librarians because of handling difficulties. The matter is discussed more fully under the heading Binding music (p. 26). Briefly: suitable works may be bound together to make a single volume, or single items can be treated by sewing into stiff manila or paper covers, or else laminated or covered with a plastic film. If a work is likely to be very rarely in demand and so warrants minimum expenditure, the spine can be strengthened with linen tape and the copy filed. There appears to be an even balance of argument between the merits of box and vertical filing. The former method permits greater portability and allows more readers to consult an extensive system at the same time; the latter has the advantage of requiring less floor space, though some libraries make the best of both systems by using box files and storing them in cupboards or on open shelves beneath the ordinary shelving--since this space is usually regarded as too low for normal public use. Local circumstances and personal preferences may be allowed to influence the decision as to which method to use.

Biographies and fiction present questions of an entirely different type from others discussed in this section and are related to the problem of music classification. There are also

administrative problems--whether to shelve books on music
and musicians with musical scores or to leave them with other
biographies, autobiographies, and novels. Since it is difficult to write a life of a composer without some reference to
the music and because music lovers are the people most likely to be interested in these lives, it is recommended that
such lives be shelved with the rest of the books on musical
history. The case for fiction is weaker though the Library
of Congress scheme, for instance, does make provision in its
schedules for such novels to be classed separately.

The majority of British public libraries tend to shelve
discs of nonmusical material in the music department, but as
this area of stock grows and as audiovisual items play an increasing part in the library service, a decision will need to
be made as to the location of such items. There has been an
assumption in many authorities that the music librarian can
undergo a sea change and become the library's audiovisual
specialist, without even the need of a magic wand to achieve
this transformation. In some cases, such a metamorphosis
may well be both possible and highly successful--but this
will certainly not always be the case. As the collection
grows in size and scope, there should come a time (again,
depending on the physical limitations of the building in which
the collection is housed) when the poetry and plays in recorded form are transferred to the literature or other department where the texts are to be found. A separation of this
nature was made at the new central library in Washington DC
when the building was opened in 1972.

Such a transfer should cause little difficulty, but what
about recorded documentary and other nonmusical materials?
These may not be so easily dispersed, and to separate them
into a series of small collections (of railway engines, of national history, etc.) could be both inconvenient and self-
defeating. It may well be that the music department will
still prove to be the best location until there is enough material in any one broad subject area to make separation both
logical and desirable.

Similar problems will need to be faced and solved with
audiovisual material. If the library appoints a technician,
there is likely to be an understandable tendency to keep the
relevant material under the eye of this specialist, but as
these materials become commonplace, then some sort of subject

division may well become desirable and, at a later stage, necessary. In short, it will no longer be the music librarian who has all the sound recordings under control, but a number of other specialist colleagues will each have a number of these items in their respective stocks--and all these subject experts should be equally adept at handling, checking for damage, and in the other routines that the librarian in charge of sound recordings may have to exercise alone until these "foreign" items are transferred to other departments.

This is no more than an extension of the problem faced with books in a departmentalised library. In Detroit:

> First claim on musical biography is made by the Biography Collection. Sometimes both Biography and Music & Drama will have the book--in two distinct numbers. Sometimes a book is just too scholarly and complex--with tables, bibliographies, appendixes, etc., for the Biography Collection and priority is yielded to Music & Drama. We miss the biographical material much less than anticipated (the policy is a few years old) but we worry about the minor figures who have importance for us but may mean nothing to the people in charge of the destinies of the Biography Collection. Musical fiction is in our fiction collection and has never presented any problems for us [156].

Indeed, a departmentalised library may be regarded as a mixed blessing in that there are, almost inevitably, gaps between departmental stocks as well as subjects which spread themselves over several areas, such as biography and fiction (mentioned in the previous paragraph), television, etc.

ACCOMMODATION AND EQUIPMENT

Location

The question of the location of a separate music department or of a music section in a general library is an academic one for most librarians but, in cases where some degree of choice is possible, certain factors should be taken into account.

The situation preferred should be in a quiet part of the library, but not difficult of access. There should be room for the provision of tables and chairs at which users can read periodicals, or browse through books or scores. Where the library lends sound recordings of music, the music collection should be located in the same area, if this is possible. If the shelves for scores and sound recording bays are simply part of a department or a general library, the music collection should be sited to allow adequate oversight from the staff enclosure and should take into account the daily traffic of the department. A constant stream of borrowers walking through or past the music section to get to the fiction shelves, for instance, might possibly draw the attention of the occasional user to the fact that music is available, but is also likely to be a disturbance and a hindrance to reading or use of the stock by music lovers.

Space Required

One may feel, a trifle sourly sometimes, that the space required and the space actually allotted to a music section often bear no apparent relationship, particularly in cases where those with the power to make decisions have minimal or no interest in music. In any case, it is virtually impossible to make hard and fast rules; so much depends upon the size of the stock (both present and potential), the services offered, the incorporation of sound recordings and/or other audio-visual materials in the same section of the library. For a public library serving a population of about 50,000 an actual figure for one such authority has been quoted--about 170 sq. ft. (i.e., a little over 16 sq. metres) for a section which did not make provision for sound recordings. For music scores, somewhere around 50 ft. (15.25 m.) of shelving was suggested, 35 ft. (10.65 m.) for a good basic collection of miniature scores, a length of 25 ft. (7.63 m.) for books on music and 12 ft. (3.65 m.) for music reference books. All these figures are on the conservative side, and the two for books are not really adequate. Even the very small library will need to provide no less than half of these suggested shelf lengths. Recommendations are not made here for academic and college libraries, not least because there will be considerable variation between two libraries serving the same number of staff and students if, on the one hand, music is a major field of study and, on the other, where the subject is an optional extra of small importance in the curriculum. [76]

If figures are difficult to quantify for the open shelves, they are equally so for the reserve or stack shelving. Because, proportionately, far fewer music scores are discarded than are books in many other classes (assuming that the original selection has been well made), the size of the stock off the open shelves is likely to be quite high, and one might suggest that this is only to be expected. Reserve stock will include seasonal music (particularly relating to Christmas and Easter) that emerges annually into the daylight of the open shelves, worthwhile items that are not popular but which are too important to discard, duplicate copies that are needed sufficiently often to be worth keeping, and scores that have grown shabby externally and which, for any reason, have not been replaced by new copies. Even though the material in stack should be checked periodically to assure the music librarian that there is little that can safely be thrown away, it seems likely that there will be a steadily growing body of material, even if the number of books and scores borrowed from the department also grows.

To work out, very roughly, how much space is required for music is something that the librarian should be able to do fairly accurately. Bound vocal scores will probably average about fifteen to a foot (30 cm.) of shelving, piano and organ works should be provided for at twenty-four to the foot, and instrumental items that have a separate piano part in a rear pocket inside the binding will use about a foot of shelving for sixteen average-width volumes (1.9 cm. each). Finally, sets of chamber music parts will require approximately an inch of shelf space (2.5 cm.) each. For a different set of estimates, and a review of the whole topic, there is a useful booklet by Robert Michael Fling [72].

Shelving

The need for special shelving for scores is self-evident. Some librarians prefer adjustable shelving because of its flexibility but the extra cost may not be justified. If fixed shelves are provided, a distance of 14 inches (35.5 cm.) between shelves will be sufficient for nearly all sheet music to stand upright, and a depth of 12 inches (30 cm.) should

be equally adequate. Because bound music tends to be
awkward to handle and is heavy in bulk, upright partitions
should be provided at frequent intervals; a minimum of 6
inches (15 cm.) and a maximum of 10 inches (25.5 cm.) between such partitions is recommended. These divisions, both
with wood and metal shelving, should extend flush to the
front edge to minimize possible damage to the scores. As
with ordinary bookshelves, it is advisable to restrict the upper and lower shelf limits; the lowest shelf should be about
18 inches (46 cm.) from the floor and the top shelf about
63 inches (160 cm.), allowing three shelves to the case.

Miniature scores present their own problems and the
best solution would seem to be the provision of special
shelves, about 9 inches (23 cm.) high and some 7 inches
(18 cm.) from front to back. This height and depth will
be suitable for the great majority of scores of this type,
although there are a number (such as the Vaughan Williams
symphonies and some of the optimistically titled Hawkes
"pocket" scores, which require a "poacher's pocket" to contain them) which are too tall for the 9-inch (23-cm.) shelf.
These will either have to stand on their fore-edges or else
be arranged in a separate sequence on rather taller shelves,
about 10 inches (25.5 cm.) high, and underneath the smaller
ones if the miniature score shelves are tiered. Either solution is an unhappy one.

Floor space will be required for vertical files if sheet
music is stored in this fashion; where pamphlet boxes are
preferred, special shelves may be required and the boxes
bought to a standard size. It has already been mentioned
that some libraries, rather than waste the space between the
floor and bottom shelf, make the front panel hinge so that
the space under the shelves becomes a cupboard. Orchestral parts and sets of anthems are usually kept in reserve.
Shelving for sound recordings is discussed in Chapter V.

If the music library is housed as a separate department its catalogue will be there also. Where the collection is
obviously separated from the remainder of the lending stock
but is not an independent department it may be thought an
advantage to have the appropriate sections of the catalogue
adjoining the books and scores. With a classified catalogue
this would simply entail the removal of the appropriate subject entries en bloc; with a dictionary catalogue a similarly

self-contained unit would be easily available if the catchword
"Music" is used before all subject headings for scores, but a
check of subject headings would be needed for books on music. It would be much more difficult to extract individual
entries for composers and writers on music and there are
definite advantages in leaving such entries in the normal
author sequence. With mechanised catalogue reproduction,
the problem should not arise.

Staff Enclosure

It seems unfair to the public, where there is a separate department for music, to expect them to use the main desk for
the issue and return of scores; gramophone records require
ample room if adequate checking of discs for damage is to be
carried out. Yet the current tendency, in both the USA and
UK, is for all material to be charged out and taken in at a
single desk in the entrance foyer, and for these tasks to be
done by clerical personnel. It is undoubtedly a less expensive method in terms of staff cost than the maintenance of a
separate counter in the music section; it could also well be a
false economy, but this is extremely difficult to prove. It
may be argued that this method builds up a general sense of
staff responsibility to music and records. If the library allows patrons to listen to sound recordings and to handle the
discs, cassettes, etc., then good oversight of the listening
facilities is needed.

Hours of Opening

Hours of opening present a problem. If the music library is
to be open for similar hours to those of the general lending
library a staff of two will be inadequate without assistance;
three people at least will be needed for the department to be
entirely self-contained except for holiday periods and absences
through sickness. Late evening hours of opening are likely
to preclude the possibilities of gramophone recitals, live music, and similar activities; early closing will be to the disadvantage of the local library user. Where gramophone records
are loaned it should be stipulated that records must be returned ten or fifteen minutes before closing time to allow
checking of the condition of each disc to take place.

The hours of opening are naturally affected by local
demand and use. It may be said that, in general, American
libraries are very much more generous in this way than those
in Britain. The music library at Boston, Massachusetts, was
for many years open from 9:00 a.m. to 9:00 p.m. each week-
day and from 2:00 p.m. to 6:00 p.m. on Sundays. British
libraries may open as early in the day but generally close at
7:00 p.m. or 8:00 p.m. (much earlier on Saturdays) and do
not open on Sundays.

STAFF

A high proportion of librarians and assistants seem to have a
liking for classical music and some knowledge of it; this is
true both in Britain and the USA. Alice Bryan's The Public
Librarian has some pertinent information upon this point, for
she attempted to discover the vocational interests of librarians by means of a test devised by Edward K. Strong, Jr.,
Professor of Psychology at Stanford University. The median
ratings for fifty-four professional men showed the highest
preference for "musician," though Bryan cautiously points
out that this surprising result might not be general if a
wider sample were taken. Since "musician" was excluded
from the choice of professions for women no comparable figure can be given [32, pp. 124-126]. A strong interest in
music among British librarians of both sexes was indicated
by the answers given in Landau's Who's Who in Librarianship
[116] since nearly 400 qualified librarians out of the 2,000
or so listed give music as a major interest. Such a high proportion seems incompatible with the equally high proportion
of inadequate music stocks in our public libraries. A personal impression is that few public libraries lack at least one
staff member who is interested in classical music and all professional members of the staff should be able to answer simple and direct queries.

Recruitment, Standards, and Qualifications

Where there is a post of Music Librarian, it should automatically be on a professional grade and require a professional
qualification. This applies whatever the title of the position,
e.g., Music & Sound Recordings Librarian. The necessary
qualifications for an Audiovisual Librarian, mentioned else-

where, are still far from universally agreed. If the post
covers a wider area than music only, such as Fine Arts Librarian, Music & Arts Librarian, Music & Drama Librarian,
or something similar, it seems certain that the holder of the
post will be either a music librarian with a secondary interest in other fine arts, drama or whatever subjects are covered by the department, or the situation will be reversed,
and the music section less adequately managed. As Lester
Asheim has written:

> The specialized background required of a good art
> librarian or a good music librarian is such that there
> is hardly time for the librarian to prepare for either
> field, let alone both. The work he will do in one
> department differs in many ways from that in the
> other. There is an entirely different set of refer-
> ence tools in the field of music; an entirely differ-
> ent group of master works and standard titles; a
> different sort of administrative problem; and an al-
> most completely different clientele to be served [10,
> p. 152].

The answer, for the really large library, is suggested by
John C. Larsen: "At present, it is safe to say that the
supervisor of a general art/music collection, when selecting
personnel, will attempt to balance his staff with some people
whose major strength is in the visual arts and others whose
primary interest is in music."

> A distinction might be made between the subject
> background needed by the general art/music li-
> brarian in the public library and the general art/
> music librarian in the academic library. Although
> the similarity of subject training between the two is
> much greater than any difference, the public librar-
> ian must be more crafts- or hobby-orientated in his
> knowledge than the librarian in the academic world
> where many liberal arts institutions do not have stu-
> dents pursuing practical studio courses [120, p. 534].

In contrast to the situation in the large library, in the
small system (particularly when there is no separate music
department), the choice is almost certainly to be made between one who is a qualified librarian but who lacks a music
qualification and another who has a degree or diploma in

some musical area but who is not the possessor of a library qualification. The preference in this case is likely to be in favour of the qualified librarian who should be able, if the need arises, to adapt quickly to work in another department and who, it is assumed, will widen previous musical knowledge and background in the course of daily employment. The musician with little library knowledge could well be a misfit in this situation.

Nevertheless, the larger the department, the more important a good musical education becomes and librarianship qualifications may be slightly less important. It is, however, increasingly recognized in public libraries (and rather more slowly in academic ones) that the real need is for a dual qualification.

Otto Kinkeldey wrote, over forty years ago:

> In the first place, and above all else, a music librarian should be a good librarian. I mean by this, that he or she should be a person adapted by nature and temperament to general library work. So far as systematic training goes, he or she would have received a large part of the knowledge which we expect of anyone who is connected with a library. A music librarian who is not thoroughly acquainted with the organization and operation of a general library as we know it today, who feels that his work is a domain unto itself and who is disinclined to make his work fit smoothly into the larger mechanism, is more likely to do more harm than all the good a great special knowledge will bring. I do not believe that it is possible to exaggerate the importance of this point [112, p. 461].

A slightly different viewpoint was taken by Otto Luening when he suggested the following criteria for qualification and knowledge:

> The ideal music librarian has had both library and musical training, is community minded, and is able to work effectively with community music leaders, musicians, and music-lovers. A person with all of these qualifications is hard to find. It is of primary importance, however, that the music librarian be

community-minded and have the ability and knowledge to meet and to discuss music with professionals and laymen alike. Such a person need not have had both types of specialized training to be a successful music librarian, although one or the other is necessary. In a few towns which had had an active musical life for some time, an active adult education programme, and well-conducted school and college music courses, the library music department is often widely used in spite of inadequate leadership [127, p. 54].

A different approach to the ideal was expressed by Donald W. Krummel:

> What then must a music librarian be today? He must know what to buy--when to depend on a creator's or publisher's name, when to wait for a review, and when even to ignore the review. He must know where entries will be found in the catalog, and why entries will not always be found in places where one might expect to find them. He must know enough not to bind the four parts of a quartet together, and he must have enough wits about him to know what to do with his copy of Stockhausen's Klavierstuck XI [30]. He must understand the problems and talk the language of performing musicians from combos, symphonies, church choirs....
>
> He must also, if he is worth his salt, be an administrative nuisance. Besides demanding money for his collection, he will pester the cataloging department for adequate indexing, the order department for the advantage of placing orders with firms that specialize in music, the circulation department to make sure all five parts of a woodwind quintet are returned, the reading room next door because his earphones aren't always soundproof enough, the supply officer because twelve-inch records won't fit safely on five-inch shelves. The price of excellence is high, but perhaps not higher than that of excellence in other special library fields [114, p. 81].

Luening's emphasis on work with persons and organizations outside the library itself is much less stressed by other writers. Appreciably more concern is expressed over adequate qualifications. Fairly detailed suggestions for those

required by the competent music librarian were presented by
Guy Marco at the 1966 midwinter meeting of the Music Library Association. Marco's concept--that the basic requirement is for the librarian to have "rapport with the collection"
--was elaborated later in an article [135]. Seven years later,
at Indiana University, the same topic was discussed at length
and it was clear that the knowledge considered necessary had
increased noticeably in the interim. Still more recently, a
detailed appraisal of these needs has been given by the Music Library Association's Committee on Professional Education
[148]; only a brief outline of the points made seems necessary here. This statement would seem to represent something of a consensus among a wide variety of opinions expressed at a number of the Association's meetings. The text
"is concerned with the minimum qualifications ..." and has a
threefold aim. It is intended, first, to offer guidance to employers or supervising librarians; secondly, to prospective
music librarians themselves; and, thirdly, to those engaged
in the field of professional education. There are four main
sections--I. Knowledge of the materials of a music library;
II. Abilities to perform the most important kinds of music
library work; III. General background; IV. Conclusion: The
education of a music librarian.

The first area (knowledge of the materials) is subdivided into four major headings and nineteen subheadings.
The larger areas are concerned with reference books on music, books about music in general "musical edictions" (i.e.,
scores, performance parts, etc.), and sound recordings.
As has been indicated, each of these headings is subdivided
to provide annotations that clarify the committee's intentions.
For example, the last four of the seven headings concerned
with sound recordings indicate that the qualified music librarian should know "the peculiarities of cataloging of sound
recordings" and collection maintenance (i.e., bindings, circulation, storage, environmental control and durability) on
the one hand, as well as technical aspects (i.e., sound com-
ponents and systems and their maintenance) and legal aspects (i.e., copyright of sound recordings, performance
rights, restrictions on copying, etc.) on the other.

The second main area is headed "Abilities to perform
the most important kinds of music library work" and is concerned with service to readers, selection and acquisitions,
cataloging and classification, and administration. British

librarians might be a little startled to read item C.6 which
expects the music librarian to "Use all three of the major
music classification schemes (Dewey, LC, Dickinson), and select the appropriate one for a newly formed music library,
on the basis of its particular advantages"--partly because
the music librarian could well be directed by higher authority as to which system to use, and partly because Dickinson
is virtually an unknown scheme on this side of the Atlantic
and one would have thought that the British Catalogue of
Music scheme at least deserved some consideration.

"General background" places the music department in
the context of the library as a whole, recognizing that the
music librarian and music section must fit into the library
services of the system. "Basic musicianship" is perhaps
more demanding than some readers might expect, while
"Music history" knowledge is considered to be a major priority. The music librarian should, in the eyes of the committee, "For purposes of breadth, have taken at least one
course devoted to a chronological survey of music history
(not a general music literature or music appreciation course).
This course should preferably be one designed for music ma-
jors and taken before formal training in librarianship." Additionally, the librarian should have taken at least one course
dealing with a special period or genre and another--a "graduate music bibliography course, taught by a qualified music
librarian or by an experienced musicologist." To make sure
that the good music librarian has satisfactory width of interests, there are requirements on "popular music, current
tastes, ethnomusicology." The final conclusion, in part,
sums up the earlier sections but adds, "A familiarity with
foreign languages, especially German, Italian, French, and
Latin, is extremely useful."

The required qualities may be well beyond the competence of anyone without considerable experience; even after
a lifetime's work, the most devoted librarian is likely to have
gaps in knowledge and skills. The important point is that
the music librarian has a series of targets at which to aim,
however few may be achieved over the years. A careful
rationalization of these targets, following the terminology and
concepts of Benjamin S. Bloom, has been offered by Michael
Ochs [170]. Ochs adds detail and support for the principles
expressed in the MLA statement. A similar prescription, in
brief outline format, has come from the Commission on Educa-

tion and Training of the International Association of Music
Libraries [51].

Despite the ubiquitous suggestion that the music librarian should be knowledgeable on technical aspects of
sound recordings, this in itself is a specialist area and the
need for technician support has already been mentioned. In
the larger system, with more than two or three professional
members of staff, it would be desirable to attempt to appoint
librarians with complementary specialities (different musical
periods, different types of music, etc.) to allow some approximate subdivision of responsibilities and the chance for
each to continue to develop personal interests in particular
aspects of music history, of repertory and other of the multitude of topics in which the musical users of the library are
interested. Yet wherever it may be, any professional post
in a music library, academic or public, really calls for a fair
knowledge of foreign languages. Both Savage (in Britain)
and Kinkeldey (in the USA) have stressed the importance of
a good working knowledge of French, German, and Italian.
The MLA committee have added Latin as a useful addition,
and a strong case could be made out for the music library
to have a Russian specialist on its staff to transliterate and
catalogue a title page correctly. The poor linguist can often
manage to translate a title page and publishers' catalogues,
using a restricted vocabulary painfully acquired by experience, but this is barely adequate for professional competence.
A useful guide to the vocabulary, in English and in French,
German, Italian, and Latin, is offered by one of the Music
Library Association Technical Reports. [212]

Kinkeldey is unyielding on this ability to read a foreign language [112] for he has written: "Although we say
that music is a universal language, the foreign vernacular
with which it is associated is a great stumbling-block to the
linguistically deficient musician.... In fact, the librarian
who wishes to rely for his knowledge of journals, histories,
encyclopedias and dictionaries in English only cannot go very
far." On performing ability he added:

> It does not seem to me to be necessary that a music
> librarian should be a good performer or composer.
> To be sure, one who sings well and plays an instru-
> ment well and one who is able to create an actual
> musical composition, is more likely than another to

understand the peculiar nature of the material in his charge as a librarian. But he may be a wholly adequate librarian without these accomplishments. On the other hand, a reasonable acquaintance with musical theory in the widest acceptance of the word; a knowledge of its principles and technical terms is a fair requirement. A music librarian who did not recognize a fugue when he heard it, or saw it on paper, or who did not know the meaning of the term double counterpoint, would be as useful as a literary librarian who did not know the difference between an epic and a sonnet ... [112].

Status and Salaries

The preceding sections have tried to demonstrate that the music librarian should possess both a music qualification and one in librarianship, plus an ability in foreign languages and a good general musical background in addition to academic studies. "Such people are not to be found in the hedgerows; they must be sought after and retained by satisfactory salaries and proper opportunities" [129, p. 47]. That was McColvin in 1937, but the reality then and now is, with the occasional exception, depressing. In Britain, it seems to have been a constant policy to pay the music librarian (where such an appointment existed; it took many chief librarians a very long time to recognize the need and potential value of such a post in every authority serving a population in excess of 100,000) on a lower salary scale than most other specialists, particularly reference and technical librarians, but also cataloguers and children's librarians. There appears to have been an implicit assumption that the music librarian's skills are more easily acquired than those in other subject fields (which is utterly untrue, as this particular volume should show), that this is a position of lesser status and that anyone entering this avenue of service is clearly doing it for vocational reasons and therefore, by some peculiar logic, should be happy to accept the post at a salary lower than it is really worth. These unflattering assumptions have had far too long a currency--not least because there have been dedicated and well-qualified librarians who have taken music library posts at salaries which have varied from the tolerable to the disgraceful.

Not only is the financial reward lower than it should
be (and a small salary clearly depresses the status of a music librarian vis-à-vis other specialists) but, for too long,
the chances of promotion within this particular speciality
were very small, simply because there were but a handful
of local authorities of sufficient size to provide a department
that needed a number of professionally qualified librarians
for proper staffing. The dramatic change in the local government scene in Britain since 1974 should have provided opportunities in public libraries for a much better career structure
for specialists. Many authorities which previously had no
music librarian now include several in their establishment,
but such posts have often been unfilled through financial
restrictions. However, in the long term, reorganization
should prove an excellent fillip to this area of the profession.

To British eyes, the American scene appears distinctly brighter. In the United States, a music librarian entering the service of a public library or an academic library
will be compensated at the same level as colleagues with
other specializations. The compensation is based on the
status of the position on a salary scale that applies to the
entire staff; an individual's place on the scale depends upon
some combination of degrees held and experience--not upon
subject specialisation. It is true that the higher salary
steps are reserved for administrative positions (director,
deputy director, etc.), and that qualification for such posts
may not be related to the usual background of music librarians, but of course this is not different from the situation in
Europe.

Professional Associations

There is no group or section within the Library Association
in Britain that is specifically intended for the music librarian;
the nearest, in terms of subject interest, is likely to be the
Audio-Visual Group, particularly if the individual's duties
include any responsibility for sound recordings. A major
reason for the unwillingness of the Library Association to
make special provision for music librarians was almost certainly the fact that the United Kingdom branch of the International Association of Music Libraries had already been
set up (in 1953) before the LA really developed a series of

subject-orientated groups. IAML membership covers academic and college libraries, as well as those in the public field and also has some members from the music trade. As a result, it can undoubtedly claim to be far more representative than any section based on LA membership could hope to be. The British librarian interested in music librarianship should certainly belong to the IAML branch. All members throughout the world receive copies of Fontes artis musicae and British members also receive Brio as a tangible return for their subscriptions. These journals are considered in Chapter II.

The Music Library Association makes an interesting contrast. It was founded in the USA in 1931 "To promote the development of music libraries; to encourage studies in the organization and administration of music in libraries" and its membership has grown to about 2,000. From personal observation, it would seem that a very high proportion of university and college librarians in the field of music are members, but there are fewer public librarians although their numbers are rising. There are also members among nonlibrarians, particularly from the music trade. The Association has twelve regional chapters covering the areas with the largest and/or most active membership. As with the UK Branch of IAML, but on a much wider geographical scale, membership is irregularly spread throughout the country.

The Association's professional journal, ambiguously entitled Notes, cannot be overrated in importance and is considered at some length in the next chapter. The strength and success of the MLA perhaps explains the fact that membership of the IAML in the USA is smaller than one would expect, although there is a joint committee between the two groups, and similar linkage with the American Musicological Society as well as the Musical Publishers Association.

It seems highly unlikely that Britain will ever have enough music librarians, whatever the type of library in which they work, to make possible an independent association such as the MLA, but it could be argued that the success of the IAML is a much more important objective, since the greater its international strength, the better for music librarianship as a whole.

OTHER ADMINISTRATIVE ASPECTS

Music Tickets, Charging Methods

It used to be common for public libraries to issue, upon request, special tickets for use with music books or scores
only. This practice is now almost obsolete owing to the continuing trend towards fewer restrictions on book borrowing.
Libraries that do issue special tickets for music have to ensure that their use is limited for that specific purpose and
the most effective method would seem to be the adoption of
a different coloured manila from that for other types of
ticket. Automated systems (which, in some cases, are programmed to restrict borrowing on any one ticket to a limited
number of items) and photocharging may effectively allow unlimited borrowing, although in Britain it is customary to restrict the number of items borrowed at any one time.

The need for a special ticket for use when borrowing
sound recordings is much less generally accepted than it was
a few years ago, but there are still many local authorities
which limit the loan of recordings to such tickets, not least
because this gives a greater measure of control over the number of recordings borrowed by one person and over the borrowers themselves. The matter is considered more fully in
Chapter V.

Generally speaking, charging methods for books and
scores will be exactly similar to those for other types of
material. It is sometimes difficult with unbound music to
find a suitable place for the date label and pocket, where
these are used, but the problem should not be insoluble.
Volumes that include separate parts in a rear pocket, etc.,
will take longer to issue and discharge because of the need
to check the presence of loose parts at each transaction.

Issue Statistics

Although the collection of issue statistics is much less common than it was, at least beyond a total figure to indicate
generally increasing or decreasing use of the library, there
are advantages in keeping fairly detailed figures, and they
deserve consideration. Statistics by categories of issues

can often confirm general impressions, although abrupt changes in borrowing habits by a library's users are unlikely to occur. In a general library, detailed statistics may well be required to reinforce the case for the provision of a separate section or department, or the reverse. However, comparatively little use of the music books and scores may be due to several reasons--an inadequate stock, one in poor condition, a badly sited section in the main library, a complete absence of any musically knowledgeable staff, a constant failure to add new items to stock--all these, and other causes, are possible. The librarian will need to investigate carefully the reasons for lack of use. There are examples of good collections receiving much less use by the local public than is deserved by the quality and range of the music provided, but this is not frequent. If the number of books and scores is quoted separately, a comparison with the stocks and amount of borrowing in other libraries is easily made, although it should be borne in mind that some libraries count the loan of twenty copies of an anthem to a choir as one issue, while others inflate their figures by counting such a loan as twenty issues--arguments can be produced in favour of either method.

Stationery

As far as possible, the music department is well advised to use standard stationery, for economy and also for consistency within the library system; a specially printed or duplicated request form may, however, be useful to ensure that readers' requests are answered correctly and satisfactorily. When a book is requested and the reader knows the correct author and title, few problems are likely to arise; but if an assistant notes that a patron wants Beethoven's seventh symphony, without further details, several points arise needing solution. Does the reader want a miniature score, an arrangement for piano duet or for organ? If the request is for Verdi's Nabucco is it a vocal score that is required? Will the enquirer be satisfied with a score showing the original words only; or is an English translation needed; or should both the original Italian and a translation be supplied? Such problems can be frustrating if not correctly answered, and this type of query is very common. A special form helps to eliminate most of the possible alternatives. There are arguments both for and against such a form being completed by the enquirer or filled in by the member of the staff answering

the enquiry. The type of form suggested is that devised by
J. F. W. Bryon for use at Eccles, and subsequently copied by
a number of other libraries. The form's reverse, intended for
staff use only, was used as a record of the steps taken in
order to prevent duplication of effort in answering the query.
Several of the questions on this all-purpose form [40] are
useful for music requests:

> <u>Level</u>. Introductory/Elementary/Intermediate/Advanced/
> Research
>
> <u>Language</u>. German/French/Spanish/Italian/...

while the questions relating to music only are:

> <u>Music score</u>. Vocal/Miniature/Instrumental/Full/Parts/
>
> Arranged for.........................

Rules and Regulations

There would appear to be no particular need for special
rules and regulations for the music library or section. The
standard period of loan for books should suffice for music
and also for sound recordings. In any case, borrowers
could well find it confusing to borrow items in these different formats at the same time, but not have the same dates
by which they should be returned. For societies and choirs
the position is different, since the sets of scores and/or
parts are generally borrowed, if it can be arranged, for a
sufficiently lengthy period for the work to be learned and
possibly performed in public. For this reason, loan may be
requested for a matter of several weeks or as many months.
Most libraries that supply parts or multiple copies make allowance for this. The former West Riding County Library,
for example, permitted a maximum loan period of up to eight
months without renewal and, after that period, the loan
could usually be renewed for a further lengthy period unless needed by another group. There was also the proviso
that works on long loan could be recalled before the expiry
of the period if necessary. If fines are charged for the late
return of bulk loans, special rates are likely to be considered necessary as the normal fee, based on a unit of a single
copy multiplied by the number borrowed, would be prohibitive.

The very large music library will normally accept requests for bulk loan of copies some months ahead of the actual date required. This will help both the society and the
music librarian. Every library, whatever its size, is usually willing to receive reservations for individual items in
stock.

Separate rules and regulations may be considered necessary for a sound recordings library, and a specimen set
is included in Chapter V.

Publicity

The largest printed catalogue of music published by a British Public library is probably that of Liverpool, with v.1
issued in 1956 and v.2 in 1981. It provides other libraries
with a useful check list and reference aid (nearly always
quoting the name of the publisher of each item in v.2, but
not in v.1). Other large systems have also issued good
catalogues (one might instance the sectional lists of Not-
tinghamshire), and such examples have both practical and
publicity value, for they permit partial revision as required.
Although the costs of printing a comprehensive music catalogue are likely to be appreciably less than the total cost of
sectional ones covering the same stock, the financial advantages to both library and users (assuming the catalogues to
be for sale, rather than issued gratis) should not need
specifying.

Selective lists of available stock are published by many
authorities, usually limited to the categories of music in
most general demand. Whether printed or duplicated, they
should be as well produced as possible; if sold for a small
sum, the more attractive examples are likely to recover a
fair proportion of the original cost. The larger the list, the
less likely it becomes that it can be sold at an economic
price, which is possibly an additional argument in favour of
a selective rather than a comprehensive publication.

What must always be remembered is that a list produced simply for the sake of publication is unlikely to be a
success. The librarian should aim at preparing a "tailor-
made" compilation and should have a clear mental picture of
the type(s) of user to be served by it. Thus, in addition

to publications showing the library's holdings in a particular
musical field, it might be relevant to publish a list of books
and scores relating to an individual composer who has just
died (assuming that the library's holdings warrant this
treatment), or whose birth or death centenary, etc., is
about to occur. These and similar occasions should provide
ample opportunities to draw users' attention to the library's
holdings. If the compilation of a list also brings attention
to unexpected and previously unrecognized gaps in holdings,
this may be regarded as salutary, providing that action is
quickly taken to make good the omissions.

There should never be a dearth of ideas for booklists
and displays. At the same time, such lists should not be
produced so frequently that their numbers dull the impact
on the library's users. Again, no list should be produced
unless there is enough relevant material in stock to make
publication worthwhile. If works are put out on display
and such items can be borrowed (as one hopes would be the
case), then gaps on the display stand should be filled as
quickly as they occur, which will not be possible if the subject chosen is poorly represented in the library's stock.

A simple and permanent display may be made of music
due for performance on the radio or on television during the
week ahead. Once users become used to the idea, the selection should receive regular use--providing that the scores
displayed are checked daily and items broadcast during the
previous twenty-four hours removed and returned to the ordinary shelves and any other available works added for the
week ahead. Such a scheme is operated in a number of libraries and appears to justify the time and trouble taken.

In addition to this semi-permanent display, occasional
ones can be organized for particular local activities, concerts,
anniversaries etc. There should also be a notice-board in a
music library displaying posters of forthcoming concerts that
are taking place within reasonable travelling range of the
town (or of festivals that may be visited during holiday
periods), prospectuses of gramophone societies and similar
local groups, perhaps an "amateur exchange" to put instrumentalists and vocalists in touch with one another with a
view to combining forces and, of course, notices of any musical functions that are being organized by the library itself.
Accessions lists, already mentioned, may prove a useful

reminder to users of the scope of the collection as well as
providing information to individuals of additions to their own
particular sphere of interest. The small and medium-sized
library would probably find one or two lists a year sufficient;
there is no point in producing them more frequently unless
there is a large number of accessions. If the library produces a general bulletin of recent additions, then music
should naturally be included. Where there is a separate music library it should receive individual mention in the annual
report.

Otto Luening's ideal of what a music library should do
is as follows:

> The department maintains a bulletin board for pro-
> gramme announcements, musical news, events, con-
> tests, scholarships, and so forth, and makes book
> lists in connection with concerts, new musical motion
> pictures, and radio broadcasts. It also prepares
> reading and listening lists for groups of clubs and
> for general distribution to all library agencies in the
> region. The library sends out music on inter-library
> loan whenever this is feasible [127, p. 59].

British libraries, at least, participate in the last of these
suggestions even if too many do not follow the other practices mentioned.

A library with space and sufficient local interest may
consider the idea of an exhibition of music and related material. It is not usually difficult to borrow suitable items
for display, and ideas may be obtained from an illustrated
article by an American librarian, A. Beverly Barksdale, which
provides much useful information to anyone staging such an
exhibition, under the headings Planning, Procuring, Presenting, and Promoting [12].

Extension Work

A number of British public libraries hold recorded music recitals in the building, which should provide excellent publicity both for the collection of recordings and of scores. Recitals may be presented by members of the library's staff,
by outside recitalists, or a combination of both. Busy city

libraries have found lunchtime presentations popular, particularly in places where it is made clear that members of the
public are free to come and go at any time during the concert, providing that a minimum of disturbance is caused.
Evening recitals organized by the library are now very much
less popular than they were at one time, but recorded music
societies (or groups with similar titles) are usually pleased
to have the advantages of using library premises as a venue
for meetings. In some cases, the local librarian is an officer or committee member of the society, and there are advantages on both sides where this is the case. It may be
possible for the society to store its equipment on the premises (which is a considerable help), to be able to provide
light refreshments during the interval (an invaluable aid to
social contact) and for the library authority to allow the
premises to be used, if not free of charge, at least at a
figure which does no more than cover the additional care-
taking, heating, and lighting costs incurred. Some of these
points are discussed in greater detail in Chapter V.

Library activities need not be limited to recorded recitals if there is a good hall or theatre in the building. The
idea that public libraries should do all they can to promote
and sponsor the arts has gained great impetus in recent
years--not only in the field of music, although that is the
immediate concern here [83]. Mention has been made of library use for music appreciation groups, etc., but in places
where accommodation is available, lecture-recitals and concerts become feasible. Bolton and Bradford are two northern
towns that regularly present recitals by internationally known
soloists and chamber groups. Both work in cooperation with
the BBC and some recitals are broadcast. A library may be
able to sponsor concerts by young local musicians. The le-
gality of making an admission charge, where thought necessary or desirable, is now beyond doubt through Section 20
of the 1964 Public Libraries & Museums Act. It should perhaps be mentioned that young professional artists are usually members of the Musicians' Union and therefore expect to
be paid at the appropriate rate. It is only proper that payment should be made by the library.

The librarian who has to arrange a series of concerts
whether professional or amateur will, one hopes, develop expertise with growing experience. Among the necessary skills
are estimating the likely size of an audience, how much to

charge for admission, and the probable deficit on a series of presentations. Fortunately, in addition to the hazards there are compensations and rewards in helping to bring good music to a wider audience. All Regional Arts associations have a staff member responsible for musical presentations, and such an officer will usually be very willing to help, advise and guide the music librarian when requested to do so.

Many music librarians both in Britain and the USA write programme notes for local concerts and recitals. It is, one may mention in passing, a decidedly more difficult undertaking than might be imagined by those who have never tried it, unless the level of musical knowledge in the audience is much the same from one listener to the next. The task of providing this help to listeners certainly strengthens links between the library and music making; the opportunity should be taken to indicate, at the end of the notes, which of the works performed is represented by one or more recorded performances in the library stock and for which items scores are available, thus drawing attention to the library's holdings and facilities.

Finance

In Britain the discount on sheet music has apparently been progressively reduced. James Duff Brown wrote in 1893: "When ordering music it will often be found of some advantage to approach the publishers directly, especially if the selection made from the list of one firm runs into a respectable amount. Discounts ranging from 25 to 50 per cent will generally be allowed on a fair order, and all the bother of employing an intermediary will be saved" [31, p. 3]. Between the two world wars it had become the custom to order from a music dealer and public libraries were allowed the same discount as that granted to professional musicians and music teachers, 2d in the shilling (16.67%). This professional discount was further reduced after World War II to the 10 percent which was and is the normal discount on books allowed to public libraries by those booksellers whose names were on an individual library's book licence issued by the Booksellers' Association. With postal charges added to the invoice total, libraries are in little better position than an individual purchaser when buying scores. There is no standard rate of discount in the USA, so libraries have to

obtain the best terms that they can. It would seem, however, that American librarians have frequently found it very
much cheaper to import music direct from European publishers, rather than through the American agent whose mark-up
in price is sometimes extremely high, so that direct purchase
from the publisher or even through a non-American music
dealer can save much money. A useful series of articles in
Notes has compared prices in the American and European
markets for various categories of musical editions [96].

A library, academic or public, should have its stock
and ancillaries (such as catalogues, accession file) as well
as the building and furniture, covered by insurance. The
figures should be checked at least every two or three years
(probably annually if the prices of replacement copies continue to rise as rapidly as in recent years) to ensure that
coverage is adequate--not only for the stock that might be
lost, but also for the re-cataloguing, etc., that a major disaster would necessitate. At the time of writing it would
seem that the depreciation in the value of scores which are
available for loan is almost fully offset by the steadily increasing costs of replacement. In comparison with books, a
much higher proportion of music scores will need to be rebound before being put on the shelves for loan, and this is
a figure which should be approximately calculated in terms
of likely cost. If an allowance has to be made for wear-and-
tear of stock (as the insurance company may reasonably demand), the librarian can work out this figure, volume by
volume if really necessary, particularly if the library stock
has date labels which will tell how often the item has gone
out and, judging from its current condition, what its likely
life will be. Failing that, the music librarian will need to
check when a number of items were bought and judge the
respective condition of each volume when inspected; from
these two values, the stock's potential worth can, one
hopes, be reasonably assessed. This rule-of-thumb is
clearly to be ignored when dealing with rare (possibly
unique) items and with manuscripts. In such cases, however, one trusts that the library has already made special
provision for their safety against fire, flood and theft.

For sound recordings, much depends upon the care
(or lack of it) with which items are inspected on return
from loan. Again, once the section has been operational
for some little time, it should not be difficult to work out

an estimate of the average life expectancy of a disc or cassette. It seems fair to estimate the life of a book on the open shelves at between five and ten years, for between ten and fifteen years for a bound score, two to three years for gramophone records and three to four years for cassettes. In all cases, allowance should be made in the sum insured for the proportion of stock in each category likely to be on loan at any one time and which would, one hopes, escape any calamity that befell the library.

This chapter has attempted to show the need for a well-developed music section, even in the very small library. It has also given some suggested answers to certain problems that are likely to arise. Finally, one point must be stressed again. Money spent on good classical music is never wasted, even though it may be a very slow process to persuade the right sort of potential user to come and take full advantage of the services offered by the public library.

Chapter II

REFERENCE BOOKS AND PERIODICALS

INTRODUCTION

There are thousands of reference books dealing with various aspects of music. There are also hundreds of current periodicals concerned with musical topics [71]. A limited number of major works, together with a selection of periodicals, are described here; emphasis has been placed on the aid they can provide towards the choice of new material for the music library or department. Nearly all the reference books mentioned should be found on the shelves of a medium-sized library and one would also expect a reasonable proportion of the listed periodicals to be displayed and, when their respective currencies have expired, to be filed.

The exclusion of all but a handful of works in foreign languages is deliberate since a more generous selection is unlikely to be found except in large libraries. The value of these works must be limited by the abilities of users to understand the language concerned or their willingness to work doggedly through each article of interest with the aid of a translating dictionary, which is unlikely to be a very satisfactory procedure. Yet it must never be forgotten that a French encyclopaedia, for example, is not only likely to contain possibly the best articles on major French composers but will also have entries for a large number of minor musical figures who might well be omitted entirely from British, American, German or other non-French encyclopaedias. Students should not restrict inspection to our small sample, but are warmly recommended to use the selection of reference books on music to be found listed and annotated in Sheehy [202], Walford [224], Duckles [58], and Marco [132]. A bibliography of special value is the International Basic List of Literature on Music of the International Association of Music Libraries [103]. This work includes approximately 500 items, the great majority of which have been published since 1945, "selected from six national basic lists compiled in Denmark, England, Germany, Holland, Hungary and the U.S.A." All works found here are in English, French, or German, the three official languages of the IAML. Updates appear regularly in issues of Fontes artis musicae [73].

The first part of the chapter deals with reference works under the following headings: General dictionaries and encyclopaedias; Special dictionaries; Bibliography; History; Opera; Vocal music; Chamber music; Discographies; Thematic catalogues; Periodicals. Works relating primarily to sound recordings are discussed in Chapter V. The second part of this chapter is devoted to brief appraisals of a handful of periodicals, roughly grouped according to subject. The final section is devoted to a brief consideration of enquiry work in the library.

GENERAL DICTIONARIES AND ENCYCLOPAEDIAS

Though music dictionaries and encyclopaedias may vary considerably in size, the scope and arrangement are usually similar; the main differences concern the amount of detail provided and the inclusion (or exclusion) of bibliographies for the more important composers. Contents usually include composer biographies (although the Harvard Dictionary of Music specifically omits them) together with full or condensed lists of the works of major figures, and briefer entries for minor composers and others (such as publishers and impresarios) who have some importance in the history of music. Living performers are normally excluded or entered extremely selectively, while it is only the outstanding virtuosi of former days who are likely to be found--and then, often, because they were also minor composers. These dictionaries include, as well as definitions of musical terms, descriptions of both current and obsolete instruments and, in some cases, epitomes of the plots of the more frequently performed operas. All dictionaries of this type will show some degree of national bias, both in the choice of subjects for entry and in the relative lengths of articles. As already indicated, this may be regarded as a useful feature and is an excellent

reason (there are others) for a library to ensure that its
stock of music reference books includes some published in
other countries, however great the temptation to limit coverage to works produced in one's own land or language.

Where possible, students are strongly advised to compare entries for the same composer in different dictionaries.
Not only will this bring to notice variations in treatment,
scope, evaluation, method of entry, etc., but may also serve
to underline occasional differences of a more material nature.
The dates of birth and death given for particular composers,
for instance, do not always coincide--although they obviously should. Again, the student might find it interesting
to try to decide the original surname of the composer we
know as Jacques Offenbach by checking different works,
including the Oxford Companion to Music.

> EVERYMAN'S DICTIONARY OF MUSIC, 5th ed., com-
> piled by Eric Blom, revised by Sir Jack Westrup with
> the collaboration of John Caldwell, Edward Ollesen and
> R. J. Beck. London: Dent; New York: St. Martin's
> Press, 1971. 793 p.

The first edition was published in 1946 and appeared in the
standard Everyman format of the period. By the time that
the second edition was issued, there had been some alterations in the series, which now had a slightly enlarged page
size and rather clearer print. The fifth edition is further
improved in general appearance and legibility although its
price is distinctly higher than earlier editions.

When one takes into account the small bulk of the volume it incorporates an amazing amount of information. Entries for composers show forenames, with brackets to indicate unused ones or the subject's preferred use of initials,
e.g., Moeran, E(rnest) J(ohn). Full dates and place of
both birth and death (if applicable) are given; this is followed by brief biographical details and a condensed list of
the most important compositions. Some compression is
achieved by the frequent use of abbreviations. The following excerpt from the entry for Joseph Lanner is taken
from the dictionary's earlier editions: "Anxious to cond.
an orch. he began by getting together a stg. 4tet, in which
J. Strauss, sen., played va." One change in the current
edition, mentioned by the reviser, is a simplification of ab-

breviations. Thus, in the current edition, "string" is
printed in full, and the last word is shown as "vla"; users
will doubtless decide for themselves whether this is an improvement and, if so, whether worth special mention.

Two other changes noted in the preface are more important. For the first time, there are now musical illustrations to demonstrate certain technical terms, such as "Fugue"
or "Phrygian cadence." Living performers are no longer excluded; they were not altogether absent from earlier editions,
but they were only included then if they were also composers
of some merit. Two useful features are details of national
anthems and a series of entries under major literary figures
showing which of their works have been used by composers
(the entry for Shakespeare extends to nearly three pages).
There is a listing under "Paintings, &c., Music based on,"
and an entry for "Collective works"--defined here as those
"in which more than one composer had a hand," followed by
a series of titles to which the reader is referred.

Students should note that the alphabetical arrangement
is on the "word by word" principle and not "all through"
("letter by letter"). In the preface to the first edition,
Blom wrote that "This is not a manual for specialists: it is
a book to be used for quick reference by anybody who is at
all interested in music ...," and that seems to be a fair assessment of a work that has proved to be an excellent tool,
particularly in the branch or school library that has no more
than a few shelves of reference books.

HARVARD DICTIONARY OF MUSIC, 2nd ed., revised
and enlarged/by Willi Apel. 1969. Cambridge, Mass.:
Belknap Press of Harvard University Press; 1969.
London, Heinemann, 1970. xv, 935 p.

This was first published in 1944, and appeared in England
under the Foyle imprint in 1948, later issued by Routledge.
The work was reprinted, in the USA, eighteen times. Since
a major feature of the dictionary is the complete absence of
biographical entries, this considerable success might appear
a little unexpected. The work was fortunate in its time of
publication, for American musical horizons were then expand-
ing. Also there was a considerable amount of information
packed into a comparatively small bulk. The arrangement
appealed strongly to students, since the method of breaking

up major articles into sections, with an indication of the
level at which certain parts were presented made it very
convenient to use. Because of this unusual method of approach, the compilation of the Harvard Brief Dictionary of
Music in 1960 [7] (a work intended specifically for amateurs)
was apparently fairly simple.

The second edition (the British issue using the American sheets with a different title page) shows a very considerable increase in bulk, and the use of an appreciably larger page has made the work much more attractive in appearance than its predecessor as well as allowing considerably
more space for articles. Although the title page might well
lead one to believe that the work was entirely Apel's, the
dust jacket corrects any misconceptions by stating that
"Mr. Apel and 88 other ... scholars" are responsible for
the "thoroughly revised, updated and substantially enlarged
edition." The first edition apparently had twenty-seven
specialists contributing articles.

There are no photographs, but a number of line drawings of instruments are included; some readers are likely to
prefer these to photographs because of their clarity. The
accent throughout the dictionary is on the historical and musicological approach. Walford comments that it is "valuable
for the enquirer who seeks to go beyond general summaries
to the basic science of musicology" and adds: "Its brilliant
resumés of the technical and historical fields are well supported by music examples and bibliographical references to
source material and periodical articles." [224] As with
Scholes and Blom, the approach is not always impartial;
some readers will find the viewpoint more to their liking
than others. In the course of an article, one may meet a
word with an asterisk. This indicates that the subject so
marked is covered in another article "whose exact title
sometimes differs slightly from the starred word." As Walford has indicated, major articles have bibliographies, sometimes quite substantial; if an item consists entirely or mainly of music, a double obelisk is printed to indicate this.

The publishers draw attention to the fact that the article on ethno-musicology is greatly expanded, yet it is still
only one and a half pages in length. Much more pertinent,
we suggest, is the entry for "Historical editions"; this "cor-
responds to the German term Denkmäler," a clear indication

of the musicological approach of the dictionary. It lists
fifty-three collections, with brief information about the contents of each. This may be more than adequate for the
smaller library, but for detailed lists of contents and immensely wider coverage, the librarian will use Heyer's work,
given a brief separate comment later in this chapter [93a].

The dictionary provides good definitions. It contains
a number of title entries, each with a brief descriptive comment. In the case of operas, it supplies the date and place
of first production, and usually adds a note on the period
and setting of the work, but omits all mention of the plot.
There are some useful cross-references (e.g., from "Songs
without words" to "Lieder ohne Wörte"), but some seem to
be completely redundant. One finds "Con fuoco see Fuoco"
and even "Un peu [F], un poco [It] see Peu; Poco" (this
entry is to be found after "Unit organ" and "Unmerklich"
and before "Unruhig," since the dictionary uses the "all
through" spelling arrangement); on the other hand, there
is no reference from "Capo" to "Da capo." Russian opera
entries are supplied with a transliteration of the title (e.g.,
"Golden cockerel Rus. Zolotoy pyetushok"). The work lists
a number of periodicals, with primary arrangement under
country, but we are unsure as to its reliability. A glance
at the British titles included would suggest that the house
magazines Chesterian and Augener's Monthly Musical Record
are still in existence when, in fact, they ceased publication
nearly a decade before this edition of the dictionary was
published--in 1960 and 1961 respectively.

Although it seems that there has been a conscious
attempt to make the work more truly international in approach, the American bias is still strong. ASCAP is mentioned, but not Performing Right Society; the article on
Festivals lists sixteen American and eight British, with no
mention of either Edinburgh or Aldeburgh which are two
well-established internationally famous examples.

There seems to have been some lack of editorial control, to be seen when a user compares the lengths of some
of the articles in relation to their relative importance. The
Harvard Dictionary allots twenty columns to the organ but
four to the violin; it has fourteen on the USA but eleven on
Gregorian chant. However, despite the criticisms made
above, an overall verdict would be strongly in favour of

Apel and this work, together with Baker's Biographical Dictionary of Musicians as its natural complement, would make a useful alternative to Thompson's much larger encyclopedia.

In 1978, the same publishers issued the Harvard Concise Dictionary of Music, compiled by Don Michael Randel [179a]. Although many of the definitions would seem to be based on those in the Harvard Dictionary of Music itself, the later work has one major difference in that its coverage contains a large number of entries for composers. Other types of musicians, particularly executants, continue to be omitted. The facts of individual lives are given briefly but adequately, and for major composers the most important works are noted. Coverage of twentieth-century writers, particularly those of the USA, is good. The dictionary is completed with some examples in music type and a number of illustrations.

THE INTERNATIONAL CYCLOPEDIA OF MUSIC AND MUSICIANS, editor-in-chief Oscar Thompson (1887-1945). 10th ed., ed. Bruce Bohle. New York, Toronto; Dodd Mead; London; Dent, 1975.

This reference work was first published in the USA in 1938, the same year that the Oxford Companion to Music originally appeared. Thompson supervised the first four editions, Nicolas Slonimsky the next four, Robert Sabin was editor of the ninth edition, and the tenth sees another change in control. It is claimed that this latest version provides "one of the most wide-ranging revisions in the Cyclopedia's history" and attention is drawn to the fact that there are new survey articles on African and Latin-American music.

As is to be expected, entries vary from the minimal one or two-line note, e.g., "Brewer, Thomas (b.1611), English composer of many fantasias for the viol, songs, catches, rounds, etc."--the entry might lead one to believe that the composer was still alive since there is no indication of his date of death--to major articles, such as that for Mozart which occupies ten pages and something in the region of 7,000 words. As in earlier editions, composers and subjects of major importance always begin at the top of a left-hand page, with the subject's name boldly displayed, followed by that of the author of the contribution. The type face for the body of the article is slightly larger than that

used for the bulk of the cyclopedia, and this is an additional
visual aid towards making these articles stand out. Each of
the biographies on major figures is followed by a chronology
of events and a more-or-less complete list of works, arranged
in classified order. Less important figures have only partial
lists of works appended, usually those which are best known.
Minor composers are treated on the style of Thomas Brewer,
quoted above, but usually at slightly greater length.

An unusual feature of this volume is the large number
of title entries, which for major works will often outline the
music's programme. Unfortunately, there seems to be no consistent plan of entry. For example, there are entries for the
three Respighi suites, Fountains of Rome, the Pines of Rome
and Roman Festivals, but not for the same composer's The
Birds, Botticelli Triptych, and similar works which apparently
have equal claim. Moreover, there is no reference from the
biographical entry under the composer to these title entries,
and indeed Guido M. Gatti in the article on Respighi briefly
discusses the Fountains of Rome and includes facts that are
not to be found in the title entry.

In many cases, the major articles (and many of the
minor ones also) are unaltered from the first edition, but
this is not invariable. Karl Geiringer's essay on Haydn has
been partly revised to take into account recent additions to
our knowledge of the composer and his works. The previous
edition's entry for Shostakovich has been deleted entirely
and a new one substituted by another writer. Large-type
entries have been included, usually at rather less than two-
page length, for a number of "new" composers, such as
Berio and Elliott Carter. The latter one might expect, for
the entire reference book is strong on North and South
American composers, an aspect of the work that is particularly valuable for European libraries. Credit should also be
given for a much large number of entries on contemporary
executants than is customary.

A number of articles, such as that for "Recorded
music" are in more than one part, and each section is
signed. This piecemeal approach can be misleading, e.g.,
on p. 1786 one reads that, "... In England the method of
financing records by subscription has been successful, the
Hugo Wolf, Schubert and other societies bringing out album
after album." The use of "has been" is ambiguous, and the

unknowing reader might feel that "society" issues were still
in being, and not realize that the article refers to pre-1939
days. In cases like this, the entry would have been much
improved by the addition of a brief introductory paragraph.

If American coverage is good, that for British subjects
should not be accepted uncritically. To offer two examples,
the footnote at the beginning of the article on Handel suggests "the the editor can see little but affectation in frequent printing of the name as Händel on programs of today
in America and England." Insofar as Britain is concerned,
that comment would be untrue even when the first edition of
Thompson was compiled, and it is ironic that the heading
gives the composer's Christian names as "George Frederick"
which was not, of course, Handel's own usage in England.
Incidentally, the bibliography appended to this article remains unaltered, with no item in it later than 1933. The
second example is the entry for the Griller Quartet, which
gives no indication that the group disbanded in the late
1960s; contrarily, none of the younger string quartets currently well known in Britain receives mention.

The useful appendices, mentioned in the first edition
of this book when describing the 1956 edition of Thompson,
have long since vanished. On the other hand, there is an
article on "Libraries of music" that was not included twenty
years ago. This is an excellent idea, but the list is set out
very badly, so that it is difficult to use quickly--and librarians may notice a reference to "McColvin and Reese."

Despite the "wide-ranging revision," some shorter biographies have not been reset to include the date of the
death of the subject at the beginning of the article. For
example, one could excuse this "postscript" idea in the ninth
editon to show the date of Eric Coates in 1958--but the subsequent version remains unaltered, and this date of decease
could be easily overlooked. Even less forgiveable in this
particular case is the statement that "After 1918 he devoted
himself principally to composition." It is this part of his
life that deservedly made Coates a household name in Britain,
and the brief list of works omits most of those for which he
is most famous. On a very different topic, one notices that
the article on "Piano playing" ends in the 1930s, so that
there is no mention of such techniques as string plucking,
nor is there any reference to the prepared piano, although
there is a brief entry under that topic on another page.

One's final criticism is of the centre four pages, where
there are eighty portraits of composers and performers--a
selection that some readers will find a little odd in places.
Some of these illustrations are photographs, but a number
are freehand drawings which vary from the good to the poor.
In many cases, one would feel sure that photographs were
easily available.   Other illustrations in the work are limited
to a disappointingly small number in music type.

After these criticisms, it may seem a little unexpected
to declare this to be the best of the one-volume encyclopaedias, but such is the writer's opinion.

THE NEW GROVE DICTIONARY OF MUSIC AND MUSI-
CIANS.   Ed. Stanley Sadie.   London, Macmillan; Washington, D.C.:   Grove's Dictionaries of Music, 1980.
20 vols.

For some years before eventual publication this work was often referred to as "Grove VI"; the choice of amended title
reflects both the enormous expansion compared with the fifth
edition and also the almost entire rewriting of the whole work.
One might feel that the change might have been carried a
step further and the work called an "encyclopaedia" rather
than a "dictionary" for that is what it is.   The current figures are most impressive: 22 million words; 22,500 articles;
2,300 contributors, whose writings were overseen by both
senior advisers and a team of fifty editors.   Although one
may be tempted to still think of Grove as an English work,
this is no longer correct.   For instance, there are more
contributors from the USA than from any other country--a
reflection of the work of the editorial committee which tried
(rarely without success) to enlist the services of an acknowledged expert, irrespective of nationality, for virtually
every person and topic.

A quick glance at previous editions gives some ideas
of the work's expansion and longevity.   At the time of publication of the first edition, Sir George Grove was Director
of the Royal College of Music in London, and he was a typical Victorian polymath.   The dictionary originally appeared
in twenty-five fascicules between 1877 and 1880; it was reprinted in four volumes in 1890.   The second edition, edited
by J. A. Fuller-Maitland and published in five volumes made
its appearance between 1904 and 1910.   An American Supplement was published in the USA in 1920 and was reprinted

with some amendments as late as 1952; its contents were not,
surprisingly, incorporated into the parent work in the latter's third and fourth editions, published respectively in
1927-28 and in 1940 respectively. The fifth edition of 1954
showed considerable expansion to nine volumes, with Eric
Blom as editor. He, although Swiss born, displayed a strongly chauvinistic attitude, particularly in his dislike of German
polysyllabic musical terms when they were translated into
American-English. Students are advised to read the editorial
preface under the heading "Language" to see the depth of
prejudice displayed. A supplementary volume to the nine
was issued in 1961. However, there was strong disagreement between editor and publisher, and the project apparently slumbered as a result.

    In 1969, a new editor was appointed in the person of
Stanley Sadie, and work progressed steadily. Despite this,
there were delays and (ironically for a set issued by a British publishing house), the volumes eventually reached American bookshelves first, towards the end of 1980 and British
libraries early in 1981. This resulted from the fact that the
earlier volumes were printed in Hong King, but the last six
were produced by American presses.

    One half of the entries in this encyclopaedic work are
for composers and the general rule has been that no such
entry is shorter than 100 words: major composers have received book-length articles of up to 25,000 words and an unexpected dividend has been the separate publication of some
of these. At the end of all entries, except the shortest, is
a bibliography. Where there are more than a handful of references, these are divided into sections, each with its own
heading. It is not difficult to find references as late as
1979 and 1980 included, which is a decided asset. Less satisfactory is the decision, with books, to cite the place of
publication but not the publisher; librarians, in particular,
will find this to be frustrating. Entries for periodical references are numerous and show examples in many languages;
unfortunately the pagination of articles is not provided.

    Composers' lists of works are often satisfyingly de-
tailed, but better editorial control would have ensured that
a standard order of genres was followed, even though an
exact pattern would have been impossible. Jazz is well
covered. There are numerous entries for major figures in

this area and also for that of pop although, as was probably inevitable, argument has raged because one singer or instrumentalist is included while another, claimed by supporters to be at least of equal rating, has been omitted. There are articles on the music of most countries around the world as well as separate ones on major cities of importance in musical history. The publishers claim that over one million words are to be found in articles on non-western and folk music. In short, the dictionary is as universal as can be expected, particularly when one takes its history and background into account. It is well illustrated--there are apparently over 4,500 illustrations comprising portraits and pictures of instruments, places, etc., supplemented by more than 3,000 examples in music type.

The work does not escape criticism. "The most serious defect is lack of an index" [132, III, p. 5]. And this edition, it could be argued, is much more for the professional musician and the knowledgeable amateur and these are well catered for elsewhere. There are no title entries as in the fifth edition, and it must be said that the change of level and approach is certainly not all gain. Several entries (one may cite those on Gestalt psychology and postage stamps, to which attention was drawn in the earlier edition of this book, as well as a number of those for persons) have been deleted. One regrets that the opportunity was not taken to make one or two line entries for all those persons, mainly British, who have appeared in earlier editions but whose names have subsequently been deleted. Such brief references could save an enquirer's time in searching fruitlessly for a now forgotten name; it is certainly in only a handful of libraries that all five editions of Grove are likely to be found. In the present edition, biographical entries should not necessarily be accepted as gospel. There appears to be at least one "ghost" entry (that for Dag Henrik Esrum-Hallerup, a Dane untraceable elsewhere). On a different level, one notices that the story of the young Handel playing the clavichord in secret at home is noted as though it were proven fact rather than the legend which is now its generally accepted status.

An extremely long review in the Inter-American Music Review [209] draws attention to a number of errors and omissions in entries concerning persons and places relating to the Americas, North, South and Central. To sum up, New Grove is the most comprehensive music reference work, yet small libraries should be cautious when considering purchase of the set. It is an expensive work (costing over Ł1,000 in 1983), takes considerable shelf space and may be often found too esoteric in approach by many non-specialist readers. Finally, if a librarian can find room, the fifth edition (where in stock) seems worth keeping in reserve.

> THE OXFORD COMPANION TO MUSIC, by Percy A. Scholes. 10th edn., revised and reset; edited by John Owen Ward. London, New York: Oxford University Press, 1970. 1,189 p.

This encyclopaedia was first published in 1938 and was regularly revised by its compiler up to the ninth edition, which appeared in 1955. On the basis of the number of copies sold (over 200,000), the publishers claim this to be the most popular work ever in musical reference. There was a long gap, caused by the death of Scholes in 1958, before the tenth edition was produced. John Owen Ward, an assistant to Scholes during the latter's lifetime, had the very difficult task of retaining the highly individual flavour of the original compiler, yet amending some of the more outrageous comments and adding a series of new entries. He seems to have succeeded admirably in both respects.

The work would appear to be aimed primarily at the amateur music lover, but Scholes suggested in his original preface that "The experienced and well-instructed professional musician ... has need also of a one-volume encyclopedia to which he can turn ..." and implies that the Companion fulfils that need. Long articles are divided into numbered paragraphs, each with its own subtitle to assist the discovery of a particular aspect of a subject, and also to allow the author both to dispense with a separate index and to provide a large number of cross-references in the text (e.g., Lavender Cry. See Street music 2). Additionally, these major articles have each a synopsis at the beginning listing the numbered paragraphs. Thus "Harmony" has no fewer than twenty-four subheadings--highly necessary with an article covering thirteen pages and approaching 10,000 words in length.

Entries under composers give forenames, year of birth and of death, plus a statement of the composer's age at death.

Scholes justifies this feature: "The extent and value of a
contribution an artist has been able to make must always
have depended greatly upon the span of life allotted to him;
it is a factor to which the intelligent reader will give attention and there seems no reason why every user of the book
should be left to make his own calculation...." These biographical entries usually mention major works in passing;
there is no list, even in summary form, at the end of each
entry indicating something of the bulk of a person's writings, as is customary in dictionaries of this type. Because
of this lack, as well as the absence of the date and the
month for all births and deaths, the Companion cannot be
recommended for a small quick-reference collection which has
room for only a single volume dealing with music; the Everyman dictionary, for instance, would be much better for that
particular purpose. On the other hand, the volume has its
own unique virtues. For example, there are several hundred
illustrations (arranged in roughly classified sections), generally quite small but adequate for most users. Additionally
there are a number of imaginative portraits of major composers drawn by Batt (Oswald C. Barrett) which made their
original appearances in the Radio Times. These pictures
are particularly noteworthy for the authentic details of the
backgrounds, the result of much painstaking research by
the artist.

    Not the least unusual feature is that "the actual work
of writing this encyclopedia, rather longer than the Bible,
was Dr. Scholes's own. The only articles he farmed out
were those on tonic sol-fa, which he could never quite manage to his own satisfaction, and the plots of operas, which
he found too boring to engage his attention." Thus Mr.
Ward. The synopses, which Scholes found "too boring" to
do, were written by W. R. Anderson and entries are interspersed in the general sequence under their English titles
(with the occasional exception); they include the operas of
Gilbert and Sullivan. Scholes's style is extremely readable
and the viewpoint is highly personal; this work, probably
more than any other dictionary of music, tempts one to read
for pleasure as well as for information. The field covered
is wider than might be expected. Mention should be made
of the article "Ragtime and jazz" in earlier editions, for
some writers thought it excellent while other critics considered it to be outstandingly bad. In the tenth edition,
the two subjects have separate entries which are apparently

the work of the editor. Attention should be drawn to a
fourteen-page introductory section of "Tables of notation
and nomenclature" which deals with such topics as clefs,
note values, staccato marks, etc.

We were given a copy of the first edition of this work
in 1938 and have always owned one since. Regular use has
given an appreciation of and affection for the Companion; it
has also caused an awareness of its limitations. We are
strongly in disagreement with William A. Katz, whose verdict
is that "Despite its rather long life, it is far from a first
choice for any reference library--it is noted here as much
to warn off the libraries, as anything else. This, by the
way, is an excellent example of a title which has gained
deserved fame from its past performance but is now long
past retirement" [108].

As this book goes to press, the New Oxford Companion
to Music has been announced. Edited by Denis Arnold, it is
a very different work from its predecessor; it is in two volumes, has a multitude of contributors and is much more expensive than the original work.

Brief comments are made next on half-a-dozen foreign
language reference works; two each in German, Italian and
French. Pride of place must be given to Die Musik in
Geschichte und Gegenwart [155]. Appearing in a series of
fascicules, the first instalment was published in 1949, while
sections 136 and 137 completed the bulk of the work in 1967.
Together, these issues form fourteen volumes. Since then,
there have been two supplementary volumes covering the letters A to D (1973) and E to Z (1979). A proposed general
index to the encyclopaedia is still unpublished in 1983, as this
comment is written.

The method of publication in sections is a mixed blessing, and one must never forget that, unlike Grove and other
multi-volume works dealing with music, MGG (to use the widely accepted abbreviation) did not make simultaneous appearance from A to Z. The work itself is highly scholarly, with
an impressive international roster of contributors. Major
composers, for instance, are often dealt with in sufficient
detail for the articles to be of book length. Lists of compositions at the ends of articles are generally exhaustive (giving the publishers of works still in copyright, or of the

complete works of a composer, where applicable), while the
bibliographies are also lengthy and international in coverage.
Nevertheless, the small type used for these appendices and
the publisher's apparent determination to leave the least possible space unused results in listings that appear as discouraging blocks of nearly solid type that are most trying to the
eyes after a short period of continuous use.   Indeed, the
overall appearance of pages is a deterrent despite the inclusion of many black-and-white illustrations. A further handicap to those whose German is very limited is the major use
of abbreviations (reminiscent of the style of the Everyman's
Dictionary of Music), although they are explained.   Attention
is drawn to the valuable articles on music history in various
countries and towns.

There are, according to Stanley Sadie [193], 9,414
articles in the fourteen volumes (compared with a probable
22,500 in the New Grove, because the latter "is a dictionary
as well as an encyclopedia," and the distinction is worth
bearing in mind, as is the generally musicological approach
of MGG).

The other useful and important German work chosen
for comment here is the Riemann Musik Lexikon, whose first
edition appeared in 1882 and which has always held a high
reputation.   The current issue is the twelfth, with two volumes (A-K; L-Z) dealing with biographies (Personenteil)
edited by Willibald Gurlitt.   These appeared in 1959 and 1969
respectively.   The third volume, limited to subjects (Sach-
teil), edited by Hans Eggebrecht, was also published in 1969.
A different editor again (Carl Dahlhaus) has been responsible for the two supplementary volumes which appeared in
1972 and 1975.   The size of these appendices is probably unexpected; the original biographical volumes ran to 986 and
976 pages respectively (ignoring the preliminary pages),
while the supplementary pair occupy 698 and 964 pages.   The
contributors are mainly German.   For composer entries, the
lists of works and the bibliographies are clearly separated,
and publishers of the works are shown where appropriate.
Riemann is strong on entries for performers, and its choices
in this field seem to be more adventurous than is usual, so
that one can often find an entry for a young executant who
has not been included in other music encyclopaedias.

The two Italian examples are alike in their use of

excellent paper, good sized print and generous margins, and
frequent inclusion of illustrations, a number of them in excellent colour. The works have a general appearance that
is most attractive. La musica, edited by Carlo M. Gatti
[151], is most unusual in presentation. Published between
1966 and 1968, the first four volumes (with between 860 and
881 pages each) are described as an encyclopaedia, while the
last two form a dictionary. The first half contains 196 articles, each beginning on a fresh page, with the appropriate
heading for the name of the author. The average length,
therefore, is somewhere between fifteen and twenty pages.
There are, in this section, about 1,500 examples in music
type, some 1,400 monochrome illustrations and thirty coloured ones. There are major articles on such topics as
acoustics and physiology, on the history and development of
music in a number of countries (which are often extremely
useful) as well as the expected biographies, which total
eighty-one of the 196 articles. The great composers of the
past are understandably here, but so are some non-Italian
twentieth-century figures such as Bartók, Berg, Schoenberg
and Webern. Each article has a bibliography appended,
while those for composers give complete lists of works in
classified order and are extremely well set out.

        The last two volumes (Dizionario) provide both an in-
dex to the four volumes of the Enciclopedia (so that the entry
for Beethoven, for example, is simply a reference to the full-
length article in volume one and also a dictionary as such.
This means that if a library has the first part, the Dizionario
is valuable, not least because some of the entries supplement
the information given in the first four volumes; the fifth and
sixth volumes alone, however, are of much more restricted
value. Whereas the biographical articles in the former are
lengthy and critical, those in the latter tend to be neither.
Lists of works supplied in the Dizionario are as cramped as
those in the first part are well set out. At the same time,
it must be said that the number of biographical entries in
the Dizionario is very high, and one has a fair chance of
tracing a minor composer not listed in other reference works.
To show the different treatment between the two sections,
one might instance Corelli who (in volume 2) is allotted about
seven pages, of which a total of about a page is used for illustrations), another for the composer's works, and a third-
of-a-page for bibliography. In contrast, Britten is allotted
a quarter column in volume 5, but to this must be added a

whole column listing his works and a bibliography of seven
items. However, this is an imbalance which is of a different
type to that found in the Harvard Dictionary. The Italian
proportions probably reflect the relative importance of the
two composers in the eyes of the editor; the American work,
with twenty columns on the organ to four on the violin,
fourteen on the USA in contrast to eleven on Gregorian
chant, suggests some lack of editorial control.

The other Italian work briefly considered is Enciclopedia della musica, compiled by Claudio Sartori [62]. There
are over 15,000 entries from 232 contributors, most of them
Italian. Major articles are signed, and bibliographical coverage is good. As a subject dictionary, this work is distinctly
better than Gatti and has a more consistent system of cross-
references from foreign words and alternate forms.

A famous French firm which has produced a number of
important reference books has included Larousse de la musique
in its coverage [118]. The two volumes, edited by Norbert
Dufourcq, appeared in 1957. It claims to be the first "committee" dictionary in its field in France, on the grounds that
earlier ones were the product of a sole compiler. Coverage
is quite wide--names (both biographical and geographical),
technical terms, including both records and acoustics, important manuscripts and music libraries are among the items
covered. Entry for minor composers take preference over
those for major executants. Living composers covered are
generally those of the older generation, and French music
receives the expected good coverage. There are appendices
with bibliographies to articles, and analyses of works (including major themes by way of illustration); the work in
general is well illustrated indeed. The dictionary has one
very unusual feature; two seven-inch discs, one in the
front cover of the first volume, the other in the rear cover
of the second one, which illustrate respectively instrumental
sounds and gamuts, and selected musical terms. As a
summing-up, we feel that the work is generally concise and
accurate (if not always as up-to-date as its publication year
might lead one to expect), but that it does not always con-
vey what might be called the flavour of a topic. Mention
must also be made of the fact that Larousse has three columns to a page and the type is appreciably smaller than that
used for any of the other five works in this section of text.

The last foreign-language dictionary appraised is
Encyclopédie de la musique, edited by François Michel and
others [63], published in three volumes between 1958 and
1961. It contains a mixture of very brief articles of two or
three lines and other long, exhaustive ones. The first volume devotes approximately its first third to a "Livre d'or"
which has some facsimiles (of manuscripts, etc.), portraits
of a few modern composers (French, or with links with
France, e.g., Stravinsky), and some letters on musical subjects. After this appear a series of entries on a wide range
of subjects, such as musical festivals (with international
coverage); radio stations, which provides the wavelengths
for all major European stations including Britain and Russia
(and which is now, in part, out of date); music periodicals;
music publishers, and secondhand music dealers throughout
Europe. Other topics include copyright (as applicable in
France), and there is a synchronous chronological table covering the period 999 to 1951, with six parallel columns to allow one to see what was happening in a number of different
topics at the same period. The first deals with rulers, popes,
etc., the second is concerned with major historical events,
the third with ideas, the fourth with art, the fifth with literature and the sixth with music. The last enters composers
under their respective years of birth and death, and makes
entries for major musical compositions. This is a very useful means of seeing how the arts interact at a given time.

The work has been praised for its coverage of modern
music, but rather more coolly received in other respects.
There are bibliographies, and subject articles are generally
stronger than those on composers. The work's monochrome
illustrations are generally not of the highest quality.

When commenting on Gatti, we chose to compare the
length of the articles on Corelli and Britten, the former as
an Italian composer of recognized standing as a minor figure,
whereas Britten has claims to being the most important British writer since Purcell. Like Elgar's (for whom some people
would claim equal musical stature) the music of Britten, except for a handful of works such as Peter Grimes and The
Young Person's Guide to the Orchestra, does not seem to
have exported well. Having made the comparison with one
Italian dictionary, we then proceeded to check the same two
names in the other works, with interesting results. MGG
dismisses the British composer in less than two pages; the

article includes a photograph of the first page of the manuscript of The Rape of Lucretia.   The list of works is selective and the bibliography tiny.   However, as the article
dates from the late 1940s, allowances are perhaps necessary.
What is surprising is that there is no additional entry for
the composer in the supplement.   In contrast, Corelli receives an article of over five pages, of which the equivalent
of a page is taken up with three illustrations, and there is
a half-page bibliography.   Riemann devotes about a half-
page to Corelli, plus a further quarter-page bibliography;
Britten, on the other hand is given over a page, with a
third of the space taken up by a fairly detailed list of
works.   In the first volume of the supplement this is extended by nearly a page devoted to further published works
and additional items in the bibliography.

Sartori has a rather more even balance than Gatti, for
Corelli receives a little more than three-and-a-half pages,
with music illustrations; Britten has a page devoted to him,
with a half-column listing of works and a bibliography of
four items.   Dufourcq allots a quarter-column to Britten,
mentioning some works in the course of the brief article;
Corelli receives one and a quarter columns.   Michel gives
the Italian twice this space (with a bibliography of three
items); Britten, in contrast, is given an article requiring
a full column, with the last inch devoted to a list of works
(with "Billy Bud" as the solitary misspelling).

Students who have access to any of these dictionaries/
encyclopaedias, or others in languages outside English are
invited to choose their own topics and to make similar comparisons; it should be a means of helping one to draw con-
clusions as to the relative merits of works which, nominally,
all cover the same subject area.

SPECIAL DICTIONARIES

HAROLD BARLOW and SAM MORGENSTERN.   A Dictionary of Musical Themes.   New York: Crown, 1948;
London: Williams and Norgate, 1949.

HAROLD BARLOW and SAM MORGENSTERN.   A Dictionary of Opera and Song Themes, Including Cantatas,
Oratorios, Lieder and Art Songs.   New York: Crown,
1966; London: Benn, 1976.

It is probably best to begin with a clarification of the bibliographical information given above. The first work, from its
fourth British impression of 1952, appeared under the Benn
imprint. A ninth (corrected impression) was issued in 1970.
On p. xi it is stated that, "The call for a further impression
has provided the opportunity, wherever possible, to revise
the dates of birth and death of composers, and to make a
few other corrections." One understands what is meant, but
the phraseology is ambiguous. As for the second of these
works, it originally appeared under the title A Dictionary
of Vocal Themes (Crown, 1950; Benn, 1956); the change
of title and the appearance of a "second edition" in 1976
regrettably do not result in any change in the contents.

Each of the dictionaries is in two complementary parts.
In the first half of each volume are single-stave excerpts
(i.e., the theme is quoted without harmony or accompaniment) varying in length from three to ten bars; the themes
are arranged first under composer and then under the actual
work. In the second half is the notation index by which it
should be possible to identify any of the themes quoted. The
earlier volume limits itself to orchestral and instrumental music and will be described first. All the works indexed in it
have appeared in recorded form in the USA and probably in
Britain also.

Composers are arranged alphabetically by surname;
forenames and the years of birth and of death are shown.
The works indexed are also entered in alphabetical order
and not in a chronological or classified sequence; the themes
are quoted in the order in which they make their appearance
in the particular work. For example, the opening of Elgar's
Pomp and circumstance march no. 1 is shown as "theme 1";
the trio (better known in its vocal form as Land of hope and
glory) as "theme 2." To the right of these two melodies are
the index numbers E 38 and E 39 respectively. A fresh sequence of numbers is begun for each letter of the alphabet,
so that Elgar themes are numbered from E 1 to E 79, George
Enesco items from E 80 to E 103 and those of Franz Erkel
from E 104 to E 107. The next composer indexed is Manuel
de Falla, so themes from his work begin a fresh sequence
starting at F 1. At the top left-hand corner of each page
is listed the name(s) of the composer(s) represented and on
the right are the running numbers of the themes on that
page, so that page 178 shows Elgar-Enesco and E 77-95 respectively.

In order to index the various tunes all are treated as
though they were written in the key of C. The time value
of the notes is ignored; for the purpose of the index long
and short notes are of equal importance and no differentiation is made. To exemplify the result one may cite the Elgar trio mentioned in the previous paragraph. Though actually written in the key of G major it is indexed as C B C
D A G--E 39. Normally the first six notes of a theme are
given in the index but a duplication between the notes of
two or more tunes may cause a longer entry to the point of
difference, with a maximum entry of eleven notes.

This excellent dictionary suffers from two obvious
drawbacks; the user must be able to understand music notation sufficiently to be able to write out the tune or to
work out the notes in it (and there is a "transposition key"
to assist in the task of rewriting the theme in the key of
C), and secondly the enquirer must start the tune on the
same note and beat as the compilers if he or she is to run it
to earth in the index. With most tunes the starting note is
definite enough but this is not always so, particularly when
the theme is a subsidiary one that appears in the middle of
an orchestral movement. This is fortunately an infrequent
problem, and for the librarian or enquirer whose musical
knowledge is up to the standard indicated the dictionary is
a wonderful instrument for identifying tunes.

The range of composers represented is extremely wide;
for instance, such comparatively unfamiliar names as Aubert,
John Bull, Platti, Paradis and Locatelli are indexed in addition to the obvious classics. The representation of contemporary American composers is excellent though many of them
and their works are still unfamiliar in Europe. The dictionary's limitation to works that had, at the time of compilation,
appeared on disc has produced some strange results upon
occasion. Minor works may occasionally be found with major
ones omitted. The holy boy of John Ireland is included but
his more important Mai Dun does not appear since it was not
available on gramophone records at the time of the dictionary's compilation.

The Dictionary of Opera and Song Themes includes the
salient and remarkable themes from operas, cantatas, oratorios,
Lieder and art songs, as well as many miscellaneous vocal
pieces not belonging to the categories above. In this volume
over 8,000 themes, together with their words, are quoted.

There is a separate index of first lines and of titles in addition to the musical index. Folk songs are included only where the music has been edited and arranged by a recognized authority such as Béla Bartók or Ralph Vaughan Williams.

In compiling this dictionary the two musicians found the gramophone record repertory of the period insufficient for their purpose--the long-playing record was only just in the market when the work was written, or that complaint would not have been valid (for more than two or three years) --so that works that are found with some regularity in recital programmes, though not then available on disc, are included. Many of these extra items have subsequently appeared in recorded form, but recital programmes governed the choice of items to be included in the case of composers such as Bach, Handel, Schubert and Wolf. The inclusion of the complete vocal works of these and some other important composers in the field of vocal music would have resulted in a volume that would have been twice the size of the actual dictionary. The listing of the individual themes is carried out in simpler fashion than in the earlier volume. In this newer work each page starts with the first theme lettered "A," the second "B," and so on. The notation index then simply refers to a page number followed by the appropriate letter of the theme. Because of copyright difficulties a number of works are indicated in the first half of the book by blank staves (tunes from Porgy and Bess, Merrie England, etc.), but the missing tunes are duly indexed in their proper places. It would seem that listing the notes only, and in the key of C, does not infringe the copyright.

The two volumes may be regarded as part of a single work, and the need for such an index has long been recognized--but no satisfactory solution had been produced until these two particular compilers came together. As has been indicated, the major drawback to its general application is the prior requirement that a user must be able to read music. The work's coverage has also been criticised. It is most unfortunate that, thirty years after the original publication, no new edition has been produced, omitting some of the works that have virtually disappeared from the repertory and introducing not only compositions that were not written when the Dictionary was compiled, but others that were missed at that time. One such, for example, is Rachmaninov's

Rhapsody on a Theme of Paganini and, particularly, its famous eighteenth variation.

> DENYS PARSONS. The Directory of Tunes and Musi-
> cal Themes. Cambridge, Eng.: Spencer Brown, 1975.

The two major drawbacks to the general use of Barlow and
Morgenstern (see previous entry) have been tackled by
Denys Parsons. In his preface, he comments on the earlier
dictionary to the effect that it "contains about 17,500 themes,
but they include a number of works that would nowadays be
considered of academic interest only." The terminal date for
the American volumes were 1947 and 1949--in the one case,
just before the LP disc was introduced and in the other, too
soon for the recorded repertory "explosion" to have taken
place. The coverage in recordings now is so very much wider
than would have been thought possible in the days of 78rpm
discs. Parsons continues: "As a basic guide to today's repertoire I have used The Gramophone Classical Record Catalogue, and aimed to include nearly all items represented by
two or more recordings, as well as many listed only once,
and works not represented at all in current recordings which
seemed worthy of inclusion." Despite this implied claim of
completeness, there would seem to be a little over 11,000
entries made, plus a further 3,000 to 4,000 for popular
works which are entered in a separate sequence in the book.
For these, the date of publication is usually given and, if
the tune comes from a musical show or a film, its title.

As with Barlow and Morgenstern, the time values of
notes are ignored, but the compiler here enters melodies on
the bedrock of the shape of a tune. He uses three symbols:
D (down), R (repeat) and U (up). The first note of the
sought tune is always shown by an asterisk, after which up
to fifteen succeeding notes are shown, divided into groups
of five for easier understanding. So the first index entry
reads: *DDDDD DDDDD DDDDD, i.e., fifteen consecutive
falling notes to follow the opening one. This tune is identified
as coming from "Saint-Saens piano concerto/ 4 in E mi op44 2m
1t"; the last section indicates that it is the first theme in the
second movement. Readers who know the concerto will recall
that this section opens with a rapidly descending scale passage from the soloist, which duly results in the form of entry in the directory. For popular music, the compiler has
limited the index entry to a maximum of fourteen notes.

Barlow and Morgenstern, it may be recalled, give only the
first six notes unless exact duplication of tunes requires a
lengthier entry when it is continued until a thematic separation occurs or eleven notes are reached, whichever happens
first. If two or more tunes listed still duplicate each other
after eleven notes, the enquirer will need to refer back to
the first part of the dictionary to see what they are. One
cannot do this with Parsons, "but in these cases the style
of the music will almost always enable the searcher to pick
out the right answer from one or more alternatives." With
the restriction of three symbols, compared with the notes of
the scale, a longer index entry is almost compulsory for
identification purposes.

On the face of it, the Parsons solution is almost too
good to be true, but the utterly simple approach appears
to be generally successful. Indeed, because of the fact that
the interval between two successive notes is often immaterial
in identifying a melody, the user can still get the right answer on occasion when the tune has been incorrectly remembered. Providing that one recalls accurately when it goes
up or down, the chances of identifying the tune will vary
from the modest to the near certainty. Such a result would
be virtually impossible with Barlow and Morgenstern if one
was a little unsure of the exact tune requiring tracing.

For those who can read music, Parsons offers no entries for the selected melodies on staves as the American
dictionaries provide, so that one cannot check as to whether
the index has been correctly used, nor is it possible to use
the book as a means of reminding oneself as to how a tune
goes--which can be done with the transatlantic works, assuming that the melody one seeks is included in the coverage. Short of noting every entry and arranging the entries
in composer order, it is quite impossible to see what Parsons
has included or omitted, although a spot check suggests that
his choices are generally excellent.

To sum up, the two works seem to be complementary
rather than rivals. Parsons is unique in his inclusion of
tunes relating to the popular music of several decades; Barlow and Morgenstern offer a wider (if not necessarily better)
coverage of classical music. Even the small reference library
should have both American and British volumes in stock.

BAKER'S BIOGRAPHICAL DICTIONARY OF MUSICIANS.
6th ed., ed. Nicolas Slonimsky. New York: Schirmer,
1978.

Theodore Baker's work was first published in 1900, quickly
established itself in its field, and reached its fourth edition
in 1940. Slonimsky took over as editor for the fifth edition (1958), in which he rightly claimed that "the present
edition is virtually a new book, with most of the entries re-
written, radically edited, and greatly expanded." He further
suggested that "the proper title of the book ought to be
Baker's musicians, librettists, publishers, impresarios, and
sundry other men, women and children who have to do with
music." A supplement to this edition was published in 1965,
superseded by a second one issued in 1971 which incorporated
the 1965 entries. The 1978 edition was entirely reset, using
a more condensed type on a slightly larger page size. Even
so, it runs to 1,982 pages compared with the 1,854 of its
1958 predecessor, and this fact indicates a noticeable expansion in the length of text.

To a large extent, entries for the sixth edition repeat
those found in the fifth, with most of the extra bulk coming
from additional names. One important difference is in the
considerable number of composers (compared with a handful
in the previous edition) whose entries now include a separate
section on "works," nearly always in classified arrangement.
For condensed lists, the style of entry is similar to that used
in the Everyman dictionary, already discussed in this chapter.
Many entries are supplemented by bibliographies; for major
composers, entries are unexpectedly long.

It is, almost inevitably, not quite 100 percent accurate,
but is remarkably close to that ideal and should be regarded
as a basic reference book for any but the smallest library.

BIBLIOGRAPHIES

THE BRITISH CATALOGUE OF MUSIC, 1957- . London: The British Library, 1957- .

This invaluable work is considered in two sections below.
The first part deals with the serial from its inception in

1957 to the end of 1981, the second from 1982 onwards.
The reason is simple: with the first interim issue of 1982
there were major changes in coverage, in classification as
well as in other lesser details. The first part of this survey was written in 1977 and has been left unaltered. It
must therefore be read in conjunction with the second; from
these two parts, the reader should gain a balanced picture.

For its first two years, BCM (to use the commonly accepted abbreviation of its title) had three interim, paperbound issues, published quarterly and cumulating with the
issue for the last quarter of the year into an annual, clothbound volume. The interim issues have never been cumulated, so that one should not discard the first issue when
the second one of the year appears, but needs to retain the
interim issues until the appropriate annual volume is published, when the paperbound sections can be disposed of.
For 1959 there were only two interim issues, reverting
to three for 1960 and back to two intermediate ones for 1961.
Since then, this plan of two interim issues, each covering a
period of four months, has been retained. At first, the annual compilations were very dilatory in appearing but in recent years timeliness has improved considerably. Even so,
this means a gap of at least five months between the second
interim issue and an annual volume with details of works deposited in the British Library during the last four months of
the year. This delay must be frustrating for music librarians and reduces BCM's value as a selection tool.

Three other changes may well be mentioned here. For
the first nineteen years, the work was published by the
British National Bibliography, with the Music Department of
the British Museum, the UK Branch of the International Association of Music Libraries, the Music Publishers Association
and the Central Music Library (in Westminster) shown as as-
sociate publishers. With the formation of the British Library
in 1974 (including BNB and the Department of Printed Books
of the British Museum as two of its constituent parts), this
new body has been shown since the first issue of that year
as the sole publisher. From the 1971 volume, the page size
was slightly increased to the internationally recognized A4.
A small reduction in the size of the type face also played
its part in marginally increasing the number of entries to a
page. The third change related to the index. It was originally printed in a single sequence at the beginning of each

issue, but is now to be found in the customary position and
appears in divided form, as indicated below.

The Catalogue is officially described as "A record of
music and books about music recently published in Great
Britain, based upon the material deposited at the Copyright
Receipt Office of the British Library, arranged according to
a system of classification, with a Composer and Title Index,
a Subject Index, and a list of music publishers." (Capitali-
zation is that of the original.) The classification scheme by
which the entries are arranged is, of course, BCM's own and
is discussed in Chapter IV of this book. Under BCM, all
books about music have places in classes A or B--the latter
being devoted entirely to individual composers and their
works, with the exception of the last section (BZ...) which
is provided for non-European music. Entries for books are
exactly the same as those already published in BNB, except
for the different classification and a possible difference in
feature heading. The same BNB identifying serial number
is used; for scores, the running numbers begin at 50,000
each year, so that there should be no difficulty in distinguishing between books and scores, however ambiguous the
title. In passing, one must not overlook the fact that there
are a number of volumes, mainly instructional in intent,
where the choice between classifying as a book or as a score
is not simple. This could, perhaps, be counted as a tiny
point in favour of a scheme which uses the same symbol for
music and a book dealing with that same music.

It should be mentioned that "recently published in
Great Britain" is interpreted generously in one way, re-
strictively in another. Many items emanating from overseas
are included, but only if the item concerned is imported to
Britain by a branch of the parent publisher or else is
brought in under a "sole agency" agreement, whereby one
firm or an individual acts as the exclusive agent for the
original publisher. This means that one can only buy such
scores through the appropriate appointed agent, which may
be regarded as a mixed blessing. This restriction will normally apply only to music in copyright. Direct ordering
from the overseas publisher or a foreign dealer is, in such
cases, theoretically useless.

There would appear to be, in fact, some inconsistency
in the treatment of overseas publications. In some cases,

there are gaps in publishers' series as they are listed in
BCM, which suggests that not all issues have been deposited.
Indeed, one wonders in certain instances whether deposit was
necessary at all or whether the volume concerned had any
legitimate place in the bibliography.

   The restriction is in the exclusion of the great majority of "pop" items and similar ephemeral material. BCM
seemed perfectly happy to include albums of songs, partly
(we assume) because of the more permanent format, perhaps
also because the very publication of a volume suggests that
the items within have successfully survived the early death
that most ephemeral sheet music expects and deserves. A
major difficulty for the compilers of the bibliography could
well be the very much higher status that pop enjoys today
when compared with its standing in 1957 when BCM first appeared. Yet, as time passes, changes in coverage become
no easier to make; any idea of comprehensive inclusion in
this field faces not only the need for some rethinking of the
classification (since pop is a culture of its own, and a single
all-embracing place would justifiably meet with well-deserved
scorn), but also in cataloguing. Interest in pop music often
rests primarily in the performer(s) rather than in the words
or the melodies; one is reminded of the music hall songs of
the earlier years of the century, when the cover would often have, below the title, "As sung by ...," with a photograph of the star concerned. Secondary interest is in the
title; with few exceptions, the composer is usually a very
minor figure and the arranger is often at least of equal importance. There appears to be no cataloguing code which
makes adequate provision for pop.

   The exclusion of much of this lightweight contemporary
music distorts the overall picture of music publishing in this
country as seen through the issues of BCM; in contrast, the
Library of Congress Catalog of Copyright Entries can be
equally misleading for the opposite reason, in that it includes all music registered for copyright purposes; fortunately, a high proportion of this is unpublished and may
well never appear on the shelves of a music dealer.

   From 1957 to 1967, entries were in the form dictated
by the Anglo-American Code of 1908. The acceptance by
BNB (and BCM) of AACR 1 in 1968 resulted in some minor
changes in entries. AACR 2 seems likely to be used from

1981 onwards. One problem concerns the treatment of composers' names. Pre-1981 entries list Haydn as "Joseph"
rather than "Franz Joseph," while Russian names were
treated by use of the exception to AACR rule 44B1 (i.e.,
by systematic romanization), but 44B1e itself was used with
such names as "Tchaikovsky," since this form "has become
established through common usage."

Under the AACR 1 regime, the Library of Congress
and the British Library went their different ways in their
treatment of Russian names. Whereas LC was unbending in
its application of romanization, BL had a short list of exceptions so that names could be the more easily found. In
other words, the British Library's Tchaikovsky was not
matched by LC's Chaĭkovskiĭ. With computer on-line systems almost certain to be adopted, BL apparently decided
to follow LC rules totally, except for emigrés such as Stravinsky or Tcherepnin. However, at LC the cataloguers
appear to have thought that the British system of certain
exceptions was worth imitating and have adopted this
scheme. The situation is certainly Gilbertian! BL has
adopted "Chaĭkovskiĭ" while LC uses "Tchaikovsky." As
Slonimsky rightly says (in the Introduction to Baker's Biographical Dictionary, p. xxi): "Variants of spelling of
celebrated musical names cause uncertainty."

In 1982 there were considerable changes in the bibliography. The most immediately obvious, perhaps, is the
non-inclusion of books on music; one can still find them in
BNB. On the other hand, many scores of "music acquired
by the British Library from foreign publishers who do not
have agents in Great Britain" are now included. Descriptive cataloguing of entries is to full AACR 2 standard (including uniform titles). Entries are still arranged in classified order, but the classification is now that of the proposed revision of class 780 Dewey Decimal Classification;
the BCM class mark is retained also, and is shown at the
foot of each entry. Class 789 of the new classification is
not used, since this is for works on individual composers,
and books on music are excluded. So there is no need to
decide which of the various alternative arrangements of 789
is to be adopted. Subject indexing is by chain procedure
still; in contrast, all other departments of the British Library appear to have adopted the PRECIS system of indexing.

THE CATALOGUE OF PRINTED MUSIC IN THE BRITISH
LIBRARY TO 1980. Munich: Saur; London: Bingley,
distributed in Western Hemisphere by Gale, Detroit,
1980- .

The Music Department of the British Library had a variety of
collections in its stock, and this multitude of scores was incorporated in the British Library in 1974. The collection, in
total, is one of the largest and most important in the world--
yet it has never before been possible to check, with ease and
assurance, just what is held. So much material, particularly
in the field of ephemeral music, has been deposited under
copyright regulations but filed away under the year of accession, uncatalogued and then virtually forgotten. The position is explained in the preface to the catalogue considered
here. "Although nearly a century has passed since the publication of the first General Catalogue of Printed Books, no
complete catalogue of the music in the same department has
ever appeared. Instead, there has been a chequered history
of partial publication." Those in authority in the past had
"... an unfortunate notion that popular music did not merit
the cost of cataloguing"; from 1885 no entries were made for
music judged to be ephemeral. This practice has continued
to the present time so that although arrears have been over-
taken to the year 1909, much secondary music from 1910 remains uncatalogued.

The idea of an amalgamated catalogue of music has long
been suggested, but without success until this current attempt, in progress as these words are written; twenty-one
volumes had appeared in mid-1983, incorporated in a sequence
that was expected to finally occupy some sixty volumes. An
enormous amount of work was involved, for: "This great
mass of material was difficult to organise into one sequence
because of the different cataloguing procedures over the
period of development of the two existing catalogues." Because of the different styles of entry, and also as a result
of the many manuscript alterations to the text, it was found
impossible to produce a satisfactory catalogue by direct pho-
tocopying, so all entries were edited as necessary and then
retyped. This was both expensive and time consuming, but
the result fully justified the effort. Cataloguing is in accordance with British Museum rules, so that editions of collective manuscripts which do not show a compiler's name are
entered under the name of the library which holds the volume or its equivalent.

REPERTOIRE INTERNATIONALE DES SOURCES MUSI-
CALES / International Inventory of Musical Sources.
Published for the International Musicological Society
and International Association of Music Libraries.
München: Henle; Kassel: Bärenreiter, 1960- .

There are two sequences in this publication; volumes in
Series A appear under the imprint of Bärenreiter and those
in Series B from Henle. The work is generally known, from
the initial letters of the French title, as RISM and its immense design proposes the listing of approximately 200,000
entries from some 1,000 libraries. About 8,000 composers
are expected to be included, as well as a host of unattribut-
able composers and writings. The intention is to cover all
musical material from the earliest times to the closing date of
1800. The work is making reasonable progress and is undoubtedly one of the finest examples of international cooperation, for libraries in thirty or so countries are taking part,
with a representative person or institution in each supplying details of the appropriate holdings of libraries within
their respective national boundaries. In the case of Britain,
Schnapper's British Union-catalogue of Early Music Printed
before the Year 1801 ... [28] has provided nearly all the entries. This will have saved considerable trouble, but at the
expense of repeating numerous errors. This highlights the
greatest weakness of RISM: accuracy and musical knowledge
of a specialist kind is needed from the contributing libraries,
and it is not always there; additionally, considerable skill
and care are needed at the editorial stage when combining
entries into appropriate sequences and preparing them for
the press. Possibly through shortage of time, scarcity of
financial resources or other limitations, editorial supervision
has received criticism.

        Series A provides "The alphabetical catalogue of all
music printed between 1500 and 1800 which is now preserved
anywhere in the world," and the ultimate intention is to supplement it with a catalogue of pre-1800 manuscripts, to bear
the series designation A/II. The foreword to the first volume, the source of the above quotation adds: "Collections
are excluded. So, too, is music published in periodicals,
methods, textbooks, treatises and other kinds of printed
music." The alphabet was completed in nine volumes from
1971 to 1981. All are entitled "Einzeldrucke vor 1800"
(Single works up to 1800).

Whereas Series A is in alphabetical order of composer, Series B is classified into volumes containing different types of material in each, such as printed collections, tropes and sequences, etc. Because of this arrangement, "B" volumes are published when ready. The title page of any volume can be in English, French or German (the three official languages of IAML), with no translation. Choice apparently depends upon the nationality of the compiler. In contrast, the preliminary information is in all three languages.

From these comments we hope that something of the series' potential value to the academic and large research library can be recognized. Most libraries today would be able to supply copies in microform of works they possess; to study a photographic reproduction is much less attractive than examining the original, but immensely more useful than having no copy at all.

VINCENT DUCKLES. Music Reference and Research Materials: An Annotated Bibliography, 3rd ed. New York: Free Press; London; Collier-Macmillan, 1974.

This work was noted in the first edition of this book as A Guide to Reference Materials on Music. In its present form, there are 1,922 items, the majority of them in English. The actual number of titles entered is slightly less than this figure because a few works appear more than once, under different headings. There are eleven broad divisions, listed below with the number of items in each, so that it should be possible to visualize the relative size of each section:

Dictionaries and encyclopedias	(1-375)
Histories and chronologies	(376-507)
Guides to systematic and historical musicology	(508-532)
Bibliographies of music literature	(533-797)
Bibliographies of music	(798-1138)
Catalogs of music libraries and collections	(1139-1563)
Catalogs of musical instrument collections	(1564-1635)
Histories of bibliographies of music printing and publishing	(1636-1734)
Discographies	(1735-1812)
Year books and directories	(1813-1833)

Miscellaneous and bibliographical
tools   (1834-1922)

Adequate bibliographical details are given for each
work quoted. In a number of cases, where a work is considered of sufficient importance, reference is made to major
reviews. Most of the works have brief annotations, usually
explanatory but occasionally evaluative. One may quote entry 1821, which is for <u>Hinrichsen's Musical Year Books</u>,
1944- , and where the comment is; "A series of volumes
edited by Max Hinrichsen, issued at irregular intervals, remarkably varied in content. The articles range from trivia
to substantial contributions by recognized authorities. Most
of the volumes contain bibliographies ..." and the annotation
concludes with a note of the theme of each of the last four
volumes published. A more limited (and typical) example is
1704: Ted Ross. <u>The Art of Music Engraving and Processing: A Complete Manual</u> ..., which, for some reason, repeats the book's subtitle as part of the annotation, but adds,
"Full of historical and technical information. Well illustrated."

This compilation has always been extremely valuable to
music (and other) librarians. The current edition is as indispensable as its predecessors and, because of the large
increase in the number of entries, should be regarded as a
necessary purchase even if an earlier edition is in stock.
One has, at the same time, to accept that the work has its
share of errors and weaknesses. For instance, in entry 5
(for Blom's <u>Everyman's Dictionary</u> ...), the annotation comments: "Excludes living performers," which is no longer
true. It is particularly unfortunate that, on the first page
of the new introduction, the special attention drawn to three
"distinguished new works that have come into existence during the past five years" should quote incorrect entry numbers for two of them, although these mistakes are not repeated in the index. The subject index is not good. For
instance, one finds entries for "Music, Danish" and "Musicology in Denmark" on the one hand and "Danish music,
Literature of," on the other, not to mention "Libraries and
collections, Denmark," "Musicians Denmark," and "Printing
... Danish." The entries under these heads are all different books, yet there is no link among the entries, related
as they are. Coverage of Latin America and of popular music is weaker than is expected in a book originating in the
USA.

GUY A. MARCO. Information on Music: A Handbook
of Reference Sources in European Languages. Littleton, Colo.: Libraries Unlimited, 1975- . [132]

This major reference tool should eventually occupy seven
volumes but, at the time of writing, only the first three
have appeared. These deal with "Basic and universal
sources," "The Americas" (1977, with Ann M. Garfield and
Sharon Paugh Ferris), and "Europe" (1984, with Sharon
Paugh Ferris and Ann M. Olszewski). Those still to come
are expected to cover Africa/Asia/Oceania" (v.4), Special
topics (v.5), Individual musicians (v.6) and Musical editions (v.7). On the face of it, Marco is going to cover
much of the same ground that Duckles has already tilled but,
as the Introduction to the present work states: "I have
sought to correlate my efforts with those of Dr. Duckles
avoiding unneeded duplication of content in several areas,
and bringing out certain features of the books he cites which
I thought could use particular emphasis" (p. xv). Two
other quotations from the same page may help to indicate the
approach of the compiler. "If one book can serve the purpose, I have not thought it desirable to present the names
of a dozen" and, in the next paragraph, "I have posited a
user who is able to draw facts from books in French or German as well as English, and those languages account for the
bulk of the inclusions."

The first volume has six major sections: The language
of music (items 1-57); Direct information sources (58-167);
Universal biographical sources (168-205); Guides to other
sources of information in general categories (206-361); Lists
of music (362-455), and General discographies (456-503).
The running numbers of the items in each category are
quoted above. The work is completed by an index of "Authors, titles and selected subjects." Annotations are generally longer than those found in Duckles and, where the same
works appear in the two compilations, there may be appreciable differences in comment, usually in Marco's favour. An
interesting comparison can be drawn by quoting here the annotation for the Hinrichsen series already used as an example
when considering Duckles: "Began life as an annual, with
attention to events of the preceding year (e.g., accounts of
London concerts in 1943-44, 1944-45 appear in the issue for
1945/46; obituaries listed, etc.) but transformed into a collection of essays--some quite valuable--by musicologists.

Seems to have suspended publication with <u>Hinrichsen's</u>
<u>Eleventh Music Book: Music Libraries and Instruments</u>:
<u>Papers Read at the Joint Congress, Cambridge, 1959, of</u>
<u>the International Association of Music Libraries and the</u>
<u>Galpin Society</u> (1961).   That volume contains a cumulative
index to the whole set."   (Duckles 1821; Marco 0165.)

Where applicable, an item carries references to one or
more of half-a-dozen bibliographic source works, including
<u>American Reference Books Annual</u>, the 1974 edition of Duck-
les, and Winchell/Sheehy.   The Library of Congress classification is supplied as part of the entry and, from volume two,
an indication is given of the language(s) of the text.

The second volume shows Ann M. Garfield and Sharon
Paugh Ferris as co-authors with Guy Marco.   There are
three chapters: 1--Update of volume I (0504-0531); 2--
North America (0532-0838); 3--Latin America (0839-1332).
The second chapter is subdivided into General, Canada,
United States; the third has its General section, followed
by entries for twenty-eight different countries, in alphabetical order from Argentina to Venezuela.   There follow
revisions for volume one, a combined author/title index for
the two volumes to date, and a subject index.   The latter
supersedes that provided in volume one, which Marco admits
was unsatisfactory.

As an aid to quick discovery of a particular aspect of
the music of a country, provision is made for a full series
of subheadings, although it is highly unlikely that all of
them will be needed for all but a handful of places.   The
main divisions under each place are: The language of music; Direct information sources; Biographical sources; Guides
to other sources; Lists of music; Discographies.

In all, these first two volumes (the third volume was
not yet available for examination) give promise that the set
is going to be of real value when it is complete and, since
it complements rather than duplicates Duckles, will be a useful addition to stock even if one has the other work.   One
small correction is needed with both bibliographies, for each
suggests that <u>BCM</u> has three interim issues a year; both are
wrong--but the point is made here simply to suggest to students, in particular, that the reference book without a mistake seems to be almost impossible to produce.   The same

error appears also in Sheehy in 1976 [202, BH25]. The
wise student will, whenever possible, go back to the original of any listed work rather than accept without question
the information found in a bibliography or other reference
book.

THE MUSIC INDEX. Detroit: Information Coordinators, 1949- .

The Index is published monthly, about nine months later
than the periodicals indexed. There is also a bound annual
cumulation which, despite editorial hopes of improvement,
regularly expressed, remains obstinately belated. The compilation for 1976 was not issued until 1983. It remains expensive in British currency and this financial discourage-
ment, combined with the late appearance of cumulations, are
presumably the reasons for the fact that--valuable work as
it is--very few British reference collections include it.

The Index's aims are expressed in its subtitle: "A
subject guide to current music periodical literature." The
first issue of the guide, for January, 1949, indexed forty-
one periodicals, all of them in English. Over the interven-
ing years, this number has grown to more than 300, with
truly international coverage. There is the expected pre-
ponderance of American titles (which is also a tribute to the
musical vitality of that country), but on a single page of
the list of serials covered one can find entries for items
originating in Argentina, Austria, Belgium, Italy, Poland
and Venezuela--and this random selection is typical.

A valuable feature of the Index is its help in tracing
book reviews. In addition to quoting these sources, the
work helpfully provides bibliographical details for each work.
All reviews are entered under the general heading, "Book
reviews," then in alphabetical order by author. A typical
entry reads: "Dance, S. The World of Duke Ellington
(N.Y., Scribners--London, Macmillan. 312p. $8.50 P.3.50)
CODA 9: 8-9 n22 1971 DOWN BT 38:30 Jun 10 1971; ; HI
FI/MUS AM 21: MA 30 Nov 1971...." The full title of the
reviewing periodical can be traced from the preliminary pages,
so that the unknowing can quickly learn that "DOWN BT" is
Down beat. The number first quoted is that of the volume,
then (after the colon) the page number(s) and the date of
issue.

If one looks under the author's name (Dance) in the general sequence, the entry reads: "DANCE, STANLEY. The World of Duke Ellington. S. Dance. See Dance under BOOK REVIEWS." The limitations of computer typesetting result both in some repetition and in pages that are not ideally clear, but this is a small price to pay. The index is occasionally a source of unexpected information, e.g., "MELBA, DAME NELLIE (r.n. Helen Porter Mitchell)." The inclusion of the singer's real name is something of a surprise; the computer is apparently unable to treat the singer's title as other than a Christian name; this solecism is shared by the author of the article concerned, which he called "Boating with Dame Melba." One hopes that he would never refer to "Sir Beecham" which would be an equivalent error.

Entries under individuals as subjects provide helpful identification, e.g., "WOODS, JOHNNY (singer, harmonica player)," and subjects often have detailed subdivisions. In the 1971 cumulation, the entry for "Woods" is followed later, on the same page, by those for:

WOODWIND BANDS

WOODWIND ENSEMBLE MUSIC--Lists

WOOD INSTRUMENT MUSIC.   See also CHAMBER
   MUSIC--WIND INSTRUMENTS; DUET MUSIC; WIND
   INSTRUMENTS; music for particular woodwind instruments Woodwind scoring practices in the symphonies of Beethoven.   [an entry from Dissertation
   abstracts]

From this brief description, the importance and value of the work should be evident. As has been mentioned, very few British libraries have this work in stock, mainly because of the cost, one imagines, but also because few of the periodicals whose articles and reviews are included in the index are taken and displayed.

REPERTOIRE INTERNATIONALE DE LITTERATURE
MUSICALE ABSTRACTS.   New York: International
RILM Center, 1967-   .

This serial provides an obvious comparison with Music Index.

The work is produced under the sponsorship of the International Musicological Society, International Association of Music Libraries, and the American Council of Learned Societies. The quarterly issues of this outstanding index have an annual cumulation, and make considerable use of computing techniques. Five-year cumulated indexes have appeared for 1967-1971 and 1972-1976. Entries are in classified order, using RILM's own scheme of ten major classes with up to nine subdivisions in each, making available an immediate maximum of one hundred categories, although further subdivision would be possible if needed. The abstracts themselves are often made by the authors of the original articles. There are obvious advantages in this system, but users must also be aware of possible handicaps--one is perhaps illustrated when an abstract is signed "Author, abridged." In cases where the author has not made the abstract, the name of the person or body responsible is usually shown.

Usually, index entries are much more quickly produced than abstracts, so it is a major point in favour of the RILM Abstracts that they appear more quickly than Music Index. However, though both Music Index and RILM Abstracts are produced in the USA, there is much less overlap than might be expected. A single example must suffice: the revised Harvard Dictionary of Music was reviewed in a Swedish periodical and this is quoted in RILM. That critique is not shown in Music Index, but the latter has three that are apparently not in RILM.

Not all readers of this chapter will be familiar with the abstracts, so a copy of one might be helpful:

> 860   CHARLES, Daniel (Paris, F).   Sonates et inter-
> ap   ludes pour piano préparé [Sonatas and inter-
>   ludes for prepared piano].   M Tous Temps 52
>   [Supplement 2] (Dec 1970) 6-9.   Port.   In Fr.
>   Brief study of the 16 sonatas and 4 interludes
>   composed by John Cage in 1946, with an ex-
>   planation of the composer's artistic and philo-
>   sophical ideas.   (Pierre Caillard)

The number 860 is the running number in this issue for the entry, while "ap" indicates that the abstract is of an article in a periodical or yearbook. The entry is filed in class 28, which is the symbol for "Twentieth century, history." There

is a cumulated author/subject index, which refers to the appropriate page number of each issue. So the reader looking
for this article or another on twentieth-century music history
is referred, in this particular volume (for 1971) to pages 54,
178 and 281.

A comparison of entries for the same work, as listed
in RILM Abstracts and Music Index could be found useful by
readers who do not have access to one or both of these
guides. First, from RILM:

> 4557 SEEGER, Charles (Bridgewater, Conn., USA)
> ap   Reflections upon a given topic: music in uni-
>   versal perspective. Ethnomusicol XV/3 (Sept
>   1971) 385-398.
>   Examines the resources of speech communication
>   with the intent of applying these to the art of
>   music. See RILM... (Staff)

In contrast, Music Index offers:

> SEEGER, CHARLES LOUIS. Reflections upon a given
>   topic; music in universal perspective. C. Seeger.
>   ETHMUS 15: 385-98 n3 1971.

Comment should not be necessary, except to repeat
that there seems to be room for both indexes. One might
add that the range of coverage is wide, although Music Index has much better representation of pop music items, even
if many of these items are of limited value. The final point
is to note the existence of a third index, but this is a German production--Bibliographie des Musikschrifttums, which
goes back to 1936.

> UNITED STATES. Copyright Office. Catalog of Copy-
> right Entries (1891-). Washington: Government
> Printing Office, 1891- .

The differences between those parts of the catalogue dealing
with music and sound recordings and the British equivalent
(BCM) of the former (there being no British bibliography of
recordings) are wider than might perhaps be expected. Additionally, LC produces printed cards for much music published in either printed score or recorded form, and this aspect of publication is also considered later in this section.

The passage of new copyright legislation in the USA
has brought the law more into line with international practice. In Britain, a composer need take no steps to copyright any original work; if it is published and made available through the normal channels of the book or music trade,
the publisher is under legal obligation to deposit a copy with
the British Library Reference Division (the former British
Museum) and is likely to be required to supply five other
copies for the other libraries in Britain and Dublin that have
copyright deposit privilege. Making such deposits, however,
does not affect the legal position of copyright except, perhaps, that this would be one means of proving both the publication of a work and of its date of deposit, should there be
any dispute. In the USA, any music for which copyright is
desired needs to be sent to the copyright office of the Library of Congress together with the appropriate application
form completed and also accompanied by the statutory registration fee. Until all three conditions are fulfilled, the work
is not protected against infringement. It may be added that
music was added to the list of materials open to copyright as
far back as 1831.

Between 1909 and 1977, any registered item was given
copyright protection for twenty-eight years, after which
(upon payment of a further fee) the registration could be
renewed for a second spell of twenty-eight years. Fifty-
six years after the original registration (which would normally be about the same date as publication), the work automatically entered the public domain, irrespective of whether
the composer was alive or dead. In Britain, copyright has
existed for many years with protection throughout the life of
the composer and for fifty years thereafter.

American copyright law, however, altered in 1978. All
new material registered for the first time generally follows
the same rule as in Britain--lifetime protection plus a further
fifty years, extended to 31 December of the appropriate
year, for administrative tidiness. There are minor exceptions, but these need not concern us. Items in their renewal period (the second twenty-eight years) at January
1978, automatically have copyright extended for a further
nineteen years, making the total coverage seventy-five years.
The works first registered between January 1950 and December 1977 will still require reregistration at the end of twenty-
eight years (when the extension will be for a further forty-

seven years;) otherwise, copyright will lapse. Sound recordings are discussed separately later.

So, while BCM restricts its entries to published music
and only includes a limited percentage of items originating
in Britain and some foreign items (as has been explained
earlier when making an appraisal of BCM as a bibliographical tool), the Catalog of Copyright Entries, in the section
concerned with music (Part 3, Performing arts) contains a
high proportion of unpublished music. Much of this, for
better or worse, is likely to remain in manuscript. So the
Catalog, published at six-monthly intervals, has greater
bulk in a single issue than several years' combined cumulations from BCM; moreover, the American publication lists
all pop and similar ephemeral music for reasons already indicated; this is another fact which underlines the contrast
with the British publication.

In its present form, this section of the Catalog dates
back to 1 January 1978. It may be useful to summarize
briefly the history of the Catalog. LC has produced printed
copyright catalogues since 1891. Music was included from
the start, and the original series of entries covered the
period July 1891 to June 1906. The second sequence of
Catalog of Copyright Entries was designated the "New series"; the music catalog was Part 3 of the set, issued monthly and with all items entered under title. There was an annual index to each year's issues. The third series was inaugurated in January 1947 and retained the same title as before, but music became Part 5 of the Catalog. Until the end
of 1956 there were three separate sections in each six-
monthly issue of this Part: published music (5A), unpublished music (5B), and renewal registrations (5C). Sections
could be bought individually, if so desired. From 1957 (vol.
11) to the end of June 1973 (3rd series, vol. 27, part 5,
no. 2) entries were made under the titles of works so that,
for instance, there were usually a number in each issue to
be found under such words as Concerto and Sonata as the
first word in the transcript of the title page. Somewhere in
the entry would be found the name of the composer--a much
less satisfactory situation than previously, with the main entry under the name of the composer. The change of emphasis, in fact, seems to have resulted from the use made of the
Catalog by publishers, music agents, and the trade in general.

From the second half of 1973, the arrangement has
changed again. Entries are now in numerical order. At the
end of the sequence of original registrations comes a second
part which lists renewals. Entries, after the identifying registration number, are still under title. Each volume is completed with a single index for composers, copyright owners,
librettists, etc. Most importantly, it also includes title entries; without these, the searcher would have to work through
the numerical sequence until the required item was found.

The change to the current system has been dictated
by the fact that the entire cataloguing operation is now performed online on computer terminals. Entries in the Catalog
are in reduced facsimile typescript form, evenly printed--a
great improvement on the previous ones which where photo-
copies of typewritten ones, with varying degrees of black-
ness, giving a somewhat spotty appearance.

From the beginning, as a supplier of catalogue cards
based on the copyright entries, LC has covered music in a
limited way. As a result of this, entries can be found for
books and scores dating back to the turn of the century (in
fact, before Class M was officially published in its first edition). These printed cards have always been a valuable
source of cataloguing guidance for librarians, and provision
has been made for all added entry cards (as considered
necessary by LC) to be purchased as well, so that a library
could use LC's expertise, if desired, in at least three ways.
It could buy the volumes of entries for music and recordings
for which cards were available. These cards were photographically reduced (but still perfectly clear) and arranged
in composer order. The librarian could use these entries
solely as a guide, and ignore the card service itself; secondly, the library was able to buy the main entry card from
LC for use in its catalogue, and make such added entries as
was thought reasonable or desirable. Since the main card
would carry tracings of all the extra entries to be found
with a complete set, the cataloguer had a useful aid here.
The third choice which might be made was to buy the complete set of cards relating to a particular book or score
added to stock. There seems to have been some resistance
to this policy, particularly from smaller libraries, where it
was felt that LC made too many added entries and that the
cost of the cards was too high.

The reduced facsimile cards are to be found in the cumulative catalogues for the period 1898-1942 (in 167 volumes) and also in the supplements for 1941-1947 (42v) and 1948-1952 (24v).   In 1943, the original plan was made more comprehensive in order to cover a wider range of music than the fairly strictly standard repertory material previously listed.   Ten years later, LC's catalogues published in book form were reorganized; one resultant change was the cataloguing of a limited number of sound recordings and the production of printed cards for them.   Coverage was still restricted, both for books and scores, to cards for classical and semiclassical music.

With the introduction of these printed cards for sound recordings, it was decided to publish the cards for music and what LC dubbed "phonorecords" in a separate catalogue, entitled Music and Phonorecords and amended, in 1973, to the more comprehensive Music, Books on Music and Sound Recordings [218].   From 1953 Music and Phonorecords has appeared twice a year, the earlier issue covering January to June and the second combined with its predecessor to form an annual cumulation.   There is also a quinquennial cumulation.   For the third quinquennium, covering 1963-67, the music volumes are not numbered, i.e., they are treated as being in a separate sequence and have expanded to three volumes.   LC, unlike BCM, does not limit its coverage to items it has received itself but also adds entries supplied by seven major participating libraries who supply details of items in their respective stocks that are not to be found in LC.

So far, we hope, the sequence is fairly simple to understand.   Complications arise, regrettably, with the issue of The National Union Catalog Pre-1956 Imprints, which is intended to supersede the LC catalogues and the NUC for 1898-1957 while, for good measure, it includes some material not in either of the two earlier works [163].   There is a note in the foreword of this mammoth set to the effect, if we comprehend it correctly, that titles listed in 1956 and 1957 were reprinted in the NUC for 1958-62 (mentioned above), which would therefore be more correctly titled as covering 1956 to 1962.   This might seem to suggest that all that the librarian needs for full coverage will be this set of 685 volumes, together with a supplement (in progress) and later NUC cumulations from 1958 onwards.

Unhappily, this attractive state of affairs apparently does not apply to the music and phonorecords volume 27 (also mentioned earlier) for 1953-57, for the foreword to volume 1 of the pre-1956 set states: "Before discarding ... it should be noted that volume 27 of the National Union Catalog ... 1953-57 include[s] Library of Congress cards for phonorecords which are not included in this catalog nor in the NUC 1958-62. The above volume is separately available for libraries that may want it." If our understanding of this is correct, it would appear that, for the library that wants complete coverage it will be necessary to have the NUC pre-1956, NUC cumulations 1958 and also volume 27 of the NUC 1953-57, since the latter volume alone records music and sound recordings issued in 1956 and 1957.

In 1972, a change in American law brought sound recordings into the categories of material which could be copyrighted. In general, the position is similar to that applying to scores, giving coverage of 75 years (whereas it is 50 years in Britain). Since the passing of the 1956 Copyright Act in Britain, nearly all record manufacturers show (on the disc, on the sleeve, or on both) the year of issue, preceded by the symbol (P), analogous to the copyright symbol for books, © etc. American publishers of sound recordings now have to do the same thing, but also add the name of the copyright claimant after the date.

When the initial set of printed catalogue cards for records made their first appearance in 1953, about 300 items were listed during the year. The change in US law and the wide coverage of Part 14 of the LC Catalog means that some 10,000 recordings are now listed annually, including about 500 "foreign published sound recordings." There is a fair proportion of cassettes, many of them nonmusical and instructional. However, printed catalogue cards are still provided only for classical and semiclassical music, so the great majority of items in that annual figure of 10,000 recordings are still excluded from the card service.

The final comment from an English viewpoint is that the sooner sound recordings are included in the British legal deposit system, and a British media record published, the better for all concerned with music librarianship.

HISTORY

THE NEW OXFORD HISTORY OF MUSIC. Ed. Jack A.
Westrup, et al. London: Oxford University Press,
1954- .

This work is intended to replace the original Oxford History
of Music which was first published in six volumes between
the years 1901 and 1905 and which made a tremendous impact upon the musical ideas and thought of the time. Five
authors were responsible for the entire work. Between 1929
and 1939 a second edition was published; in this an introductory volume was included to cover music in the ancient world
and to extend the information on the art in the Middle Ages
which had been the starting point of the original first volume.
Some new material was added to the first two original volumes
in this new edition, while minor corrections were made to the
contents of the third volume. The fourth, fifth and sixth
volumes were not revised, while a new seventh volume completed the scheme by carrying the history from its earlier
limit of 1850 forward another fifty years to 1900. The second edition, therefore, had two more volumes than the first,
one at each end of the original six.

Such has been the expansion of knowledge, particularly of music in the eighteenth century and earlier (one has
only to think of how views of Haydn changed between the
1930s and 1970s, or to consider the fact that there is now
available a large recorded repertory of pre-fifteenth century
music, in contrast to the paucity in the days of coarse-groove
recordings) to appreciate that the original Oxford History is
of very limited value today except, perhaps, as an indication
of the "state of the art" nearly fifty years ago. The publisher's decision to commission an entirely fresh work was
clearly the right one. As with other "Oxford histories"--
we recall the Oxford History of England and the Oxford History of Art (there are other examples)--complete publication
is stretching over a very long period. Volume 2 began the
series in 1954, followed by volume 1 in 1957. Nearly thirty
years after the inauguration, the series still lacked volumes
6 and 9, together with volume 11, scheduled to include the
index to the complete set.

Each volume consists of a number of essays, each contributed by an expert, with a specialist in the period acting

as overall editor. The team of writers is truly international, and the writing is well supported by many illustrations (both pictorial and musical) and with bibliographies. The work is primarily intended for the teacher and serious student; it is probably too demanding for most general readers, but highly rewarding to those who combine the necessary stamina with musical knowledge.

Because music can only be fully appreciated as sound, the hearing of a brief item can often be incomparably more rewarding than reading many pages of text; in this belief, the set was supplemented with an aural complement in the form of a series of gramophone records, under the general title of "The History of Music in Sound." Each set of two or three LP discs covered the same period as the appropriate volume of The New Oxford History and carried the same title. There was a substantial booklet, well illustrated and with considerable detail about the musical examples. Because EMI (RCA in the USA) were responsible for the discs, but Oxford University Press for the booklets, the latter were not supplied with the discs, but had to be purchased separately, while the sleeves of the discs simply noted the items on each record and identified the performers. When the recordings were made, care was taken to ensure that the chosen examples were not otherwise easily available on disc. Beethoven was thought to be so well represented in the general catalogues that no example of his music was included in this series.

As time passed, so the monophonic recordings became outdated in many cases and a growing number of the musical examples were superseded by new recordings and, in many cases, by better performances. Libraries that have the booklets may face a difficult decision when the records are withdrawn; one feels that the texts should be retained in stock but problems are possible with some borrowers who cannot understand why the library has the booklets and not the recordings.

Still very valuable, but unfortunately never completed in its coverage, is the American Norton History of Music, of which eight volumes were published [168]. Here, in contrast to the current Oxford compilation but harking back to the first edition's five-man team in that each American volume has a single author, is a series written by musicologists

of the standing of Manfred Bukofzer, Gustave Reese, and
Curt Sachs. Bibliographies are good, if now rather outdated, while ample illustrations in music type increase the
set's value.

The small library collection might be thought no place
for books so far listed in this area. If so, one can warmly
recommend three one-volume histories, also well worth the
attention of the librarian or student for a personal collection.
All are likely to be enjoyed by the music lover who desires
a good, fairly succinct history of the development of occidental music that generally demands little more than the basic
technical knowledge that the keen music lover will have acquired almost unconsciously. The first work is Donald Jay
Grout's A History of Western Music, first published in 1960
and appearing in a second edition in 1973 [88]. The work is
well illustrated with both photographs and musical quotations.
There is an extensive bibliography and also a chronology.
Paragraph headings in the margins help the quick discovery
of a topic, but result in a bulkier book than would otherwise
be the case.

The nearest British equivalent of this was probably
Man and His Music: The Story of Musical Experience in the
West, by Alex Harman (with Anthony Milner) and Wilfrid
Mellers [92]. The history was originally published in four
volumes between 1957 and 1959, with the two major authors
taking responsibility for the first two and last two volumes
respectively. The work's success was such that it was
quickly (1962) reissued in a single volume of over 1,200
pages. There were some minor textual alterations in this
form and the volume was reprinted at least three times; it
was both a surprise and disappointment that the publishers
allowed the work to go out of print in the late 1970s. However, a superb alternative appeared in 1979 in Gerald Abraham's The Concise Oxford History of Music [1]. It offers a
somewhat more scholarly approach than either Grout or Harman and Mellers produced and is apparently aimed at a slightly more musically mature readership. This work is well illustrated in black and white and carries numerous examples, often deliberately unfamiliar, in music type. The author cites
dozens of references; it is particularly helpful to have each
quoted at the bottom of the appropriate page, so that the
user can read or skip at will, and lose no time. As for content, Abraham states in his preface that "Far from being a

condensation of The New Oxford History of Music, which
would be impossible, this book is not even based on it."
The author has paid far more attention than is customary in
a work of this sort to non-European music, while the narrative bibliography at the end of the book is subtitled "Suggestions for further reading, by specialist scholars"; in several chapters recommendations of suitable books go in tandem
with another on editions for scores. In all, this is a truly
outstanding work that should be in stock in both lending and
reference sections in all but the very smallest library.

NICOLAS SLONIMSKY. Music Since 1900. 4th ed.
New York: Scribner, 1971; London: Cassell, 1972.

This work was first published in 1937 and covered the period
from January 1900 to December 1936. The second and third
editions were almost entirely concerned with extensions to update the work. The fourth edition continues the process,
carrying its reportage from the end of 1948 (where the third
edition closed) to 20 July 1969; it also shows many new items
in the pre-1949 section. Despite the compiler's own dictum,
"When in doubt, do not delete," there have been quite a number of excisions--entries which are no longer considered to
be of sufficient importance to justify retention. "Importance"
is not perhaps quite the right word, for Slonimsky has a
keen eye for the offbeat and ridiculous, or one would find it
difficult to explain some of the inclusions, such as that relating to the underwater playing of a harp.

The major part of the volume (1,281 out of 1,595
pages of text, plus nineteen of preliminaries) is a chronology
of important dates in music history. Again, "dates" is an
inadequate description for there are not only records of
births and deaths, but also of first performances, of important publications and a variety of other events. The preface
states that "This is a book in the first place of materials, in
the second of evaluation." To illustrate, the entry for 27
January 1955 reads: "The Midsummer Marriage, opera in
three acts by the 50-year old English composer Michael Tip-
pett, to his own libretto, dealing with two pairs of lovers
... set to music in a capaciously diatonic idiom diversified
by opulently terraced dissonances, is produced at Covent
Garden in London." From the entry one can gain a number
of facts--the barest skeleton of the plot, the librettist, the
place of performance. There is an assessment of the music,
but such ratings are not invariable.

Two other examples, taken from facing pages, will show the difference between what might be called penny plain and tuppence coloured entries: "2 November 1960 Malcolm ARNOLD conducts the British Broadcasting Corporation Symphony Orchestra in London the world première of his <u>Fourth Symphony</u> in four movements, cast in his customary infra-modern hedonistically vigorous style ... "; "17 November 1960 <u>Second Violin Concerto</u> by Paul CRESTON is performed in a world première by Michael Rabin and the Los Angeles Philharmonic."

One idiosyncratic aspect of the entries that the examples may not have made explicit is the compiler's limitation of each entry to a single sentence. This, at times, results in highly convoluted English. Biographical entries include some for major performers, and those for composers often have a terse summing-up that show a highly developed and critical sense. Thus the entry recording the birth of Britten adds, "magus of modern English music, whose operas, symphonies and chamber music are imbued with the imperishable spirit of music Englishry and marked technical expertise, astutely incorporating the most viable elements of cosmopolitan modernism, is born in Lowestoft." One might be surprised at the word "symphonies" and feel that the more general "orchestral music" would be more accurate, but that is a minor point.

In the three earlier editions, the closing date for entries was the end of the year prior to publication. In this case, "Even a history of the future must have a temporal finish. I have resolved to mark it by the romantically realistic landing of men on the moon." To placate those readers who feel that this event has nothing whatsoever to do with music, the compiler claims that this is related to the music of the spheres!

Although additions to the post-World War II chronology have a fairly strong American bias, Slonimsky has softened the third edition claim of, "the objective truth that during the last decade the center of creative music has gradually shifted from Europe to the United States" to: "As a natural corollary of the commanding lead that America is beginning to assume in the world of music increasing representation of works by American composers has been given here." Many European readers would continue to disagree.

The second part of this substantial volume (pp. 1283-

1419) is allotted to letters and documents. It begins by reprinting the Motu proprio of Pope Pius X on sacred music
(i.e., the regulations that govern the choice of music in
Roman Catholic services), and includes many letters to
Slonimsky himself from Charles Ives and others. One of
these is from Arnold Schoenberg; in a letter dated 3 June
1937, Hollywood, the composer writes about the origins of
the twelve-tone method of composition. Part 3 (pp. 1423-
1502) is a dictionary of terms where one can find definitions
of such topics as Aleatory music, Game music (which is very
much older than is often realized), Metric modulation (which
is not an abstruse contemporary means for translating music
from inches into centimetres), Microtonality, Serialism and
the like. Mention must also be made of a tongue-in-cheek
entry for "Macropolysyllabification."

The work is completed by a substantial index (pp.
1505-1595). Under a composer's name the indexed life
events are in chronological order, the titles of works in alphabetical order. One's overall reaction is one of admiration
for the sheer effort of compilation. As the name of Slonimsky is synonymous with chronological accuracy, one should
be able to rely implicitly on the information given in these
pages. If there is a conflict of dates between Slonimsky and
another writer, one cannot imagine the former being wrong.
In short, here is a reference book that fulfils its stated function admirably. It does not, obviously it cannot, include all
the dates that one is liable to need at one time or another
over the years, but the basis of selection is sound and the
judgements expressed command respect, even when one disagrees with any of them.

OPERA

THE NEW KOBBE'S COMPLETE OPERA BOOK. Ed.
and rev. the Earl of Harewood. 9th ed. New York:
Putnam, 1976.

Gustave Kobbé was an American music writer and critic who
died in 1918 as the result of a boating accident involving a
seaplane. He had left the material for the first edition of
this book in a fairly advanced state of preparation at the
time of his death, so that only a limited amount of editing
was necessary before publication, which took place in 1919

in the USA and 1922 in England. Subsequent reprints increased the work's coverage, but a thorough overhaul became necessary and was provided by the Earl of Harewood.
The second edition was published in 1954, and this next
major revision is, as can be seen from the heading, described as the ninth. In this form it has been completely
reset and, in the words of the publisher, has "Accounts of
91 operas given for the first time, and the text has grown
from 1246 pages to 1670, not counting a greatly enlarged
and improved index. The book now contains details of over
300 regularly performed operas." One may perhaps quibble
over the "regularly," but still be delighted by the coverage.
The illustrations are a completely new set compared with
earlier editions, and there are nearly 100 new musical examples.

The book is divided into three sections. Part I, dealing with opera before 1800 has a chapter on Gluck and another on Mozart, the latter running to sixty-five pages. The
first part extends to p. 142; Part II, "The nineteenth century" is from p. 145 to p. 990. The arrangement is first by
nationality and then chronological by composer, with separate
chapters for major figures who are also given a brief general
introduction. The substantial large section, Part III, is devoted to the twentieth century and has nearly 700 pages--
from p. 993 to p. 1670 to be precise.

Before each synopsis is a brief note of the opera's
form and origin, e.g., "Opera in five acts and seven tab-
leaux by Sergei Prokofiev. Libretto by the composer from
a novel by Valery Briusoff (published in Russia in 1907).
First complete performance in concert...." Details of the
first performance--the place, date, main singers and conductor are provided; this is followed by similar details relating to first performances in other major countries and
cities. This historical background is succeeded by a cast
list, indicating the type of voice required by the composer
in each case. The preliminaries end with a note of the time
and place in which the opera is set, and then comes the
synopsis itself. For major works, there is a generous selection of themes provided in music type. Although there
have been a number of excisions in the second edition and
again in this major revision, they are of works unlikely to
be revived. The headings for individual entries have been
prepared by Harold Rosenthal, an acknowledged expert in
the field of opera history.

   Libraries that have an earlier edition of Kobbé would
still be well advised to buy a copy of the current one. If
the older one is retained, it should still be borrowed fairly
regularly, since the majority of requests for the outlines of
plots, etc., are likely to relate to works that are in the well
trodden repertory. There are numerous other books of opera plots and students may like to compare any of them with
Kobbé as a useful exercise. A useful index to books of
plots, guiding the user to the synopses of individual operas,
is available [56].

   ALFRED LOEWENBERG. <u>Annals of Opera, 1597-1940</u>;
   <u>Compiled from the Original Sources</u>. 3rd ed., rev.
   and corrected. London: Calder; Totowa, N.J.: Rowman and Littlefield, 1978.

It is perhaps best to begin this survey with a bibliographical note. The first edition was published in Cambridge at
the beginning of 1943, by Heffer's. It was in one volume.
The second edition, thanks to help from Theodore Bester-
man, appeared in 1955 in Geneva, from the Societas Biblio-
graphica. It was in two volumes--the book's four indexes
forming the second of these. In fact, there was little difference in bulk between editions; the first publication had
twenty-three introductory pages and 879 of text. The second edition comprised twenty-six pages of preliminaries and
878 pages of text. The latter were not numbered separately; instead, pages were divided into two columns and each
of these was numbered, to give a total of 1756. The com-
parative figures are a little misleading, for the 1955 version
was from reset type and was appreciably fuller than its
predecessor. The third edition has exactly the same pagination as the second. The major alteration is the appearance of a number of asterisks, explained below, and to describe the work as "Third edition" seems quite unjustified.

   The second edition was printed in a single volume by
the New York firm of Rowman and Littlefield in 1970. The
same company, now based in Totowa, N.J. issued the third
edition contemporaneously with Calder.

   The purpose and scope of the book is well described
in the preface as "a skeleton history of opera, in dates and
other facts. It is therefore arranged chronologically, but
by means of copious indexes it can also be used as a dic-

tionary of opera.   There are no descriptions of plots, no
musical analyses, no personal critical comments." On this
last point, Loewenberg apparently deceived himself, as will
be shown.   The material is based upon information gleaned
from a wide variety of sources--original scores and librettos, playbills, contemporary newspapers, diaries and the
like.

Some three to four thousand operas are listed (the
estimate is that of the compiler) and inclusion has been limited to works that have actually achieved production.   Older
operas have been selected, in general, if they are still in
the repertory or have historical importance.   For modern
works the chosen criterion is usually that of performance
outside its native country.   The earliest work included is
Peri's La Dafne (probably 1597) while the last is Izaht by
Villa-Lobos (1940).   Arrangement is strictly chronological
by the Gregorian calendar and this has produced some apparent inaccuracies in the cases of English operas produced
before 1752 (when the Gregorian calendar was adopted and
eleven days were "lost") and with Russian works prior to
the similar change made in 1917.

Each entry included the composer's surname and the
original title in the language in which the opera was first
performed.   Russian names are transliterated in accordance
with the British Museum rules, and the transliterated title
is followed by its original in Cyrillic script and an English
translation.   German, French and Italian titles are not
translated, unlike those in other foreign languages; neither
is translation made when the title is that of the principal or
other character in the score.   The date and place of first
performance follow the heading of composer and title.   Only
the date and month are quoted since the year is shown at
the top of each column.   The remaining information about
each opera is shown in smaller type.   It begins with the
librettist's name and a note indicating the original source of
the text.   First performances in other countries are then
listed.   If, in such cases, the work has been sung in a different language to that of the original, then the name of the
translator is generally quoted.   Finally, important revivals
are noted.   Much of this information has been incorporated
into the ninth edition of Kobbé, described above.   In the
third edition of Loewenberg is to be found a number of titles marked by an asterisk.   Such works "indicate an entry

with additional information in the supplementary volume being prepared by Harold Rosenthal, which will cover the period 1940-1978." These symbols would appear to be almost
the entire "revision" in this edition.

Loewenberg's claim that there are "no personal critical
comments" is open to challenge. To describe Richard
Strauss's Der Rosenkavalier as his "most popular opera" is
acceptable, based upon the number of performances received,
but impartiality seems breached with "One of the chief works
of modern dramatic music" (Wozzeck) and "Pfitzner's most
important work" (Palestrina), even if one agrees with these
judgments. There are many others of a similar nature. On
facing pages (for 23 March and 20 May 1851) one finds references to "The Duke's first greater success" and "Petrella's
first greater success." Greater than what?

The second part of the Annals contains the work's four
indexes. The first is that for titles, with the composer's
name in brackets, followed by the year of first performance.
Users should note, in passing, that there is no entry for
Maid of Orleans except under the original title of the
Tchaikovsky work. Less expected, perhaps, is that A Vil-
lage Romeo and Juliet is missing, in favour of Romeo und
Julia, as the opera was first performed in German. So this
part of the indexes really requires knowledge of the original
titles of operas. As no more precise information than the year
of first performance is supplied with each entry, there may
be a slight delay in tracing a particular work in a year in
which a large number of new operas were presented.

The second index is one of composers. This supplied
what might be called the "standard" forenames (e.g., Wolfgang Amadeus for Mozart, not his complete forenames) with
the year of birth and of death quoted in brackets. Under a
composer's name is a list of those works included in the Annals; again, these are chronological and not in alphabetical
order. Where the composer has written the libretto, alone
or in collaboration, the fact is indicated by an asterisk against
the title of the opera. The third is that of librettists and
includes authors whose works have been used as the bases
of librettos; examples of the latter category are quoted in
italics to distinguish them from librettists proper. Christian
names but no dates are given, and after each name is the
year in which the opera was performed; in the case of the

Tchaikovsky opera quoted above, the Schiller entry includes a reference to 1881 and Zhukovsky's name is also included in the index with the same year noted. The fourth and last is a "General index containing (a) persons not mentioned in Indexes II and III; (b) a small selection of subjects, and (c) countries and towns; under the names of the latter only events considered to be of significance" are noted, such as important first productions, openings of theatres, etc. Subject entries are made for such items as "American operas in Germany," "Ballad opera," "London promenade concerts." References from this index are to the appropriate column of the first part where the particular item can be found; this is the only index which does not refer to the year and so is the easiest to use.

Loewenberg's is a major work in the field of opera. The term "opera" is used in its widest sense so that one finds entries for Smetana, Stravinsky, Sullivan, and Suppé all included. The amount of research and cross-checking that preceded publication was obviously tremendous and the result is a permanent mine of information, unlikely to be superseded, for all interested in the historical aspect of opera.

Our attention to the immense reference literature of opera has necessarily been limited. Two recent bibliographic works--neither available at this writing--appear to offer useful access to that domain of publication: Andrew Farkas, Opera and Concert Singers; An Annotated International Bibliography of Books [68]; and Guy A. Marco, Opera: A Research and Information Guide [134].

VOCAL MUSIC

MINNIE EARL SEARS and PHYLLIS CRAWFORD, eds. Song Index: An Index to More Than 12,000 Songs in 177 Song Collections Comprising 262 Volumes. New York: H. W. Wilson, 1926. Song Index Supplement: An Index to More Than 7,000 Songs in 104 Collections Comprising 124 Volumes. 1934.

With a solitary exception, the 281 collections indexed in these two volumes were published in either North America or Great Britain. The anthologies do not include any devoted to the works of a single composer but are all collections of one type

or another. The two volumes also exclude from their scope
hymnals, children's and unaccompanied songs (but see the
last paragraph of these descriptive notes). The major effect of the restriction to anthologies is to exclude almost all
modern composers whose works are protected by copyright,
for these are rarely found in mixed volumes; on the other
hand, there is an excellent selection of folk and traditional
songs.

Before the index of individual songs which forms the
main body of the work, the collections themselves are quoted
in classified sequence under the following headings: General,
National, and Folk songs (divided alphabetically, e.g., English, French, German, Hawaiian, etc.) Chantey, Christmas
carols, School and college songs.

The index to individual songs follows. A search for
the song "Ma belle Marianne" shows the English translation
"Pretty Marianna" given in parentheses and the description
"Folk song from Alsace." The letters "e.f. FTF" indicate
that both English and French words are to be found in the
album symbolized as FTF whose full name can be traced in
the "key symbols" section. The supplement is arranged on
the same principle as the original volume. Where new information has been found about any song, this is indicated by
special brackets.

The usefulness of these volumes should be clear. One
can find, within their stated scope, the authors of the words
of over 19,000 songs, in what collection(s) these words can
be found and (assuming that the tune is not traditional) who
composed the music for any individual song. In some respects, the index supplements Granger's Poetry Index, especially for anonymous folk songs.

Two years after the publication of the supplement one
of the gaps was filled by the Children's Song Index by Helen
Grant Cushing [45]. This work indexes 189 collections in
222 volumes and only eleven of this total have been already
included in the Sears and Crawford volumes. The layout
and arrangement is on the same lines as earlier volumes.

After a gap of more than thirty years, a much needed
supplement to Sears appeared. This is Songs in Collections:
An Index, by Désirée De Charms and Paul Breed [49]. The

compilers thought that "an index of solo songs with piano accompaniment was the primary need ... collections of art songs and operatic arias were ... considered the most important for inclusion in this index." They attempted to include all noteworthy collections published between 1940 and 1957, and incorporated a few others which had been omitted from earlier works in this field. A handful of folk song anthologies were considered to be of sufficient merit to warrant inclusion, but the generally high standards demanded meant that only 411 volumes were listed, covering a total of 9,493 songs. As for arrangement, "the compilers decided to depart quite radically from the practice of previous song indexes. Works by identifiable composers are entered under the name of the writers, but a geographical arrangement is preferred for folk songs." This main section is followed by separate sections for sea songs and carols, while the work is completed by a combined first line and title index, and a second index for authors.

The compilers themselves used the Barlow and Morgenstern system of transposing all anonymous melodies into the key of C, and this helped "to discover some songs with different texts but the same melody" (p. x). The collections included are arranged by the compiler's name or the work's title, as appropriate. Information is given as to the publisher and date of each volume, the pagination and the number of songs included.

CHAMBER MUSIC

W. W. COBBETT.   Cobbett's Cyclopedic Survey of Chamber Music, 2nd ed.   New York: Oxford University Press, 1963.   3 vols.

Sir George Grove was originally a civil engineer who erected lighthouses in the West Indies. Walter Willson Cobbett (1847-1937) was by turns an insurance underwriter, foreign correspondent and, finally, "an exploiter of certain patents, one of which turned up trumps" [235]. This success enabled him to retire as a comparatively wealthy man at sixty, to find his real vocation as a tireless propagandist for, and generous patron of, chamber music. He successfully called upon some 150 people for contributions to his cyclopedia which was published in two volumes in 1929. His distinguished international

team of writers included such names as Alfredo Casella, E. J.
Dent, Vincent d'Indy, Willem Pijper, D. F. Tovey and Egon
Wellesz. Chamber music here is interpreted as ranging from
duos to nonets; the editor has also included such topics as
Oboe in chamber music, Plagiarism, and Restaurant and Café
music, to take three examples found within the space of less
than a hundred pages. All contributed articles are signed
and, from this fact, one can quickly see that the editor himself wrote a considerable portion of this guide.

Articles on individual composers are generally detailed
and profusely illustrated (in the case of major figures) with
musical examples. Such entries usually begin with a list of
compositions in the field, followed by a series of analyses
and descriptive comments. After the signature of the writer, there is frequently a postscript by the editor in which
he gives his reactions as an amateur string player to the
particular composer's music. For example, after Wilhelm
Altman's article on Reger, Cobbett remarks that "Many of
Reger's works are very heavy going ... but from that view
I was converted by hearing the very beautiful and original
quartet, op. 109 ... "; this quotation is typical of his personal and informal approach.

The second volume contains a supplement listing relevant composers who are considered insufficiently important
in this musical area to warrant individual entry in the body
of the text. So one finds entries such as: "AVISON,
Charles, c, 1710-70. English. Eighteen trio sonatas, one
republ. (Simrock)"; or "BRUNMAYER, Andreas, 18th to 19th
cent., Austrian organist." There is a bibliography of books,
periodical and newspaper articles, arranged alphabetically
under the writers' names. The work is rounded off by a
contents list which simply repeats in convenient form the
headings used in the text, together with a detailed list of
contributors. The two volumes total over 600 pages and
were photographically reproduced for the second edition
which is completed by a third volume (of a little over 200
pages) to cover the period 1929 to 1963. Where this last
volume contains additional material relating to composers who
have already appeared in the original volumes, an asterisk
is shown against the 1929 entry, while a bold "C" in the
third volume refers one back to the earlier contribution.
There is, therefore, a two-way reference for all such entries. Additions to, and corrections of, dates shown in the

1929 volumes are noted by means of an obelisk and these amendments are listed at the end of the third volume.

The supplementary volume, edited by Colin Mason, has proved to be something of a disappointment for many users. Instead of maintaining the expected dictionary plan for entries, the text is in narrative form in virtually three chapters. Mason himself deals with European chamber music, including Stravinsky, but excludes Soviet Russian music from his survey as that is the subject of a separate contribution by I. I. Martinov. Chamber music of the United States and of Latin America are the province of Nicolas Slonimsky. The content of this third volume is "more selective in its coverage of the available material" and confined "to composers who have acquired some considerable international reputation" (these quotations are from the foreword). The Martinov article is quite restricted in its choice of composers, as is that of Mason, whereas Slonimsky has preferred to cover a wide range of writers but to compensate by limiting the number of works receiving comment. The article on Soviet music suffers from an approach that appears to be completely uncritical, offering nothing but praise for both the composers and the works discussed. The new volume has its own appended selective bibliography, and also an index of composers whose names appear in volume three; this is needed because of the arrangement of the text.

One can summarize by saying that Cobbett is unique and will always be of value, even if a more up-to-date compilation should appear at some future date.

A useful guide to the standard repertoire of chamber music is Ella Marie Forsyth's Building a Chamber Music Collection [75]. It describes the important works for groups of two to thirteen instruments, giving publisher, duration, level of difficulty, programme notes and references to critical literature. Librarians will find this to be helpful in selecting stock as well as in answering enquiries about works in this genre.

DISCOGRAPHIES

"The term discography is used here to define a wide range of related activities, problems, and products involved in the

analysis, description, enumeration, and bibliographical control of the artifacts of recorded sound and the sounds preserved on and transmitted by those artifacts." This definition, which opens an admirable article by Gordon Stevenson
[208] indicates something of the wide range that the topic
now encompasses.

The word "discography" itself has come into general
use over the past twenty years or more, despite some criticisms of its unsuitability, particularly since the spread of the
cassette (i.e., tape, not disc) format. However, the term is
widely accepted and is generally taken to be the audio equivalent of "bibliography" in the book world. A claim has been
made that the first example dates back to the RCA Victor
catalogue published in January 1912, "a completely self-
indexing alphabetical catalog which gave biographical material on composers and artists, listed operatic selections by
acts and in the order in which they came in the opera, and
combined the familiar catalog 'subject' headings with an en-
cyclopedic cross-indexed listing of the recordings then offered for sale by Victor" [141, p. 677].

As with bibliographies, an increasing number of books
and articles on musical topics now include a discography almost as a matter of course; there is also a growing body of
separately published works in this field. The standard guide
for tracing most of these compilations will be the Bibliography
of Discographies [17].

We do not think that "discography" should be applied
to selection tools in the field of sound recordings, so these
are considered in Chapter V. The works listed below are
primarily of historical importance, but their value as reference works is permanent.

> FRANCIS F. CLOUGH and G. J. CUMING. The World's
> Encyclopaedia of Recorded Music. London: Sidgwick
> & Jackson, 1952. Second Supplement (1951-52), 1953.
> Third Supplement (1953-55), 1957.

The original volume contains almost 900 pages of which the
last 160 form the first supplement, mentioned on the title
page; the second supplement has a mere 262 pages while the
third adds another 564 pages to the series. Within these
four sequences are listed recordings of almost all music of

permanent value issued between 1926 and 1955, with the omission of some less important versions. Thus, in general, one
has a survey of the 78rpm era from the early days of electrical recording to the "death" of the format, together with
listings of the first five or six years of LP. Despite
the all embracing title, coverage is limited to music of Europe
and North America.

     Arrangement is by composer and then, if there are but
a few recordings, alphabetically by title. As the number of
recordings increases, so the compilers have made ad hoc classification systems. For major figures, a brief synopsis of the
scheme devised is given; for one or two composers (such as
Debussy and Liszt), a title index is also supplied to show the
set of works from which an item comes. This can be of general use to the music librarian as a finding aid. WERM (to
use the accepted abbreviation) is no more than a list; it
makes no attempt at judgement of either performance or recording.

     The work is unlikely to be superseded as the best in
its particular field. Its standards of accuracy and completeness have been the criteria by which many later discographies
have been judged. The cost of typesetting the work must
have been extremely high and sales, though reasonable, were
apparently not good enough to allow a fourth volume to be
published, and attempts to obtain a subsidy towards the issue of material duly collected were unsuccessful. Clough and
Cuming's own entries were deposited with the British Institute
of Recorded Sound (now the National Sound Archive) and it
is understood that the slips have been regularly updated
since then; however, the longer the period without publication, the less the likelihood of this happening.

     A different sort of discography is the Index to Record
Reviews, compiled and edited by Kurtz Myers and published
in 1978 by G. K. Hall [157]. It is a conflation of the assess-
ments provided in Notes from about 1948 to early 1977, so
follows much the same form. There are some 30,000 entries;
one-composer discs are entered under the appropriate name;
records with two or more works are considered as "composite"
and are arranged by manufacturer/label name, then numerically. To allow the enquirer to trace individual works there are
indexes arranged by performer, by manufacturers' numbers
and, for composite records, by composer and title. So, "it

is fair to say that a very high percentage of the world's recorded classical music since 1948 is indexed here. Even
without the analysis of reviews, the opportunity of finding
most records of the past thirty years by looking in one
place is an advantage we have not enjoyed since WERM was
new" [60].

A series of works of permanent value has the general
title "Voices of the Past," edited by John Reginald Bennett
[16]. The volumes are primarily listings of records issued
by The Gramophone Company (HMV) and its related companies. The information is presented in tabular form, in numerical order under the appropriate prefix for the manufacturer's various series.

THEMATIC CATALOGUES

BARRY S. BROOK. Thematic catalogues in music: an
annotated bibliography, including printed, manuscript,
and in-preparation catalogues, related literature and
reviews, an essay on the definitions, history, functions,
historiography, and future of the thematic catalogue.
Hillsdale, N.Y.: Pendragon Press, 1972.

The compiler has certainly provided a very full subtitle, to
which one might add that the work is "Published under the
sponsorship of the Music Library Association and RILM Abstracts of Music Literature." There are 1,444 entries, arranged (where appropriate) in composer order, but, as the
subtitle indicates, there are numerous entries for what
might be considered "fringe" works, and these have a different method of entry in the sequence. Although it is expected that any cataloguing code which includes music within
its purview would have a rule relating to the entry of thematic catalogues, many students seem unaware of what these
works contain, or of their considerable importance in music
librarianship. So a preliminary comment might be helpful
before briefly appraising Brook's work.

Such a catalogue in the modern sense (since the original thematic catalogues of Breitkopf and Härtel had very different purposes from those of today) is a complete list of the
works of a particular composer, giving a variety of useful
information, such as when and where a particular composition

was first performed, the writer of any words, the publisher of the first edition, the whereabouts (if known) of the original manuscript, and a number of other points of interest. Musical themes are quoted for the opening of each work and, in some cases, intermediate themes also. With multimovement compositions such as many symphonies and concertos, the catalogue usually provides the incipit (i.e., the first few bars) of each section, indicating any tempo marked by the composer. These musical illustrations, invaluable for identification purposes, may be given on one stave or on two. Brook maintains that all other means of identification are liable to mislead, particularly with older music, and he suggests that "incipit index" is a more accurate definition than "thematic catalogue." One should also remember those special catalogues, exemplified by the two from Barlow and Morgenstern [13, 14], considered earlier in this chapter.

There are two major methods of arranging a composer's works: chronologically or in a classified sequence. If the order of composition is fairly clear or can be established with a reasonable degree of certainty, the chronological method is probably to be preferred since, in general, it will tally with the opus numbers allotted by a composer, assuming that the works have been so identified. Chronological arrangement was chosen by Köchel for his catalogue of Mozart's works although despite his best endeavours and considerable research, he made quite a number of errors. As a result there is, in the third and later editions of Köchel, what might be called a list of corrected Köchel numbers allotted by Alfred Einstein, but musicians and the public in general remain faithful to the original identifications, and many Mozart lovers can quote "K numbers" for the more popular works of the composer.

The alternative arrangement by musical form is well exemplified by the Schmieder catalogue of the works of Johann Sebastian Bach. In this case, the sequence starts with the composer's cantatas and the selected order is that of the Bach Gesellschaft volumes. This is a matter of convenience, in that many users will be aware of some of the numbers and there was no real virtue in allotting a different sequence, for many of the cantatas cannot be assigned to a particular time with any precision; Bach did not write dates on his autograph scores, and several could have been composed at quite different periods in his life--so a classified sequence is the more sensible one.

In most cases a thematic catalogue identification is
added to the title of a composer's work by a combination of
the initial of the compiler's surname and the appropriate
number in sequence in the catalogue. So, Mozart's works
are identified by a "K," Weber (for whom many works have
opus numbers) by the further addition of a "J" number (for
Jahn's catalogue), Purcell by a "Z" and so on. In the case
of Bach, Schmieder apparently prefers the use of a "BWV"
(Bach Werke Verzeichnis) number, but one finds compositions sometimes identified by an "S"; the numbers are the
same as those for "BWV", so no confusion should be possible. With a handful of composers, two examples being
Vivaldi and Domenico Scarlatti, there is more than one
identification system, which tends to confuse. In a few
cases, although the works of a composer are generally well
established with opus numbers that fairly accurately represent the order of publication, a thematic catalogue may still
be produced to tidy up the loose ends and to provide the
musicological information that should be so useful in the well
compiled catalogue. Finally, before reverting to Barry
Brook's list, it might be added that even the small library
should buy any recognized thematic catalogue that it can
afford. In general, these are works of permanent reference
value that will never become outdated, although there may
be some minor amendments over the years in certain of the
catalogues.

Brook's bibliography includes "listings for all manner
of printed and manuscript thematic indexes, dictionaries,
compilations, and tables of contents, as well as for collections of true themes and motives ..." (page x), so that the
coverage is very wide indeed. The general arrangement is
alphabetical by composer or author, as is appropriate; the
names of the former are in bold capitals, the latter in light
capitals. The text is apparently entirely typewritten, but
with an unusual variety of type faces to make light of the
expected limitations. For those entries referring to collective catalogues, listing is under the name of the place, followed by that of the library, the publisher or the compiler
of the work, according to circumstances. Location abbreviations use the same sigla as RISM, a help to quick recognition. Indeed, there are a number of entries under the heading RISM, subdivided by country, and indicating some items
that will be included in the A/II manuscripts sequence of
RISM when that eventually becomes available.

Brook's work replaces an earlier compilation of the Music Library Association, A Check-list of Thematic Catalogues (1954) but is itself unlikely to be superseded for a very long time, particularly if (as one hopes) supplements are issued periodically to keep the work updated.

PERIODICALS

Most better quality daily and Sunday newspapers in Britain, together with a number of literary and other periodicals, publish reviews of a small number of books on music during the course of a year; in addition, they may include critiques (often too brief to be of any real value) of a handful of sound recordings.   There tends to be a considerable, if un-derstandable, overlapping in the works reviewed by different newspapers and the criticisms are unlikely to be of more than marginal use to the music librarian, not least because the books and recordings considered are probably those which the librarian has added, or will add, to stock as a matter of course.   Much more relevant as aids to selection are the many periodicals specifically concerned with one or other aspect of music, or with individual genres of instruments.   A vast num-ber of periodicals have appeared in the field of music.   Imo-gen Fellinger lists about 5,600 titles in her New Grove arti-cle [71].   A good brief review of periodical publishing, with comments on 39 selected titles, was contributed to the Ency-clopedia of Library and Information Science by Dominique-René DeLerma [52].

Such periodicals have at least two possible spheres of usefulness in the music library or music section.   They are, or should be, of value to those library users who have per-sonal interest in all or part of the musical area covered by a particular periodical; they are also of considerable potential value to the music librarian in offering specialist reviews of books and scores with an expertise that is often outstanding, even if occasionally a little unbalanced and intemperate.   It is primarily from the librarian's viewpoint that comments are made when discussing individual titles below.

The library should try, within its budget limitations, to offer a range of journals suited for most kinds of music interest--from church choirs to brass bands, from music history to the activities of a variety of singers, instrumentalists and conductors of international stature as well as some whose fame is generally restricted to one's own country. University and college libraries should not restrict coverage to material within the syllabi of music courses offered by the individual educational establishment (though this range must be the primary objective), for music students will certainly not limit their interests solely to those concerned with the examinations ahead.

As Ruth Watanabe, of the Sibley Music Library, Eastman School of Music, Rochester, N.Y., has written: "No music collection is complete without some representative periodicals to give news of the concert world and to provide the latest results of research on a variety of topics of interest to both the professional and the layman." She lists nine categories of material and gives a brief explanatory annotation on each. Her classification is as follows:

A. Current events periodicals; concentrate on the national scene, and include signed reviews of concerts which, ideally, should discuss both the music played and its performance.

B. Learned journals; articles will contain musical examples and bibliographical aids. Reviews of books or scores are intended for the professional musician and the specialist rather than the layman.

C. Journals of music education and pedagogy.

D. Audio magazines.

E. Journals of performing media; will have articles on instruments or the voice. Reviews tend to focus on specific medium of the periodical.

F. Church music journals.

G. New music journals.

H. Professional or propaganda magazines; would normally be issued by a composers' group or a national information centre.

I. Non-music journals which have the occasional music article or a regular music feature [227a].

For small libraries (which Watanabe considers to be those that have stocks of fewer than 5,000 volumes of music material), six periodicals are suggested. These are: <u>High Fidelity and Musical America</u> (D,A); <u>Musical Quarterly</u> (B); <u>Music Educators' Journal</u> (C); <u>Opera News</u> (E); <u>Instrumentalist</u> (C,E); and <u>Audio</u> (D). For medium or average music libraries (extending up to 20,000 volumes) the range is considerably broadened by a further forty-two recommended titles. Whereas the basic list is understandably limited to titles published in the USA, the first extension shows a much wider outlook, with twenty-four American-published titles, eight from England, seven from Federal Germany and one each from France, Holland and Switzerland. Suggested periodicals for the large music library cast the international net still further afield with recommended titles from East Germany, Sweden, Argentina, Austria, Australia and Denmark. The list specifically omits recommendations of yearbooks, although the article names several examples which could usefully be considered for stock.

Librarians of authorities which are too small to have a separate music library may find it worth considering the periodicals listed and described below when extending or revising the list of publications taken. The suggestions here do not coincide with those in Watanabe's article, not least because of our different national backgrounds. Branch libraries could, with profit, take a different selection of magazines and periodicals from those found on the racks of the central or district library, rather than duplicate the titles already taken. If, despite what has been written above about the shortcomings of some reviews, it is felt that the comments in journals taken in branch libraries should nevertheless be checked, this can be done by the appropriate member of staff; alternatively, the periodical can be sent to the music librarian once its currency has expired, and so provide the opportunity to see if any book, score or recording has been well reviewed in the periodical in question but which, up to that time, had been overlooked in making additions to the library's stock.

Because of the ever-present possibilities of changes of editor, of alteration of format, coverage and style of approach (particularly if the ownership of a journal changes hands), the brief descriptions given below may well be incorrect to a greater or lesser extent, by the time they appear in print. Indeed, individual periodicals may have ceased publication through changes in economic or artistic circumstances, so

students pursuing courses which expect some knowledge of
relevant periodicals are strongly advised to try to inspect
two or three recent copies of any titles of interest, partly
to aid the memory but, equally important, to check that the
comments here are still generally accurate and that they have
not omitted any important points.

Every library possessing scores and recordings ought
to subscribe to at least a few periodicals in the area of music. Librarians of larger systems should need no encouragement to display and file as many journal titles as possible,
particularly those indexed in Music Index and Répertoire de
Littérature Musicale. A good case could be made out for the
assertion that the range of holdings of periodicals and their
treatment provide one of the best indications of the compara-
tive richness and strength of a music library.

Periodicals receiving mention below are divided into
three groups: scholarly, mainly instrumental, miscellaneous.
Magazines primarily concerned with sound recordings are not
described here, but comments can be found in Chapter V.

Scholarly

EARLY MUSIC, 1973- . (Quarterly). [59]

Published by the Oxford University Press, this contains long,
signed reviews of books and also of music scores within its
subject field. Coverage is international. Articles are by experts in their respective spheres, and contributions are frequently illustrated with photographs and by musical examples.
Coverage includes some practical articles, as well as those
dealing with such aspects as history and interpretation. One
might instance an article on making reeds for the baroque
oboe, or another on gut strings. As a final comment, it
should be noted that the magazine is distinguished by excellent typography and superb production.

FONTES ARTIS MUSICAE, 1954- . (Quarterly). [73]

This is the official publication of the International Association
of Music Libraries. There were two issues annually for over
twenty years, but the long-expressed intention was to produce three issues a year as soon as finances permitted. So

the first copy was nominally a double one covering eight
months, e.g., "1973/1-2/Januar-August." The German version of the first month results from the fact that the journal
is printed in that country. The periodical carries a note to
the effect that "<u>Fontes</u> is a private publication and only available to members of the Association. The subscription price
is covered by membership dues." In other words, all members of the Association receive <u>Fontes</u> or, put yet another
way, it is necessary to join the IAML as a corporate or individual member if one wishes to have the journal.

In 1976, there was a change of editorship, with some
resultant alterations in the periodical. One very pleasant
one was the fact that there were four issues during the
year. As before, each number continued to contain articles
with a musicological bias, to supply reports and book reviews usually--but not always--in one of the Association's
official languages of English, French, and German. Only in
the case of articles apparently considered to be of major importance is a brief summary in each of the other two languages provided; official announcements are made in all three
languages; book reviews are in one language only. From this
description, it should be clear that the monoglot librarian is
at an appreciable disadvantage, and one could wish that all
articles could carry an abstract in each of the three languages recognized.

We had long thought that one of the great values of
each issue was the selective lists printed at the end of each
number. These provided brief details of books and scores
published throughout the world, arranged under countries
(in the French form of their names), subdivided in each case
into five categories, in alphabetical order of composer or
author under each heading. The five chosen divisions were
these: Théatre et films; Musique instrumental; Musique
vocale; Folklore; Ouvrages sur la musique et ouvrages
didactiques. The lists provided a simple but potentially
very valuable (albeit incomplete) check upon important
foreign publications. Under each country was given the
name of the compiler of the list, in some cases an individual,
in others an institution such as Donemus.

However, the lists were dropped in 1976 "because of
the large percentage of members who considered it one of
the less useful regular sections of the publication." Never-

theless, the decision met with disapproval in Canada, and a
"Liste sélective" for that country appeared in the last 1976
issue, suggesting that the matter was by no means finally
settled. The members of the Canadian Music Library Association pointed out "that for countries not so fortunate as to
have a national music bibliography, the list offers the only
comparable alternative for surveying recent music publications on a national basis." This is a good illustration of
the way that changes of policy take place in serial publications, and the need for students to check the latest issues
in order to ensure awareness of such changes. In recent
years, similar selective lists for Belgium and France have
appeared.

For British members of the Association, there is also
Brio [25], subtitled "Journal of the United Kingdom Branch
of the International Association of Music Libraries" and published twice yearly. Receipt is included as part of the subscription to the parent body. The magazine usually includes
two or three articles of particular British interest, reports
of meetings and a number of reviews.

MUSIC AND LETTERS, 1920- . (Quarterly). [145]

This is one of the most scholarly of the music periodicals
published in Britain. The main body of each number consists of articles on various musical topics and a high proportion of this information would seem to appear later in book
form. References to discoveries of material relating to famous composers appear with surprising frequency and facsimiles and illustrations in music type are to be found in
many of the issues. Book reviews (both of domestic and
foreign publications) vary considerably in length, but 1,500
words is not uncommon and even longer appraisals are found
upon occasion. Because of this thoroughness, only a limited
number of books is selected for review in each issue but
those chosen are usually those that may be regarded as the
most important. Initials at the end of each review indicate
the writer. A limited number of music scores is also appraised and, again, these comments are also over the name
of the particular reviewer. Items may be considered individually; on the other hand, shorter notices may be grouped
for comment under a generic heading, such as "New music
for voice."

An index has been published for issues from 1920 to
1959. Both articles and reviews are incorporated, but in
two separate sequences. The main compiler was Eric Blom;
after his death, with the work left well towards completion,
the compilation was rounded off by Sir Jack Westrup, and
published by the Oxford University Press.

MUSICAL QUARTERLY, 1915- . (Quarterly). [153]

The most important American periodical of its type dates back
to 1915 and is published by G. Schirmer, Inc. The work has
been described as "... the standard scholarly periodical in
music of the United States and is found in nearly every
music library" [228, p. 186]. The body of each issue usually consists of long articles, normally illustrated by examples
in music type and, when relevant, with other illustrations.
Book reviews are limited in number, but are lengthy; the
average is about 1,500 words, but much lengthier appraisals
are to be found, particularly when the general tenor is critical.

Gramophone record reviews are also very limited in
number and tend to concentrate either on early music or on
contemporary works. The individual critic (whose name will
be shown at the end of a review) is likely to concentrate
upon the music performed and on its place in musical history. The edition used (for early music) is also likely to be
discussed. The actual performance often seems to be considered of lesser importance, and the quality of the recording is unlikely to receive more than brief comment.

There is an index to the first forty-eight volumes,
covering the period from 1915 to 1962 [79]. It includes book
reviews as well as articles in its coverage.

MUSIC REVIEW, 1940- . (Quarterly). [150]

This periodical began life during World War II, in 1940; it is,
superficially at least, intended for the same segment of readers as Music and Letters. Each issue contains a number of
book reviews, by no means restricted to English works.
Each review is initialled, and a separate guide identifies
those writing in a particular number. A small number of
gramophone records is also covered, and there may be

reviews of one or more recent concerts, often limiting coverage to a single unusual item in a program. That is considered at some length, with the work often given more emphasis than the performance.

NOTES, 1934- . (Quarterly). [169]

This is the official journal of the Music Library Association (of the USA). It is surprising and disappointing that its circulation in Britain is so small; that many American libraries also are nonsubscribers cannot be accepted as an excuse. The total circulation figure is under 4,000 copies. Notes is basically a bibliographical and reviewing periodical for librarians, produced by librarians. The journal first appeared in July 1934 in duplicated typescript and subsequent issues were published irregularly. The present series of well-printed, quarterly issues dates back to December 1943--a somewhat unlikely date for such a major change.

Each issue usually contains one or two bibliographical essays in a specialist area of music, but as indicated in the previous paragraph, the bulk of the content is a series of reviews. There are a number of books considered, in critiques which usually run to a maximum of some 500 words, but which may well exceed that figure considerably if the book is reckoned to be sufficiently important to justify such treatment. On occasion, where there is felt to be a strong subject or other link between them, several books are reviewed as a batch. Items considered are not restricted to those published in the USA but include also a wide range of European publications. As the reviewers are highly qualified librarians, they show an awareness of the sort of information and opinion about a book that other librarians require. Bibliographical citations, as one would expect from such a source, are excellent.

"Books recently published" lists such works in alphabetical order of language, except that English is given precedence. The ISBN, pagination and LC catalogue card number are all supplied if possible. Twice yearly a list of "Announced reprints and facsimiles of music and musical literature" appears. It may be mentioned that an immense number of books, many of them British in origin and long out of print, are reissued in the USA at what appears to this writer to be very high prices indeed. Moreover, one has doubts in some cases whether the books are worth reprinting at all, but must assume that the publishers in this field know what they are about and sell enough copies to make the business profitable.

"Index to record reviews, with symbols indicating opinions of reviewers" is a long-standing feature, compiled and edited by Kurtz Myers. Between fifteen and twenty periodicals, all of American or British origin, are indexed. Entries are in two sequences--in composer order for discs containing works by a single writer, and under the label name for anthologies. In all cases, full details of the contents of each record are given, often with the LC catalogue card number. Each of the selected periodicals which has reviewed a particular disc within a certain period is shown by means of a mnemonic abbreviation; to the right of each is a note showing the issue and page(s) of the review. To the left is the rating assessment. "Three primary grades of opinion are indicated: + excellent, • adequate, and - inadequate. On a different plane, the symbol ■ indicates that the review, whatever else it might supply, offers no clear statement on the performance and recording, and the symbol ⏉ indicates a review of sufficient length and probity to warrant special attention."

A criticism of the choice of periodicals used for the compilation of the lists appeared in Notes itself: "One supposes, upon reviewing the list, that the choice has been made on the basis of easy availability, coverage of special subjects, and quality of 'reviews.' With the exception of Disques, which was in French, all of the periodicals indexed are in English. This fact ... leads to the omission of several major reviewing media. Of these, it is probably the German publications that are most missed" [21]. One may accept these criticisms but, at the same time, recall that the index is a one-man compilation, requiring a great deal of reading and evaluating, and probably as much time again in listing and arranging. For British librarians, the lists are probably of little help for domestic issues that are later released in the USA, but extremely useful to indicate outstanding American productions. Those from the major companies are likely to find their respective ways quite quickly into the British catalogues, and the most favourably reviewed of those from minor labels may be thought worthy of special importation by the enterprising librarian.

Reviews of music follow the same pattern as for books --they are often lengthy, cover publications from a number of countries, and are signed. Not the least asset of these reviews is that the librarian critics are often prepared to voice an overall judgment, rather than remain politely neutral, and this is clearly most helpful to less expert colleagues. The December issue of Notes used to contain an annual survey of "Piano music for children," classified by grade of difficulty and annotated. Its value should be immediately apparent; unfortunately, this listing seems to have ended in 1974. Even the "Popular music" feature, once an annual list (as its introductory note still suggests), no longer appears in each issue. The coverage was described as "A survey of books and folios with an index to recently reviewed recordings."

Types of music included were "Country and Western music, Soul, MOR (middle of the road), musical comedy, and various forms of rock...." Discs, cassettes and cartridges were listed in a single sequence, arranged by name of artist. It was rather like the lists of Kurtz Myers in this same periodical, but there was no symbol to show an overall verdict on the record. "Folio music recently published" listed albums of popular music, giving pagination and price, together with contents. It should need no stressing the value of such a section, and how unfortunate it is that it is no longer included.

Nevertheless, from the comments made earlier in this appraisal, the immensely valuable nature of Notes is apparent. One final point about this serial is that all back numbers are kept in print.

Mainly Instrumental

The guitar player is well catered to and, in turn, the librarian has little excuse for failing to keep abreast of new music and recordings in this particular magazine area. Guitar: The Magazine for All Guitarists is a monthly publication. It has undergone a distinct change of emphasis since the end of 1982. At that time, the subtitle quoted above still applied, after which it began to concentrate on classical and other fingerstyle guitar playing/players. The policy of articles and interviews on rock and jazz guitar began to dwindle and now seems to have virtually dried up. This is implicitly acknowledged with the adoption of a new subtitle in November 1983, "for professional and amateur players."

It still indexes the year's issues each July, and continues to publish pieces for performance; there are five or more pages of signed reviews of concerts, music scores, books and records, running approximately between fifty and 500 words. For the librarian in the United Kingdom, it has the obvious advantage over Guitar Review (see below) that items noticed should be fairly easy to obtain; for American librarians, the reverse is likely to be true.

Mention is cautiously made of Guitarist, a monthly publication which first appeared in June, 1984 [90a]. It is apparently attempting to fill the gaps left by Guitar's omission. At the time of writing, only two issues have appeared, so that the following comments may not continue to be relevant. Emphasis is strongly on rock/folk/jazz players, instrumental equipment, etc. Articles include interviews with well-known performers, instructional articles on playing and also on instrument/equipment maintenance, signed concert, record and book reviews, usually at some length. If the magazine survives it gives every hope of becoming a British equivalent of the well-established American Guitar Player magazine [88a]. This last, published monthly since 1967 is readily available in Britain and has extensive coverage of all aspects of guitar playing, but has its main emphasis on pop and jazz players and playing. It carries interviews with players together with equipment reviews and tests, instructional articles and signed record reviews of American issues. This is perhaps the best and most interesting guitar for the nonclassical player, even taking into account its obvious and expected American bias.

Finally, for this section, mention must be made of Guitar Review whose three issues a year are published by the Society of the Classic Guitar [89]. This periodical is, at one and the same time, erudite and beautifully produced. The magazine has reviews of books (including tutors), of compositions for the instrument and of recordings. The width of coverage is broad, from renaissance lute music to that for contemporary guitar, the latter including both bossa nova and flamenco. Publications reviewed stem from a number of countries, including Britain, France, Germany, and Italy. Tutors of different approaches (including the peda-

gogic), books on various types of guitar and music scores
all receive comment; classical and folk guitar tutors have
also been included in the periodical's review pages. These
critiques, like those on books, usually average between 300
and 500 words each, sufficient space for a critic to expand
a little on such aspects as technical difficulty, the apparent
effectiveness (or the reverse) of a tutor, and the standard
of playing needed to obtain full benefit from the guide.

The periodical is nominally published three times a
year; in practice, issues seem to be much more erratic.
The appeal of the magazine can perhaps best be illustrated
by the fact that the first six issues (from 1946-1948) have
been reprinted in a single volume, as have numbers seven to
twelve (1948-1951). These reissues are as handsomely produced as the originals, and are correspondingly expensive.
Issue no. forty (dated Winter 1976) was devoted mainly to
Gaspar Sanz, to coincide with the publication 300 years previously of his Instrucción de música sobre la guitarra es-
pañola, and the idea of a major theme for an issue is not
uncommon.

For the librarian selecting books and/or scores within
this instrumental field, all the books listed above are valuable
aids.

A different sort of stringed instrument is the subject
of The Strad, a magazine whose history goes back to 1890
[210]. Its subtitle is "a monthly journal for professionals
and amateurs of all stringed instruments played with the
bow." The reviews of new music provide, in narrative form,
brief but useful thumbnail appraisals of the items listed.
The standard of playing ability required for effective performance is shown by the reviewer. There are occasional
exceptions to this rule. The reviews are, therefore, particularly helpful to the librarian who is looking for worthwhile items to add to stock--a description which should apply to all who are responsible for selection.

Recorder and Music Magazine includes reviews of both
books and scores [180]. When a work whose coverage is
wider than that implied by the title of this serial, the review
will generally comment only on those sections relevant to the
recorder family, and ignore the remainder. As an example,
one might quote the September 1974 issue, for it contains a

review of the third edition of Arthur Jacobs' A New Dictionary of Music. The reviewer has looked at the entries in the
dictionary relating to early instruments and also has searched
for the names of current composers who write for these instruments. These are admittedly a very limited range of
topics, but from this specialist viewpoint, the dictionary has
clearly failed to impress its critic. Reviews of new music
are brief, but signed.

Miscellaneous
We begin by considering a group of periodicals which may
be described as catering for the intelligent music lover. If
we adopt a roughly classified order, then Musical Opinion is
the first to consider [152]. This is a monthly journal, dating
back to 1877, which provides a useful complement to The Musical Times. Separate critics usually deal with reviews of
books, of new music, and of gramophone records. Comments
are usually fairly brief, but there is enough room for the
individual critic to present a view of the work under discussion and to give reasons for it. The second part of each
issue is entitled "The Organ World," and is allotted about one
third of the available space. Indeed, the same publishers
produce The Organ; a Quarterly Review for Its Makers, Its
Players and Its Lovers [173].

    The Musical Times [154] is a mixture of three aspects
of music publishing. For most readers, the work is simply
a highly reputable journal aimed to interest the informed music lover. It is also, however, a house journal; evidence to
this effect used to be shown each month by the insertion of
a reduced facsimile of an anthem or part of a larger choral
work (always a composition published by Novello). The Musical Times has a continuous history since 1844 which makes
it of greater antiquity than any other periodical considered
in this section.

    Reviews are given for books, for recordings, and for
music. In each field, there is usually a panel of several
critics. Comments are a mixture, in the case of music
scores, of long single reviews and much briefer appraisals
of groups of related works such as early romantic piano.
For the rest, there are articles on a variety of musical
topics, and the magazine also reviews some London concerts
and, in general, keeps its readers au fait on current events.

If one excludes The Musical Times which is, as has
been explained above, something of a special case, the last
of the British "house magazines" is Tempo, a quarterly which
emanates from Boosey & Hawkes [211]. This very well produced magazine has been in production since 1939. It contains major articles often illustrated with musical quotations.
Tempo includes reviews of books and of music. The two
other journals from British music publishers which were apparently defeated by rising costs were the Monthly Musical
Record (published by Augener between 1871 and 1960) [140]
and Chesterian, the organ of J & W Chester; this existed
from 1915 until it ceased publication in 1960 [38].

Opera [171] is more specialist in appeal. Possibly
because this art form plays a much smaller part in British
musical life than do orchestral and other concerts, the editor's horizons are worldwide. This international outlook is
reflected in the reports of performances in many different
countries, often illustrated with photographs of singers,
stage settings and of works in performance. Recordings of
complete operas, together with some recital discs, are reviewed; the critic is usually named at the end of each appraisal. Coverage is usually limited to about 200 to 300
words. Within each issue of the periodical is a section on
tinted paper listing coming events, and this is worldwide in
scope. A popular American journal on opera is Opera News,
issued by the Metropolitan Opera Guild [172].

Jazz and popular music have their own specialist periodicals, of which an important one is down beat (the lower
case typography is that used by the publishers) [57]. It
hardly needs to be said that the magazine is American; frequency of publication is now monthly. The importance of
the magazine in its chosen field is illustrated in part by the
fact that its articles are included in the coverage of Music
Index. Each issue contains a number of record reviews, often lengthy. The arrangement is by manufacturers' labels
(many of them available in Britain). Shorter, and of lesser
importance, are book reviews, concert notices, brief notes
on new equipment and occasional instructional articles.

Another valuable serial in this field is Jazz Journal
International, which began life as Jazz Journal in 1948,
adding "International" from May 1977 onwards [107]. It
has always been catholic in its coverage, and it has a well

deserved high reputation as a reviewing medium. This fact can be particularly useful to the music librarian whose knowledge of jazz is small, and the journal's slightly conservative approach as to what it reviews is no disadvantage for such a librarian.

Reviews of discs are arranged in alphabetical order of soloist's, leader's or group name, as considered most appropriate, or by the disc's collective title if that is felt to be best. Reviews, generally some 200 to 300 words in length, are signed. It should be mentioned that there is a separately available annual index to articles and to record reviews. For the librarian hard pressed for time and with only a small budget for jazz record accessions, this selection of reviews could be extremely useful.

For current events in the pop world, and for reviews of some of its plethora of recordings, there are a number of periodicals available. For the librarian, there are three periodicals which cover much the same ground; all are issued weekly and at least one should be bought if the library stock includes pop. Melody Maker was first issued in 1926, before World War II, and was generally recognized as the standard serial in the field of British jazz [139]. Unfortunately, in the early 1980s jazz coverage almost disappeared. Pop is still covered, but it sometimes seems that the reviewer's writing style is more important than the content!

The second work is New Musical Express which is a much younger periodical, dating back to 1952 [165]. Although coverage is not unlike that of Melody Maker, there are distinct differences in approach. One may suggest that "NME" appeals to a narrower spectrum of readers, as is evidenced by its use of a number of writing styles which will be familiar to the regular reader but possibly not to the casual buyer. For example, not all music (or other) librarians would understand the comment on one disc that "the riff is so simple, the hookline so utterly mindless." Such remarks give the periodical its own individual character, and are perhaps attempts to build up a selective readership. The potential audience would appear to be younger than that for Melody Maker, and these readers may appreciate the apparently cynical approach to some aspects of the pop scene. Reviews of albums (i.e., 12-inch discs) are signed and are often lengthy. Singles generally receive shorter notices.

The third weekly periodical discussed here is <u>Sounds</u> which was first published in 1970 [206]. Originally it appeared to be modelling itself closely on <u>Melody Maker</u>, but in the last few years it has emphasized "new wave" music. This may be regarded as an indication that it, too, appeals to one particular sector of pop fans, with a still lower age than those whose first choice would be one of the other two periodicals considered in this section. <u>Sounds</u> would now appear to have the edge for LP reviews, for they are still signed, and they are concise and to the point. Chart information in any of these weeklies is inferior to that provided in <u>Music Week</u> (considered below), which means that the latter is a more effective selection tool. It should be noted that none of these three consider MOR ("Middle of the Road") recordings. For these, the librarian will still need to rely upon the appropriate section of <u>Gramophone</u> and other classically biased monthly magazines, considered elsewhere in Chapter V.

<u>Music Week</u> [150a] (incorporating <u>Record and Tape Retailer</u> and <u>Record Business</u>) is, as its subtitle suggests primarily for the retail market. For every librarian working with a collection of audio material that is not entirely classical in its musical coverage, it does have considerable use as a selection tool. Its weekly listing of new LP releases gives artist/title/label/item number/distributor/trade price, and shows whether the record is domestically produced or is an import. Clearly, the number of releases varies from week to week, but is generally in the range of 50 to 150. It should be stressed that all types of music are included, with the important exception of classical music.

For those librarians selecting, the excellent "Top 100" LP chart included in each edition gives full details of each item, including cassette equivalents, where applicable, so that it is simple to order up-to-date best-selling items, without having to trace manufacturers' numbers in other discographical sources. This makes a pleasant contrast with the pop weeklies, where charts are usually restricted to the top thirty to fifty and omit discographical details, presumably on the basis that their readers will ask for records by artists or titles, and expect the dealer to check numbers as necessary.

There are some reviews each week. Although brief and

unsigned, they are usefully classified under such headings
as "Folk," "Top 50," "Nostalgia," "Budget," etc. A star
rating system is used, but this refers to the estimated selling power of a record as distinct from an assessment of
quality.

Mention should also be made of Music Master [149],
which is bought on annual subscription, which includes provision of the supplements and the annual master volume.
There are monthly editions whose appearances have been
highly erratic in the past. Music Master could be characterized as "essential but frustrating." Lists used to contain
deleted discs a long way back, but in mid 1984 this has
been amended to the inclusion of nothing more than three
years deleted, so that earlier volumes will need to be retained if the tracing of older deletions is a relevant factor
in selection policy. Further observations about this periodical are made later.

Now, there is a single alphabetical listing under artists, under which details of all LPs and singles by these
artists are to be found. A titles list of singles is retained,
and the intention is to produce cumulations incorporating
six months' releases, from January to June and for the second half of the year. As indicated above, lists are cumulated from February to May, and then made into self-contained
unit, so that (except for these biennial volumes), a month's
issue can be disposed of as a cumulation appears. The serial
has recently began a separate listing of compact discs. The
great majority of LPs include a listing of individual tracks,
and sometimes brief descriptive notes provided by the record
companies.

Music Master is, understandably, not inexpensive but
is good value for what it offers and so is an important tool
for anything but the small record library. It is not as useful for selection as Music Week, simply because cumulation
makes production less immediate. However, for retrospective
selection and for general enquiry work, there is really nothing to compare in the non-classical music fields.

Music Master also publishes annually a labels list,
which incorporates an alphabetical list of labels, record companies, and distributors giving access to a variety of information. From this a librarian can check whether a particular

label actually exists, who distributes a particular label, what labels a particular distributor supplies, which parent company owns a particular record label, etc.

ENQUIRY WORK

The separate chapters on music cataloguing and classification which are provided in this book are indicative of our firm belief that these areas present particular difficulties of sufficient importance to warrant consideration of their particular problems at some length. With reference, or information work, we are much less convinced that equally detailed treatment is either possible or necessary. It is freely acknowledged, however, that there are many questions likely to be put to the librarian of a music department which will require a wide range of specialist knowledge if the right approach toward finding the correct answer is to be pursued; indeed, musical expertise is often required in order to understand the question posed.

Despite the variety of queries, a limited number of categories cover the great majority of requests; without trying to put these in any order of priority or relationship (not least because some of the headings overlap), we would suggest that those indicated below are most common. It may strike a reader as paradoxical to begin with questions that have a musical context but which require no particular musical knowledge or even, in many cases, any specialist background. To be asked when the Sydney Opera House was opened should be no more difficult than a similar question relating to the Sydney Harbour bridge--one can be completely ignorant about matters operatic but still be able to find the right answer, quite quickly, from one of several possible sources, not necessarily in the music section of stock. Similarly, one might deal with a question concerning the winners of the National Brass Band championship in a particular year or information about the various attempts to invent successfully what might be called a musical typewriter.

Of the enquiries immediately related to music, the most common is likely to be concerning stock--has the library a copy of a particular work? If the questioner accurately provides three pieces of information, there should be no difficulty. The necessary data concern the composer and the

title of the work; the other vital factor would be the medium
for which the work was wanted. With this firm basis, the
answer should easily be found by straightforward use of the
catalogue by the enquirer or any member of staff, however
junior in status. The usual complication is that, all too frequently, minor errors are included in the question, sometimes in the name of the composer or in the medium required
but, far more frequently, in the inaccurate transmission of
the work's title. The musically competent librarian will often
be able to correct the error without hesitation through personal knowledge of the library's stock and the standard
repertoire. One would know that the "Consecration of the
horse" is a Beethoven overture and that the last word should
be "house." On the other hand, a great deal of time was
once spent in a music library trying to discover the composer
of the "Dardarina" overture, when no other information was
supplied; after a fruitless search, the staff could only wonder if Rameau's Dardanus was the right answer. These errors in transmission are common in any subject field connected
with the arts--with paintings, novels and plays as well as
with music--and can occasionally be very frustrating.

A related, and almost as frequent, request is for the
composer of a particular work. This seems to be an area in
which there is no adequate substitute for experience allied
with a wide musical knowledge. There is no musical equivalent to the Cumulative Book Index or the various Whitaker
publications with their plethora of title entries. In any case,
music enquiries will often relate to parts of a work only. It
could be quite difficult to find the composer of "Fairies and
giants" if nothing but these three words was known about
the work; the title, taken at face value, suggests music for
children (and, quite likely, bad music at that). In fact, it
is a movement from Elgar's Wand of Youth Suite, no. 1.
But how can the inexperienced librarian discover that? The
enquirer can be politely crossexamined, but even the most
patient interrogation may not provide enough clues for the
work to be traced. A recent help, and one that is going to
become of increasing value as time goes on (but is also going
to take that much longer to search as the file lengthens) is
American Catalog of Copyright Entries, Part 14, which relates to sound recordings and which has been briefly described earlier in this chapter [217]. Its multitude of title
entries will help to fill a gap in most libraries' catalogues.

The librarian may be asked to supply the name, and perhaps the address, of the publisher of a work. This should not be difficult if the work is still in copyright and the composer is of some standing, even if the issuing firm is located in another country or even another continent. Mention has been made of the lists given in such reference tools as MGG and Riemann. Addresses of musicians or of their agents may pose no problem or be almost impossible to discover, according to circumstances. Many of the more famous figures in all musical fields may well not appear in the appropriate area telephone directory, yet may have provided a telephone number by which they may be reached in Who's Who or other guides of like nature.

Illustrations may be required of a composer or performer, of an instrument, of a stage setting or perhaps a page (usually the first) of an individual manuscript. Such questions can vary, like so many others, from the immediately answerable to the virtually impossible. Queries about recorded music concern the same matters that are liable to arise in connection with scores; the additional hurdle here is the fact that performers are also involved. This opens yet another wide area for error--this time in the name of the artist(s), in the name of the label under which the recording has been issued, or in the musical content of the recording. Questions on musical personalities may be answered from encyclopaedias (such as those described earlier), from biographical directories, from various musical yearbooks and directories, from recent issues of periodicals (particularly if the subject of the enquiry is a new star in the musical firmament), or from one or other of a number of possible musical sources. The librarian's skill (or good fortune) will be shown in the selection of the right reference tool at an early stage of the search. Quite often, a little extra time spent in questioning, to ensure that the enquiry being put is as clear as it is possible to make it, can well save a lengthy spell of fruitless searching. To take a single example, it should be almost the first question on being asked about an individual whose name is unknown to the librarian, to discover in which musical field the subject is or was engaged. Performers of, say, twelve-tone music and of the latest successes in the "charts"--those all-important tables of relative public interest in a particular week, as demonstrated by record sales of pop music--are unlikely to be found in the same reference sources.

Enquiries are certain to be received concerning songs
that were popular many years previously. Here, a file of
gramophone record manufacturers' catalogues and of the
quarterly cumulations produced by Gramophone and of the
Schwann monthly equivalent (considered in Chapter V) may
well provide a partial, if not complete answer. Films and
the music for them are another frequent source of questions.
In this area, the librarian could well redirect the problem to
the appropriate colleague who supervises the library's books
on films. The stock there is more likely to provide the
answer than are specifically musical works of reference.
Again, the Gramophone popular catalogues can often be
helpful, since the film soundtracks of a fair proportion of
successful issues are later released on disc and/or tape.
The pages of Gramophone itself include, from time to time,
the sources of music used for series of television or radio
programmes. In Britain, both the BBC and commercial radio
stations are generally most helpful in supplying details of
works which they have relayed. As for those who ask the
librarian to identify a tune, much will depend upon the accuracy with which the melody can be sung or whistled and,
if not immediately recognized, whether it can be traced
through those guides mentioned earlier in this chapter--
Barlow & Morgenstern, and Parsons.

The wise librarian will keep an indexed file of concert
programmes. It is one thing to be asked for a musical analysis of a work in the standard repertory, but a very different
matter if the composition concerned is recent or rarely performed. In these cases, analysis may be absent from the
usual guides such as Tovey, Biancolli, Newmarch, and the
like but could be found in a concert programme. For example, we found a long note on Litolff's overture Robespierre,
otherwise untraceable, in a programme given by the Bridling-
ton Symphony Orchestra (a body now very long defunct) in
1908. As has been suggested, an index to works analysed
is needed and the programmes themselves need to be retained
in an organized sequence. Yet published concert guides and
articles in musical journals do cover a very wide range of
repertoire. Two useful indexes to programme notes and
criticisms of individual works are available, by Voorhees
[223] and Diamond [54].

For current events, reference will usually be made to
the appropriate periodicals or to the arts pages of certain

newspapers--an important reason for having a wide range of
the former in stock, and keeping them on file for at least
several months, and preferably much longer. Finally, there
are those questions which do not fit into any of the loose
categories listed in the foregoing pages. There will always
be a fair number of these unclassifiable queries. For all
out-of-the ordinary and difficult questions, the wise librarian
will maintain a file, adding the correct answers and, equally
importantly, the source of the information found. The file
should also be used to record questions which remain unan-
swered, together with a note of the sources used in trying
to trace the answer. If the same question, or a closely related one, should be raised again the librarian who tries to
answer it can see at a glance what works were consulted
previously and so avoid wasteful duplication of unsuccessful
effort.

This section is no more than a superficial glimpse of
the potential quagmire through which the reference librarian
has to struggle. There is no vade mecum or operational
short cut; a wide knowledge of the appropriate works in the
stock, a retentive memory, a lively curiosity, a love of a
wide range of music and, for good measure, the occasional
stroke of serendipity, will all be necessary if the librarian
is to achieve a high percentage of successful answers to
questions on music and to enhance the library's reputation
as an information centre.

It seems to us that the good librarian should be ready
to admit failure on an enquiry at an earlier rather than a
later stage, but should not regard this as the end of the
process. There may be colleagues within the library system
or elsewhere who may be reached by means of a local telephone call. The temptation may well exist to fob off the
enquirer, when the librarian has failed to find the answer,
with the vague suggestion that other sources should be tried.
It is, or should be, a matter of professional pride (as well
as good public relations) for the librarian to make the approach elsewhere on the enquirer's behalf. In this way,
there is a greatly increased likelihood of a definite answer
to the question. If three or four professionals cannot hunt
down the solution, there is a much stronger probability that
it is unanswerable. Colleagues, within or without the library,
may themselves be willing to pursue the matter further.

If the answer is found, it certainly needs to be recorded for future possible use. The librarian may, possibly unconsciously, build up a fuller picture of the scope and stock of other libraries within the area. Such a plan may well result in an informal network of librarians within an area; again, the special knowledge of individuals will be better realized and appreciated. There is ample scope for much more active co-operation than generally exists today. Additionally, any scheme of this nature, whether it be formally constituted or not, should not restrict itself to any one type of library. Public and academic libraries can provide invaluable support for each other, given the opportunity and the willingness to do so.

Finally, the interested reader is referred to the most comprehensive modern examination of the reference process in libraries, in the second volume of the work already cited by William Katz [108].

Chapter III

CATALOGUING

INTRODUCTION

This chapter falls into three sections. First is a brief survey of some of the problems likely to arise in cataloguing music, with possible answers. Second, there comes a section which briefly outlines some of the rules relating to music in certain of the published codes; this is intended to be of concern mainly to librarianship students. The third part of the chapter is devoted to some practical suggestions for music cataloguing: the comments there, it must be stressed, are not for the expert but are included to help the cataloguer whose knowledge of music is small and who lacks specialist guidance from colleagues. The need for a fair degree of musical expertise, if scores are to be correctly entered in a library catalogue, is still by no means as widely appreciated as it should be, and it can easily happen that the cataloguing staff (and "staff" may well be one person) in a small public or college library includes no qualified member who has an understanding of key signatures or the difference, say, between a string trio and a trio for two violins and a viola.

Some guidance may be found from inspecting appropriate entries in the cumulations of The British Catalogue of Music or other national equivalent, but it is most unlikely that the searcher will be fortunate enough to find entries for all the works presenting problems that have to be solved if cataloguing is to be done well. In any case, the small library may not subscribe to BCM, and its funds may be too restricted to buy one of the other major cataloguing aids-- despite the fact that one could argue that the need for such assistance is greatest where musical knowledge is poorest.

Cooperation between libraries has made appreciable advances during the past few years. In the USA, OCLC (originally Ohio College ... but now Online Computer Library Center) was founded in 1971 and has over 2,000 members at the time of writing. It is a computer-based network with two major uses. Its original, and main, function is cataloguing; its database of ten million items includes 200,000 sound recordings and nearly as many music scores. It also acts as a location guide when a library is checking for a copy of a wanted work. Other services are also being developed.

In Britain, the network idea is advancing more slowly. Four academic libraries (in 1984) belong to OCLC; public libraries are more independently minded. There are also the UK-based cooperatives. They are BLCMP, based in Birmingham, SCOLCAP in Scotland, and SWALCAP which is largely confined to academic libraries in the southwestern counties of England. The biggest network in the UK is, however, BLAISE LOCAS, the British Library's Local Cataloguing Service. Even this has well under 100 members, including a number of government libraries. It has a rather more centralised structure than the others.

THE PROBLEMS

The cataloguer who normally deals only with books and similar printed materials may reasonably wonder why one claims that music needs special treatment and that it poses particular problems. There are four difficulties which are normally found only in scores and not with other printed material. The first problem with music concerns the title for, contrary to standard cataloguing practice, this may be considered partly irrelevant--in that copies of the same piece of music can present what could, at first sight, seem to be a very different title if published in, say, Germany compared with other editions emanating from the USA, Italy, or Russia. It is now generally accepted that the old tag to the effect that music is the only universal language is no more than a half-truth; nevertheless, the borrower who knows no German may well take out a German edition of some Bach organ works and play the music, even though the editorial comments in the foreword cannot be understood or appreciated. The same person would be at a complete loss with a German edition of

Heine's poems; to read this verse would require an English
translation (whose title page, one hopes, would make it immediately obvious that the volume was not in the original
language). The comparison is admittedly inexact since, in
the case of vocal works, the language in which the words
are presented may prove to be an insuperable barrier to
performance in another tongue by a native of a different
country: few British singers, for instance, would be capable of singing songs to a Czech text without some form of
guidance both to meaning and pronunciation. Provision has
to be made in a code of rules, therefore, for all entries relating to the same piece of music, whatever the language of
the title page, to appear together in the catalogue, or, at
worst, to be linked by some means of references. This latter alternative is unlikely to be readily acceptable to either
users or library staff.

The second problem concerns arrangements; a musical
work may be available in several different forms, e.g., the
library's stock could well contain a miniature score of a
Beethoven symphony, an edition of the same work arranged
for piano solo, another for piano duet, and a fourth for
violin and piano. The music collection could also contain
simplified versions of compositions, modified to suit children
or adult performers of very limited technical accomplishment.
Good cataloguing practice requires an individual entry for
each item, but the different versions should be filed in immediate proximity under an appropriate heading. Only in
this way can a potential user see quickly what are the available alternatives in stock, and then select the one most likely to be suitable for his particular purpose.

The third difficulty relates to excerpts. Separate pub-
lication of extracts from longer works is very much more common with music than with books. One can hardly imagine an
enquiry for an individual chapter of Wuthering Heights, but
the music librarian is not surprised if a pianist asks for
Wedding Day at Troldhaugen (which is one of the numerous
Lyric Pieces by Grieg), nor if a singer requests Songs My
Mother Taught Me, completely unaware that this is one of
Dvořák's Gypsy Songs. The soprano who wishes to learn
One Fine Day might be painfully surprised if she found her-
self forced to buy a complete vocal score of Madama Butterfly
to achieve this ambition, though she could well be happy to
borrow such a score from her local public library if this aria

were not available separately. The nearest analogy in the world of literature is probably the request for an individual poem, which may be published in a volume of the poet's works or in an anthology of verse.

The fourth handicap has been the lack of clear direction for nonmusicians until recent years in most codes, and the equal absence of standard examples that can be followed as guides. The difference between what have been called the bibliographic orientated and the retrieval orientated types of catalogue is very real. It could be argued that the library whose clientele requires the latter is one in which fairly simple music cataloguing is likely to be found adequate, but there is little indication in the published codes as to what information is basic and indispensable and what might be desirable but can be omitted if economies are required. As will be shown, even where such help is nominally given in a code, there seems an inescapable tendency to slip into unnecessary detail.

A fifth problem could be met in libraries which integrate entries for books, scores, sound recordings and other audiovisual media into a single catalogue sequence. The desirability of achieving this is usually well understood, but one can appreciate that many libraries are still wary of an amalgamation of individual sequences because of the difficulties, real or imagined, involved.

Before suggesting answers to the questions propounded above, reference should be made to two very different and specific matters which need provision in a cataloguing code that includes rules for music; these are thematic catalogues and librettos. The purpose of a thematic catalogue and its possible methods of arrangement have already been described (on pp. 130-132) so need no repetition. Librettos, however, have not been the subject of discussion in an earlier section of this book, so will be dealt with here.

Librettos (or libretti, if one prefers the correct Italian plural) are the texts for operas and similar works with words. There are basically three choices under which these writings can be entered. These are the composer of the music, the writer of the words, or the title of the opera. Each possibility has its own advantages and limitations which are indicated below in order that no more than a passing reference is needed when appraising individual codes.

In the great majority of cases, music lovers have no
idea who wrote the words which a composer has set, and it
was regrettably common until recently for the text to be of
very inferior literary quality. Yet to make the main entry
under the name of the composer is contrary to a basic tenet
of cataloguing; the unwary user, checking the files less than
meticulously, is quite liable to overlook the fact that the entry refers to a copy of the words only and not to the music.
Indeed, it is quite possible that the library has only the
words and no score. Additionally, many of the librettos of
the eighteenth century were used not by one, but by numerous composers (thanks in part to the lack of copyright protection then); texts by Zeno and Metastasio, to name but
two of the more popular writers, were used time and again
by different composers over the years. It is perhaps fortunate for present day cataloguers that most of these operas
have disappeared entirely or else continue to collect dust in
some archive.

Entry under individual librettists is correct practice in
terms of intellectual responsibility, but if these names are unknown to music lovers, they are unlikely to be sought headings. Entry under title may be regarded as an excellent
compromise, but for the decision involved as to which title
to use if the original is not in English. There is often a
best known form in the case of more popular works, but
this is by no means always the case and consistency seems
impossible to achieve without pedantry. As can be easily
shown, customary usage is erratic--we would find it odd to
use an English title for La traviata, Così fan tutte or Der
Freischütz (all of which are nearly untranslatable), but
would be equally perplexed by the original title of almost
any Czech opera, and rarely meet the German form of such
works as Flotow's Merry Wives of Windsor. Russian opera
titles are sometimes found in transliterated form, sometimes
in French or English translation. Once again, consistency
would only be achieved by forcing titles into a mould of
Procrustean inflexibility.

In practice all three possible solutions to the puzzle of
how best to enter librettos are to be found in one or other
of the codes considered in this chapter, indicating a lack of
general agreement among cataloguers, and perhaps among musicians also. This fact also shows, one would suggest, the
need for more than a single entry in most cases, so that the

item can be easily found whichever approach is adopted by
the enquirer.

SOME ANSWERS

We now return to the other difficulties posed a little earlier
in this chapter. The best overall solution is almost certainly
the employment of a good cataloguer who has a fair knowledge, or more, of music. Where the staff establishment includes a music librarian, it is important that cooperation
should exist between music and cataloguing departments,
even though complete agreement may not always be possible
between the specialists in the two sections. The idea that
the music department should have its own cataloguers, a
scheme which once operated in some large city systems such
as Detroit and Manchester, has long vanished from public
libraries as far as the present writer is aware (but does
nevertheless still exist in some academic libraries), yet it
had very real advantages. It could patently have its difficulties also, for the cataloguers could easily find themselves
with divided loyalties if, as was usual, they were nominally
members of the cataloguing department but were on longterm
secondment to the music library.

The answer to the second question posed earlier
would appear to be a sound code of rules applicable to music and to nonbook media, sensibly applied.

The confusion arising from the common problem of the
same piece of music being stocked in different editions with
varying title pages, because of publication in one or other of
a number of countries, has been solved with a high degree
of success by the use of what was called (in the 1941 MLA
code) the conventional title, but is now called (in AACR) the
uniform title. By this means, the principle of copying the
title page (ignoring any irrelevant material) has been retained, yet the language in which that title has been printed
becomes of limited importance, while excerpts, arrangements
and other related versions are duly brought together.

Once propounded, particularly in the 1941 preliminary
version of the 1949 ALA code (which had a wider circulation
than the original MLA rules), the virtues of this method of
overcoming the problem were quickly apparent, and it is now

standard practice in the well catalogued music collection.
The MLA code identified five different types of title, but
this was perhaps being over scrupulous. The basic thinking behind the method can be simply explained. If a work
is written in a standard musical form or one which has an
internationally accepted meaning--categories which include
such works as symphonies, sonatas, nocturnes, serenades--
then the uniform title is presented in English, or the local
language where this is not English. If, in contrast, a composition has an individual and distinctive title (as is the case
with most operas, song cycles and certain orchestral and instrumental works, such as tone poems), then the uniform title is that given by the composer to the work. Some of the
difficulties that this broad distinction fails to solve are considered later in the chapter.

     In any library that stocks scores and/or recordings,
the cataloguer will require an adequate supply of reference
books to help elucidate some of the various queries that will
undoubtedly arise. No two librarians are likely to agree exactly how many are adequate, although it would be a very
large collection, one imagines, that required as many as 243
items--the number listed by Minnie A. Elmer in the bibliography to her thesis of 1946 [61]. In practice, Miss Elmer
marked those items which she considered to be of basic importance. A library may reasonably economize by supplying
the cataloguer with the previous edition of appropriate nonmusical publications, withdrawn from the reference department
or elsewhere. The cataloguing section could also usefully retain at hand, if space permits, one or two older music dictionaries and encyclopaedias which might help to trace minor
historical figures whose names no longer appear in current
reference books. It will have to be accepted that, for many
library systems, the prices of books have risen so astronomically in recent years that the service can afford no more
than a single copy of an expensive reference work, and that
such a volume will be shelved in the most appropriate public
or other department. If a cataloguer needs to use a book of
this nature, he will have to make the occasional foray to
wherever the work is filed, in order to make the necessary
informational checks. Only if this has to be done so frequently that the time involved makes the process demonstrably uneconomic, can the cataloguing department hope to make
a valid claim for an extra copy to be bought for its use.

CATALOGUING CODES

Older codes will be dealt with briefly. Students who wish for, or need more detailed surveys than those provided here are recommended to seek additional sources, such as John Horner's book [98].

British Museum

The famous ninety-one rules were printed in 1841, and have formed the basis of most subsequent codes. The revised edition of the Rules... appeared in 1936 [188] and the work includes a page-and-a-half appendix headed "Catalogue of music." This directs that entry should normally be made under the name of the composer, and added entries are to be provided for editors and arrangers. Operas, oratorios, songs, and the like have added entries made under their respective titles. Anonymous items (which, in the context of the code, include any work in which the composer's name does not appear on the title page, even though identifiable through other sources) in the field of instrumental music, have an entry under title. For similar vocal works, the first line of the words is used, with a reference from the work's title (which one might have expected to be the preferred choice, partly for consistency but also because it is at least as likely to be as well known as the opening words). If an anonymous instrumental work has no title, it is to be entered under the name of the class of music.

Collections of psalms, hymns or Christmas carols are entered under the name of the musical editor or collector, with a cross-reference from the class heading. If the anthology has a title but lacks a named editor, form entry is to be used. However, the code gives no guidance as to whether an added entry is to be made under the collective title; one imagines that this would be expected.

Unusually, the rules make specific provision for programmes and "word books." These may be solely textual but are, nevertheless, entered under the generic heading "Programmes." In practice, there are few such entries in the library's own catalogue, and the great majority of those that are there relate to the nineteenth century. Similar subject entry is to be made for periodicals. The interested

reader may like to inspect the appropriate volumes of the
British Museum catalogue to see how this particular part of
that library operated its own rules.

Cutter

In Cutter's Rules for a Dictionary Catalogue [46] there is a
single rule for music which suggests double entry under composer and the author of the words. Cutter adds a note that
short and medium entries would probably dispense with the
author of the words but that in the case of famous authors
(e.g., Shakespeare) the double entry should continue to be
made. At the end of the rules is a section entitled "Cataloguing special publications and other material" in which the
second subhead is "Music." This particular section of the appendix is the work of O. G. Sonneck of the Library of Congress, and is divided into sections for Author, Title, Imprint
and Notes. "Author" is a variation of the single rule already
quoted; "Title" deals solely with the problem of those musical
scores which have a title page common to the whole series,
the individual score at hand being distinguished by a pen-
cilled or printed line under the appropriate entry on this
multiple title page. This form of printing was an obvious
economy for the publisher but is rarely met with today when
it is the custom to print a separate and distinct title page
for every piece of music issued. "Imprint" devotes a page
to the dating of music; it emphasizes the importance of publishers' plate numbers (those letters and numbers usually to
be found at the bottom of every piece of music published
later than the eighteenth century). With rare or old music
the date is often extremely valuable but it is of much less
importance with modern music; and public library patrons
are not normally worried if a score was printed in 1925 or
1955 providing it contains the required music. Copyright
dates, however, may be usefully added for modern composers whether or not they use opus numbers. The final section of this appendix, headed "Notes," gives some useful
information to the music cataloguer particularly with its
elucidation of the word "score" which is still often used in
an imprecise way. Four examples are given but one may
doubt if they are particularly helpful. Sonneck apparently
favoured the exact transcription of the title page, a form of
cataloguing that can often be misleading as is indicated later
in this chapter.

Anglo-American Code, 1908

This was the major set of rules [37] used in both British
and American libraries for almost sixty years, yet music
cataloguing is dismissed in three brief rules (although Horner usefully reminds one that "Other rules throughout the
code can be invoked for application to music" [98, p. 86].
One can perhaps reasonably infer that the music section in
most public libraries was very small or imperfectly catalogued;
it could well have been both. The first of the three rules
(no. 8 in the code) is a general one that instructs the cataloguer to make author entry under the name of the composer,
with added entries for any editor or arranger, and also for
the librettist when words have been set to music. In practice, few librarians have ever troubled to make entries for
the author of the words which composers have set to music,
even when the librettists or poets are such important figures
as da Ponte or Hofsmannsthal, although Shakespeare may be
treated exceptionally. Editors and arrangers are also usually
ignored, unless they are famous composers in their own right
or are very well known as executants. Even in these cases,
the majority of libraries make no added entries for such persons, with little apparent handicap to the majority of the users of the service.

This same rule has a subsidiary section which directs
the cataloguer to enter a set of variations written by one
composer on a theme taken from another musician's work under the name of the writer of the variations and not under
the earlier one. This is patently sensible; only rarely is the
original theme of intrinsic interest--it is what the later composer has done with the melody that matters. A secondary
catalogue entry under the writer of the original theme may
be of some value in those few cases where more than one
later composer of standing has chosen to use the same frag-
ment of music as a starting point. The best-known example
of multiple use is the extract from Paganini's Caprice op. 1.
No. 24 (written for unaccompanied violin) which has prompted,
among others: a) Brahms (a set of piano variations); b)
Rachmaninov (the famous Rhapsody on a Theme ...); c)
Boris Blacher (an orchestral set); and d) a brief high-
spirited two-piano work by Lutoslawski. In a case such as
this, an added entry under Paganini would clearly be useful to some enquirers.

Rule nine relates to librettos and recommends added entry under the composer of the music but main entry under the writer of the words. The third of the rules relating specifically to music is number ten, devoted to thematic catalogues. The code provides for entry under the individual composer concerned, with added entry under the name of the compiler. This means, in fact, that the entry under the composer is really a subject one.

Music Library Association

These rules of 1941-1942 were discussed at some length on pages 114-118 of the first edition of this book. There seems no point in repeating those comments here, as the code has been superseded by the MLA/ALA rules of 1958, considered a little later in this chapter.

American Library Association, 1949 [2]

The preliminary edition of 1941 included, as an appendix, the first chapter of the then newly-published MLA code, whose thirty-one rules dealt solely with headings, but presented in the 1949 ALA code as a single rule. Again, comment is superfluous, since this same rule was reproduced again as part of the 1958 code.

Library of Congress Rules for Descriptive Cataloging [219]

These also date from 1949 and are twelve in number. Rule nine deals with music; it is both lengthy and detailed and is divided into five sections. The latter concern, respectively: conventional titles; transcription of title page; imprint; collation; notes. As has already been mentioned, conventional title became uniform title in AACR.

In 1952, a supplement (rule 9A) was issued to deal with "phonorecords," an umbrella term produced by LC to incorporate gramophone records, wire and tape recordings, cylindrical records and player-piano rolls. This rule was reproduced, without amendment, in the 1958 MLA/ALA code, and therefore is considered there.

As an aside, it might be mentioned that these rules direct the cataloguer to enter a libretto under the name of the composer of the music, with an added entry under the name of the librettist. However, a footnote allows for main entry under the librettist if preferred, with title entry to be made for an anonymous text.

Music Library Association/American Library Association

The Code for Cataloging Music and Phonorecords [147] has five chapters, occupying some ninety pages. The first chapter is a reprint of rule 12 of the 1949 ALA code. Chapter II brings together aspects of description that formed chapters II to V of the 1941-1942 MLA code. No fewer than sixteen pages are devoted to Conventional titles, an indication both of the importance attached to this device and also of the problems that can arise in its use, e.g., differentiating between the complete works of a composer and of a similar publication but limited to chamber, instrumental or vocal works. Excerpts, following the usual American custom of dictionary catalogue entry, are apparently arranged in alphabetical order; it would seem better to enter such extracts in the order in which they appear in the parent work, but there are arguments on both sides.

When a score lacks publication date (a common situation), printing or copyright date, the code suggests identification by plate or publisher's number. The former "appears at the foot of the page of most engraved music" whereas the publisher's number is restricted to the title page and seems to be generally accepted as the more useful means of checking. Just how important it is to give a date is open to question. To this writer it would seem a minor matter, except for those scores which are primarily of antiquarian or musicological interest.

Considerable detail is recommended in the Notes, including such items as "the name of the author and title of a work on which the text may have been based ..." (unless the cataloguer is sure, of what value is a dubious attribution?), and duration of performance. Again, if such an item is included in the entry, the authority for this figure should invariably be given also: timings may vary widely from per-

former to performer, and possibly with different performances by the same artist(s). Composers themselves have
often shown that, when performing their own works for
which they have given approximate timings, the difference
between precept and practice can be surprisingly wide.
Hall or room ambience is another cause of modified tempi
which will affect the overall playing time. A reverberation
period as lengthy as that of, for example, St. Paul's Cathe-
dral in London must be taken into account by any performer
playing there, or music presented at a fast tempo, even if
the speed has been prescribed by the composer, could well
be utterly blurred for the listener.

Chapter III, "Phonorecords," is considered later in
this book as part of the chapter on sound recordings.
Chapter IV, "Simplified rules," offered a completely new
departure in codified guidance at the time of publication
and it should be said immediately that, in our opinion, this
section offers excellent pilotage for the cataloguer with little musical knowledge, although some of the suggestions contained in the chapter seem open to criticism, as will be indicated. The preamble begins: "The rules in this section are
written on the premise that the library using them wants to
catalog its music as quickly and yet as efficiently as possible.
It is assumed that some searching will be done, but that it
will be the minimum to establish a satisfactory heading and
title which do not conflict with others already in the catalog." The compilers also expect that the cataloguer will
maintain an authority file in which decisions are duly recorded and used, to ensure consistency of approach. It is
admitted that, using these rules, the conventional titles
"will not completely integrate with those established according to the rules in Chapter II." The differences, however,
are rarely more than minor.

The tenor of the rules is immediately apparent when
the cataloguer is instructed: "Make added entries for arrangers and editors only when the work is likely to be
known or cited by their names." Folk songs are to be entered under the name of the arranger, with added entries
under the titles, while librettos are to be entered "under
the composer of the music, with added entry for the librettist."

On the vexed questions of transcriptions, arrangements,

and similar reworkings, the decision as to entry under the original composer or the adaptor is left to the cataloguer to decide, with the comment that the right answer "depends on the amount of new musical material added" and the rider that, in case of doubt, the original composer is to be preferred.

In the choice of conventional titles, welcome advice is interspersed with recommendations that seem less desirable. For distinctive titles, the suggestion is to prefer English "if a choice of language is possible." This might be acceptable for the first example quoted (The Marriage of Figaro) but much less so for Afternoon of a Faun which, in England at least, is always quoted in the original French. Where a composer has used the same title more than once, but relating to different works (an example would be the three sets of Images by Debussy, two of them for piano and the third for orchestra), the rules give the order in which the identifying elements should be quoted to ensure that the catalogue entries clearly show that the scores are not simply duplicate copies of the same item.

Rule IVB1c (the code's method of numbering seems unnecessarily complicated) deals with titles "in languages not employing the Roman alphabet" and gives an example of a work by "Kabalevskiĭ, Dmitri Borisovich, 1904- ," quoting the exemplified work's title in Cyrillic script with, fortunately, an English translation also. This reflects LC practice in the use of systematic transliteration. British librarians would almost certainly prefer "Kabalevsky" to the admittedly more accurate transliteration, "Kabalevskiĭ," quoted in the code, but one might ask if the second forename is really needed, or the year of birth? There is only one composer of this surname known to current Western music dictionaries. Systematic transliteration is now generally used in the British National Bibliography and the British Catalogue of Music (following AACR rule 44B, though it should be remarked that this rule also allows the alternative of following precedent or a standard dictionary), but dates are not included. These differences, incidentally, lead to awkward results in shared cataloguing.

As for the use of the Russian alphabet in the example quoted from the code, it would be a major task for many cataloguers to transliterate the title page of a score and then

decide, quickly, or slowly and painfully, what the work is.
The assumption that the title and imprint would be copied
on the library's entry in its Cyrillic form would appear to
be utterly contrary to the general intention of simplification.

Under IVB 2h is the suggestion that excerpts which
have distinctive titles should be entered directly under them.
Jesu, Joy of Man's Desiring is an example; a good case can
be made for such an entry, since many enquirers for the
item will have no knowledge of its original context. Nevertheless, to omit any mention whatsoever of Cantata 147 (from
which the excerpt comes) seems a little too cavalier, particularly if the library should also have in stock a score of the
complete cantata. Again, the recommendation to include the
plate number in the imprint if no publication date is quoted
on the copy is not, in our view, "simplified" cataloguing in
any way. For many who borrow scores for performance themselves, or to follow one by other artists, the date of publication is usually irrelevant. In contrast to this proposed exactitude, one reads on the next page (rule IVD1): "For
most publications of music, collation may be omitted without
destroying the value of the entry."

One may sum up this chapter of the code by suggesting that it is generally excellent and that a cataloguer should
soon discover which of the rules can be ignored with minimum
loss of effectiveness and, one suspects, a considerable saving
in both time and temper.

The final section concerns "Filing rules for conventional titles." The first entry under a composer's name will be
for the complete works, using the heading "Works," followed
by different categories of composition (Works, organ; Works,
piano), i.e., a semi-alphabetical order. After these entries
are titles beginning with the letter "A"--thus beginning a
separate alphabetical sequence. One hopes that the casual
user of the catalogue is not misled into thinking that the library does not have a composer's symphonies because the
first entry encountered under the musician's name begins
with "W." Clearly, there is a strong case for making brief
reference in the main alphabetical sequence under "Organ
works," "Piano works," and "Works" to offset disadvantages
of the three sequences of entries.

The next rule calls for the interfiling of singular and

plural entries under musical forms, so that one does not have one sequence under "Sonata" and another under "Sonatas" at the end of it, but have the two terms treated as if they were one. This needs human supervision and, as Horner suggests, makes these filing rules unsuitable for machine ordered arrangement. He believes that the compilers should either have "allowed singulars to come before plurals as in ordinary alphabetical filing" or else have chosen to use either the singular or the plural form consistently, irrespective of whether the volume concerned included one, two or more works [98, p. 98].

Because the heading may be qualified to indicate selections, arrangements and the like, as well as sound recordings, the need for a standard filing order is highly important: an invaluable auxiliary to this end is the careful use of punctuation. Six items are listed which must be used in a stated order for filing purposes. This prescribed arrangement may appear to be rather fussy at first sight; it could certainly be some little time before use became a matter of habit, but the care which this part of the system has been given requires equal conscientiousness from the user.

Finally, the code includes a glossary of cataloguing and musical terms used in this subject area. This list is useful and helpful, if occasionally wayward; for example, to describe a miniature score as a "... pocketsized, low-priced listener's full score of an orchestral work, chamber music, or vocal music with orchestral or chamber music accompaniment" is clearly wrong. Price is irrelevant (and some miniature scores are decidedly expensive), and the definition should surely include instrumental music, since the Lea scores (to quote but one example) list a number of solo keyboard compositions. However, despite criticisms, this is generally an excellent code and chapter IV remains the best available published guide for the non-specialist library cataloguer.

International Association of Music Libraries [102]

IAML, soon after its foundation in July 1950, set up a committee under the chairmanship of Kay Schmidt-Phiseldeck to prepare a code of cataloguing rules suitable (it was hoped) for international acceptance. The original intention was to publish three volumes--the first concerned with the author catalogue, the second with limited cataloguing and the third with full cataloguing. It was later decided to add volumes dealing with manuscripts and with sound recordings respectively. Publication has been slow; volume 4, on Rules for Cataloguing Music Manuscripts, by Marie Louise Göllner, was published in 1975, nearly twenty years after the first, while the last volume has only recently been announced. Each volume has a different compiler which may well account for the distinct lack of uniformity between them.

The first volume (The Author Catalog of Published Music) was prepared by Franz Grasberger. Although dated 1957, it does not seem to have appeared until 1958. The format is upright--some 28 cm. high by 22 cm. wide, with text in two columns on each page--the original German on the left and the English translation in parallel on the other half of the page. The work has a flap as part of the back cover (a pocket would have been much better) which provides a precarious haven for a dozen leaflets used to illustrate examples and the problems they raise. In addition, there is a pamphlet with the work's text in a French translation, which suggests that the third language was an afterthought. Subsequent volumes are printed in an oblong format, so that the three languages are displayed side by side.

The suggestion (on p. 15 of volume 1) that "Indexing the contents of music periodicals and yearbooks is unavoidable for libraries of any size" arouses a wry smile when one thinks of the number of libraries that have evaded this unavoidable task. A section on librettos considers the three possible ways of entry, and comes down in favour of titles; the declaration, "Above all, the contest between composer and text writer is thereby diminished, emphasis is placed on the subject matter which is served equally by music and text," exemplifies the somewhat opaque English that makes understanding difficult in places. The author of the volume regrets the neglect of programme note collections which have bibliographical, social and local historical importance--an attitude with which we entirely agree.

After this, section D (dealing with printed music) considers it to be "quite natural that music publications are separated from other printed material and that they are collected in separate catalogs." This is but one example of a standpoint that is contrary to that generally held in English-speaking countries, while to write (on p. 19), referring to sound recordings, that "Collecting these new, highly technical materials, presents entirely new problems for libraries and their solutions have not yet been found" seems to have been (even in 1957) unnecessarily pessimistic as well as unappreciative of the many years that recordings had been incorporated most successfully, into the stocks of American, British and Scandinavian libraries.

The second chapter of the code begins with an historical survey (in which it appears that the compiler considered James Duff Brown to be an American) and comments briefly upon particular points of individual codes, e.g., that a Spanish set of rules of 1902 enters vocal music under the writer of the words, with added entry for the composer. Under "Principles," readers are told that "The contents of a main entry consists of the following parts ... "; after listing these, there is comment on the actual items included and their order as seen in different library catalogues and codes. Some problem areas are listed with recommendations as to the best procedure in each. There are twelve of these items, of which only the first eight are numbered (there seems no apparent reason for this inconsistency); the sequence in which they are dealt with seems to be arbitrary. As for "Catalog organization," the compiler illustrates that both alphabetical order of items and the alternative classified arrangement each have their pros and cons. A third approach, mentioned but not recommended, is to arrange composer entries by opus or thematic catalogue order. The compromise proposal, "For a composer of light music it may be advisable to arrange by title, but for the voluminous work of a master of serious music the system of instrumentation will be advisable if it replaces security of alphabet and opus numbers by methodical regulation in all details" (assuming that the reader can understand this; the present writer thinks it refers to a classified approach) seems highly inadvisable, if only because of the difficulty of deciding which composers are "light" and which "masters of serious music."

As has already been stated, the volume contains twelve folded sheets as an appendix: on each of these is a photograph (much reduced in size) of a title page, and under each example is a list of problems that are thought

to face the cataloguer. On the other half of each of these
individual folded sheets is a set of typewritten copies of
catalogue entries, showing the heading and information given
in the main entry in several libraries. The number of catalogue entries for each title varies between three and ten,
and it is certainly interesting to notice the differences among
the specimens. For British librarians, it seems unfortunate
that the only British library represented in the code is the
then British Museum, which is certainly not typical nor, one
feels, the best example of national practice.

The volume under consideration ranges far more widely than its title would suggest, and one may argue as to how
far this is desirable. There are some excellent points in it;
for example, the comparison of national practices which are
sometimes quoted can be illuminating to the student. On the
other hand, irrelevant items could have been omitted with advantage and, as one or two quotations may have shown, the
meaning is not always crystal clear--although this could be
partly due to faulty translation.

The second IAML volume, published in 1961, is Limited
code, compiled by Yvette Fedoroff (whose surname is shown
as "Fedorov" in the first volume). The work gives the original French text as the first column of each page with parallel German and English versions.

The preface includes the comment that "The librarian
to whom this set of rules is addressed is assumed to have a
knowledge of the cataloguing of books. But when he turns
to the cataloguing of his music he may be bewildered, music
presenting particular characteristics which differentiate it
from the book. This code is intended to aid him." For reasons which will be explained, our view is that the code is
only partly successful in this admirable aim. Some of the
ideas expressed must appear odd to a British or American
librarian; one might quote "Generally it is difficult to bind
music ... " (paragraph 3); or the recommendation, (in the
next paragraph) for "... the arrangement of works on the
shelves not systematically, but simply by format, giving a
saving of space and better preservation along with a simplification of the call numbers. If the library cannot establish
a subject catalogue, it is obviously necessary to have a methodical system of classification. But the latter system, less
and less used, is not recommended." Both points are likely

to arouse a sense of horrified disbelief among British and
North American librarians. Whether a classified or a dictionary catalogue is used, the scores will be arranged in
appropriate order on the shelves in accordance with the
scheme of classification adopted. Format will play its part
with such items as miniature scores, but this method of
separate sequences is usually restricted to as small a part
of the department's stock as possible.

For works of joint authorship, separate entries are
recommended (paragraph 8) but, above a certain number of
collaborators (the figure to be chosen by the cataloguer)
the recommendation is that "the work is considered anonymous." In practice, joint works are comparatively rare in
the area of standard music. Suggestions for the treatment
of anthologies, collections of anonymous works and the like
follow. For the thorny problem of transcriptions and arrangements, the cataloguer is referred to the first volume
of this code: alternatively, "a completely mechanical rule"
is offered which requires entry under the original composer
and also under the arranger. This sidesteps the problem,
yet is probably the most sensible recommendation for the
cataloguer with minimal musical knowledge.

The suggestion for cadenzas is "to arrange them under
the name of their true composer, but making a cross-reference
to the author of the concerto" (paragraph 16). This is directly opposed to the suggestion in the first volume of this
code: "Heading: composer of the concerto. Cross-reference:
composer of the cadenza." There are other examples of this
lack of consistency, which suggests that the two volumes
were prepared entirely independently. Librettos are to "take
as the heading either the author of the text or the title. It
would be interesting (sic) to make a cross reference to the
musician who has used the libretto, if his name appears,
though there is nothing of the composer in the libretto"
(paragraph 17).

With multiple imprint, the recommendation is that the
first named publisher is sufficient. This seems good advice,
but for a simplified code, one could argue that there is too
much detail in the points about dating music (paragraph 24),
and that plate numbers are unlikely to be regarded as important by the unmusical cataloguer, and probably rightly so.
Size, if one follows this code's recommendations, is to be

quoted as octavo, quarto, etc., rather than in centimetres,
although the latter is recommended when describing the format of an oblong score (paragraph 26).

Section B of the code is devoted to "Secondary catalogues" for the authors of words, for subjects and for titles
and incipits--this last providing entries for vocal works both
under their respective titles and, where necessary, under
the opening words. Such a title entry will include a reference to the volume in which the work is to be found, assuming that it is included in an anthology. These catalogues
"can be placed in their own special cabinets or, following the
practice of certain libraries, principally American, interfiled
in the author catalogue, according to the principle of the
'dictionary catalogue'" (paragraph 33). By "Subject catalogues" the compiler apparently assumes an alphabetical,
dictionary arrangement with multiple entries. "There is,"
one reads, "an increasing tendency to abandon" the classified catalogue, and it is given short shrift here. Part III
of this volume of the IAML code is concerned with "Arrangement of the author catalogue" which acknowledges the American idea of the conventional title. If one does not wish to
use this plan, then a semiclassified arrangement is apparently recommended, but it reads oddly: "Theatrical works,"
"Instrumental works," "Pedagogical works," "Cross references." The explanatory notes for these headings are far
from clear, and the nonmusical cataloguer is unlikely to find
any salvation here.

There are three appendices, the first dealing with
manuscripts; this seems to be quite unnecessary, for the
suggestions are in very general terms, and the word "music" is not mentioned once. Appendix B explains how to
form conventional titles, although these are not used in the
examples quoted in the body of the text. The explanation
given here is, in fact, both less full and less clear than that
given in chapter IV of the MLA/ALA code. The last appendix is a "Plan for the systematic classification of a subject
catalogue," based on Hofmeister's Jahresverzeichnis which
has no notation and would be very difficult to apply to a
collection. Why the compiler has ignored all the schemes
that are in use, even if only in a handful of libraries, is
a mystery.

It must be said that the English translations, in both

volumes, are not always accurate, although the cataloguer is likely to understand what is intended, except perhaps in paragraph 13 of this second volume where "editeur" is rendered as "editor" when "publisher" would seem to be the compiler's meaning.

Volume 3, <u>Rules for Full Cataloging</u>, was compiled by Virginia Cunningham of the Library of Congress, and published in 1971. Understandably, it shows much greater awareness of North American and British practice than that of the two preceding volumes. Indeed, its roots are clearly founded in <u>AACR</u>. There are five chapters, dealing respectively with choice of entry; filing titles; elements of description; added entries and cross references. There are also three appendices, for examples, glossary of terms, and "Abbreviations used in filing titles for thematic catalogues."

The compiler states (on p. 9) that "These rules provide for the part of a catalog entry which identifies a work and describes an edition of the work. Schemes for the classification (i.e., shelf arrangement) of music will not be considered; the area of subject headings likewise lies outside the scope of these rules." Provision is included for added entries, but the code (as the last quotation shows) omits all reference to subject work, so that "full cataloging" in the title is misleading. One major claim is that "The basic rules are written so as to result in entries which can be interfiled in international listings, even though emanating from different countries" (p. 10), and are based on the so-called Paris principles [104] promulgated in 1961, which have not been superseded and which have coloured subsequent ideas on cataloguing very considerably.

Filing titles have long been recognized as desirable; this code makes the point that there have been various ways suggested in which one can try to ensure consistent and correct order and, if a cataloguer uses these IAML rules, a filing or conventional title is mandatory. The rules accept that, if possible, the original language is first choice for such a title and there should be "the minimum number of filing elements in the title." In the context of this code, "original language" means that used for the first edition of the work, but accepts that, for "local libraries," the title may be translated into the vernacular when the original language is unlikely to be known to any but a small minority

of the library's users. "Assigning a filing title in the plural
to a single work may seem semantically objectionable, but
there are great practical advantages" (p. 12). We have
made the point earlier in this chapter, and thoroughly agree.
After the work's title, this code prefers to qualify by use of
the opus or thematic catalogue number. There are two obvious objections to this: a fairly large number of works, with
no identification of either type, is likely to be found in all
but the smallest collection. Secondly, even if all items could
be specified in this fashion, the enquirer may not have the
necessary information to hand, but is much more likely to be
aware of the particular forces for which the desired work is
set, or for what medium it is required. AACR's preference
for quoting the medium of performance as a "distinguishing
element" before the use of an opus number seems much more
practical, e.g., "Sonatas, piano."

Description "is taken primarily from the publication and
is recorded in its language" (p. 13). The minimum entry
recommended here incorporates the title (given, as indicated
above, in the language of the original publication), edition
statement, first-named place of publication and publisher,
followed by collation. For this last-named, "only the term
'score' (with modifications) and 'parts' are used" (p. 14),
with any additional description of the physical makeup of the
music being relegated to notes, which this writer would not
consider to be a desirable solution. Librettos are normally
to be entered under the name of the music's composer, unless the library "has a long tradition of treating a libretto
as a literary work and entering it under the name of the
author" (p. 14). The code provides an alternative which
allows librettos to be entered under title (p. 14). As has
been suggested earlier in this chapter, any of the three
possible solutions may well appear foolish in certain cases,
but without a uniform approach there would assuredly be
considerable confusion.

All the comments on volume 3, so far, relate to the
introduction; it is here that the compiler has explained her
reasoning in formulating rules. If a reader turns to the
main body of the text, it will be quickly noted that a number of the rules have explanatory examples appended. These
are brief, but perfectly adequate to illustrate the particular
point being made; however, the code also quoted in a number of cases the appropriate full composer entry. The ex-

amples are given in Appendix 1 in the same order as they are found in the text, so that it is possible to check speedily and exactly what is being recommended and how the proposed form of entry appears.

Section 1.3 (p. 21) deals with "works of authorship of mixed character." In the first edition of our book, we attempted to explain the differences between a transcription and an arrangement, accepting the McColvin basis of approach (as used in the original edition of <u>Music Libraries</u>). It was unfortunate that <u>Grove</u> (one of the few music dictionaries that treats the two words--correctly--as having different meaning and not as synonyms) should give definitions that reverse those provided by McColvin. This hurdle has been avoided in volume three of the IAML code by copying <u>AACR</u> and using the terms "arrangement" and "adaptation," with the advice, "In case of doubt, catalog as an arrangement."

Cadenzas published separately (section 1.34) are to be entered under the name of the writer, with added entry under the composer of the concerto for which the cadenza is intended: comment has already been made on this suggestion. The rule for liturgical works (section 1.42) clearly separates "officially prescribed" compositions from any "composed setting of a sacred text," under which, to offer a simple example, a Haydn setting of the Mass is entered under the composer's name.

Chapter 2 deals with filing titles and is, understandably again, related both to the previous volume in this series and to the MLA/ALA rules. The use of such a title is necessary "when a work is published with the title in a language other than that of the first edition, or varying from the first edition; when a composer has written more than one work having the same title or when the publication consists of an excerpt from a longer work." This suggests that one does not supply a filing title when it would coincide with the title page of the work in hand--a situation akin to that recommended in chapter four of the MLA/ALA rules. In the case of music in standard forms, the filing title is given in the languages of the cataloguing library, so that an English-speaking country would use "Symphony," "Quartet," rather than "Symphonie," "Quatuor," etc. For titles in a type other than Roman, the recommendation is to transliterate.

Alternatively, a footnote allows the reverse procedure for
libraries which contain "primarily publications in non-roman
alphabets"; this is a necessary provision if this code is to
be genuinely international in scope. At the same time, it
should be remarked that there are a number of countries
which have more than one official language, but none of the
codes considered in this chapter makes any reference to this
possibly inconvenient fact.

Chapter 3, "Elements of description," has some facsimile title pages incorporated into the text to provide examples. Unlike the first volume where, it will be recalled,
similar examples were provided on loose sheets, here the
copies used are printed in the body of the text, which is
much more practical. The rules for imprint are sensible.
The first named place of publication is usually adequate,
"unless another place is distinguishable by type or position
as being the actual place of publication." Should more than
one place of publication be shown, the abbreviation "etc" is
used in the entry to indicate this fact. The name of the
country, state, or the like is usually omitted; only if its
absence is likely to cause ambiguity or difficulty should it
be listed. Similarly, (section 3.42) only the first-named
publisher is to be given, adding "etc" if others are shown
on the title page. An exception is to be made if one of
these additional names relates to the country of the cataloguing library. In such a case, the imprint is extended
on the entry to incorporate both the place and the name of
the domestic publisher. Where no date of publication is
shown, the "date of printing, legal deposit or of copyright"
may be substituted. One is left to assume that, if none of
these is shown, the cataloguer gives an estimated date or,
if that is too difficult, the abbreviation "n.d."

Examples of added entries are given in chapter 4, using a unit card system applicable to a dictionary catalogue.
Chapter 5 is concerned with cross references: from transcribed titles to filing titles, from alternative titles to those
used in the catalogue (as, for example, would be necessary
with Fingal's Cave and The Hebrides, as Mendelssohn's overture has both titles), from excerpts to the appropriate complete work, and for spurious works.

Appendix one, as has been mentioned, gives examples
of full entries under composers' names. In the left-hand

margin of the type we find quoted the number(s) of the
rule(s) illustrated; several of these examples have already
been used in the body of the text, but in abbreviated form.
Appendix two is a glossary of terms, compiled by Meredith M.
Moon.   The trilingual basis of the code presented problems in
some cases when it came to expressing English terms in French
or German, so "the translations supplied here are approximate
rather than literal."   By no means all the terms that a music
cataloguer may meet are explained, only those used in the
code "where a certain amount of ambiguity or divergence of
meaning exists in both the musical and bibliographical fields."
There are therefore definitions of such terms as "chamber
music" (which follows LC practice in deciding that two is the
minimum number of performers in this category, whereas other
authorities argue that three is the basic figure), "full score
order," "monumenta," and the like.   The definition of "small
orchestra" gives ten as the minimum number of performers,
but makes no mention of the maximum beyond which the group
ceases to be "small."   The third appendix follows the separate
translations of Moon's definitions, and consists of "Abbreviations used in filing titles for thematic indexes."   It proves to
be a somewhat erratic list in its inclusions and omissions.
For example, in addition to the universal "K" used to identify
Mozart's works, this same initial is listed for Beethoven (Kin-
sky), Dittersdorf (Krebs) and Michael Haydn (Klafsky).
Michael Haydn also has Perger's catalogue listed, yet there
is no reference to Kirkpatrick's list of Domenico Scarlatti
sonatas.   A word of warning about Vivaldi thematic catalogues
would also have been useful, and several generally accepted
listings relating to other composers are not mentioned here.
Finally, students should find the code's index of interest in
that entries in all three of the official languages are interfiled into a single sequence.

No appraisal is made here of volume four of the Code
(Rules for Cataloguing Music Manuscripts), since this class
of material is considered to be of peripheral interest in the
context of this book.   Comments on volume five are to be
found in chapter five of this book.

Anglo-American Cataloguing Rules, 1967 [4]

Both the British and American texts of this code were published in 1967 by their respective national library associations.

The minor differences between the two versions need not concern us here, but the appropriate rules are treated in some detail despite the fact that a second edition of the code appeared eleven years later. Although the later work has a very different layout, it may well be regarded as a consolidation of the first edition, so that the latter cannot well be dismissed in the course of a paragraph or two.

It may be recalled that the ALA code, which eventually appeared in its final version in 1949 (after a preliminary edition of 1941), had received full British participation until the beginning of World War Two in 1939, but was not officially a joint production when it was published. An entirely fresh start was made for the 1967 code; a brief look at some of the major principles upon which it was compiled may be helpful. As Sumner Spalding, general editor of the work, wrote on page four of the Introduction: " ... each rule dealing with a specific problem is to be understood in the context of the more general rules.... The relevant general rules apply to any aspects of a particular problem that are not dealt with in a specific rule." Thus, the general rules for entry (chapter 1) and for description (chapter 6) apply equally to chapters 13 and 14 which provide the special rules for music and phonorecords respectively. Again, quoting from the same page of the Introduction: "Rules for types of publication ... have normally been included only when such types involve special problems in authorship responsibility or require special headings that could not be dealt with satisfactorily in the general rules."

Thus, as is mentioned below, there are no individual rules for thematic catalogues or for librettos. Problems of entry applicable solely to music are, as indicated above, treated in chapter thirteen. These concern vocal compositions of various types: ballets; added accompaniments; arrangements; transcriptions, etc.; and cadenzas.

Because of its physical separation by thirty pages of text, it is easy to overlook the important note at the beginning of Part III of <u>AACR 1</u> (which quickly became the accepted abbreviation for the first edition, once the second had appeared): "The rules of entry, heading, and description for books ... are applied also to the cataloguing of nonbook materials ... unless they are specifically contravened or modified" (p. 198). This warning is reinforced by the

"introductory note" at the beginning of chapter 13 which reminds users, again, that the general rules for entry (chapter
1) "apply equally to musical compositions." The result of
this, as has been mentioned earlier, is that there is no rule
for librettos to be found in chapter 13; such publications
are treated in accordance with chapter 1's rule 19, "Related
works." To quote from P. K. Escreet (on p. 82 of his Introduction to the Anglo-American Cataloguing Rules, 1971):
"The question is ... one of deciding whether a given work
is to be catalogued in its own right or as one in some way
dependent on another work. The rule is a remarkable feat
of compression." [64] The distinction made by rule 19 is
whether or not "a work has a title that is indistinctive and
dependent on the title of another work." It may be remarked
here that AACR 2 has abolished the distinction. Librettos
provide excellent examples of this type of problem. On its
own, a libretto is a text which one might normally expect to
enter under its author. With music written for it, the libretto
becomes a related work; the composer of the music is normally given preference.

A quick glance at rule 19 is therefore indicated. The
code prefers entry for a libretto under the name of the librettist, with an added entry under the name of the composer, but the first "optional exception" to this rule allows
for "entry under the name of the composer and/or title of
that work. Make an author-title entry under the librettist."
If the latter method should be chosen, an exception to the
exception follows, directing that "a libretto published as a
literary work without reference to a particular musical setting" should be listed under the writer of the text.

Another familiar musical species not to be found in
chapter 13 is the thematic catalogue. This, again, counts
as a dependent work and so, presumably, one follows the
MLA/ALA code ruling of entry under the compiler (or publisher, if the compiler's name is not known), with a subject
entry under the composer whose works have been tabulated.

The specific rules dealing with music begin by considering "Musical works with authorship of mixed character,"
i.e., vocal compositions of various types, and ballets. There
is no surprise in the suggested treatment: author/title added
entries are indicated for "the other persons who share responsibility for the work," but this is not considered neces-

sary in the case of a single song. The chapter recommends
an explanatory reference if the text is based on the work of
another writer, e.g., an entry should be made under Chaucer when cataloguing Walton's Troilus and Cressida, as well
as under the name of the librettist.

Comment has already been made in this chapter of the
difficulties liable to be faced when dealing with arrangements
and transcriptions. AACR considers the two terms to be
virtually synonymous (as do most music dictionaries) and
uses the heading "Related music" for what McColvin would
have considered to be a transcription, but which is defined
here as an item "that represents a distinct alteration of another work" and which is therefore entered, if one does not
use the unit entry method, under the composer's name. This
rule (232B) includes a section on cadenzas published separately and written by somebody other than the composer of
the concerto. It seems crystal clear that such a work has no
independent life and to remark, as the code does, that "when
cadenzas are for a particular work ..." is nonsensical. A
cadenza exists solely for use in a particular concerto (unless,
perhaps, it is written for a film, play or similar entertainment).

Uniform titles are covered in nearly nine pages of text
and examples--rules 233 to 242. This is a clear indication of
the importance attached to this aspect of music cataloguing.
We feel it to be a fair complaint that this section of the code
is obscure and muddling, particularly in comparison with
other rules in which similar complexities are treated; one
might instance numbers 108 to 113 (Bible) or 87 to 91 (Con-
ferences). This confusion, fortunately, has been tackled in
AACR 2. Similarly, the inconsistency of rule 239, under
which complete collections are to be entered under the broad
heading of "Works," while partial collections of music in a
single category are entered under the form, with appropriate limitation, e.g., "Concertos, piano" (239C) and "various
types of music for a particular medium are entered under the
name of the medium," e.g., "Piano music" (239B) has also
been successfully faced in the second edition of the code.

Another potential source of confusion was the discrepancy between rule 240E, dealing with "Three or more excerpts published together" (in which the word "Selections"
was added to the conventional title) and rule 239D for

"Incomplete collections," which used the qualifying term "Selections" also. Here, again, the revised edition has clarified
the ambiguity.

Anglo-American Cataloguing Rules, 2nd Edition, 1978 [5]

For those who have little, if any, interest in the earlier part
of this chapter and who have come directly to this section,
it may be helpful to place AACR 2 (as it has quickly become
identified by librarians) in context. For nearly sixty years,
most British libraries used the 1908 Anglo-American code as
the basis of their author cataloguing. The 1949 A.L.A. code,
although largely a joint effort, was mainly ignored on the
eastern side of the Atlantic, despite the considerable improvements on its 1908 predecessor. Further development,
again, was to be found in AACR 1 of 1967. As with the
1908 code, there were one or two points upon which the two
committees failed to reach agreement, so that slightly different American and British editions were published.

The latest edition appeared at the end of 1978. This
was a fully agreed international code, since it was prepared
and accepted by the American Library Association, the British Library, and the Canadian Committee on Cataloging, as
well as by the Library Association and the Library of Congress; so it represents a wide consensus indeed. Comment
here, although concerned mainly with this later edition, occasionally looks back at its 1967 predecessor which, in many
ways, represented at that time a major step forward in its
coverage of both music and sound recordings. To a large
extent, the criticism of its weaknesses and inadequacies have
been taken into account and rectified in 1978. This is particularly true of the rules relating to nonbook materials;
these are considered in a later chapter.

AACR 1 was arranged to deal with entry and heading
(chapters 1 to 5), description (chapters 6 to 9) and nonbook
materials in chapters 10 to 13. In effect, this meant that
the code traversed a catalogue entry from top to bottom; it
also gave the impression that nonbook materials were something alien which deserved no better than relegation to an
extended appendix.

An entirely different stance is adopted by AACR 2.

Although there have been no revolutionary changes, the new
structure is appreciably more logical. Its method of numbering the rules (a system, incidentally, proposed with AACR 1,
but rejected during gestation in favour of a straightforward
consecutive sequence) will not be to the liking of every user,
despite all the arguments produced in its favour. The new
code also works from the centre outwards. "The rules follow the sequence of cataloguers' operations in most present-
day libraries and bibliographic agencies ..." (0.3, p. 1).
So the first thirteen chapters give instructions for making a
description, followed by rules for the assignment of headings
(chapters twenty-one to twenty-six). Chapters fourteen to
twenty do not exist, and may never do so; the gap has been
left to allow for any future nonbook materials that may be in-
vented and will then require consideration. Additionally, nonbook materials are no longer treated as though they suffered
from some contagious disease; they are now, rightly, considered as a normal part of library stock. The basic set of
general rules for description (chapter 1) applies to all formats, while later chapters amplify these for particular types
of nonbook materials--a system previously demonstrated with
the LA/NCET rules. So chapters five and six (which relate
respectively to music and sound recordings) elaborate chapter 1 in their specific fields. The new code uses International Standard Bibliographic Description (ISBD) style and
punctuation, an illustration of efforts to make the rulings
more universally acceptable; it also makes entries more easily compatible with the MARC format. MARC is a specialized
topic, outside the scope of this volume. Interested readers
are referred to the study by Seibert [200], which gives the
relevant references. But as an aside, it should be pointed
out that there will have to be some alterations and additions
to MARC fields, e.g., Field 245 for General Material Designation, Field 300 for Specific Material Designation; and one
wonders if a new edition of the MARC manual will be quickly
produced to fill a gap that badly needs removing. There is
also the problem of noncompatibility, if a library adopts AACR
2 with existing headings/uniform titles, etc., when attempting
to interfile new entries into an AACR 1 database. For example, one medium-sized English county has something like
1,500 entries with titles that begin with the word "Symphony,"
whereas AACR 2 requires "Symphonies" as the filing word in
all cases. The need to decide upon the appropriate level of
description is briefly discussed later when considering practical cataloguing.

The "general material designation" (entitled "Material
designator" in <u>AACR 1</u>) is an optional addition, to follow immediately after the title, should its inclusion be desired.
One would use, as appropriate, "printed music," "sound recording," or "multimedia" (5.10). Parallel titles, i.e., books
and scores with titles pages which carry the name of the
work in more than one language, are entered with an equals
sign (=) to accept the provision which publishers may include
with the hope or intention of selling more copies of an item
in a number of different countries. Further title information can be provided if available and thought to be useful in
such cases, the procedure is laid down in chapter 1, section
1E. Chapter 1 deals with description in a general way,
whereas each succeeding chapter covers a particular area--
so the rules follow the normal procedure of moving from the
broad to the particular.

"Statement of responsibility" (5.1F) amends the method
specified in the first edition; no longer does one use "by"
between author and title when that word is omitted on the
title page; the cataloguer has now to provide an oblique
stroke--"/". This is simpler, quicker and probably just as
effective in those cases where "by" or its equivalent in another language is omitted from the title page. On the other
hand, where the word is supplied by the publisher, the oblique stroke is still required, preceded by the word "by."

Section 5.4 relates to imprint, with a brief set of rules
provided to standardize punctuation (5.4A1) and the inevitable
reference back to chapter 1. It is interesting to note in the
short rule concerning early printed music (5.4B2), that the
definition of such items is "published before 1821." This is
an unexplained alteration to the long-accepted cutoff date of
1800, a choice whose origin certainly dates back many years,
and is in the British Museum rules. Rule 5.4D1 allows the
option of adding, after the publisher, the name of the distributor. Where no date of publication is shown, but a copyright date is given, the latter is to be quoted. In such a
case, square brackets are not used, but the cataloguer is
instructed to put a lowercase "c" before the date. Some users of the cataloguer might misinterpret this and read it as
"circa," but the staff should find no ambiguity. Some reasons for trying to include a date on a catalogue entry deserve mention here, since it is a point of importance for
academic and scholarly libraries, if not necessarily for others.

With monographs, one expects the date of publication to be
supplied, and usually the date(s) of any reprinting to be
given. The equivalent in music is very rare (Faber Music
and Bärenreiter are honourable modern exceptions). It matters to the scholar that he knows the date, since new editions or reprints may include minor corrections or even, perhaps, alterations to the musical text. Although a copyright
date is not the same as a date of publication, the two are
usually sufficiently close for the former to make an acceptable substitute for the latter. Rule 1.4 of the code allows
for this matter of including either an established or estimated date.

        Several pages of text are occupied by section 5.5
which concerns the physical description area. This begins
with "specific material designation" (5.5B1) such as "score,"
"vocal score," or "miniature score" (with a note that this
qualification is to be used "for scores reduced in size and
therefore not primarily intended for performance"), and
makes provision for noting the number of scores or parts.
This is a section of the code that students should study carefully until they are sure that they understand the terms used.

        Two or three examples may be found helpful. Music
for piano, organ, solo violin and similar unaccompanied items
have no specific material designation, since none of the terms
given is applicable in such cases. The collation would be
"11p of music" (or whatever the number of pages may be).
The term "piano score" is limited purely to orchestral music
arranged for performance as piano solo, such as those editions of Beethoven, Haydn, and other symphonies intended
for domestic use and very popular in the days before sound
recording and radio. A song for voice and piano is to be
shown as "score," but a song for voice with orchestra that
has had the accompaniment arranged for piano solo is to be
shown as "vocal score."

        It must also be realized that the number of parts is
not necessarily the same as the number of copies. One
might cite Samuel Barber's Adagio for strings which has
five parts, but an orchestral librarian could well have a set
of 8 8 7 6 3 copies, and would supply the information in a
note. In the code 5.5B3 shows: "1 score (viii, 278p) + 24
parts" (which is almost the same as rule 246B in the first
edition). The rule relating to the number of parts is 5.7B20

--a wider separation of the two closely related aspects of collation than might be thought desirable.

The contents of an album are to be listed (5.7B18), and there is no suggestion in the code that there is to be any limitation upon the number of items so treated. Such completeness is highly desirable, but one feels that many librarians will ignore this, to a greater or lesser extent. If it is wished to include the publisher's number of the plate numbers for a particular volume, this should be done in the form of a note. In passing, the code fails to define either term in the glossary. The publisher's number is usually shown at the bottom of the title page; plate numbers are quoted at the base of each individual page throughout the score, slightly reminiscent of the signature to be found at the beginning of each section of a printed book. A music publisher's number for a volume will usually be quoted in the firm's catalogue, almost like a form of standard book number, but a practice followed for many years before the SBN plan was devised.

Chapter 6, on sound recordings, is considered in a later chapter. In AACR 1, chapters 13 and 14 (dealing respectively with music and phonorecords) include instructions for dealing with entry and, in chapter 13, with the formation of uniform titles. It must be remembered, as we have already emphasized, that rules for entry and description in these two chapters merely supplement the general rules in chapters 1 and 6.

AACR 2 distributes some of these items, e.g., uniform titles for music are now considered in Part II of the code (headings, uniform titles and references) along with such titles for all other kinds of work. Another example of this separation is shown in 21.4A--Works of single personal authorship, where one of the examples quoted is Brahms' fourth symphony. So the music cataloguer may need to make frequent reference to chapters 21 and 25.

Rules 21.18 to 21.22 relate to musical scores; 21.23 is concerned with sound recordings, so is considered here in chapter 5. The general rule is 21.18, indicating the scope and application of the rule, while 21.18B deals with arrangements and transcriptions. It is similar to rule 231 in the first edition of AACR, with rule 21.18C covering the same

ground as the earlier edition's 232. The reasons for decision between treating the work as an arrangement or as an
adaptation remain much as before, with "a distinct alteration
of another work" being necessary for the resultant composition to come within the purview of rule 21.18C. It has been
pointed out that an etcher, for instance, who copies another
artist's painting and so changes the medium, is counted as
having primary intellectual responsibility, but in music the
primacy of the composer remains and the arranger is considered of lesser importance. It is a minor inconsistency in
the code.

Musical works that include words are covered by 21.19.
The general rule (section A) is virtually the same as 230A in
the 1967 edition, except that it provides for an added entry
for the writer(s) of the words, instead of an explanatory reference. Section B (pastiches, etc.) is also similar to the
earlier edition's 230B1, except for ballad operas. Whereas
the main entry was formerly under the dramatist, it is now
under the work's title, which is probably a more effective
decision and is in accordance with the code's principles of
entry. AACR 1 originally entered collections of previously
existing (our italics) works under the compiler. A later
amendment replaced this with entry under title. Hence the
difference between 21.19B1 and B2: the former is for works
such as The Beggar's Opera, where Pepusch used tunes from
a variety of sources, some traditional and others contemporary; 21.19B2 is for similar works, which have the music
specially composed and not gathered, magpie fashion, from
the works of others. The text refers the cataloguer to 21.6
(works of shared responsibility), which is the relevant heading for all the section of the chapter considered here. Mention must also be made of 21.19C which provides for the
works of one writer set by two or more composers and issued
in a collection. In such a case, the revised rule for collections applies, i.e., the main entry is under the title of the
compilation with added entries for the author concerned and
for the first-named composer on the title page.

Ballet music (21.20) is treated as in rule 230D of the
earlier edition, with entry under the composer of the music,
but in the newer code the cataloguer is instructed to make
added entry rather than an explanatory reference for the
choreographer or the author of the story to which the ballet
or pantomime has been set. Added accompaniments (21.21)

repeats the old rule 230E, so that if one has Paganini's unaccompanied Caprices in the version for violin and piano (the
accompaniment being supplied by Schumann), the main entry
would be made under Paganini and an added entry provided
under Schumann. That there are these similarities between
many of the rules in the two editions of AACR shows that
there has been a desirable element of continuity, rather than
demolition and replacement by something different, unless a
complete reappraisal of a rule has been considered necessary.

Liturgical music (21.22) shows some changes from the
earlier edition. Form headings are no longer used. Instead,
one is instructed to follow rule 21.39 for officially prescribed
parts of the liturgy, which means that entry is made under
the heading for the church, etc., followed by a uniform title. One outstanding omission from this section would seem
to relate to cadenzas when they are written by someone other
than the composer of the rest of the concerto. Up to, approximately, the time of Mozart it was customary for the
executant to provide original cadenzas at the appropriate
points in a concerto. Modern editions of such works usually
provide a cadenza, often composed by a nineteenth or twentieth century executant, for major works in the form that
lack this item. The concerto then becomes, in cataloguing
parlance, a work of "mixed responsibility." Cadenzas are
mentioned in 21.28 (related works) and, amid a numerous
series of examples, is one for Mozart's two flute concertos,
composed by the flautist George Barrère. According to the
rule, the main entry for the concertos is made under Barrère;
Mozart is given an added entry (name-title). Not all cataloguers will agree with this ruling since, without the original work, there would be no point in composing a cadenza.
However, as both composers are to be entered in the catalogue, the choice for priority between the two may not be
regarded as being of vital significance. Nevertheless, one
is surprised that the distinction drawn in AACR 1 between
a) works with a dependent title, and b) other works, has
been dropped. Cadenzas would certainly seem to come into
the former category. The interested reader is referred to
rules 19A and 19B in the first edition of AACR. At the
same time, it has to be admitted that the problem of a cadenza only arises when this part of a concerto is published
separately, which is not a common occurrence. However,
there are collections of cadenzas, such as those composed
by Beethoven for use with Mozart piano concertos, or those

prepared by Reinecke to a number of concertos by different composers. The problem of headings for related works only arises when one tries to choose a _main_ entry.

The rule on works of mixed responsibility also covers librettos (21.28A), and is similar to that found in the 1967 edition, i.e., the preferred choice in the code is to make the main entry under the librettist with an added entry for the composer, but the rule allows the original amendment to be reversed in an alternative that applies only to this specific type of literary product. If this amendment is adopted, then the main entry will be made under the composer, with added entry under the librettist. "If, however, a libretto is published without reference to its musical setting, enter it under the heading for the author of the libretto." Since this rule, like that for cadenzas, postulates multiple entry, it may be felt that the choice as to which is the main one has little practical significance.

The last section of the code with specific reference to music is found in chapter 25, which deals with uniform titles. The compilers have clearly thought it best to bring together all rules for dealing with this particular problem, whatever the format of the item concerned, so that the section dealing with music follows that for laws, treaties, and "parts of sacred scriptures and additions," to be found in chapter 4 of AACR 1. The general rules (25.1--25.6) are to be used where applicable and "are not contradicted by the following rules." Since 25.26 deals with definitions of musical works, an annotation defines "work" and "title," the latter very narrowly indeed. Thus, among the examples quoted is "Five little pieces for piano," in which "Little pieces" is considered to be the title. Similarly, "Four orchestral pieces" is, from the code's standpoint, titled "Pieces."

This would seem, to us, to be a rule likely to result in bafflement and inconsistency. The rule itself (25.26A) states that title "means the word or words that name the work exclusive of ... numerals (unless they are an integral part of the title)." The problem is how one is intended to interpret the word "integral." We would accept as integral any example where a number is the first word of a title, provided that it was so named by the composer himself, and is not a title given to a collection of works originally published at different times. One assumes that Peter Maxwell

Davies' Eight Songs for a Mad King and Haydn's Seven Last
Words on the Cross would be entered under their titles--but
what should be done with Verdi's Four Sacred Pieces (Quat-
tro pezzi sacri), which were written over nearly a decade at
the end of Verdi's life and which form a group, admittedly a
somewhat odd one? Is the cataloguer likely to know whether
the overall title was supplied by Verdi or the publisher?

Selection of titles is covered by 25.27, similar to rule
234 in the earlier edition. However, the preference for the
original language is now more strongly recommended, but the
use of English for such generic terms as "sonatas" and "quintets" remains; although the example of the Bach prelude and
fugue for organ being entered as "Präludium und Fuge ..."
could be found more confusing than helpful. Works with title consisting "solely of the name of one type of composition"
are to be entered under the English form of the name (25.27B).
One assumes that preludes and fugues are counted as two
types; this is true, even though the two types are very frequently found in harness. The uniform title is to be given
in the plural, even if one is cataloguing but a single work.
This aids consistency in filing, but can mean an enormous
amount of alteration to existing files. The remainder of 25.27
is concerned with rules for particular problems, such as
duets, trio sonatas and works with very long titles.

"Additions" are detailed in 25.28 and concern (in
25.29) the medium of performance when it is not immediately
apparent what this is. Thus, unless otherwise stated, one
assumes that a symphony is written for an orchestra of
strings and wind, and is likely to include brass and percussion in the instrumentation. Where this assumption is wrong,
as with synphonies for strings alone (such as the juvenile
Mendelssohn ones) or for organ solo (a favourite form with
several French composers since the nineteenth century), the
medium is listed in the entry. Other examples quoted include chorale preludes, masses, overtures and "Songs,
Lieder, etc." Where a set consists of work for which more
than one specific instrument is acceptable, such as the Handel sonatas published as his opus 1 (nominally for "a German flute, hoboy or violin") then the medium would simply
be shown as "Sonatas."

Rule 25.29 is concerned with the terminology of individual instruments. Although preference is expressed for

the form in English, both British and American sensibilities were taken into account by the acceptance of either "cor anglais" or "English horn" for this instrument. While the rule, in general, stems from AACR 1, there are some changes in detail. There are alterations where uniform titles are concerned, many of them made in the interests of computer filing. A comparison, in a simple sequence, between AACR 1 and AACR 2 should demonstrate this. Under AACR 2, the cataloguer is expected to use "flutes (2)" in contrast to the earlier "flutes 2," while it is now "Scherzos, flutes (2), clarinets (2)." In the earlier publication the word "and" would be used to link the two instruments, but that is now omitted in the interests of clarifying the filing order. For example:

AACR 1	AACR 2
flute and clarinet	flute, bassoon, horn
flute, bassoon and horn	flute, clarinet
flute, clarinet and horn	flute, clarinet, horn

It may be helpful to take a longer sequence, as under:

        Concerto, flute
        Concerto, oboe
        Concerto, piano, no. 1
        Concerto, piano no. 2
        Concerto, 2 pianos
        Concerto, 2 violins

That is what might be called "human" filing; give the sequence to a computer, and the probable arrangement will be:

        Concerto, 2 pianos
        Concerto, 2 violins
        Concerto, flute
        Concerto, oboe
        Concerto, piano, no. 1
        Concerto, piano, no. 2

To evade an obvious difficulty, AACR 2 puts the type of composition into the plural (unless a composer has written but one work of the type) and, if there is more than one of the same instrument, names the instrument before the number. The sequence then becomes:

       Concertos, flute
       Concertos, oboe
       Concertos, piano, no. 1
       Concertos, piano, no. 2
       Concertos, piano (2)
       Concertos, violins (2)

In this way, the logical sequence is the same as the filing
sequence. Notice that plurals, e.g., concertos, are used
when the composer has written more than one work in this
form, even though only one may be for a particular solo
instrument. So, under Brahms, will be found [Concertos,
violin] and the examples in AACR 2 even have "Concertos,
orchestra" under Bartók.

It is probably worth separate comment that the definition of "title" in uniform titles is also tightened up. Anything that can be removed, is. This happens to the extent
that, for example, Fünf Orchesterstücke becomes [Stücke].
AACR 1 allowed translated titles to be used on occasion, but
AACR 2 insists on the original so that, e.g., The Golden
Cockerel will be found (or not found, as the case may be)
as [Zolotoi petushok]. If, however, the title consists simply
of the name of the type of composition, then English may be
used. This concession is hedged about with qualifications
and exceptions, since English usage is often multilingual, as
in études, divertimenti, concerti grossi.

Slight expansion is to be found in 25.29H, on vocal
music, if one compares this rule with 236D of the first edition. The code now accepts that there may be a need, in
addition to the standard range of voices from soprano to
bass, to allow for "high voice" and "countertenor." Another new provision is at 25.30, "Sketches," although many
smaller libraries are unlikely to find this of any practical
value.

"Other identifying elements" are to be listed in a prescribed order--a serial number, opus number of thematic index number, and key; each element is to be preceded by a
comma. One would have preferred "opus number and/or
thematic catalogue number," since there are cases when both
can be usefully quoted. In any event, there is usually a
period of several years, at least, when the balance is tilting
from the former to the thematic catalogue number. At the
time of writing, Dvořák's opus numbers (which are misleading

in a number of cases, if one assumes that they follow a direct chronological/published order) are slowly being replaced
in general use by Burghauser's chronological catalogue numbers, published in 1960. Until the latter identification is accepted as readily as, say, Deutsch numbers now are for
Schubert compositions, there is a strong case for showing
both opus and thematic catalogue numbers on each Dvořák
entry. Although the new code rule is apparently like the
first edition's number 237, there are differences. One might
cite "pre-twentieth century works" (23.31A5) compared with
"1700-1900," in the earlier edition's rule 237D. The 1978
version also collates, at this point, some miscellaneous rulings from the 1967 code, e.g., 241 Arrangements, 242 Adap-
tations, and 243 Reductions. The wording has also been
slightly amended to improve clarity.

Another section of 25.31B is concerned with librettos
and song texts (25.31B5). If such publications are entered
under the name of the composer of the music, then the qualifying word ("libretto" or "text") is to be included as part
of the uniform title. This appears to be a completely new
provision in the code, unrepresented in the earlier edition.
As it now stands, there is a parallel in "General material
designation" in 1.1C. It may be regarded as a natural development of the "Early warning media designator" which
concerned some American cataloguers several years ago.

Section B6 and B7 of this rule provide for the language to be added to a title (one example given is of Messiah with words in both the original English and in a Dutch
translation). Language as a filing element is a nuisance, but
one that has to be accepted as, because of the need for machine filing in many libraries, alphabetic order of languages
is the only practical method. However, filing order is outside the scope of AACR. The code's method for music is in
line with that used for non-musical uniform titles, and consistency is what one would expect. "Parts of a musical work"
are covered in 25.32 and this is very similar to the old rule
240. For two works published together (25.33), main entry
is to be made under the first, and added entry under the
second. The musical section of this chapter is completed by
25.34, "Collective titles," which has a strong relationship to
AACR 1 rule 239, but is somewhat expanded. Provision is
made, as before, for works of various types of the same
broad medium, as Instrumental music, of a specific medium

(e.g., Piano music), for works of a specific type of music (Quartets, string), and for selections.

ISBD (PM) [106]

This is perhaps a point at which one can make brief reference to the International Standard Bibliographic Description for Printed Music, usually abbreviated to ISBD(PM). It was published by IFLA in 1980, and runs to 53 pages. It appeared some two years after AACR 2 and, fortunately, is generally in agreement with that code. One immediate difference is that, while the General material designation (GMD) is optional, as it is in AACR 2, this new volume prefers [Printed music], rather than AACR's [Music], "or its equivalent in other languages." A "Printed music specific area" is inserted between the Edition area and the Publication, distribution, etc., area. There is a similar device to be found in AACR, but there it is not for music but is intended for cartographic materials and serials. This area "consists of statements indicating the special music format of a work distinguishing it from other formats of the same work." The statement is to be given in the terms used on the title page of its substitute. Similar information is repeated in the Physical description area, and it bears a strong relationship to that given in AACR 2. In ISBD(PM), however, the terms are taken from a list which has minor differences compared with AACR's choice in 5.5B1, which reads: score; condensed score; close score; miniature score; piano [violin] conductor part; vocal score; piano score; chorus score; part. ISBD uses the same terms except that "miniature score" is not used, and "piano score" is absorbed into "piano conductor part" (or appropriately for other instruments).

Another minor difference between the two guides is that, in AACR, the plate number is quoted in the note area, but as that whole section is optional, there is choice for the cataloguer to provide or omit as is thought best. In ISBD(PM), the plate number is incorporated into the standard number area, referred to in the text as "International standard number (or alternative), plate number, and terms of availability area." The ISBN or publisher's number must be quoted, but the inclusion of plate number(s) is optional.

SUBJECT CATALOGUING

Subject headings will already be in use in libraries using a
dictionary catalogue. If they are considered to be badly
chosen, inadequate, etc., the headings for music entries
may be revised and some recataloguing undertaken. The
largest list of subject headings is that of the Library of
Congress, first published in 1897 [221]. Because this sequence comprises actual headings in use for LC's immense
collection, there is considerable detail in both headings and
subdivisions. A smaller and simpler list, based on this publication, is to be found included with the books for all other
subjects in Sears' List of Subject Headings [199].

If the LC headings, in their entirety or in part, are
used in an English library, it is almost certain that the terminology will have to be modified, as required, to follow normal British usage. As no list of subject headings intended
for use in British libraries appears to have been published,
a library inaugurating a dictionary catalogue would probably
have to make an ad hoc set of headings.

PRACTICAL CATALOGUING IN THE SMALL LIBRARY

The publication of the MLA/ALA code, and also of AACR,
has transformed the situation compared with twenty years
ago. If the cataloguer is genuinely seeking guidance, and
is also willing to amend practices which can now be seen to
be wrong, or are at best less satisfactory than is possible,
guidance is not difficult to find. At the same time, one has
to accept that there is an understandable innate inertia in
most people; it is usually very easy to think of good (and
often genuine) reasons for continuing with long established
practices. Even small amendments of practice can have far
wider reaching effects than originally envisaged. Nevertheless, a careful appraisal of each stage of what is currently
being done and, more importantly, why the particular procedures being used were originally selected can prove very
valuable. Arguments which were valid years ago may no
longer be operative; in any case, cataloguing standards have
risen markedly in all types of library over the years. Even
some simplification of what is currently being done may well
be an improvement. On the other hand, it must be said that
the general standard of music cataloguing (in the light of a

variety of catalogues we have inspected over the years in
several different countries) is generally poor to middling;
the really good catalogue is met but infrequently.

As a general standard, the music cataloguer in the
small library might follow chapter four of the MLA/ALA code
(the simplified rules), with AACR used as a secondary guide
when the older code is not entirely intelligible, when it offers no guidance, or when fuller instruction is wanted. This
is particularly likely to be the case in the construction of
filing titles.

Composer Entry

There is normally very little difficulty with western names
usually quoted in Roman script. There might be a tendency
to file Vaughan Williams under "W" because there is no hyphen
between the two parts of his surname, but reference to a
standard music dictionary should ensure correct entry.

With Russian and other names written in Cyrillic script,
problems are of long standing and seem likely to remain for
many years. The cataloguer must decide, or perhaps have it
decided by higher authority or by precedent already firmly
established, whether to use systematic romanization or established forms (AACR rule 44B offers the choice). As Nicolas
Slonimsky has lamented:

> The transliteration of Russian names is as insoluble
> a proposition as the squaring of the circle, because
> of the non-correspondence of the sound represented
> by the letters of the Cyrillic alphabet and those of
> the Latin vocables. Since Russian music was first
> published in Germany, Russian composers became
> embedded in German matrices. Tchaikovsky was
> Tschaikowsky in American concert halls, even though
> the initial Russian consonant of his name has the
> exact phonetic equivalent in the English diphthong
> "ch" .... The introductory "T" persists in the com-
> mon American spelling of Tchaikovsky, even though
> most library catalogues list him under "Ch." But
> familiarity breeds respect, and Chaikovsky looks
> queer [203, p. xiii].

Even reference books may change from one edition to the next, and the cataloguer will have to decide whether to retain the old form or to alter all existing entries. With the growing influence of MARC and of the joint cataloguing axis of Library of Congress and the British Library, there will be continued emphasis on systematic romanization. One recalls the efforts made by the British Broadcasting Corporation in the 1930s to introduce "Chaykovsky" and its firm rejection by the music loving public at large. Attitudes may be modified, particularly if the reasons for the proposed alterations are understood; the swift change of accepted numbering of the Dvořák symphonies exemplifies this.

If the cataloguer decides to follow a standard music dictionary, such as Grove, Thompson, or the Everyman, a check will need to be made when a new edition is bought to see if suspect names have been changed. In any case, the cataloguer should certainly keep an authority file of all doubtful cases with a note as to the solution selected, so that consistent entry can be achieved. For a composer using a pseudonym, it seems best to accept the generally recognized form of the name; how many music lovers realize that, for example, neither Meyerbeer nor Palestrina is the name with which the respective composers started life? A reference from the unused form may not be worthwhile. Again, a single forename will usually suffice unless confusion is likely to result, as in the case of the Bach family. We were surprised to notice that the generally recommendable Nonbook materials ..., by Jean Riddle Weihs and others, quotes full Christian names not only for composers (all four for Mozart), but also for conductors, etc. [229]. This seems a considerable waste of time and effort. For non-European names the problem remains virtually minimal for musical compositions. Until recently, almost all music outside the western tradition has been anonymous/traditional, so that any scores would be entered under the title, with added entry for the compiler, editor or arranger, etc. One might instance a collection of Kwontong melodies in Cheve notation: Yin Yueh Chyuu Shyuuan, compiled by Seen Shahng-Dar.

Title Entry

Any library with more than a handful of music scores would now be well advised to use the device of the filing title,

perhaps also adapting the MLA/ALA suggestion (rule IVB,
p. 55) that this additional line be omitted when it agrees
with the transcription of the title page, but leaving in such
cases a blank space where the filing title is normally inserted. Not only is this consistent, but it permits the addition of the filing title if, at a later date, it is decided that
these should be provided for all scores.

The choice between the language of the title page, the
language of the library, and the language of the original
(assuming the three to be different), is dealt with at length
in AACR 1 (rules 233-243). For the smaller library, a simplified rule will cover most cases. If the title is of a standard musical form (symphony, string quartet, concerto) then
the language of the country in which the library is situated
should be used. For works with individual titles, then the
original is generally to be preferred. In cases of doubt
(and there may be a fair proportion of these), the cataloguer
must decide after checking any reference sources to hand.
It is relatively unimportant whether the cataloguer enters
Tchaikovsky's opera under Pique dame or Queen of Spades,
providing that a reference from the unused form is made to
that selected.

If one follows either of the two suggested codes, then
musical form will precede the name of the solo instrument
when cataloguing a concerto. This means for example, use
of the style "Concerto for piano and orchestra" rather than
"Piano concerto." The latter saves both space and time because it is the shorter entry, and it will result in a different scheme of arrangement for the entries under an individual composer, emphasising the instrumental aspect at the expense of musical form. There are sound arguments in favour
of this approach, and in the first edition of this book, recommendation was made in favour of this style, to correlate "Violin concerto," "Violin sonata," etc. Twenty years later, our
personal opinion has changed, mainly because of the difficult
cases over which the instrumental approach stumbles. For
instance, the accompaniment in a concerto is not always
scored for full orchestra; it may be for strings only, for
wind instruments, for chamber orchestra or other limited
groups. Poulenc's Organ Concerto (if one prefers that
form) can be misleading, for the full title is Concerto for
Organ, Strings and Tympani. Whichever form of entry is
preferred and chosen, the cataloguer should make every

effort to achieve consistency in entries. In passing, rule
239C of <u>AACR</u> (for "Concertos, piano") for collections can
raise problems.

The key in which a composition is written should be
given in the language of the library users. For works
written between 1700 and 1900 (the dates are very approximate), one can usually decide the key of a work with little
difficulty, even in cases where it is not quoted. The key
signature will offer two alternatives--a major key or its relative minor; e.g., no sharps or flats suggests either C major
or A minor, and the simplest way of determining which of
the two is applicable is to look at the end of the work. If
it ends in a chord based on A (even in A major), then the
key is almost certainly A minor. One custom which saves
both space and time is to use a capital letter if the key is
major with lower case for minor keys, so that "b" would
represent B minor. The drawback is that in a number of
works (mainly modern), although they have a definite tonal-
ity, may be shown on the title page to be, say, "in G" and
to be ambiguous in key--the work may be regarded as being
in both G major and G minor. Nevertheless, at least in the
small collection, this lack of definition is not likely to occur
often (since so many modern works do not state any key)
and it can probably be ignored without real loss in cases
where it does occur. With computer produced catalogues
that give upper case only, this suggested distinction between major and minor keys is not feasible.

Over the past twenty years, there has been a noticeable increase in the number of works (usually without opus
numbers, but by no means invariably so) that are precisely
identified by means of a thematic catalogue number. For
instance, there is now a much wider acceptance of the Hoboken numbers for Haydn works; there would probably be
much more general use if the numbers were in the usual
single numerical sequence. Instead, the Hoboken series is
divided by a classification and then by a number. The
cello concerto in D (once thought to be by Anton Kraft, a
member of the Esterhazy orchestra and a pupil of Haydn)
was always identified, until fairly recently, as "op. 101."
The "H" number is VIIb, no. 2, which is not straightforward. With Buxtehude there is more than one thematic
catalogue currently available but, at the time of writing,
none seems to have firmly established itself as the standard.

Sooner or later, one of the present contenders (or a fresh compilation) will emerge as that generally accepted by the musical world.

As with ruling monarchs, the first in a series only adds "I" after the name when a second appears. Thus no number is required to pinpoint the symphonies of, for example, Franck and Sullivan; each wrote only the one work in this form. So, for twenty-five years, one could refer to the Walton symphony; from 1960, the original work had become Symphony No. 1 and catalogue entries will be entered in numerical order, not alphabetical. If one used the latter, "five" would come before "four," which would precede "one," "three" and "two." For the great majority of catalogue users, this would be utter nonsense, and rightly so.

Imprint

The name of the publisher should always be given with the main entry for a music score, however simplified or curtailed the practice followed for such entries in other respects. Students may have to study a particular edition while the reputation of different publishers of the same work may vary considerably in level, and the editions themselves may be equally at variance with one another. Although one would like to see (where applicable) both the names of the original publisher and that of the importer, where these are shown on the title page, it is appreciated that many cataloguers would feel this double listing to be an unnecessary lengthening of the entry. If that is the case, we would recommend that the original publisher's name be preferred. There should be little difficulty in tracing the appropriate dealers or publishers when music is imported under sole agency arrangements into a country. Again, the place of publication is usually easily inferred from the publisher's name; only in cases of ambiguity (as with Peters) should the city or town of publication be a necessary part of the entry.

As for dating the music, it is becoming usual practice for works in copyright to carry the date of registration, although this is not necessarily the date of the issue of the copy in hand. For other works, we remain unrepentant in our belief that the date of the copy (unless it is one issued in the early nineteenth century or before) is irrelevant. As

Asheim and Byler suggest, "In most music libraries, the
music is in reprint and the date is not so important; certainly it seldom repays the amount of time required for its
verification" [10, p. 183]. With music apparently printed
before 1820 or so, completely different criteria apply. Such
items as plate numbers, watermarks, the address and exact
form of the publisher's name and other aids towards precise
dating are then immensely valuable--but such scores are not
likely to be made available for indiscriminate lending and may
well be part of the local or other special collection.

Collation

AACR 246A suggests that collation should follow the normal
rules, unless the item is issued in parts or in the format of
a score and parts. There is, we suggest, some reason for
giving the number of pages in a score, since this figure will
give a very approximate guide to the probable length of the
music. The page height, though also useful upon occasion,
does not seem worth measuring unless the score is of unusual
dimensions; even oblong scores, such as are often found with
organ works, are very doubtful contenders for the description "unusual."

For works issued in parts, but with a score included,
collation should make this provision clear. With chamber music that includes a piano in the ensemble (the piano quintet
is perhaps the most common example), the piano score often
includes the string parts in small, light type. This allows,
among other things, for the piano score to be used by a
listener to follow a performance. Again, where a piece of
music is written or arranged for two pianos it is clearly vital to indicate the presence (or the absence) of the second
copy. The cataloguer in the small library is unlikely to need
to include a series note, but "Notes" (AACR 248) form a vital part of many entries, since these should elucidate any
lacunae in the title statement, or possibly include information
omitted by the cataloguer as part of the title statement in
the belief that such items are better shown in the form of
notes. This is often a very difficult decision, and one is
reminded of shelves filled with books or scores. Those on
the top and bottom shelves are less likely to attract attention and be borrowed than items that are around, or a little
below, eye level. In the same way, different persons refer-

ring to the catalogue may have varied needs in mind, and
the problem of where to put certain information in the entry
is never likely to be solved to the satisfaction of every enquirer. The cataloguer is perhaps best advised to make
independent decisions, providing that they are defensible on
rational grounds. Consultation with users might bring consensus, but could as easily result in strong disagreement
among music lovers.

A plea must be made, however, for contents notes for
volumes which contain more than one work that cannot easily
be covered by generic title. "Preludes for piano" will need
any limitations to be indicated--they may be from a single
opus number, when the composer has written others, or they
may be a selection brought together by an editor or compiler.
"Selected piano works," in contrast, must have the contents
listed if the volume is to achieve optimum use. It is likely
to need a fair amount of patience to check the volume(s) with
such general titles on the shelves; if the required item is not
found, the music lover will either have to reserve any other
likely anthologies, in the hope that the required piece of music is in one of them, or else check the shelves at intervals
to see if any of these missing volumes have been returned.
Neither prospect is likely to be found encouraging nor to
raise the estimation of the library in the user's eyes.

Chapter IV

CLASSIFICATION

<u>INTRODUCTION</u>

Music presents many problems to anyone who would prepare
a scheme of classification: a few of these are noted here.
First, should books and scores share the same sequence of
symbols or should there be two separate (but, one hopes,
related) sets? James Duff Brown in his subject classification, and Melvil Dewey's decimal classification (DDC), up to
the fifteenth edition, used a single sequence of symbols, so
that (to offer a simple example) an album of Schumann Lieder
had the same class mark as a book of comment on and appraisal of those songs. Some librarians using either of the
two schemes would ensure differentiation in the subject catalogue by prefixing scores with "M," "S," or other identifying
symbol. A different idea, applicable only to DDC, was to
move the decimal point one place to the left for scores, and
so ensure both separation and ease of recognition between
the two types of publication. Whatever method was used,
format clearly divided the two sequences--books and scores
--since it has always been general policy to keep the two
types of material apart, if only to save the considerable
waste of space that would amost certainly result if they were
shelved in a single sequence.

Thus, although one could achieve this separation with
the same class marks for both books and scores, it has become generally accepted that it is much better to provide
separate sequences for the two types of material, if only because (as mentioned in the previous paragraph) they are
highly unlikely to be shelved cheek by jowl and the different class marks should make it virtually impossible, even in

those cases where format is deceptive, for a book to be
shelved as a score, however much first appearances might
mislead. If the two class marks show an immediately apparent relationship, as is the case where the British Catalogue of Music scheme (to quote but one example) is used,
then library users should have little trouble in mentally relating the two.

A second problem concerns the choice of characteristic,
or the order of division of music scores. One writer has
listed eleven "characteristics of scores which determine or
affect classification": 1) Size; 2) Format; 3) Alphabetical
arrangement; 4) Medium; 5) Form; 6) Subject content; 7)
Character or content; 8) Language of text; 9) Geographical;
10) Style relating to a historical period; 11) Opus and thematic numbers [35]. But usually the question is whether
the primary arrangement should be by form or by medium.
The major schemes have chosen the latter and so have brought
together all works for the voice, those for individual instruments, for orchestra, etc. The implied judgement is that this
is the most useful plan for the majority of library users. It
is not difficult to argue the case in favour of division by form,
when all sonatas would be brought together, be they for piano, organ, unaccompanied violin, two clarinets, or whatever.
Alphabetical division by composer (which is, of course, not
really classification at all) was chosen by Ernest Savage for
the large music collection in the public library at Edinburgh.
Although the Library of Congress scheme, with a fair amount
of modification, was used in most other departments, the LC
music schedules did not find favour with Savage and he has
explained how he grouped collections of scores at the beginning of the sequence for each individual composer, with single scores following in alphabetical order of title; books
about the composer were grouped together at the end of his
works. Savage claimed that

> ... alphabetical arrangement by composer [is] the
> simplest, the most convenient and the most logical.
> The simplest obviously. The most logical, because
> we must group music, as we group literature, by
> the most tremendous thing in it--the personality of
> its begetter.... The most convenient, because play-
> ers today are far outnumbered by students who lis-
> ten, and who are more interested in the music than
> its form.... If convenience demands (as it does)

that we mix small books with large scores, we should
mix them and make no bones about it [195, p. 104].

There is, in practice, rather more of the LC scheme
to be found in the arrangement of the department than Savage's article implied. A somewhat similar scheme can be seen
today in the Central Music Library in London, which may be
taken as another indication that this method has been found
suitable for a large music collection.

The schemes that divide scores by medium usually
choose musical form as the secondary characteristic: for all
but the largest libraries this may be considered an unnecessary refinement. It can be argued that a classified collection of, for example, solo piano music gives a clearer picture
of the range available to the pianist than the same collection arranged in composer order under a more general symbol that covers any sort of piano music. A common (and
effective) compromise can be seen on the shelves of (for example) the library of the Royal Northern College of Music in
Manchester where solo piano scores are arranged by composer, but, as a secondary feature, these works are carefully
organized in form (title) order, so that both staff and students using the collection will find all available versions of
Beethoven's piano sonatas together, as are the bagatelles,
the sets of variations, the German dances, etc. The arguments in favour of subdividing music by form runs contrary
to the approach of most instrumentalists. If the would-be
borrower is disappointed in his quest for a copy of Chopin's
waltzes for piano, another work by the same composer would
be a more likely alternative than waltzes by Brahms, Schoenberg or Schubert, despite the fact that these scores would
be adjoining the place on the shelves where the Chopin set
would have been found. If considered desirable, the subject entries in the classified or dictionary catalogue can be
subdivided by form even though this subdivision may be ignored on the shelves. It is interesting to note that the recommendation, in the earlier edition of this book, that all miniature scores should be arranged on the shelves, for general
convenience, in a single sequence of composers was subsequently, and coincidentally, adopted by DDC as an option in
the sixteenth edition and as a firm recommendation in the
seventeenth and eighteenth editions.

These previous paragraphs may illustrate something of

the logic and force of Savage's arguments.   The classification
maker has other problems to face.   A schedule can allocate
places for special songs such as shanties, for national songs,
for songs written for male voices only, for songs written in
four parts, etc., and promptly has to face a welter of cross-
classification.   Yet each category of song has works that fit
it specifically.   This problem and the others mentioned are
quoted not because we can offer a perfect answer (for there
is no such thing) but to draw the attention of the student
and librarian to some of the difficulties that have to be faced
and overcome as well as may be before any satisfactory scheme
for classifying music can be produced.   The student might
ponder, for example, the matter of music written for the virginals, clavichord, harpsichord and other precursors of the
modern pianoforte, and decide how to cope with that; it
might be useful to compare any projected solution with that
adopted by the various schemes considered below.

A case for a completely different arrangement has been
argued by Maurice B. Line, who claims that

> ... this primary division by medium, so far from be-
> ing as satisfactory and inevitable as its general use
> would lead one to suppose, is directly responsible
> for many of the worst features of existing classifica-
> tion.... When the student or scholar approaches a
> music library classified by existing schemes, he finds
> music of quite different periods jumbled together be-
> cause the medium happens to be the same.   This can
> cause difficulties even with classical and post-
> classical music when the medium is one for which the
> music was not originally written....   With pre-
> classical music the problem becomes really serious;
> many performing editions bear little resemblance to
> the original scoring, while the instrumentation of
> much medieval music is either unknown or irrelevant,
> and both librarian and user are at the mercy of the
> arranger, whose guesswork may or may not be in-
> spired [124, p. 352].

Line's solution to the problem is a chronological arrangement by period, with further subdivision "as the material demands"; in earlier periods he envisages this as by
musical form, but by medium with later music.   However, he
admits that chronological division is difficult "with music that

is transitional between one period and the next." He also
feels that such a scheme would be unsuitable for small or
medium-sized public libraries but, on the other hand, should
be excellent for academic and national libraries.

The plan is not, perhaps, quite as revolutionary as
its proposer would seem to suggest. The Library of Congress has a placing (M1490) provided between instrumental
music and vocal music for all pre-1700 items, arranged by
composer and ignoring medium, form, character or any other
approach. This could be helpful to the scholarly historian,
or in an academic library with music history as a major subject for study, but it seems less likely to help the practi-
tioner.

Before looking with some care at a few of the better-
known available schemes, one should perhaps consider what
the average potential user (if one can define such a character) may reasonably expect of a classification, for this should
strongly affect the choice of which scheme to select, assuming that the music librarian has such an option or the authority to reclassify, should it be sufficiently advantageous to do
so. Basically, one has to decide if the shelf arrangement of
books and scores is more important than the retrieval of
wanted works through the use of indexes--usually the catalogue.

The first method depends upon a logical arrangement
of classes, one that allows the user to work along the
shelves from one subject to a related one, so that browsing
should be a cheering experience, assuming that the stock itself deserves this reaction. To make such a scheme even
more helpful and attractive, it should be equipped with a notation that is brief, easily memorized and simple to understand. Specificity is a secondary consideration here but, if
the alternative approach is preferred, then a classification
scheme that allows for the extra degree of precision in its
class mark becomes much more valuable. In effect (to limit
examples to schemes considered in detail later), decision between DDC and the LC schemes on the one hand, and the
British Catalogue of Music on the other, could be made on
this single, but highly important factor.

If most of one's stock is not immediately available but
can only be obtained by indirect access, the lengthy but

possibly cumbersome notation of BCM is but a limited handicap since the subject index to the entries in a classified
catalogue (as already mentioned) can show a much greater
degree of specificity than is possible with, for instance, DDC.
This can probably best be demonstrated by quoting some
comparable class marks; from these examples it will be seen
that the length and complexity of the BCM symbols are not
as outrageous as some critics of the scheme would have one
believe. In each of the following BCM is quoted first followed by the Dewey equivalent:

SPME   unaccompanied violin sonatas

787.1541   unaccompanied violin music

Here it can be seen that not only does BCM provide the
shorter notation, it is also noticeably more specific.

DP/LF   Christmas carols

783.65   Christmas carols

Both schemes provide a specific place, but BCM requires only
four symbols; DDC needs five.

DP/LM   New Year carols

783.6   Songs: sacred music

DDC is no shorter, but is very much vaguer than BCM.
On the shelves, a volume of New Year carols (in a Dewey
classified library) would be mixed with all sorts of other
sacred songs.

QPK/DP/LF   Christmas carols, arranged
                          for solo piano

786.405   Scores and parts: music
                          for keyboard (class here
                          arrangements)

Again, DDC's notation does not carry one beyond a general
number for all arrangements for piano solo, whereas BCM
pinpoints the type of music that has been so arranged.

As a final comparison, here is a book on a limited subject, and one may claim that this sums up the argument:

AB/FD(YD/XLT 28/WT)   A list of recorded vocal
                             music in England, 1898-
                             1925

016.7899120942   A list of recorded music in
                             England.

The actual work involved is Bennett's The Voices of the Past: Vocal Recordings, 1898-1925 [16]. The breakdown of the BCM symbol perhaps deserves explanation in this instance. Class A is for books, and AB is for books on vocal music; the /FD indicates recorded music. Y introduces the ethnic/ locality subdivision and D is English (in this case, of course, England). X introduces a period subdivision. XLT is the symbol for 1898; 28 is quoted to show that the work being classified covers a period of 28 years, while the final WT is the symbol for "lists of objects." In short, BCM provides an exact place, except perhaps that it equates a discography with "a list of objects." DDC places the work as a bibliography (acceptable for a discography) of recorded music in England. One cannot specify either that the music is vocal, or the actual term of years which the work covers.

From these examples, it is patent that BCM gives appreciably more information in all but one case than is possible with DDC, usually at the cost of one or two additional symbols. If any reader thinks that the choice of examples is unfair or misleading, it will be found that any random comparison of class marks between the two schemes will produce similar results.

One can offer a small consolation benefit to those who feel that the balance of effectiveness cannot always lie with BCM. With some fringe topics, Dewey can offer a more specific placing. One might instance Juliette Alvin's book Music Therapy (Hutchinson, 1975). In BCM one would have to classify this book at A(ZD) which is no more precise than "Music influencing another subject," whereas in DDC, 615.837 is an exact placing in the schedules for music therapy.

A further point to remember, in the choice of a scheme,

is that a classification's impact on the positioning of books
and scores on the shelves should not be considered in iso-
lation, for one should contrast this with its effect on the
catalogue's sequence of entries. We have tried to demonstrate this, in part, above. An author (i.e., composer)
catalogue will produce a roughly classified order of titles if
one uses the uniform title approach, as suggested in AACR.
If the argument is accepted that most users are more interested in a composer or a related group of musicians (such
as Les Six) rather than in a particular musical form, etc.,
be it sonata, suite or symphony, then the case for manag-
ing without a subject catalogue has some validity, if not
enough perhaps to persuade most cataloguers (or their
superiors) to adopt such an heretical plan.

   If the author catalogue uses the citation order: com-
poser--form--medium, one can find a different order in LC
subject headings where it is often: form--medium--composer,
or else: medium--composer. Examples of the two types are:
1) Masses (equal voices); Masses (men's voices); Mazurkas
(piano), Mazurkas (string orchestra); and 2) Recorder and
harpsichord music; Recorder and piano music; Quintets (4
accordions, double bass); Quintets (bassoon, clarinet, flute,
horn, oboe); Quintets (clarinet, flute, violin, viola, violoncello). Attention might be drawn here to the fact that the
individual instruments are presented in alphabetical and not
in score or descending pitch order.

   At the risk of considerable oversimplification, it could
be argued that a library classified by either DDC or the LC
scheme and using a dictionary catalogue, will offer three different approaches to scores. On the shelves the arrangement will be: medium--form (assuming that one subdivides
works written or arranged for the same medium)--composer.
Use of the author catalogue would give one, via the uniform
title, an order of composer--form--medium. Finally, the subject catalogue would give the enquirer access by form, divided first by medium and then by composer.

   The student, therefore, needs to consider this chapter
in relation to the preceding one. The long-accepted consideration of the two aspects closely connected (as accepted by
the common British abbreviation "cat and class") is no accident. Decisions reached in the one field can, as suggested
above, affect the other. In the pages that follow, the schemes

are considered in a very approximate chronological order of
the original date of each system. This results in the sequence: Dewey, Library of Congress, McColvin, Dickinson,
British Catalogue of Music and "Phoenix" Dewey class 780.
The schemes of Brown, Cutter, and Bliss have been omitted
from consideration in this edition. There are now no libraries known to the writer which use the first named; all have
been converted to Dewey for compelling reasons. Cutter's
"Expansive" classification is still employed in a handful of
American libraries, but no more than that, while the "Bibliographic" classification of Henry E. Bliss has been revised
to the extent that the music section presents an entirely new
scheme with its roots embedded in BCM so that separate, detailed consideration would be pointless.

Any reader would be well advised, if at all possible,
to have a copy of the appropriate classification scheme to
hand when reading the outline descriptions, comments and
criticisms found in the following pages.

THE DEWEY DECIMAL CLASSIFICATION [53]

The classification of Melvil Dewey is undoubtedly the best
known and most widely used system in the world today, not
least because of its regular revision. Nevertheless, the music section of the schedules can only be regarded as unsatisfactory, both in outline and in difficulties of consistent application. Class 780 in the twelfth edition of 1927 was reprinted, with neither amendment nor development, in both
the thirteenth and fourteenth editions. Alterations made in
the fifteenth (the so-called "Standard") edition of 1951 were
generally badly received and further attempts to adapt the
class to modern needs, made in the sixteenth and seventeenth
editions, seemed only to solve some problems at the cost of
creating fresh ones. Additionally, there were introduced
such oddities (in the sixteenth edition) as a place for counterpoint (781.4) preceding melody (781.41), amended in the
next edition to making 781.4 the place for melody and counterpoint, with the latter subject alone at .42. In the eighteenth edition, melody was again given an individual place
at .41, which had been deleted in the seventeenth edition.

The tables are clearly the better for most of the revisions carried out; nevertheless, these changes only tend

to emphasize the fact that neither Melvil Dewey, despite his many virtues and abilities, nor his successors, seem to have had very much knowledge or appreciation of music.

Music is allotted the places 780 to 789 in the scheme; while this makes it a "fine art," it also sandwiches it (rather unhappily in general opinion) between photography at 770 and recreational and performing arts (formerly "amusements") at 790. Although this may seem unfortunate, one can offer a kind of defence: 770 is the last of a list of arts which exist in space while, it might be claimed, 780 begins a fresh series of arts which exist in time and which can be said to continue (if one is prepared to accept the admittedly dubious argument that recreations such as golf and fishing are also arts) into the literature class of 800. This overlap of main classes exists elsewhere in the scheme, e.g., 550 to 590 continuing into 610, or 690 carrying over into 710 and 720.

Reverting to the music schedules, inspection will show that there is basically a single sequence of placings for books and scores; this is generally held to be a disadvantage for reasons already mentioned in this chapter. From the sixteenth edition onwards, an attempt has been made to provide two parallel sequences for books and scores, usually by the addition of the figure "5" at the end of the literature number for an equivalent score. This modification appears to be a substitution for the former recommendation to affix a capital "M" before the class number if it related to a book, on an "S" in the case of a score. Music librarians may consider the latter a preferable alternative to lengthening the class mark at the tail, when classifying scores. Mary Pearson has carried the suggestion a stage further by showing the connection between the class mark on sound recordings, if these are also classified by Dewey, with those for books and scores: "The procedure is simply a movement of the decimal two points to the left. The number with the decimal one point to the left is for scores, so that they, too, will be related to recordings and books" [176, p. 58]. If one followed this suggestion, a book dealing with the lute would be classed at 787.67, a volume of lute music would be marked 78.767 and a recording of lute solos would be filed at 7.8767. Since music for performance and sound recordings are both almost invariably shelved apart from books and from each other, this modification would cause no difficulties in shelf arrangement and, in the case of printed material, would draw

attention to any book or score that had become misplaced in
the wrong sequence, possibly because of misleading appearance.

After these general remarks, the remainder of this
commentary proceeds through the class, drawing attention to
a number of placings. Number 780 is the general one for
music and is succeeded by 781, "General principles and considerations" (a rather different emphasis from the "Theory
and technique of music" in the sixteenth edition); 782 "Dramatic music and production of musical drama" (simply "Dramatic music" in the sixteenth edition); 783 "Sacred music";
while 784 to 789 are grouped together as "Individual mediums
[sic] of musical expression." The sections in this last group
are 784, "Voice and vocal music" ("Vocal music" in the sixteenth and earlier editions); 785, "Instrumental ensembles
and their music"; 786, "Keyboard instruments and their music"; 787, "String instruments and their music"; 788, "Wind
instruments and their music"; 789, "Percussion, mechanical,
electrical instruments." As the parenthetical comments show,
there has been a widening or clarification of headings first
introduced in the sixteenth edition, to the general advantage
of users.

The casual user of Dewey could well fail to realize how
many minor changes take place in the schedules from one edition to the next, even in apparently virtually static areas of
subject knowledge, and the music schedules offer a number
of examples of these minor readjustments, for better or worse.
For instance, the changes in terminology which have taken
place since the publication of the fourteenth edition in 1942
are well illustrated by 780.07 which, in that obsolete version,
was "Relations of individuals to public bodies"; in the sixteenth and seventeenth editions this symbol became the placing for "Music and society," to be amended again in the
eighteenth edition to "Relation to society." "Analytical and
programme notes," which used to be found in 780.072, were
transferred in the sixteenth and subsequent editions to
780.15. The vacated number was then allotted, in the sixteenth edition, to "Musical criticism and critics"; this was
changed to "Critics and musicologists" in the seventeenth
edition, and left blank in the eighteenth, which would seem
to suggest that books on these musical personalities should
go to 780.07.

One new placing in the eighteenth edition was 780.8 for collections and miniature scores. Miniature pocket scores alone go at 780.84, regardless of medium or kind. The idea of a single grouping, unlike the fourteenth edition's plan of separating them into the appropriate subject areas in the scheme--masses in 783, orchestral scores in 785, and so on --clearly accepts the logic of format, and it is interesting to recall that McColvin did this as far back as 1937. In his case, however, the miniature scores were allocated the very end of the score sequence to form a kind of bridge between music itself and books on the subject. Dewey's choice is less happy, particularly in a classified catalogue, as miniature scores are now widely separated from full-size orchestral, piano, and vocal scores, and will appear, somewhat incongruously, between festivals, competitions, awards (780.79), and music history (780.9).

An example of the type of change of thinking, that may infuriate or bewilder the conscientious cataloguer, is well illustrated by the matter of musical biography. In general, earlier editions of the classification had apparently preferred 927.8 as the most suitable location for lives of musicians. In the sixteenth edition, 780.92 was also provided for criticism and appraisal of works of individual musicians, but this apparently straightforward plan was then complicated by suggesting that biographies should be placed here only if the library classed biography by subject, rather than placing all examples in class 920 and, further, that a subject approach be preferred for "individual musicians working in one medium" and offering, as an example, 787.1081 as the suggested symbol for a book dealing with an individual violinist. Both the seventeenth and eighteenth editions, at 780.9, omit mention of 927.8; instead, the schedules simply show 780.92 musicians. This seems clear enough until one notices, later in the schedules, that 782.092 is also a placing for musicians, with the subheading composers, librettists, performers. 784.092 provides yet another biographical niche for musicians--this time for composers, librettists and lyricists, singers. Further confusing repetition occurs at 785.092 (musicians; composers and conductors) and at 786.1092 (composers and performers). 787.1092 is also shown to be for composers and performers, but here is added a note "including criticism, appraisal." This subsection relating to the violin and its practitioners can be

similarly applied to many other musical instruments. Subject
division of musical biography and appraisal into a number of
different places is very undesirable, in this writer's view.
Certain composers are admittedly concerned with one particular medium or form (obvious examples are Chopin, Verdi and
Wagner); most artists are limited to a single instrument or a
particular type of vocal music, but there are many exceptions.
When one considers composers such as Bach, Beethoven,
Haydn or Mozart, their respective ranges of writing are immense. Current figures such as Bernstein, Boulez and Mes-
siaen refuse to fit neatly into a single musical compartment.

In short, a good case could surely be established for
using 780.92 as the preferred placing for all books dealing
generally with the life and work of an individual musician.
If an attempt be made to separate appraisals from biographies, using 780.92 and 927.8 respectively, there is the uncomfortable fact to be faced that most appreciations have
some biographical detail, and the majority of biographies
find it necessary to make a certain amount of comment on a
composer's music. There is, of course, a practical drawback
to placing biography at 780.92; books here will come between
general musical history (780.9), divided by period, and the
related histories of individual continents, countries and areas
(780.93, etc.). Even in a small collection, the physical separation of these two aspects of music history could be considerable; if one decides that this is unacceptable, it will be
necessary to shelve musical biography slightly out of proper
sequence.

Class 781 deals primarily with musical theory: musical
forms are at 781.5 and there is some unexpected division
here. Sonata is .52, dance music .55, program music .56
and jazz and related forms at .57: it might be suggested
that jazz is more closely related to dance than to programme
music. One other placing in 781 deserves mention; this is
781.971 which is an optional number for bibliographies (hardly an aspect of musical theory!), but the schedules suggest
016.78 as preferable. This is another section of the tables
which has been the subject over the years of minor amendments which do not necessarily improve the final result. In
the sixteenth edition, a thematic catalogue of an individual
composer's works was placed at 781.9735; in the seventeenth,
this became 781.972, a placing still allowed in the eighteenth
edition, but transfer to 016 was recommended. The spine of

the library's copy of Köchel and the catalogue card amendments could bear mute witness to the efforts of the music library staff to keep abreast of these changes from one edition to the next.

The placing of 782.085 for librettos was introduced in the seventeenth edition and is clearly useful, particularly as it adjoins opera analyses (.086). The former subdivision of opera books and scores into such categories as "Epic, Wagnerian and other German" and the like has disappeared in recent editions: all are now at 782.1. At least, this appears to have been the intention, but it seems to be more confusing than helpful to indicate that comic opera should be classified here, and then, on the opposite page (under 782.8 Theater music) to have a placing for musical shows, operettas, musical comedies, revues. The dividing line between comic opera and operetta is far from clearcut; however, since the borderline between grand and light opera is equally vague at times, it would seem that there is no unequivocal answer in the Dewey classification to this problem of overlapping types.

Musical shows (782.81) are immediately succeeded, in the schedules, by cantatas and oratorios, which is a sudden transition indeed. It is made clear that these last works are all of the secular type; sacred works are classed in 783. Incidental dramatic music (another unexpected leap in subject) is at 782.83, to be succeeded in turn by places for film, radio and television music. 782.9 is for "Other forms of dramatic music," with ballet as the sole subdivision. Overall, the arrangement seems to be more than a trifle erratic and a reordering of topics might be desirable, albeit at further cost perhaps to the mental equilibrium of cataloguers and of catalogue entries and the spines of the scores involved.

From the sixteenth edition onwards, sacred music (783) makes provision for nonChristian religions, although one would not expect to find much material in an occidental library except possibly for Jewish religious music. As has already been noted, 783 to 789 has the omnibus heading "Individual mediums of musical expression"; it includes a "table of precedence" to help the user of the classification scheme when faced with that common situation of placing a score with what is called a composite subject approach. The

schedules quote, as an example, duets for flute and violin
and indicate that these should be classed at 785.7271, i.e.,
not under either individual instrument but with chamber music (785.72 duets) with the added subdivision (... 71) for
violin, since stringed instruments come before wind instruments in the table of precedence.

In 784, voice and vocal music, the long-standing confusion between 784.4 and 784.7 is still not clearly resolved.
784.4 is for folk songs, and 784.7 (other kinds of song)
includes national airs, songs, hymns. Differentiation between these categories is often far from easy, and a note
preferring one or the other in case of difficulty might help
the classifier. If a librarian decides to ignore one of the
two places, this should be noted in the classifier's authority
file. The conflation of songs for students and those for
children in 784.62 raises a smile; in Britain, at least, these
are two very different categories of works.

When considering the placings in 785, one can see
both advantages and the reverse in the different editions.
The provision of locations (in the seventeenth edition) for
jazz, and the separation of jazz orchestra (.0667) and jazz
band (.0672) presents a nice problem in semantics, made
even odder by the placing between these two numbers of
books on bands in general as well as for brass and military
ensembles of this type, together with any books that the
library might have on the esoteric art (in British eyes) of
the drum major.

The main headings and divisions that comprise 785.1
to 785.8 remain confusing, with a lack of official guidance to
help the classifier to make the correct decisions. For example, 785.34 is for "Variations and other large works," without any annotation to show what sort of large works the
scheme is designed to accept at this point. 785.4 is allotted
to "Music for small ensembles"; again, there is no clue as to
what is meant by small. The necessarily arbitrary decision
may well baffle the classifier without much musical knowledge
--and even experts are unlikely to agree as to the minimum
and maximum numbers involved. This same section of tables
contains music "for rhythm and percussion bands" whose size
may vary from a handful of performers to the pupils of an
entire school. Chamber music still intrudes between concertos and orchestral suites, while jazz scores seem equally

ill at ease fitted between miscellaneous orchestral music and
independent overtures. "Independent" in that context is
yet another unexplained word, but the intention is presumably that this is the placing for concert overtures (i.e.,
works that are self-contained and which have no opera or
other work to follow; one might offer Sullivan's Di ballo or
Ives's Robert Browning overtures as examples) and also for
operatic overtures which are both published and often performed separately (such as Rossini's Guillaume Tell or Verdi's
La forza del destino), possibly with the provision of a concert ending when, in the original score, the overture runs
directly into the opening scene without a break. Die Meistersinger is an example of a work for which the composer
made provision for performance of the overture on its own,
since Wagner wrote an alternative few bars of music to allow
the work to come to a full stop.

From 786 to 789, which deal with individual instruments,
there is now provision (as is also allowed in 782 to 785) for
using separate but related class marks for books and scores,
if desired. Additionally, in piano music--an area where
there is likely to be a large proportion of the stock in a
general music collection--there is obvious merit in making it
possible for further subdivision, even though many music
librarians would argue that a better arrangement is to place
all keyboard music in a single sequence by composer, then
subdividing by form if thought desirable. If one should follow the schedules and arrange piano music by category, the
suggested subdivisions do not seem to be mutually exclusive.
786.43, "Romantic and descriptive music," could well conflict
with 786.42, "Rhapsodies and arabesques." The same symbol is provided for fugues, whose usual formal precision
makes them surprising companions to rhapsodies, with their
structural freedom. To use the same class mark for both
ballroom and jazz music for the piano seems liable to invoke
ridicule or annoyance, and to locate these works (786.46)
between "Dances" (a place which itself contains such ill-
assorted companions as gavottes and square dances) and
"Artistic études" (whatever they may be) is again not a sequence of musical subjects likely to command general approval. However, duets and two-piano works are now duly
separated in the schedules.

Organ music (786.8) retains its old faults. 786.82
contains fugues, preludes and fugues and toccatas, whereas

preludes alone go in 786.83 and there is still no specific
placing for chorale preludes, a form that is extremely well
represented in the organ repertory. In passing, only keyboard and organ among individual instruments have separate
subdivisions for scores in the schedules, although an allow-
able minor breakdown of scores to a standard pattern is
quoted for other instruments.

Electronic organ has its own placing at 786.92, and
the tables make it clear that music for this instrument is to
be classified at 786.8, which is sensible for there are many
scores which can be played satisfactorily on either the pipe
or the electronic type of organ, despite the very different
methods they have of producing sounds.

One matter that has been touched upon earlier needs
slightly fuller comment. The classifier has a problem with
music written for two instruments. Should a sonata for
violin and piano be classed in 787.1542 (solo, accompanied)
or in 785.7271 (duets)? With Beethoven's Spring sonata the
latter number is clearly correct, but the decision may be
difficult, particularly for the classifier with little musical
knowledge. In case of doubt, 787.1542 is probably better;
indeed, the small collection may make no use whatsoever of
785.7271, as cross-classification would be most difficult to
avoid if both placings were accepted. The same problem is
also met with other combinations of instruments.

The remainder of the class needs little comment. 788
(wind) illustrates a poor allocation of notation which accordingly provides an odd sequence of topics. 788.01 is for
brass in general, .05 for woodwind, but specific brass instruments are between 788.1 and 788.4, and individual woodwind between 788.5 and 788.9. Among the latter group is
found 788.53 as a blanket number for recorder and flageolet;
this could usefully have been subdivided to take into account
the many published items for specific members of the popular
recorder family. 789.9, electronic instruments, has been
further expanded in the latest edition to make provision for
the steadily increasing number of published discographies
(which are not necessarily critical, as the annotation at this
point in the schedules would seem to imply), although the
preferred placing for these works in 016.789912, since this
would align them with other musical bibliographies, thematic
catalogues, etc.

In the foregoing pages, attention has been drawn to some of the apparent anomalies and practical difficulties met with in using the scheme, particularly for those with a limited knowledge of music. The eighteenth edition certainly shows many improvements on the twelfth to fourteenth editions, which had a long currency in many libraries (particularly where the fifteenth, and sometimes the sixteenth were ignored), but it also underlines the fact that nothing less than a complete recasting of class 780 will bring it into line with modern ideas and needs.

For British librarians, the difficulties of classifying scores are the more noticeable since BNB has been applying to books a standard, authoritative Dewey number since 1971. One may not always agree with the placings, but there is sometimes room for a difference of opinion as to the right class even between members of the same cataloguing staff. In contrast, there was no similar guidance for scores before 1982 (when "Phoenix" Dewey was included with entries); an individual classifier had to work independently.

All libraries using DDC face a second handicap. Scores do not become outdated or obsolete at anything like the same rate as do books. Even the hard wear of frequent borrowing is usually limited to the more popular items of stock. This fact is likely to result in considerable difficulties whenever a new edition of Dewey is produced. Many librarians are likely to continue with the edition already in use, simply because of the labour involved in reclassifying and amending the class marks on the spines of books and scores and on catalogue entries. One may introduce the new schedules from a specified date, but it is likely to be a very long time before the older section of the stock becomes so attenuated in numbers that the volumes that are left can be given corrected class numbers as a spare time occupation that will not take long to complete. What often happens is that certain selected numbers from the new schedules are extracted for use, because of their obvious value--but they can also result in a hotch-potch of a scheme that becomes increasingly difficult to apply with consistency and assurance.

It has already been mentioned in this chapter that a "phoenix" schedule has been prepared, produced by the Working Party of Music, Dewey Decimal Classification sub-committee of the Library Association. It is radically different

from the section it is designed to replace, but one hopes
that it will receive a full and fair appraisal by music librarians everywhere, even though it may take a little while
for the initial shock waves to subside when one studies what
is proposed. Without such a drastic rethinking, Dewey's
music schedules seem unlikely to find even the resigned acceptance that appears to have been their lot during the first
century of the scheme.

At the beginning of this section devoted to DDC, we
remarked upon the lack of alteration to the music schedules
in the thirteenth and fourteenth editions of the scheme.
History has almost repeated itself in the nineteenth edition
of 1979, for there are no more than a handful of amendments
(none of major importance) compared with the 780 schedules
of the eighteenth edition. (One can hope with increased
confidence that the absence of revision presages the arrival
of the long-awaited "phoenix" schedule in the twentieth edition.) The changes that have occurred might be briefly
considered under five headings. First, there are the amendments necessary because of changes in the standard subdivisions. Particular note here should be taken of "08" which
is no longer used for collections. As a result, writings on
music in groupings of anthologies and the like have been
transferred from 780.8 to the general placing of 780. 780.8
is now reserved for collections of scores and parts. Another
addition adopted generally throughout the scheme is the
chronological one of -905, and so provides a location for
music of the twenty-first century at 780.905.

Expansion of the tables occurs at a few points, such
as 784.12 Madrigals (a new subdivision of choruses and part
songs); country, rock, blues and soul music are listed aspects of popular music under 784.5, itself a new class entirely which gathers together material previously scattered
in the region of 784, notably in 784.3, .4, .75 and .76. At
787.67 is a placing for lute "(including sitar)" which may
cause some surprise. Admittedly, the sitar has made its
way into western music, particularly with pop groups, but
one would not expect its repertory to overlap that of the
lute in the great majority of cases, and separate subdivisions would seem desirable. Places are now found in the
schedules for dulcimer (787.94) and bagpipe (788.92). The
latter number accommodates all members of this family.

Electronic music, previously included in an unspecified part of 789.9 is now at 789.99--a possible indication that the compilers regard this as the ultimate in music? The current edition also permits subdivision of 789.912 (recordings) by the rest of 78--so that, for example, recordings of folk songs would be found at 789.91244. The last two digits have been derived from 784.4, folk songs, with the "78" deleted.

There would seem to be but a single relocation, that for Negro spirituals; these were to be found in 784.756 but now appear at 783.67. This means that spirituals are now considered to be sacred songs. In general, there has been some tidying up of the schedules, mainly by better presentation of the "Add ..." instructions.

Two final points. First, the introduction of -079 Competitions and awards in the eighteenth edition was a subdivision not specifically related to music, but could be added in the appropriate places if required. In the nineteenth edition, "Festivals, competitions and awards" is often shown in the schedules and is another example (as are biographies of musicians) of a refinement that may be regarded with mixed feelings. The smaller library could well restrict itself to a single placing, whereas the larger collection might consider it helpful to separate instrumental, vocal, and choral festivals. One may well wonder, however, what literary warrant there is for books on festivals of choral music, bagpipe music, etc. In Britain, the answer seems to be very little. Since 1971, BNB has recorded virtually nothing apart from a handful of books on pop festivals which appeared in the early 1970s. These were classed in the "general special" subdivision at 780.42; as -042 counts as a standard subdivision, it is impossible to add -079 to the end of the symbol, since editor's rules forbid the adding of one standard subdivision to another. In passing, most material of British pop festivals since the appearance of the Stevenson Report of 1973 has been mainly sociological in scope and approach, and is classed accordingly in 301.57.

At least, this new, extended meaning of -079 is intelligible, but one wonders what is now meant by -08, "History and description of the specific instrument and its music or groups of instruments and their music among groups of persons."

THE LIBRARY OF CONGRESS
MUSIC CLASSIFICATION [220]

The importance of the LC scheme of music classification is
generally accepted, but there seems to be little detailed description or criticism of it in British professional literature,
possibly because so few libraries in the country use it.
There have been attempts to provide simplified versions of
the music schedules, of which more below; in contrast, the
Music Division of LC has found the tables insufficiently detailed in a number of places and has introduced new subdivisions which do not appear in the published version.

    The first edition of the music scheme (one of the earli-
est LC classes to be published) appeared in 1904 and the
second in 1917. That remained current for over sixty years,
but a quick glance at any reprint produced during that period should suffice to bring to notice that the volume is in
two parts, the second bound in as an appendix to the first.
For instance, in the 1968 reprint, the "Subsequent additions
and changes to July 1967" needs a further forty-two pages,
plus twelve more of double-column index. This supplement
is numbered to page 113, but is printed on the recto only,
leaving the back of each sheet blank, which accounts for
the apparent discrepancy in the pagination. The librarian
was then faced with a choice between hours of scissors-and-
paste drudgery, tipping in the additions and amendments at
the appropriate places in the main body of the text (as the
printing on one side only of each page suggests was the intention) or else looking in two places every time that every-
thing that needed more than a moment's thought was classified.

    A third edition appeared in 1978; it amalgamates the
earlier text, revisions and new placings up to June 1977.
One wonders if this volume is published as an interim measure, for the printed tables of the second edition have been
superseded by a photocopied typescript that is much more
difficult to use because of its lack of clarity. Even the tables themselves seem to have received very little revision,
although the index has been expanded. Comments on the
classification schedules appear a little later in this chapter
(p. 231) and are based on the second, not the third edition.

    A condensed or simplified version may have much to
commend it for the smaller collections. O. G. Sonneck him-

self who, as Chief of the Music Division, devised the classification, thought (in his "Prefatory note" on p. 6 of the
published work) that, "A classifier of fair talent and skill
could without much difficulty 'telescope' our scheme into a
suitable instrument for any collection of any size, by can-
celing unnecessary subdivisions, by substituting subdivisions for his special purposes, and rearranging at his convenience the sequence of certain entries." Presumably,
such "telescoping" would need to be done on an ad hoc
basis, crossing out each and every classmark that the classifier thought to be unnecessary. Because the structure of
the LC scheme is not hierarchical, one cannot satisfactorily
adopt (as is easily possible with DDC) a "rule of thumb"
method or ruling that no symbol shall exceed a certain length
of, say, two figures after the decimal point, in Dewey, or
that common subdivisions will be ignored.

A possible simplification for a very small collection,
perhaps, would be to use the abbreviated form given on pp.
12-13 of the LC Outline (3rd edition, 1975) which gives
thirty-nine groups of numbers, making no mention of certain
"odd" ones such as M1490 and M5000, but providing enough
detail for the basic collection to be satisfactorily arranged;
the classifier would use, perhaps, just the first number
given for a group, e.g., the outline shows M2102-2114
"Songs for one voice." A library using this as a basis
would simply class all solo songs at M2102, and use the
other numbers up to 2114, as required, should the collection expand in this area.

In contrast, a condensation of the M Classification,
prepared by Betsy Rovelstad [187], and quoted by LaMon-
tagne [115] appears to have been so curtailed as to bear
virtually no resemblance to LC at all. We are reminded of
attempts to portray the appearance of some prehistoric mon-
ster with no more than two or three skeletal bones as a
foundation.

As with other classes of the LC scheme, the music
classifications are published as a group in a single volume
with a combined index to the three nominally separate classes. According to Sonneck's prefatory note on p. 3, the
scheme was originally devised when the collection numbered
in all about 386,000 items; it is now many times that figure.
When the second edition of class M was published, Sonneck

also declared in his second "Prefatory note" (p. 6) that,
"... I have reached the conclusion that in the interest of
all concerned it would have been better to have formed a
separate group of 'early' music and books on music." Just
where he considered "early music" to end is not stated.
According to the definition of "early music" on p. 11 of the
publication, 1800 is the dividing line (which may have been
influenced by the fact that the British Museum had chosen
that date as its musical watershed); on the other hand,
M1490 (mentioned again when we work through the schedules) takes 1700 as its limit.

The three classification sequences are M, music
scores; ML, literature of music; and MT, musical instruction
and theory. Class M is divided into four major groups. M1
to M4 are allotted to collections (in the broadest sense); M5
to M1459 is for instrumental music, characterized by size,
proceeding from solo instruments to nonets, with orchestral
music beginning at M1000. The order of instruments in the
instrumental section is keyboard, string, wind, plectral, percussion and this plan is followed for chamber music groups.

M1490, as has already been mentioned, is a special
placing, the use of which is optional, for all instrumental or
vocal music, printed or manuscript, before 1700. The suggested ordering of topics is by composer and not by form or
medium; the reason for this recommendation, one assumes, is
partly bibliographical and partly to take into account that
period when the old modes were being replaced by the key
system that was to remain virtually unchallenged for over
two centuries. In fact, early music (as Sonneck clearly saw)
is a major problem in the very large collection which owns
much material. For the small and medium-sized public or
college library, this choice is unlikely to cause much concern,
simply because most of the stock is likely to relate to post-
1700 items while music written earlier will normally be provided in good modern editions.

Vocal music runs from M1495 to M2199 (and one notices
that the major divisions simply follow on: they do not start
with a number such as M1500, to take this particular section).
Secular music is allotted M1497 to M1998, and sacred music
from M1999 to M2199.

Looking at some aspects of class M again in greater

detail, we notice that it starts with places for general collections, otherwise unclassifiable, and M3 for the collected
works of individual composers. Single works, or works of a
particular form for a single instrument, are classified in the
places that follow. M5 is the first number for instrumental
music (miscellaneous and heterogeneous collections), and the
individual instruments are then treated individually in turn,
starting with organ music at M6. M7 to M13 are subdivisions
of M6; thus M7 is for collections of organ music, M8 for
sonatas and sonatinas, M9 for suites and kindred cyclical
works, M10 for fugues (with or without pedals), while M12
and M13 are for arrangements for organ, collections using
the former number, single works the latter. A set of Handel organ concertos, arranged for organ solo, would be
classed at M12, but a single concerto from the set would be
at M13. M14 is the place for organ accompaniments to hymns
and psalms.

The harmonium provides the link between organ and
piano music, the latter being allotted the numbers M20 to
M39.5, and this music again is generally arranged by type.
M35 is the place for arrangements of orchestral music, and
M37 for concertos, arranged for a single performer. Pianoforte duets, it should be noted, do not come into this section, but are to be found in M200 with works for two instruments.

After keyboard instruments, the schedule continues
with stringed instruments, and the general subdivisions are
the same in each case. Five numbers are usually allotted,
providing places for miscellaneous collections, collections of
original works, single works written for the instrument, collections of arrangements, and arrangements of single works.
String instruments are followed in turn by wind, plectral
instruments and percussion and other instruments. The last
begins, surprisingly enough, with bagpipe and includes "Pi-
anola and kindred instruments," amended in the appendix to
"Player piano rolls."

Duos begin at M180, but other combinations are mnemonic, with trios having places from M300 onwards, quartets
from M400, and so to nonets at M900.

M1000 (itself for miscellaneous collections) begins a
fresh section, for orchestral music. M1001 is for symphonies,

M1002 for symphonic poems, M1003 for suites, partitas, theme
and variations, with M1004 for overtures and entr'actes.
From M1005 onwards are places for concertos, arranged according to the solo instrument, beginning with organ and
maintaining the same order as at the beginning of the class.
In each case, two numbers are provided; one is for full
score, the second for scores in which the orchestral score
has been arranged for pianoforte, so that the work can be
performed by a soloist together with a pianist who plays an
approximation to the orchestral parts. A full or miniature
score of Mozart's clarinet concerto would be classed at M1024,
and the same work arranged for solo clarinet and piano
would be at M1025. M1045 and subsequent numbers are for
orchestral pieces such as marches, potpourris and arrangements for orchestra. M1100 onwards is for music for string
orchestra, M1200 for (military) band (with numbers analogous
to those following M1000), and M1350 onwards for "reduced
orchestra" and juvenile instrumental music. These divisions
alone show something of the care and detail with which the
schedules have been made.

Vocal music begins at M1495, the placing for miscellaneous collections of both sacred and secular types. The latter is then classified according to the genus of composition,
beginning with operas, a term which is used embracingly to
include "serious, comic, operettas" and the like, so that the
problem of deciding into which category of opera an individual
work falls is avoided. On the other hand, the use of M1520
for "pantomimes, ballets, masques, pageants, etc." seems a
little uncomfortable, particularly for those ballets which are
independent works and have no connection with any opera.
Secondary division is by the combination for which the work
is written, e.g., men's voices, women's voices, and is further
subdivided to allow for the number of parts, e.g., duets,
solo and chorus, for which the work being classed is written.
Specific places are provided in the schedules for works to be
performed without accompaniment. From M1611 onwards songs
are classified. Here, special places are allotted for songs
with lute accompaniment, concertina accompaniment and the
like, but the general subdivisions are unexpectedly meagre.
This section is succeeded (from M1627 onwards) by one for
folk and other national songs. One is not surprised at the
very detailed classification for songs of the USA, with broader divisions for songs of other countries. "Society songs"
is the next heading (M1900 onwards), and is very minutely

divided indeed; it is primarily of American interest. The
number of listed bodies shows a tremendous expansion in the
appendix compared with those printed in the main schedules,
and we are surprised at the number of groups who have produced music related to their particular ideas and beliefs. So
we find M1920.A35 Alcoholics Anonymous; M1920.C6 Corned
Beef and Cabbage Club of America; M1920.S54 Society for
the Preservation and Encouragement of Barber Shop Singing
in America. It will be noted that the arrangement is alphabetical, and not all classificationists approve of LC's habit
of providing class numbers for proper names. The section
concludes with places for students' songs (M1940-1973) and
juvenile songs (M1990 to M1998).

       The next field covered is that of church music, at
M1999. M2000 to 2017 provides places for masses, requiems,
etc. These are succeeded by anthems, which are divided by
types of voices and also by the Church seasons of the year.
There are special subdivisions for such items as Creed, Nunc
dimittis, and a separate place for motets that are difficult to
classify elsewhere. Foreign hymnals are divided by country,
regardless of denomination, but (as is natural) American
hymnbooks are divided closely by sect. The section then
provides places for church music, liturgy and ritual. Roman
Catholic church music of this type is allocated M2150 to 2155,
with subdivisions, and Protestant churches have provision
made, such as M2164, Dutch and other reformed; M2166-3,
Scottish Episcopal church; M2166, Irish church and Church
of England. There are places for what might be called topi-
cal or utilitarian church music (gospel hymns, religious bodies with particular functions, etc.) which are analogous to
the secular society songs. These special interests are allotted the places M2198 (for collections) and 2199 (for single
works). Class M is completed with M5000, which includes
"unidentifiable" works (chiefly fragments) which may be instrumental or vocal, sacred or secular. It is not, however,
the place for anonymous works, which are classified in the
normal manner, and if necessary, entered under title.

       Before describing the other two sections, some com-
ments on class M may be helpful. First, it can be seen that
(except for the collected works of a composer, which are
classified together as a set in M3, and not broken up) the
general scheme of division is first by medium, and then by
form. Whatever criticism one might make, it must always be

tempered by the fact that the scheme was devised to deal
with the scores already held in the Library of Congress (and
the preface does not indicate any second thoughts of the "If
I had but known ..." type), and was intended primarily for
internal use rather than by other libraries. In the music library of all but the largest cities, we feel that (to quote an
example) Bach's organ works are better classed together
rather than spread over eight different places, as is possible in LC. The composition student might find the divisions
by form of use, but interest is normally first by composer,
with form as secondary interest only. The argument against
this is that having chosen this arrangement a better view of
what is available can be given if the works are divided by
form, remembering that each section is divided alphabetically
by composer. In LC, the person primarily interested in
Bach's organ works can be given the complete works, while
single items are classified according to form. Edward N.
Waters, former Chief of the Music Division of the Library
of Congress, has categorically declared in a personal letter:
"I do not believe that we neglect the interest of readers
seeking music by composer" [228a].

Against criticism of these form divisions, one should
balance pronounced approval for the provision of separate
numbers for original works and those which have been arranged for an instrument, or combination of instruments;
M12 and M13 (mentioned earlier) are examples of such numbers. At first sight, this has the compensating disadvantage of separating similar works of a composer. Dvořák's
Humoreskes would be in M24 (pieces); a copy of the most
famous of all the Humoreskes (no. 7 of this opus 101 set of
eight) would, on the face of it, be classed at M31 (two-
rhythm), although LC itself would apparently class it as
M25 as it is a single item from a set of pieces. An arrangement of the New World Symphony for solo piano would be at
M35. This last place has proved useful, particularly as such
arrangements are usually made by a musician other than the
original composer. A personal preference would be to place
all original works and arrangements under the composer, and
then subdivide by form, etc., with a separate number for
arrangements. This even wider separation, in LC, of piano
solos from piano duets is logical, but unattractive. It is
also surprising that separate numbers are not allotted for
the different keyboard instruments, such as virginals (which
does not even appear in the index), clavichord, etc., as

much early music was written for one or other precursor of
the modern pianoforte, and many musicians consider that
such pieces sound better when played on the instrument for
which they were written, though this is a matter of taste.
The difficulty here is that there is often no certainty, when
two or three different keyboard instruments were in vogue
at the same time, as to which one was favoured by a composer for a particular piece of music or set of pieces. Such
would be the case with the Bach 48 preludes and fugues.
On the credit side, LC includes a placing (M26) for pieces
for piano left hand alone, which is something missing in
Dewey; moreover, this number is easily discovered via the
LC index, which is an aid that BCM does not provide. It
will be apparent that a non-American library using this
scheme would ignore the subdivisions in a number of places,
where these are peculiar to the USA, and incorporate national subdivisions for its own use. This is a difficulty that
should be easily surmounted.

Though many people tend to regard Classes M, ML,
and MT, as a single class, this is not really true; they are
three selfcontained and semi-independent classes. ML, the
literature of music, includes such items as periodicals, al-
manacs, societies, institutions, programmes, libretti, etc.
It also includes such special topics as musical prodigies
(ML81) and women and music (ML82). Libraries that collect the writings of musicians--manuscripts, autographs and
facsimiles, etc., find the scheme provides a place for these
at ML90. The numbers ML100 to ML110 are given to dictionaries and encyclopaedias; ML111 to ML158 are for bibliography, while ML159 to ML3795 are normally divided by country,
and there is a special, detailed subdivision for Wagner at
ML410 which illustrates, yet again, how the scheme was built
round the stock held rather than in accordance with any
abstract theory. A footnote in the tables at this point suggests that a similarly detailed scheme could be used "in other
exceptional cases ... with the necessary variations." Since
Wagner wrote little non-operatic music, it seems certain that
an entirely different scheme of subdivision would be needed
for any other major composer. Places are provided for books
on orchestral, chamber and vocal music. ML3800 to ML3920
are for subjects dealing with the philosophy and physics of
music, and finally at ML3925 is an extremely useful place for
fiction. There are quite a number of novels that deal sufficiently with musical subjects to be of interest to music lovers.

The final schedule, MT--musical instruction and theory
--should be self-explanatory. It takes in all aspects of pedagogy, including such subjects as harmony and counterpoint,
orchestration, and teaching methods for various instruments.
These last are generally divided into four groups--general
observations, systems and methods, studies and exercises
and self instructors. The inclusion of the third heading
means that purely educative works as well as those composed
particularly to illustrate and exploit technical difficulties
(such as Bartók's Mikrokosmos and Liszt's Etudes d'exécution
transcendante) are to be found here, rather than (as would
be expected) in the section of solo piano works in class M.
The Liszt concert studies are often heard in recitals; they
are also completely outside the technical abilities of the great
majority of amateur pianists, so that the MT placing seems
somewhat unreal. This difficulty of deciding whether the
accent should be on "concert" or on "studies" is met, in LC
itself, by classing some copies in class M and others in MT,
a practical if inconsistent answer.

The Library of Congress scheme has been dealt with
at length because it is used with what is probably the largest collection of music in the world. The greatest proof of
its quality is the simple fact that Sonneck's scheme still
seems to meet with the general approval of those who work
with it, despite the immense increase in the size of the collection since the classification was originally devised.

THE McCOLVIN SCHEME

Because of what he considered to be major deficiencies in
Dewey's 780 class, Lionel McColvin decided to prepare a
scheme of his own, using a decimal notation which could be
adopted by a library classified by Dewey without causing
many problems. McColvin simply scrapped the DDC music
schedules and replaced them with others which used the same
numerical basis of 780 to 789. The scheme was first published in his Music in Public Libraries (1924) and slightly
modified on its second appearance in Music Libraries (1937)
[129]. One can only regret that a busy working life did not
give him the opportunity to make further modifications in the
light of experience after World War II, by which time some of
the scheme's weaknesses must have been clearly apparent.
One might instance the tremendous growth of interest in

recorder playing in schools which, in turn, has resulted in a veritable spate of music--original sixteenth century and later, modern arrangements of Elizabethan lute and other instrumental music, as well as works written by twentieth century composers in response to this considerable demand. McColvin's scheme has no separate place for recorder, yet the repertory is now large enough to make desirable individual placings for the various members--descant, treble, etc.

McColvin was convinced of the need for separate sequences of placings for books and for scores. He allots 783 to 789 for the former and 780 to 782 for the latter, a noteworthy contrast to the British Catalogue of Music scheme which uses only classes A and B (in an alphabetical sequence of 24 letters) for books, allocating classes C to Z for scores. McColvin's second tenet was that subarrangement should be for the benefit of the performer rather than the listener; clearly, however, his belief that "it is sufficient, for example, to bring together all the music for piano solo; to divide it further by form is unnecessary, confusing and often impracticable," conflicts with the views of some other classification makers. The third point is that his scheme claims to be in evolutionary order, beginning with vocal music, proceeding to instrumental and ending with orchestral items. A similar principle is followed for music literature, but there is the necessary introductory section for general books, histories and biographies and the like.

Vocal music, at 780, makes provision for collections of special types of song such as shanties, music hall songs, excerpts from operas and from oratorios, and then works through duets, trios and groups of larger size to choral items. All this material is secular. Religious music (780.5 and 780.6) is divided by form, with a place provided for music of non-Christian religions. Then comes opera at 780.7 (arranged in composer order) and musical comedies and light opera at 780.8--but here the arrangement is by title. This solves the problem of shelving a work such as Kismet, in which the Borodin melodies have been reworked by a much later composer, but presents difficulties with works such as the younger Johann Strauss's Die Fledermaus which has also been published as The Bat, Gay Rosalinda and possibly other titles as well.

Instrumental music is treated in the following order: wind, plucked string, bowed string, keyboard (which includes organ, rather than counting the instrument as a wind one), and "other," mainly percussion. Chamber music is usefully listed in two parallel sequences, one for string music and the other for piano and strings, for trios, quartets and quintets. For sextets upwards there is a single placing, and 782.6 is provided for wind music or works including wind. Again, this suggests inadequate division for the larger music collection. There are individual numbers for military and for brass bands, followed by 782.89, "other instrumental music." This last number quotes dance band music as an example of works to be classified at this placing, and the compiler envisages that both commercial dance music and jazz will be found here, which is both inadequate and wrong-headed. A separate and single place for all miniature scores was probably unique when McColvin provided it, but it is an idea that has subsequently been copied by other schemes. The user is given the choice between 782.77 (a placing that follows immediately after full scores and orchestral parts) or 782.99, at the end of the sequence of scores and immediately preceding, in terms of notation, the books on music.

Provision for encyclopaedias, periodicals, societies, musical theory and such general topics in 783 seems reasonably adequate and well founded. From 784 onwards, the scheme generally follows the same sequence as for scores, with necessary additional places for such topics as the manufacture of instruments. Because of these additional items, and McColvin's unwillingness to extend the length of the notation, the numbers for scores and books do not match up in a manner helpful to users; thus, scores for double bass are found at 781.37, while a book on the instrument is not at 785.37 but at 785.58. Aesthetics and appreciation are placed in 787, history and criticism in 788, and biography and miscellaneous topics in 789.

The author describes his schedules as "a simple scheme suitable for the average public library," and this would seem to be a fair appraisal of it. Maureen Long's Musicians and Libraries in the United Kingdom reported that 9 percent of the municipal libraries covered by the survey used McColvin, compared with 86 percent classed by Dewey; in county libraries the respective figures were 10 percent and 82 percent.

The biggest and most important user of the scheme was the Central Music Library in Westminster, where it seems the scheme was found lacking in detailed subdivision in some sections; further subdivision would have been welcome [125, p. 37]. Because of the unsatisfactory nature of DDC until its music class is completely revised, libraries with medium-sized collections could well find McColvin's alternative tables attractive and practical.

THE DICKINSON CLASSIFICATION

George Sherman Dickinson was the first music librarian at Vassar College, Poughkeepsie, N.Y., from 1927 to 1953. During this period, he formulated his own scheme of classification for music scores, using the large stock he administered as his working material. The College published his schedules in 1938; a mere 300 copies were printed and these were only made available to enquirers upon request--the compiler made no attempt to publicize his scheme. A copy of the schedules was acquired by Richard Angell soon after publication. At that time, he was music librarian at Columbia University, New York City; he adapted the Dickinson schedules for use in his library. In this amended form it has become known as the "Vassar-Columbia" and, as both the original and the variant schemes are used in different libraries in New York State and elsewhere, the student may well become a trifle confused. The amended tables were published by the Trustees of Columbia University in 1955. This version is not discussed further in these pages; consideration here is limited to the original which has been made generally available by Carol June Bradley [22]. The publication is in facsimile typescript, with a photographic reprint of the 1938 original and a commentary. The necessary explanations and guide for potential users that Dickinson did not supply are provided by Bradley.

The scheme warrants consideration in this chapter, partly because (like the Library of Congress class M classification) it is based on an actual collection of material--albeit with the intention that it would be suitable for any library of scores (but not, one must always remember, of books)-- and also because this is one of the schemes with which the Music Library Association expects the good music librarian to be familiar (see p. 53).

Dickinson offered a choice of approach, to be selected according to the type of library using the scheme; he envisaged three main ones, respectively designated as "loan and performance music libraries," "reference and musicological libraries," and "general or small libraries." However, once a choice has been made between the options available, that decision must be maintained with all future additions to stock. If the librarian later considered that one of the other approaches would be better for the collection concerned, then complete reclassification would have to be undertaken.

It would seem that American libraries which have adopted Dickinson have generally chosen the reference and musicological option, and Carol Bradley's guide is based on this approach. The survey here, therefore, is from this same angle.

If one adopts the approach that the original medium is the most important factor (an idea which is completely contrary to the standard approach of classifying according to the medium of the copy in hand, but one which Dickinson implies is that likely to be chosen by the musicologist, although we would have thought a chronological method to be more valid), the BCM method, to take an obvious contrast, is reversed. In the latter, one classifies any arrangement with a "K" to show the instrumentation of the original; Dickinson's scheme takes the opposite approach in this musicological option. "This rule is sometimes relaxed to allow major works as rearranged by their composers to class in the arranged form, especially when the arrangement is the better known and more frequently consulted form" [22]. Thus, for example, Dvořák's Slavonic Dances would be classed as orchestral works rather than piano duets, the form in which the composer originally wrote them.

A decimal base is used, and the main divisions are these:

0   Miscellaneous (collected works; manuscripts; methods; historical materials)

1   Keyboard

2   Bowed strings

3 Winds

4 Plucked strings/percussion/mechanical

5 Chamber ensembles

6 Orchestra

7 Vocal solo and solo ensembles

8 Choral ensembles

9 Dramatic; opera, action pictures, ballet

The ordering of the classes deserves at least a moment's consideration. Bradley argues that "The arithmetic sequence progresses in a musically-logical fashion from solo keyboard to opera, the largest musical form." It must be emphasised yet again that the tables are concerned solely with scores and make no provision whatsoever for music literature. "The most salient characteristic of the notation is mnemonic quality. A call number should be easily 'read' by interpretation of the factors which comprise it. It should with equal ease be 'composed' from the same factors." This mnemonic background may be easily illustrated (if one refers to the main divisions quoted above) by stating that class 52 is for string chamber music, 53 for wind chamber music, etc.

With the musicological option, the "average call number consists of four lines, five when the call number is preceded by M to relate it to the total library classification scheme." With a four-line symbol, the top one consists of the division number, i.e., the original medium of the work. The second line represents the composer's name, quoted in Cutter form (and not in the more usual Sanborn revision). The third line describes the piece in hand, and can be formed from one or other of a variety of features, e.g., "a species title indication, such as 'ov' for overtures; the first letter of the title, if distinctive; an opus number or thematic catalogue number." Where it is possible to allot more than one of these items, the preferred order is that displayed in the quotation. The fourth line provides for the initial letter of the editor's or publisher's name. Again, the former should be used if known; whatever problems that might present, there should be no difficulty with the publisher's name. One minor point to be made here is that the letter "O" is never used alone because of the possible ambiguity that could result; an effect of this practice is that a work pub-

lished by the Oxford University Press would be abbreviated
as "Ox." To show the overall appearance of a call number,
the following example is taken from p. 39:

M	[optional]
52	string chamber music
B39-4	Beethoven, cutter number, 4 players
(18/1)	opus 18, no. 1
B	Breitkopf & Härtel edition

The optional first line can be ignored; below that the
work is shown to be a piece of string chamber music. The
B39 represents the constant number that one uses to indicate
Beethoven in Cutter's scheme, and the succeeding "-4" identifies the work as a quartet; the line below quotes the opus
number, and the last symbol is the publisher's individual
abbreviation. Foreshadowing the BCM scheme, Dickinson
calls for the symbol "=" in cases where the score in hand is
an arrangement, so that 52=15 would show that here was a
piece, originally chamber music, but here arranged for organ
solo. "Following the symbol =, an 0 indicates arrangement of
the accompaniment.... In some cases the symbol =01 may
signify the addition of an accompaniment to a composition
originally lacking one."

A few comments may be made on certain placings. 07
is for methods, tutors, etc., which generally contain both
text and exercises. Technical exercises for trumpet would
be classed at 0736. 36, in the main tables, is the number
for music written for trumpet and piano; the combined number exemplifies, once again, mnemonic assistance towards the
speedy recognition of a class number. 29 is provided for
"Ancient stringed instruments" which include, for instance,
the lira but which does not offer hospitality to viols, which
apparently go in 59 "Obsolete combinations"--a distinction
which may be found too subtle for some library users.
Rather surprisingly, no separate numbers are provided for
flute and recorder, nor for oboe and cor anglais; each pair
of related instruments has but a single placing, which may
be regarded as unfortunate--particularly in the first case,
as flute and recorder have their own considerable reper-
tories. Number 46, percussion instruments, includes a special place (463) for chimes, while 48 and 49 usefully differ-

entiate between electronic music in combinations with conventional and other instruments, and for electronic music alone,
respectively.

Folk and nationalistic music (and it is wise, in this
writer's opinion, to combine these categories) are at 74,
but no distinction is made between original and arranged
music. Geographical subdivision is achieved by adapting the
appropriate Dewey classification number. Where division is
by genre rather than by location, as is the case with Z5,
the number for war songs, and Z6 shanties, these indications are used in the second line of the class mark, to precede the Cutter number for the editor's name.

Bradley's commentary provides a long and detailed
section on Notes, while collation includes the useful description vis-à-vis for piano duets with the two parts shown individually on the recto and verso pages rather than in the
alternative presentation of the two parts in parallel, one under the other. The miscellaneous information list includes
the names of sixty-one authors who are considered sufficiently important to warrant added entries in the catalogue when
settings of their words are being entered. "Robert Burne"
is a misprint for the Scottish poet, but British music librarians would probably not expect to make entries for authors
such as Christian F. Hebbel, Chester Kallman, and Theodor
Storm, as these are names generally unfamiliar here, however
well known they presumably are in the USA.

For filing purposes, numbers are treated decimally, so
that 015 precedes 04 on the shelves, and 860 follows 86 but
comes before 87. The signs for natural, sharp and flat are
filed, where necessary, in that order and not alphabetically.
To judge the scheme fairly, one needs to see it in operation
in a library but, assessed purely as a theoretical exercise,
it seems to be generally sound, although the apparent first
choice of classifying by medium rather than that of the copy
in hand means that the classification is clearly considered to
be one for use in an academic library.

The use of mnemonics seems to have been well devised
so that the intelligent user would, one imagines, quickly
learn the basis of the notation and move with confidence
among a collection of scores.

THE BRITISH CATALOGUE OF MUSIC [28]

The first issue of the British Catalogue of Music appeared
in 1957. In general, its appearance, as one would expect,
was similar to that of BNB. The classification sequence,
however, was quite dissimilar in that the older work had
used Dewey, whereas BCM appeared with its entries listed
according to a new and original scheme devised by E. J.
Coates of BNB. The bibliographical side of this compilation
has been covered in Chapter II; here we are concerned
solely with the classification scheme.

    At first, it was necessary to rely upon draft outline
schedules if one wished to study the BCM scheme; however,
in 1960 the full tables were published. To those used to a
numerically based system such as Dewey or one with a mixed
notation such as the Library of Congress, the BCM classification may well appear at first to be very strange, if not
intimidating; experience should prove, however, that it is
not difficult to apply and is generally highly effective in
operation. Coates's scheme is a faceted one (based on the
methods introduced by Ranganathan in his Colon classification) whereby one builds up a symbol which will show most,
if not all, of the essential constituents. The final result
may well be quite complicated but it is not usually difficult
to decode and (as demonstrated earlier in this chapter)
gives an exactness of meaning that is rarely possible with
older and more conventional schemes.

    The introduction to the classification outlines the
facets used. For instrumental music the major ones are
executant, form of composition and character of composition.
The executant may be vocal, instrumental or both. Since
BCM arranges scores primarily by medium, it follows that
this aspect will be the first in the final symbol. As the
rule is laid down that composite subject symbols are formed
by joining together the symbols listed for the constituent
elementary terms in the reverse order from that in which
they appear in the schedule, it follows that the executant
will come towards the end of the schedules. From this
standard reverse schedule order, we suggest that it ought
to be difficult (but not, unfortunately, impossible) for a
classifier to compose an incorrect symbol, providing that the
different aspects are correctly listed. In some cases, as
will be shown, part of the theoretically correct class mark

may be omitted--but the section relating to the executant is never so shortened.

With books on music, there are rather more facets to be considered. Here, the order is composer, executant, form, elements of music, character, technique, common sub-division. This, again, may appear a discouraging list, yet the reader may take hope from the fact that it would proba-bly be impossible to find any book that used all these facets. It will be noted that the composer facet takes priority, so that any volume dealing with any aspect of the music of a single composer must be classed under the composer. A book dealing with the operas of Verdi, if correctly classified, will automatically gravitate to a place on the shelves with all the other books dealing with Verdi's life, writings and works; it will not be with books on the history of opera or criticisms of the operas of the nineteenth century and the like. This is a major difference to remember if one is comparing BCM with any other scheme of classification.

As for executant, listed as the first facet for scores and the second for literature, it has subfacets. For vocal music, these relate to the size of the body performing the work, e.g., a single soloist or a full choir. The type of executant also receives provision, since it would be an odd classification that provided only the one placing for music written for sopranos and that composed for a male voice choir, even though the number of singers might happen to be the same. The third, and last, of these subfacets for vocal music is concerned with the accompaniment, which is ignored if it is for piano or organ. For any different sort of backing, or for a cappella music, the appropriate speci-fication is added.

Instrumental music has four subfacets. First is the type of executant, e.g., strings; then comes size or com-plexity. With a string quartet this aspect would be "quartet." After this is added the accompanying executant--for a string quartet, there would be none. Finally, provision is made, in the case of transcriptions and arrangements, for the orig-inal scoring to be shown. Thus, Turina's La oración del torero is almost invariably played in the composer's version for string quartet although it was originally written for four lutes. BCM allows the classifier to indicate this fact, if de-sired, for a score of the bowed string version or for a set of parts of the work.

The notational basis is alphabetical. There are twenty-four letters used: "I" and "O" are omitted for reasons of clarity, although they would be used in class B when dealing with books concerning such composers as d'Indy or Ives, Ockeghem or Offenbach. They might also be found in geographical schedules. "O" is also available for an alternative schedule relating to chamber music. Reference to this is made later. Numerals are included in a symbol if one applies Table 7, which allows for dates and duration; an example of such use has been quoted earlier in this chapter (on p. 212) for the Bennett discography which, it may be recalled, covered the period 1898-1925.

There are basically two sequences in the classification. Classes A and B are for books, C to Z for scores. The two series are closely related (in parallel) wherever possible. Music written for the viola, for example, would be found on the shelves at class SQ; books on the instrument are classed at ASQ. These parallel sequences are of real value both to classifier and to user. The instruction is given as part of the preface in an annual volume of <u>BCM</u>, that

	A
is followed by	A(....)
which is followed by	A/....
which is followed by	AA
which is followed by	AB
which is followed by	B & C.

The introduction of the stroke and curves means that a triple sequence is possible, though only partly used in practice. These two symbols, therefore, are a preferable alternative to a second alphabetical sequence--say, in lower case--followed in turn by a third in italics. The purpose of the stroke and curves is "to mechanize the order of subjects" (p. x).

Because scores have so great a part of the alphabetical base allotted to them, this part of the schedules will be considered first. C begins with places for educational scores of a general nature (C to C/AL) with C/AY for general collections of music; these can be divided by locality if it is considered necessary or desirable. C/AZ is for "Collections from individual composers." The remainder of C/.... is shown in the tables as being for "Collections to illustrate music of a particular character," although <u>BCM</u> (in its annual volumes) slightly amended this to "Collections illustrating music of particular form, character." It is unfortunate that such amendments and the provision of additional placings can only be discovered through keeping a close eye on the interim issues and annual volumes. There have been no published sets of official changes and expansions. These illustrative types of music in C/.... include such categories as cowboy music (C/GNF), music about the sea (C/EG) and religious music for harvest (C/LP). Anthologies of music for a particular Christian denomination are to be found at C/LJ (a placing not in the tables, and fitting most uncomfortably between C/LH Holy week and C/LK Passion). Anthologies for Christian denominations have their places (C/LS etc.), divided according to Auxiliary table 5. C/LU is shown in the tables as the place for Jewish religious music which is the only symbol available, it seems, for all religious music other than Christian. Later, in "Collections illustrating the various elements of music" we have such topics as C/NM Rhythm and C/PR Modes. This means that the scores found first on the shelves, assuming that the collection is arranged in schedule order, form a kind of generalia class.

CA is left blank, so "Music for particular media (Vocal & Instrumental)" begins at CB. This sequence, which is for choral or vocal music of one kind or another, continues to the end of class K. Instrumental music begins with class L (with a series of dance forms from LH, starting with allemandes and ending with waltzes; the use of alphabetical order reminds one of J. D. Brown's classification, for its originator normally used an alphabetical sequence when he could see no more effective method). Orchestral music is found at M, chamber music (for mixed ensembles) at N, while individual instruments and instrumental groups are ranged from P to Y. Since the notation is not hierarchical, PW is provided for keyboard instruments, with Q for piano; if one used Dewey precedent here, piano would have been allotted the symbol PWA or something similar, to show its subordination to its family group. In like fashion, the general number for music for stringed instruments is RW, with violin at S, and plucked string instruments at T, wind instruments at U, woodwind at V, brass at W and percussion at X. In passing,

the latter section has places for dulcimer, gong and rattle
but not, surprisingly, for xylophone. Y is for other instruments; its subdivisions are YR glasses, YS music produced by tools and machines, and YSS sewing machines.
One would not expect the sewing machine repertoire to be
extensive, despite critics' allegations that some performances
(particularly of the music of J. S. Bach) have as much imag-
ination and flair as if played on this humdrum instrument.
The final class, Z, is for non-European music.

The schedules also contain seven auxiliary tables; the
first allows for "Sub-arrangement under Instruments and Instrumental groups," so that these become common subdivisions that permit the classifier to specify that a work is,
for instance, a sonatina or a march (irrespective of the solo
instrument or combination for which the music was written).
Auxiliary Table 2 is a subarrangement for piano or harpsichord, and provides places for two-keyboard works, duets,
six-handed works and solos for left hand. Auxiliary Table 3
is even briefer, dealing with organ, harmonium or American
organ; while Table 4 offers three subdivisions applicable to
any other instrument.

Table 5 is concerned with Christian denominations so
that, by way of illustration, one can have a specific placing
that would separate hymnbooks say, for Presbyterian /LSF
and for Baptist /LSH congregations. Table 6 gives ethnic/
locality subdivisions 1974. Local government reorganization
in Britain means that some reallocation of places has been
needed; the table provides a symbol for every old county in
Britain, plus individual placings for Birmingham, Liverpool,
Manchester, Edinburgh and Glasgow, in addition to London.
These are all cities with impressive musical traditions and
current activities. The table, in fact, demonstrates how
rapidly political changes have altered names on maps in many
parts of the world in recent years.

Table 7, previously mentioned, lists "Chronological
references points," and the work is completed by an index
to the geographical placings in Table 6 and another index to
the classification as a whole. The suggestion in the introduction that one should metaphorically break down the subject of any published book into its various facets, also points
out that the initial term (i.e., that of the medium of the
work) should always be written down in full. After that,

the other facets follow in reverse schedule order, omitting A, C/ or L if one aspect begins with any of these letters. This is because, in a composite symbol, these symbols become redundant. Arrangements are introduced by K after the medium designation. K is always followed by a stroke, if one is following the printed schedules, and should be succeeded by symbols indicating the original scoring. Thus, using the Turina example, we begin with RX (bowed string instruments), adding NS from Auxiliary Table 1, to show that there are four instruments--thus, RXNS. As this is an arrangement, K is added, followed (if desired) by TWNS to specify the four lutes of the original. In practice, BCM itself has stopped specifying the original instrumentation since 1971. Had the Turina work been a sonata, it would have been classed at RXNSK/AE, i.e., bowed string instruments; arrangements; sonatas.

If we take an example of solo piano music, the general placing is QP (the P taken from Auxiliary Table 2), with additional letters if the music is of a particular type, e.g., QPE piano sonatas. S is the general placing for violin, SP for violin and piano and SPM unaccompanied violin. This last may seem to be a step backward, but accepts the practical point that there is far more music for violin and piano than for the unaccompanied solo instrument. It may be recalled that a similar situation exists in DDC, where 787.15 is the placing for music for violin and piano, while 787.1541 is used if there is no accompaniment.

Common form subdivisions are given within parentheses when they apply to books; for scores they are taken from C/...., dropping the initial letter as the symbol is combined with that for instrument or voices. The matter of arrangements has already been covered; the use of the stroke after the K is simply to assist comprehension. The stroke as such, examples have shown, is also used as part of the notation for certain topics, e.g., LF represents Christmas music (from A/LF) and the stroke is therefore retained whenever this aspect is applied anywhere in the schedules. Thus, to repeat an example given at the beginning of the chapter, carols are classified at DP, a subdivision of class D, choral music. If the carols relate to Christmas, then one adds /LF, while New Year carols become DP/LFM (the New Year symbol is, incidentally, not in the 1960 published tables but is an expansion found via the annual volumes). If one quotes the

entire second part of the combined symbol and writes DP/
ALFM, one gets a nonsensical number, since this would mean
carol cadenzas. Similarly, /LF appearing after K, as in
QNUK/LF indicates that this work is a reduction for two
pianos of a piano concerto. These last examples should provide a warning, perhaps, that one must follow the instructions from the introduction relating to "practical application
of the scheme," concerning the dropping of initial letters in
certain combined symbols.

Let us consider another example of number building,
which may clarify some minds (but could equally befog other
readers still further); this time we will take Smetana's Polkas
for piano solo as our example. Since it is a piano score,
there should be no problem in deciding that class Q (piano)
is going to be the first symbol. At that place in the tables
we are referred to Auxiliary Table 2, which shows that QP
is the placing for solo piano. A/H is the aspect of Musical
character for dances, so we now have QPH, dance music for
solo piano. Auxiliary Table 1 confirms that H is for dances,
and adds "(Elaborated as at LHJ/LHW in Main Table)." Faint
but pursuing, we turn back to class L and discover that
LHVH is the symbol for polkas, so we arrive at QPHVH for
the Smetana volume. If, for interest, one compares this with
DDC, there the classification would be 786.44 which includes
not only polkas, but also marches, polonaises and mazurkas.

The method of building up symbols in combination to
show the instrument, the musical form, its relation to the
scoring of the original work (if the item in hand happens to
be an arrangement), its nationality and its place in chronology allows an exactitude that no scheme built on traditional
lines can match, yet the notation is rarely unwieldy--partic-
ularly if it is broken down into groups of three letters for
easier comprehension. The scheme's design to accommodate,
without undue strain, new developments as they occur in
published material has so far been satisfactory. This is the
primary reason for the nonhierarchical notation. It was also
an important consideration in the decision to adopt a facet-
type structure since this should enable the classifier to see
where a new subject should go; a nonhierarchical notation
enables the topic to be placed at the desired point with the
minimum of complication.

Another important reason for use of a faceted structure

was its ability to allow different means of approach, all perfectly reasonable and legitimate, to be acceptable. This is
achieved by means of the system known as chain indexing,
which takes into account the various approaches; it also allows for the fact that users, all too frequently, do not ask
for the specific subject they require, but make a more gen-
eralised enquiry. If one uses a classified catalogue, the
user who begins with a heading that is wider than the topic
actually required can, by simply working patiently through
the entries as they appear in the catalogue, (and helped on
his way, one hopes, by guide cards), eventually arrive at a
specific topic, always assuming that the library includes at
least one work upon it.

Two examples, one a book and the other a score, will
show (once again) the synthesis involved in building a BCM
class mark, and illustrate how each example would be shown
in the subject index. In the hope of making these points
even clearer, the same two works will be given similar treatment, but using DDC instead of BCM. The book is William S.
Newman's Performance Practices in Beethoven's Piano Sonatas:
An Introduction, published in 1972. The respective class
marks are BBJAQPE/E and 786.10924

BBJ	Beethoven, Ludwig van
AQ	Piano
P	Solos (from Auxiliary Table 2)
E	Symphonies, sonatas (from Auxiliary Table 1)
/E	Performance (from A/E)

For indexing, we work in reverse order. Performance
would be omitted from the chain, since the likelihood of an
approach through this word is extremely remote. In any
case, it might be more practical to trace the book through
its title:

Sonatas: Piano solo: Beethoven, Ludwig van: Books	BBJAQPE
Solos: unsought	–
Piano: Beethoven, Ludwig van: Books	BBJAQ
Beethoven, Ludwig van: Books	BBJ

With DDC, the build-up of the class mark would be via the
following stages:

786	Keyboard instruments
.1	Keyboard string instruments
09	Historical and geographical treatment
2	Musicians, performers
4	Individual; Beethoven, Ludwig van

It should be plain that the final symbol is much less specific
than that found through BCM, partly because the citation
order is completely different. "Piano" cannot be indexed,
because the class number for pianos is 786.4 and not 786.1.
This fact, combined with the lack of exactitude in classing
means that indexing is very difficult:

Beethoven, Ludwig van: keyboard music	786.10924
Keyboard music	786.1

"Sonatas" could conceivably be indexed, as a further verbal
extension:

Sonatas: Beethoven, Ludwig van: keyboard music	786.10924

In practice, BNB no longer employs chain indexing,
but now uses the "Precis" method. For this particular example, the bibliography provided four access terms in the
subject index entries--Beethoven, sonatas, pianos, and music for piano. This illustrates an entirely different method
of approach which has only become economic with the use
of computers. When BNB did employ chain indexing (i.e.,
before 1971), they used their modified version of Dewey in
classes 785/789, with lower case letters, but BCM continues
to use chain indexing.

The Sonata for Trumpet, Violoncello and String Orchestra, in D Major, by Domenico Gabrieli (a very minor
figure indeed compared with the famous Andrea and Gio-
vanni of the same surname) will serve as an example of the

classification of a score. Although the possibility has already been suggested earlier that a <u>BCM</u> symbol can be presented in groups of three letters, here we list the letters in pairs for easier comprehension: RX MP WS PL SR E. This may seem excessively lengthy, but is the product of

RX		Bowed string instruments	(Medium)
	MP	Works for solo instruments and orchestra	(Size/ complexity)
	WS	Trumpet	(Executant)
	PL	Solo with second instrument (Auxiliary Table 1)	(Executant)
	SR	Violoncello	(Executant)
	E	Symphonies, sonatas	(Form)

The indexing procedure would be as follows:

Sonatas: Trumpet, cello and string orchestra	RXMPWSPLSRE
Violoncello, trumpet and string orchestra	RXMPWSPLSR
Trumpet, violoncello and string orchestra	RXMPWSPLSR
Trumpet and string orchestra	RXMPWS
Orchestral music: string orchestra	RXM
String instruments	RW

This provides a means of discovering the work under every term that is likely to be sought. In practice, a cataloguer is unlikely to make index entries both for "Trumpet, violoncello and string orchestra" and "Trumpet and string orchestra," but would use one or the other. The former is the more accurate here, but the second heading might be felt to be of greater use if the collection also included any other works for trumpet and string orchestra. It should be mentioned that the rule for such concertos is that where the solo instruments are of the same family, they are to be cited in forward order; on the other hand, if they are of different families, then retrograde order is right. Thus, a concerto for violin, violoncello and string orchestra would have the

two instruments cited in that order: RXMPSPLSRF. The
actual example quoted above has soloists of different orchestral families, so the later one in the schedules (trumpet) is
cited first in the final symbol.

If we now take the same Gabrieli composition and deal
with it according to the Dewey scheme:

785.6	Concertos (the work is a sonata, but where else can one put it?)
.66-69	Score and parts
.673	Violoncello (from Table at 784-789)
.67304	Single works

A comparison here shows that BCM gives the order: execu-
tant--form, whereas DDC gives form--executant; indeed,
concertos contains an element of both. In Dewey, strings
take precedence over wind, so that the poor trumpet is entirely lost. Again, chain indexing would be impossible here.

So far, no real mention has been made of classes A
and B. Musical literature, A, has the same basic method of
facet structure and its symbols are closely related to those
for scores (another point that has been made earlier). A
book on Christmas carols would be placed at ADP/LF while a
work on orchestral music for bowed string instruments would
go at ARXM. The common form subdivisions, from A(A) to
A(Z) include the expected ones such as encyclopaedias A(C),
bibliographies A(T), history A(X) and its related division by
place A(Y), but also include a number of unexpected topics
such as statistics A(HM), law A(J), lists of objects A(WT),
whose use was demonstrated in an earlier example, and aspects of music in relation to other subjects, branches of
A(Z), e.g., music influenced by another subject, A(ZF).

These subdivisions are followed by places for other
aspects of music--A/AM the theory of music, A/CY technique
(which includes A/D composition, A/E performance and A/F
recording), A/FY musical character (including A/G folk music, A/H dance music, A/L religious music, etc.), A/M elements of music (including A/P pitch and A/R harmony) and
A/S forms of music (which includes A/T theme and variations
and A/Y fugue). Two points stand out here. First, that

the subdivision may have a shorter notation than its containing head, and second, that many of these places use symbols related to those for the appropriate scores. On the first point, it is simply a matter of practical use; there are likely to be appreciably more books on musical composition than on the more general topic of technique. As for the second, the previously quoted example of DP/LF for a collection of Christmas carols can be connected with A/LF for books on music for Christmas.

Now follows the straightforward division of class A, from AB vocal music to AY other instruments. These topics are for "Works on particular kinds of music, designated by executants." AD is for choral music, ADP for carols; AL begins the sequence for books on instrumental music with ALH as the general place for dance forms, subdivided alphabetically from ALHJ allemande to ALHW waltz. Somewhere in the middle is ALHVH polka; here again, it is simple to see the relationship between this placing and that of QPHVH (quoted earlier) for a collection of polkas for piano solo.

Class B is for books on individual composers. Collective works on musicians are in A/D(M) which is made up of the symbol A/D composition, plus the common subdivision (M) from A(M) for "Persons in music." A(N) is for biographies, so that general biographies of composers are classed at A/D(N). For individual composers the arrangement is alphabetical using the initial letters of the composer's surname plus other letters (following the style of Cutter and other author arrangements) to bring the names into a single sequence. Thus, a life of Bach is at BBC; the first B is for a work on an individual composer, the second B for the first letter of his surname and C to arrange the name among the other composers whose names also have B as an initial letter. Beethoven is BBJ, Mozart BMS, Schubert BSF and Schumann BSG. William Schuman, the American composer, would therefore be allotted a symbol such as BSFZ to bring a book on him and his works into place in the schedules immediately before Robert Schumann. This method of interpolation can be applied at any point throughout the schedules. Here is a class in which I and O have to be used--for books on John Ireland or Jacques Offenbach and others whose names begin with these two letters. Not only biographies but any books dealing with aspects of the life or works of an individual composer are classed here. The appropriate

subdivision is taken from class A and added to the symbol
for the composer. Thus, a biography of Schubert would be
given the symbol BSF(N) and a book on Schubert's variations
BSF/T, since A/T is the class mark for books on variations
in general. Other amplifications can be made by using the
symbols from AB to AY; a book on Schubert's Masses would
be given the notation BSFADG. Such a scheme brings together works dealing with many varied topics relating to a
particular composer. This simple juxtaposition of symbols,
somewhat reminiscent of what is possible in the subject classification, is invaluable. It might be a weakness in the hands
of the unskilled classifier who could link together the various
parts of a complicated notation symbol in the wrong order,
unless he remembers the basic rule which should prevent this
happening, i.e., that symbols should be combined in reverse
schedule order (unless the schedule itself directs to the contrary). Once this is understood and practised the book on
Schubert's Masses will be correctly placed at BSFADG and
not at a place such as ADGBSF.

Brief mention should be made of the alternative schedule for chamber music in the (otherwise unused) class O, and
of the other optional schedules in classes D and E (for choral
music). BCM itself does not use these alternatives which offer a more detailed listing of executants than can be given
using the standard tables. If one takes, for example, a trio
of clarinet, violin and piano, the normal class mark would be
NUVNT, compounded from:

NUV   Clarinet, strings and keyboard trios

NT   Trios (Auxiliary Table 1)

The class O alternative would be OFV.S.Q., which is built
up from

OF   Woodwind, strings, keyboard

V   Clarinet

S   Violin

Q   Piano

The full stop between each of the instruments is required by
the scheme. The alternative schedules for classes D and E
"are designed for users of the classification who require more

precise specification than is given in the main table." Under
this alternative, one can show the number of parts in a choral work which could be of potential value to a library with a
large collection of such items.

Before giving further examples of class marks for particular works, it should be mentioned that BZ is allotted to non-
European music, which can be subdivided in the same way
that class A has been broken down. One minor technical
point not previously mentioned is that where a subject is
modified by two common subdivisions, each of which would
normally be shown in curves, then the two aspects are combined by a stroke, so that A(K/C) is used and not A(K)(C).

The two most frequent criticisms levelled at BCM are concerned with A/D(M) as the placing for collective biography,
and the provision for jazz. On the first point, this symbol
is derived from A/D composition (which would, on the face
of it, exclude collected lives of executants) and A(M) persons in music. Why a place was not provided at the beginning of class B, to be adjacent there to all the individual
biographies, criticisms, etc., seems inexplicable. Even in a
fairly small library, there is likely to be a wide separation on
the shelves between collective biography and individual ones.
As for jazz, this is placed at the end of the orchestral music
(AM) and before chamber music. One could perhaps claim
that this is sensible in that jazz groups are in combinations
of two or three to the big band of fewer than twenty. Jazz
songs are to go at KDW/HJ and music for jazz groups at MT,
which directly relates to books at AMT. Overall, the placings seem as unhappy as those in DDC for the same subject.
For individual instruments, Auxiliary Table 1 provides HX to
allow the appropriate modification to the symbol for any individual instrument, and HXJ for ragtime.

In passing, the tables give no indication of how one deals
with books on Carl Zeller, Anton Zimmermann, and other composers whose names begin with the letter "Z," since BZ is
reserved for what is today described as "ethnic" music.
BYZ is perhaps the best answer.

As we look at some additional examples, it may be noticed
that the symbols required for scores are of similar length to
those for books (an indication of how well Coates allocated
his notation), despite the fact that books are limited to the

two classes (A and B) only. We should also remind readers
that there is now a policy in the issues of BCM to ignore the
indication, with arrangements, of the original scoring. However, this provision is still part of the scheme and is used
in most of our examples.

The first of them is an arrangement for military band
of ballet music, UMMK/MM/HM. The constituent parts are U,
wind instruments; UMM military band with the added K to
indicate an arrangement. M is orchestral music and MM music for symphony orchestra. A/H is the symbol for books on
dance music, with the related A/HM for books on ballet music.
Used with a score, the A is dropped, leaving /HM to be
added and thus giving the placing UMMK/MM/HM. Our second example is a medley of hunting songs, for light orchestra. M is orchestral music, MS for light orchestra, and K
indicates an arrangement: DW is the symbol for songs, etc.,
while GT is derived from A/GT, a subdivision of A/G, Folk
music. So the three parts of the final notation MSK/DW/GT
show clearly the actual executant of the music (the light orchestra), the original executant (a singer) and the actual
character of the composition--a type of song.

VWPK/RXLF shows VW bassoon; P, piano accompaniment; K, arrangement (from) RV bowed string instruments.
L comes from Auxiliary Table 1 (K/L) which indicates a
reduction from a score for orchestra and the same instrument;
in this case the interpolation of RX before the L means that
the original orchestra was a string one. The final digit is
F, concertos, and the complete symbol, therefore, shows a
work for bassoon and piano which is an arrangement of a
work originally scored for bassoon and string orchestra.

Two final examples show the same sort of built-up notation. In XMK/QRGM, X represents percussion instruments,
XM percussion band, K an arrangement (from) QR harpsichord works and, in Auxiliary Table 1, G is suites and GM
marches: the score is therefore an arrangement for percussion band of a march originally.

Unlike the other schemes considered in this chapter
(except Dickinson), BCM is not part of a general classification scheme but is limited solely to music. It can be used in
lieu of the music section of any other classification scheme
but would probably be most useful with a large collection that

is housed in a separate department. A major music library would benefit from the detailed subdivision that the scheme permits, and the individual notation would be no handicap in a self-contained section or separate accommodation.

At two or three points in this survey, comment has been made that certain symbols are not to be found in the published tables, but have been added since. This is a necessary development, but one regrets that no lists of these additions have been published, even in the appropriate annual volumes. As for the future of the scheme, it may be limited, for it is understood that there is a possibility that BCM (as a bibliography) may cease to be arranged by the BCM classification scheme; instead, the completely revised "Phoenix" schedule for Dewey 780 would be adopted. If this were to occur, it would mean that books on music that were listed in BNB and the same books appearing in BCM would carry exactly the same class number, which would be a clear advantage both to BCM staff and library classifiers.

"PHOENIX" DEWEY CLASS 780

At first glance, the possibility of expressing BCM classification in numerals and fitting the whole scheme into a decimal basis, so that the schedules occupy class 780, seems highly unlikely. Nevertheless, it has been done brilliantly, and the schedules have been published as Proposed Revision of 780 Music: Based on Dewey Decimal Classification and Relative Index / Prepared under the direction of Russell Sweeney and John Clews, with assistance from Winton E. Matthews, Jr.

To indicate how little distortion has taken place, we now quote the titles considered earlier when discussing the BCM scheme and show the classification under the Dewey variant, as well as the steps by which these numbers are built up, and how they would be entered if one used chain indexing.

Performance Practice in Beethoven's Piano Sonatas

Music	780
Individual composers	789

1750-1824	.4
Beethoven, Ludwig van	22
Executants	1
Piano (from 786.2)	62
General principles and musical forms	1
Instrumental forms (from 781.8)	8
Sonata forms	3

This gives 789.422162183. Further subdivision is possible, but is not recommended. See the instruction at 780:

1	General principles
4	Techniques (from 781.4)
3	Performance techniques

Index entries (assuming that we do not use the optional extentions of the class number) would be as follows:

Performance techniques: Piano sonatas: Beethoven, Ludwig van	789.422162183
Sonatas: Piano: Beethoven, Ludwig van	789.422162183
Piano music: Beethoven, Ludwig van: Music	789.422
Composers: Music	789
Music	780

Note: a) "Books" is added, at the end of the index entries, in the fashion of pre-1982 BCM, since the scores would be classified elsewhere; b) Composers may be classified in no fewer than six different ways and none of the methods has official preference. The choice is among these:

(1) Chronological sequence, using all-number notation: 789.422162183

(2) Chronological sequence, using Cutter numbers   789.4B 43162183

(3) As above, but using the first three letters of surname: 789.4BEE62183

(4) Alphabetical sequence, using all-   789.15162183
    number notation

(5) As (4), but using Cutter numbers   789.B 33162183

(6) As (4), using the first three letters 789.BEE62183

Sonata for Trumpet, Violoncello and String Orchestra

Chain:

Music	780
Instrumental ensembles	784
String orchestra	.7
Featured executant	1
Wind instruments (from 788)	8
Brass instruments	9
Trumpet	2

(verbal extension) and Violoncello

(verbal extension) Sonatas

Index

Sonatas: Trumpet, violoncello and string orchestra	784.71892
Trumpet, violoncello and string orchestra: scores	784.71892
Violoncello, trumpet and string orchestra: scores	784.71892
String orchestra: Scores	784.7
Orchestral music	784
Instrumental music	784-788
Music	780

Note: 1) The classification allows only one "featured instrument," and users are instructed (at 781-788) to class in the
number which comes last in the schedules; in this case, at
Trumpets (788.92) rather than Violoncellos (787.4); 2) Strict

chain procedure has been modified in accordance with B CM's
practice, except that B CM would not use the qualifier
"Scores" or "Music." They have been inserted in the example here on the assumption that the entries would be in an
interdisciplinary catalogue: a catalogue limited solely to music would not need the extra word.

Chapter V

SOUND RECORDINGS

<u>INTRODUCTION</u>

This chapter attempts to provide a practical guide to the
provision of gramophone records and cassettes as a library
service. The emphasis is on British public library practice
but account has been taken of other establishments, both
public and academic, in the USA and elsewhere. The text
indicates certain of the problems to be faced in cataloguing
and classification and attempts to provide satisfactory answers to some of them; it also considers briefly questions of
staffing and of suitable qualifications, and offers suggestions
on other administrative matters. It is hoped that any librarian who may be faced with the inauguration of a service of
this type will find adequate guidance here; as already indicated, these pages are written primarily in a British context
but it is hoped that they will have some value for librarians
in other countries. Furthermore, each year sees a new in-
take of students entering librarianship, and one hopes that
these may find here the basic groundwork of this particular
area of service.

The first part of this chapter gives a cursory overview
of the present position, followed by a brief historical summary;
it then supplies comments upon the various types of material
which may have claim to inclusion in the departmental stock.
The main headings for the chapter are history; preliminary
factors; what to provide, and for whom; what to collect. This
last section is divided into musical and nonmusical, with a
number of subheadings.

One can consider the provision of gramophone record

collections in public libraries in Britain to be nearly forty years old, since this service really began to make its mark soon after World War II. This is long enough, one feels, to take a brief survey before going more thoroughly into the historical side.

In general, it might be claimed that libraries of sound recordings have followed a similar pattern to that of books in the nineteenth century and after. The early public libraries were often inaugurated as an antidote to the "gin palaces" and as an educational force. The result, in terms of book stocks, was the almost complete exclusion of any reading matter considered to be recreational. Similarly, borrowing was usually restricted to a single ticket, for which the completion of an application form that required a local ratepayer's guarantee, if one was not in that category, was necessary and the loan period was very rarely more than a fortnight. Renewals of loans were not encouraged, the reservation of desired titles was often impossible, and the rate of fines (in contemporary money values) often punitive.

Time passed, and with it the "indicator" (the mechanism that denoted which books were immediately available for loan and those which were out); borrowers then could go directly to the shelves to choose their books. Selection criteria were widened, and during the 1930s, a number of library authorities decided to compete with the so-called tuppenny commercial lending libraries by offering a much higher proportion of light fiction than heretofore, and so drive their rivals out of business. The number of tickets a reader could have was increased, books could be reserved for a small fee, and the whole atmosphere slowly became more congenial. Readers' suggestions for addition to stock were accepted; in many cases, a reader could use a valid library ticket in neighbouring authorities and even further afield. In short, there was eventually an active attempt to attract readers to use the library and, at the same time, to reduce restrictions to a minimum.

One might have reasonably expected those lessons to have been learned when sound recording collections were begun--but this was not so. Stock was limited almost entirely to the standard classical repertoire, issued by indirect access (although, it must be admitted, open access would have had little positive value with 78rpm discs in their brown

Films and Recordings Center, Public Library of Cincinnati and Hamilton County, Ohio. (Photo: Bill Engdahl, Hendrich-Blessing)

A busy sound recordings department at the Precinct Library, City of Manchester, England.

The Precinct Library, City of Manchester, England.

The Music Department in the London Borough of Bromley Central Library.

Another view at Bromley Central Library.

A periodical display case at the Central Music Library, London. (Photo courtesy of Westminster City Libraries)

Some of the music periodicals available at the Central Music Library, London. (Photo courtesy of Westminster City Libraries)

Another view at Central Music Library, London (Photo courtesy of Westminster City Libraries)

paper covers), loan periods were frequently restricted to a week, and the rate of fines for overdue discs was usually high. There were, doubtless, excellent reasons for these restrictions, but one must feel more than a little uncomfortable at the parallels. It took the profession a long time (and by no means all librarians are converted even now) to accept the idea that sound recordings are just another form of presentation of information, education and entertainment, and should be treated as such.

One positive result of local government reorganization in Britain in 1974 and 1975 was that there were many cases of amalgamations where one library had a sound recordings collection, and its neighbour lacked this service. Once provided, there was, apparently, no going back and equity meant that provision was necessary throughout the new authority. This resulted in almost complete coverage of Great Britain and Northern Ireland, even if the provision was sadly inadequate in many places. The relative wealth or poverty of an authority and its population is no guide to the generosity (or the reverse) of its treatment of sound recordings. Much still depended upon the ability of the chief librarian to persuade the appropriate "overlord" and/or committee of the value of a sound recordings library, on the pressure from local councillors or citizens keen to see a steady improvement rather than a gradual deterioration of the service, and on the presence of an enthusiastic music librarian, willing to provide constant advertisement and discreet propaganda for the service.

Again, as with books, there was (even after thirty years) much less standardization of basic methods and procedures than one would have expected or hoped to see. There is a continuing divergence on such topics as damage control, open access for discs and tapes, and the physical arrangement of discs and tapes that is most generally helpful to the public. We lack any set of minimum standards, such as those that have been propounded and accepted for book stocks (however far we are from matching up to them, particularly with the financial stringencies that have had such a deleterious effect since the early 1970s). There is the additional contrast with books that we still await any form of British national discography, although the need and value of such a tool is slowly becoming much more widely recognized.

On a more optimistic note, there has been a steady
emergence of schemes of cooperative purchase and the interloan of recordings. Progress has been made in the Greater
London area with the Greater London Audio Specialisation
Scheme (GLASS) for co-operative purchase of classical music
and jazz. GLASS is steadily widening its scope, to include
folk music and the provision of multiple copies of vocal scores
and or orchestral parts. The old adage of the supply creating the demand is proving true here.

As for staff in charge, there is a steady movement
away from traditional music librarianship to taking control of
audiovisual materials in general. This may be regarded as a
mixed blessing and, like a number of the points briefly made
in this section, is discussed more fully later in the chapter.

HISTORY

The first public library gramophone record collection appears
to have been in Minnesota. The St. Paul Public Library in
its report for the year 1914 included a note that "A collection
of phonograph records was inaugurated by the gift of twenty-
five records from the Thursday Club," a women's study and
social group. At that time, the library's then old building
was due for replacement, and the discs were issued from the
Children's Department. It seems that statistics were not
kept until 1916, in which year the circulation figure was
1,768. Within a further twelve months, the collection had
grown from 165 to 256 discs [239].

In 1917, the library moved to a new building and by
1919 the stock had further increased to 442, from which
3,505 borrowings had been made. In a brief report in
Library Journal for 1 February 1920, one can read that
"The collection was made simply for educational purposes.
It is, therefore, limited to reproductions of the musical
classics, both vocal and instrumental, patriotic music, and
folk songs." Loans were restricted to schools and clubs.

General acceptance of the idea of record provision by
public libraries can probably be dated from 1921 when the
Detroit Public Library collection was started and made available for individual borrowing. It was a happy chance that
an authority of this size should enter the field and so provide

a distinct stimulus to smaller cities and towns in the USA.
This collection appears to have been excellently administered
from the start, and its operational methods were copied by
many other places. By 1939 seventeen cities in the USA with
populations in excess of 75,000 had gramophone record stocks;
their number was augmented by many other smaller authorities
that had made similar provision [232].

      In that same year, there was but one British public
library, the Middlesex County Library, with a collection. It
bore some resemblance to the pioneer American library in that
the stock was limited to classical music, and loans were almost
exclusively to schools and selected groups. As so often seems
to happen in Britain, the inauguration of the new service was
almost accidental and owed much to the foresight and imagina-
tion of an enthusiastic librarian. The outline of that story
may best be told in the words of that man, Richard Wright,
who was then Librarian of the Middlesex County service.

         In the 1930s, I was informed by Mr. C. E. Bridges,
         Assistant Secretary for Elementary Education [in the
         area covered by Middlesex County Council] that he
         was busy with the provision of a record library for
         musical appreciation in schools. A committee of ex-
         perts had selected the records and he was keen to
         make it a success. Had I any ideas? I said that a
         static record library would be limited in use unless
         located in London, and even then the teachers could
         ill afford the time to travel to select the records.
         Hence my suggestion that I would carry out the ad-
         ministration inasmuch as my library van was around
         the County daily. I was prepared to do this if the
         records could be used for adult courses of musical
         appreciation or similar organisations, especially those
         connected with our branch libraries.... All expenses
         would come from Education funds [24a].

      The suggestion was accepted and the service began in
1934. It proved very successful. Record recitals were given
regularly in some of the branch libraries, but with a book
fund that never grew fast enough to be adequate for the
needs of the county library's readers, the possibility of providing a collection of discs for public use was not seriously
considered. The service remained exclusive to schools, etc.,
until after World War II.

The first British local authority to inaugurate a loan
service open to individual borrowers was Herefordshire
County Library, the result of a gift of 300 discs to the library in 1940. This was the personal collection of a local
resident who stipulated that, after her death, the records
were to be offered to the library, by whom they were accepted [233]. A stencilled catalogue was prepared and made
available to all interested users.

Herefordshire maintained its service until 1974 and the
end of its independent existence as a county, but with minimum publicity, so that its primacy in this particular field of
service remained generally unknown and unrecognized for almost two decades. The next local authority in Britain to
provide gramophone records was Chingford, in 1946. The
local library was a branch of the Essex County Library service and that system was one of the very few then remaining
that still allowed differential rating (taxation), whereby a
local authority could improve its service above that provided
by the county, if the district concerned was prepared to pay
the entire extra cost involved. There was no objection to
the Chingford authorities starting to provide discs for loan.
It reflects considerable credit upon both the local Council
and the then librarian (Eric Leyland) that they were prepared to use their relative independence to such effect.
Later in the same year, similar services were started in the
independent library authorities of Walthamstow, Westminster
and St. Marylebone in the London area.

The Library Association Record for July 1949 stated
that there were at that time thirty-seven public libraries in
England with gramophone record collections [55]. Between
1949 and the middle of 1957, the total was exactly doubled,
with Motherwell appearing as the first Scottish representative.
By no means all of these seventy-four issued records to individual borrowers, for a number restricted loan facilities to
schools and local societies, as had Middlesex in the 1930s.
Gramophone record libraries continued to be inaugurated in
the USA at a much faster rate than in Britain, for between
1945 and 1948 another thirty-two libraries in the over 75,000
population group started collections, as well as an unknown
number of smaller authorities [3].

For some years the legal position in Britain was governed by a ruling issued by the Ministry of Health (the

central government department concerned, at that time, with
public libraries) which, in reply to an enquiry from the City
of Westminster, allayed doubts.   The decision quoted in The
Library Association Record for May 1947 reads, in part:
"The Minister has consulted the Minister of Education in the
matter and is advised that as music is both a science and an
art, and a gramophone record is undoubtedly a specimen of
music, the Council have power under Section 15(1) of the
Public Libraries Act, 1892, to form a lending library of gramophone records as an extension of the present library service."   This apparently tongue-in-cheek reply (slightly inaccurate, since not all recordings were of music) caused
one public librarian to suggest that the 1892 Act would only
empower a public library to possess a single gramophone
record, solely as a museum specimen.   However, the minis-
terial decision was accepted as legal sanction for a library
to operate a gramophone records section.   At least four
authorities which provided such a service made individual
membership available only on a subscription or rental basis.
Such a limitation was entirely contrary to the accepted general idea of a free service and was therefore open to legal
challenge, but no aggrieved ratepayer took the local Council to court.   The Public Libraries and Museums Act 1964
put the matter beyond argument, in section 8 (5), which
states that, "Where facilities made available to any person
by a library authority go beyond those ordinarily provided
by the authority as part of the library service, the authority may make a charge for the provision of these facilities."
The phrase, "those ordinarily provided" was taken to refer
to books, periodicals, and reference services only.

PRELIMINARY FACTORS

The need for a librarian to make out a case for a sound recordings library much diminished with the spread of record
libraries, but the library profession itself has not always
spoken with vision or enthusiasm.   This may be exemplified
by the Library Association statement published in January
1958 [122].   Questions and answers relating to gramophone
record libraries begin at number 12:   "Should a library service continue to be provided free of charge?...   If the service should be free in respect of books and other papers,
should a charge be permissible in respect of other articles,
such as ... gramophone records?"   The Association felt that

an entirely free service was desirable. Question 13 dealt
with improvements needed "in the response of librarians to
the cultural needs of their areas." The Association considered (in paragraph 39) that "the most necessary improvements in library provision to cultural needs will lie in the
increase in the range, quality and quantity of stocks of
books...." There was no reference to sound recordings and
this absence is underlined in the next paragraph by reference to solutions "which are only indirectly concerned with
books and readers," using as illustrations "organised public
lectures, exhibition, film shows, and discussion circles."

The Association's official view at that time was that
there was "a wide and generally amorphous interest in cultural matters in all urban areas that usually lacks focus,
funds and accommodation. Where the library has accommodation, and where facilities elsewhere for group meetings are
lacking, the library could be the centre for such meetings."
The library should offer encouragement and "if necessary,
even form such groups" itself. There is, again, no mention
of a gramophone record library nor the value of well-prepared
recitals of recorded music, nor the part that a gramophone
or recorded music society could usefully play in a locality.

The body to which the LA's answers were directed,
generally known as the Roberts committee after its chairman,
took a much more positive attitude. In paragraph 118 of
their report they reaffirmed their belief in a free service
and continued, in paragraph 119:

> In recent years the stocks of a number of public
> libraries have been supplemented by the acquisition
> of gramophone records ... and some authorities have
> sought powers ... to make charges for the loan of
> them. We cannot subscribe to this discrimination
> between books and supplementary material. Such
> things as gramophone records serve the same pur-
> pose as books in that they are the media for the
> recording and communication of information and
> ideas and artistic experience. They are a legiti-
> mate and valuable addition to the resources of a
> public library and to make charges for them would,
> in our view, be a retrograde step [85].

This stand in favour of the service was reinforced in the

report of the Bourdillon committee [84]. They stated, in
paragraph 83, "We consider that the provision for loans of
non-book material, such as gramophone records ... is an increasingly important part of public library service."

These views were to be partly reflected in the Public
Libraries and Museums Act of 1964 [86]. Section 7(1) begins with the oft-quoted phrase: "It shall be the duty of
every library authority to provide a comprehensive and ef-
ficient library service for all persons desiring to make use
thereof...." In (2)(a) of the same Section, it states that
library authorities should see "that facilities are available
for the borrowing of, or reference to, books and other
printed matter, and pictures, gramophone records ... sufficient in number, range and quality to meet the general
requirements of both adults and children...." In practice,
over a decade after the Act came into force, few libraries
provide sound recordings for loan to children, but the number is slowly growing. The final reference here to official
statements is taken from the Public Library Manifesto of
Unesco, where one can read: "But science has created new
forms of record and these will become an increasing part of
the public library's stock, including print in reduced form
... gramophone records, audio and video tape, for adults
and children, with the necessary equipment for individual
use and for cultural activities" [216].

Although the librarian may quote one or more of these
statements to local officials, the initiative could well come
from a member of the authority (an influential councillor can
be a most helpful advocate), from a gramophone or music
society, from enthusiasts in the area, or from some other
source. For example, at the opening of the Motherwell gramophone record lending library (already mentioned as being
the first in Scotland), the local newspaper reminded its readers that, "... on July 1st, 1949, the local branch of the
Union of Shop, Distributive and Allied Workers had a reso-
lution endorsed and sent to the Public Libraries Committees." This motion proposed, "... that there should be in
existence within the public libraries of Motherwell and Wishaw
a section of recorded music for the furtherance of culture
and musical education amongst the general works and or-
ganisations of this Burgh" [143].

Local bodies and individuals may support the proposal

when made public. On the other hand, there could well be
disapproval also, the most frequent objection being that a
sound recordings library provides a minority service; this
seems as relevant as to protest because a library buys some
books in French, or that it stocks music scores--both of
these types of material are even more restricted in general
appeal. In some cases, there is a suggestion that those
sufficiently well off to be able to afford the purchase of a
record player are demonstrably so affluent that they can
also buy all the discs that they need. This is patently ab-
surd, although it seems true that a sound recordings library
stimulates the private purchase of discs, etc., by its users.
A listener may well borrow a library recording and find the
work and performance sufficiently attractive to wish to buy
a copy. Local dealers generally benefit where the town has
a library of commercial recordings, and any argument against
a public collection on the grounds that such a service would
reduce sales of discs and tapes seems completely without
foundation. The writer has been assured of this by a number of dealers in different towns, but documentary evidence
on either side seems to be nonexistent.

Most committees discharging public library functions
today, however, are likely to accept the principle of providing a library of recorded sound, even if they then proceed
to vote against any proposals to implement the decision on
the grounds of cost. The librarian in charge of an old building may well be in something of a quandary by advocating the
pressing need for a new library or better accommodation because the present one is badly overcrowded. This may be
true--in which case the librarian has not only to find adequate room for an audio library in a building where every
inch seems already occupied, but also possibly to explain
why this newly discovered available area has been previously
overlooked, and why it is not considered suitable for other
purposes. In virtually all new central libraries built in Britain since 1950, provision has been made for a separate music,
arts and music, or some similarly entitled department. Local
councils have apparently taken it almost for granted that the
new building would include a gramophone record or sound recordings library, whether or not this particular service was
previously available in the old building.

One of the most difficult factors in preparing a preliminary report is to estimate potential demand. The only

general rule which seems applicable is that the higher the
average standard of education in the locality and the greater
the affluence of the population, the better the chances of the
sound recordings library being well patronised [137]. Standards of selection must also play an important part.

Any attempt to restrict demand, if only for an initial
period, by limiting the use of the service to schools and local
societies only, would seem to be a misguided step; indeed, it
could well be argued that these are likely to be the worst
types of users, simply because collective responsibility usually means no responsibility at all in practice. Each body
should be required to appoint a named individual (or, at
most, two or three specified persons) to borrow recordings,
return them and pay any charges for overdue retention or
damage. Much more practical (in the author's view) is to
limit the scope of the collection rather than the categories
of potential borrowers. Access to the service could be limited originally to local residents who might also be restricted
to a single ticket apiece. Then, as the situation eases in
terms of the number of recordings probably available in the
library for borrowing at any one time, as should happen,
there is the chance to extend on all three fronts--the range
of recordings provided, the area/age within which persons
become eligible for membership, and the number of tickets
issued to each member.

WHAT TO PROVIDE--AND FOR WHOM

What type of records should the collection include? The
scope of the library and its standards of selection are basic
criteria that must be resolved at the outset. In the first
edition of this book, the matter of record sizes and playing
speeds were presented as further hurdles. These erstwhile
variables only marginally concern us; in general, the librarian buying gramophone records now buys 12-inch stereophonic
discs playing at 33 1/3rpm.

The appearance of the Compact Disc has altered the
position considerably. These single-sided discs of 120mm
(4.7") diameter, running for up to an hour or more, have
digital codes in the form of tiny pits moulded into a plastic
base which is silver coated to make it reflective and then
protected by a thick layer of hard plastic on both sides.

The playback system, using a laser light source, is completely different from that of the familiar analogue record, and so
requires a special player. This can, however, be fed into
any good hi-fi amplifier or domestic audio system. Fortunately, as with stereo but unlike video and the ill-fated quadra-
phonic sound discs, there is an agreed universal standard
for these records.

One problem from the purchaser's viewpoint is that
compact discs cost roughly one third more than the normal
LP. The choice of music is also limited, but has shown signs
of extending its range to equal that of the LP catalogue.
Duplication of repertoire is already a minor problem. Pene-
tration into the market is continuing. (The LP is also being
challenged by the increasing quality and consistency of the
cassette by the use of chrome tape and HxPro during recording, although they are easily damaged beyond repair on poor
machines and are not recommended for library use.)

The advantage of the CD disc over LP is in its incred-
ible lack of background noise and very low distortion with no
"fall off" right up to the ends of sides. There is also no
wow or flutter and the frequency range extends without res-
onance much lower than on LP. The normal surface scratch
does not reproduce as a click or pop (as so often happend
with LP), thanks to the error correction built into the system. However, the discs should be handled with care, as
finger prints can cause loss of signal or mistracking, especially on the cheaper machines. Correct treatment can
clean away the finger prints and restore the sound. The
laser does not wear the recording as does the stylus on an
LP. Thus, with reasonable handling, the CD can be played
indefinitely without any deterioration. One problem is that
the protective case which stores the CD and accompanying
notes requires a certain knack to open and this is not easily done by those with arthritic hands. Also, the case will
break if dropped or handled carelessly.

However, the disc answers most of the librarian's problems and seems likely to replace the LP as a library loan item
in the fairly near future, despite the expense.

Reverting to analogue records, the 10-inch disc was
never popular in LP history, despite the fact that it provided
an ideal format for certain works, and had virtually disappeared

by the early 1960s. The 7-inch 45rpm disc has also ceased to be produced in the area of classical music, killed by the 12-inch "bargain" record, which usually offers a playing time of at least four times that of its smaller rival, and sometimes at a lower cost. A very limited number of monophonic records are to be found in the catalogues of currently available material, with new releases approximately balancing the numbers of those deleted. The recordings are almost entirely of old issues which are considered of sufficient historic importance and interest to be worth making generally available again. A number of these performances have been transferred from 78rpm originals (frequently, it might be added, with surprisingly good sound quality and much less obtrusive surface noise than could reasonably have been expected). A proportion of these historical reissues is reprocessed in simulated stereo, but this treatment is no guarantee of improved quality. Where the sound is poor it is not necessarily a result of the pseudo stereo but is probably because the original tape has been transferred to a modern specification which often leaves the engineers with the choice between a thin and undernourished treble or a filtered, generally woolly sound. Critics and music enthusiasts, for whom the performance is often more important than the recording, may feel that the electronically processed stereo effect is less satisfactory by far than the original, but it seems that many collectors will no longer consider buying any disc that is admitted to be monophonic. Indeed, many public libraries have found that their single channel discs are shunned by the majority of borrowers, however great the merits of a performance, however good the recording and however satisfactory the general condition of the record. The time may well come, however, when there will be some slight swing in the pendulum of fashion, in the way that there is now a small but quite lively market for 78rpm discs, with as many youthful collectors as elderly ones.

Despite this, a library is currently unlikely to buy any of these old shellac discs except in special circumstances. Gifts of coarsegroove recordings may be offered to a library. For some years the general response was to reject them; indeed, where a collection of discs had been started before the LP era, there was a widespread tendency to withdraw and scrap all the coarsegroove recordings during the 1950s. Belatedly, it is being recognized that almost any old record in playable condition is likely to have some historic and artistic

value (or, one imagines, it would never have been issued in
the first place), so that the possible importance of an archival collection is slowly being recognized; this matter will be
raised again later in the chapter.

An American view of what facilities and resources
should be provided in a record library was given over thirty
years ago by Otto Luening, who declared that in the good library, "There are a sufficient number of turntables or listening rooms to make the collection available to the community,
and there is a phonograph in the auditorium for the use of
groups and classes. The record collection includes a number
of foreign language sets, recordings of literature, history
and poetry, and enough recordings of children's records to
serve local users" [127, p. 56]. It took much longer in
Britain for listening facilities to become general, but the increasing acceptance of headphone listening made cubicles
(which were nominally soundproof but, in practice, usually
allowed a worrying amount of noise to escape and were often
inadequately ventilated) unnecessary.

Record collections for children are to be found in some
libraries in the Greater London area and in a few other parts
of Britain but, unless there is a general change of viewpoint
by our profession, national coverage is going to take a very
long time indeed to achieve.

For whom should we provide? As has been indicated,
a small number of sound recordings libraries in Britain restricted use of the collection to schools and, possibly local
societies--thus limiting the service to organized bodies. Admittedly, in some cases the term local society was interpreted
very liberally indeed. The great majority of libraries allow
residents within the authority's boundaries to join, although
limitations may still be made, the most usual one specifying a
minimum age for membership. This last is reminiscent of the
high insurance premiums demanded of young drivers which
may be felt to be unduly harsh on the careful ones. With
sound recordings libraries, as with books, one wishes that
there could be devised some method of checking a potential
borrower's sense of responsibility for the material.

Libraries that make no charge to local residents for
use of the sound recordings library may nevertheless require a subscription from those who live outside the area but

who are full-time employees or students within the library's boundaries. The local authority may well require a higher fee from those who neither live nor work in the district and who, therefore, make no regular contribution to the community. Almost every library in Britain accepts valid library tickets from another authority for book loans, but only a handful of places (mainly in the London area) allow the use of their respective sound recording collections with equal freedom and generosity.

It has been mentioned earlier in this chapter that the majority of users of a collection based on classical music will be, for want of a better definition, those who have continued their full-time education to the age of seventeen, or later. This is not to suggest that there will be no borrowers from the factory floor or from behind a shop counter, but they are likely to be a distinct minority. This may affect standards of selection. If one wishes to attract a wider spectrum of the public, then it will be necessary to stock a wider range of music, with emphasis on popular appeal. This is a basic policy decision on which it is difficult to generalize; in a residential district or seaside town with a high proportion of retired people who have moved in from other areas, it is virtually certain that such borrowers will surely represent a large part of a library's clientele. Even the suggestion that there will be more male than female borrowers in the record library may not be universally true, though it is a fairly common experience [236].

The proportion of the local population registered as library book borrowers is likely to vary between 20 percent and 50 percent (although figures beyond these limits can certainly be found), with an average of around 30 percent; for gramophone record libraries the range will be equally varied --from less than 1 percent to approximately 5 percent. These figures will show a wider variation if the standards of selection are very high or are virtually all-embracing, and they will also be affected by the physical condition of the stock and by staff attitudes to members of the public using the service. It is perhaps relevant here to comment that when a survey was carried out in the London Borough of Bromley it was found that: "Out of a total of 20,000 audio borrowers registered throughout the borough, only 3,480 were found to have items on loan on the day of the count.... This represents only 17 percent of the 'paper' registration and a mere

1 percent of the borough population" [144, p. 88]. The
survey was made "during the very busy period mid-
December 1974 to mid-January 1975," and it may be remarked that the borrowing of sound recordings drops off to
a very much higher degree in summer than is the case with
books.

In a college where music is taught as a major or subsidiary subject, one would expect nearly all students to be
regular users of the collection, and listening facilities will
need to be provided on a lavish scale. The collection in
such libraries will almost certainly be closely related to the
areas of the subjects that are taught, and the stock itself
may well be for reference use only. Where this occurs, the
local public library collection is likely to receive much heavier use than would otherwise be the case, and student demands could well influence the stock selection to an important
degree.

Western Music

The Standard Repertoire

Unless the library is one of the small minority whose stock
is limited to records and tapes of the spoken word, poetry
and drama, language tuition, etc., the initial stock will presumably be based on western classical and popular music.
On the face of it, the selection of standard music presents
few problems; all that is needed is a collection that is reasonably balanced between the different categories of music
(vocal, orchestral, chamber and instrumental), generally
limited to composers already represented in the library's
stock of music scores, and with items selected from the manufacturers' catalogues of one's own country, so that there
should be no difficulties in supply. Having decided which
works one should buy, choice between competitive versions
might be solved (in Britain) by following the guidance of
such works as The Art of Record Buying [9], The Penguin
Stereo Record and Cassette Guide [177] and Notes [169].

For new issues, the librarian should read, either personally or by a musically minded proxy (who may well have
a slightly different range of interests in this area), such

periodicals as Gramophone, Hi-Fi News and Record Review,
etc., which are considered fairly fully later in this chapter.
Outside Britain, any librarian will make a choice of available
discographies and periodicals, but may well include at least
one of the British items if only because of the importance of
England as a recording centre for North American as well as
for London-based manufacturers.

    The previous paragraphs have been based on the li-
brary that is too small or unenlightened to employ a full-
time music librarian. While such authorities should no longer
exist in England, small public library systems remain in Scotland and many overseas areas. The pattern outlined, if followed, should make it possible to build up a good basic stock;
a more ambitious programme is probably best delayed until
the opportunity arrives for the collection to expand. At this
point, the librarian may have to rely upon reviews rather
more than before, and may be likely to be buying music by
a number of composers whose names may be completely unfamiliar. Although the number of new records issued each
month in Britain may run into the dozens, this figure is still
tiny compared with the number of new books published, and
it should not take a great deal of time to skim through reviews of all new and reissued records within the library's
chosen categories which, even if broadly based, still probably represent a minority of releases.

    It can easily be seen that the selector is faced with
two recurrent and irreconcilable problems in the field of selection. The library must have an adequate coverage of the
basic classics, for there will always be the borrower who has
yet to hear the famous piano concerto of Tchaikovsky (and
who may well remain in continued ignorance that the composer wrote other works in this form) and the musically immature
listener who will fail to progress beyond a colourfully orches-
trated and tuneful work such as Scheherazade or the second
of Liszt's Hungarian Rhapsodies.

    On the other hand, we are likely to have a percentage
of library users, however small it may be, who would feel it
no hardship if they were told that they would never hear another performance of such great works as Beethoven's Symphony No. 5 or the overture to Die Meistersinger for the
remainder of their listening lives--simply because these and
other masterpieces have become stale and unattractive by

being heard too frequently. Others will have their own copies of recordings of these works; these listeners may well
expect the library to make provision to allow them to hear
less common, and possibly downright rare, works that are
unlikely ever to be encountered in a concert hall and only
very infrequently on radio. It is a legitimate request for a
borrower to ask for the Busoni rather than a Brahms piano
concerto, for a symphony by Martinů rather than one by
Mendelssohn, but the library administering a small collection
on an inadequate budget may consider it quite impossible to
satisfy such requests. The selection balance will almost
certainly be tilted in favour of the popular classic, if only
because such records are certain to be in regular demand.
Where a library is run on a subscription basis, the need
for every record to justify its inclusion by regular loan is
even stronger. This might be counted as a point in favour
of the free collection.

For the smaller library, or the collection in a branch
library, there is the dilemma between alternatives when making a choice as to which version of a work to buy for library
stock. Even large libraries cannot always afford to buy as
many new issues as they would like; many have to select
with some rigor. The obvious temptation is to decide upon
a version on a medium-priced or bargain level, always assuming that a recording in either category has received respectable reviews. In this way, the limited budget may be
stretched a little further. It must never be forgotten, however, that individual borrowers have an even greater incen-
tive than the librarian to prefer to buy the cheaper issues--
for even the wealthiest patron is unlikely to have as much
money for record buying as the smallest library; this writer
knows several collectors who proudly proclaim that they
never buy top-price discs, even though this limitation will
mean that some artists and certain works (particularly less
common operas) will never grace their shelves. Understandably, therefore, some of our patrons will make it clear that
they expect to find the top-price version in the library
stock. This may be regarded unkindly as middle class snob-
bishness (but could equally reflect a good musical and critical sensibility), yet it cannot be dismissed out of hand. The
feeling that one is not getting full value for money when it
is an inexpensive disc that is borrowed rather than a top-
price one is understandable, and is sometimes true. Additionally, many listeners will wish to hear a comparatively

expensive issue and compare it with a cheaper alternative which they own, if only to persuade themselves (rightly or wrongly) that the library's dearer record is not worth its extra cost. A library will, in fact, almost certainly find that it has to buy a fair proportion of high-priced releases, perhaps getting cheaper versions when additional and alternative performances are needed.

If the original selection is conservative and unadventurous, one hopes and imagines that the base can be broadened as time passes and the collection grows. This assumes that more discs will be added each year than are withdrawn from stock, which may not necessarily be true. If the library has no discs of music by Henze or Stockhausen in its collection, how can the open-minded listener discover the music of either or both composers? Impulse buying of recorded music is not uncommon, but it appears that it rarely occurs outside the purchaser's usual musical tastes.

Once a sound recordings library has begun to function the demand for popular standard works is likely to be heavy. Rather than duplicate the particular version already in stock, it is usually preferable to provide an alternative recording even though the second performance may be less satisfactory, in one way or another, than that already bought. Comparisons between performances can provide a source of great interest and enjoyment to the music lover (the British Broadcasting Corporation for many years have provided series such as "Interpretations on record" and "Building a library" which are based on such comparisons). Listening like this is certainly a means of sharpening the critical faculties and can provide pleasure and interest, both for the interested amateur and the experienced professional musician. In any event, it is most unlikely that one particular version of a recorded work will possess all the virtues compared with its rivals to such a degree that it can be considered definitive. Even a slightly inferior performance can provide enhanced enjoyment for many listeners, particularly those whose primary interest is in the sound, if the recorded audio qualities are outstanding.

The standard repertoire (which, in terms of recorded items, seems to be a growing corpus of music) is constantly being recorded anew--partly to accommodate the stream of young performers who are making their way up the musical

ladder of fame, partly to take advantage of continuously improving recording techniques, but also to satisfy a public
that often tends to assume that the latest issue of a particular symphony or concerto must automatically be the best.
These new issues drive some of their predecessors out of
the manufacturers' catalogues, although older versions that
continue to sell well naturally retain their respective places,
often for a surprisingly long time. When discs are deleted,
a proportion of them will reappear later, usually on another
label or in a different series produced by the original manufacturers. The price of the reissue is normally lower than
that previously charged, but this is not necessarily the case.
For the librarian, this never-ending flow of new recordings
of standard works may result in pressure from certain patrons
to buy a particular issue, even though it may compare badly
with examples already in stock, both for performance and recording, and despite the fact that a version held by the library may be in excellent condition. It is poor policy to
duplicate a work that is rarely, if ever, borrowed--unless
the alternative issue is so very much better than its predecessor that it is likely to be taken out with some frequency,
and may be regarded as a replacement.

The individual purchaser is likely to be deterred from
adding a lengthy opera or other choral work to stock. It is
one thing to buy a recording of Oberon or Parsifal that is
unlikely to be played as much as once a year after the first
rapture of possession has faded; it is very different to borrow a recording of a work such as those mentioned, knowing
that if one wishes to hear it again in a year or two's time,
the library should still have a copy for loan. A gramophone
record may be compared with a motor car, in that both objects will usually be depreciating in value whether they are
being used or not, and it seems pointless to buy an expensive set of discs unless satisfied that one is likely to receive
good value from the money spent. If this thesis be accepted,
it is another argument in favour of library provision for minority interests, providing that the individual borrower who
suggests that the library adds a particular work to stock is
not likely to be the only person who will take it home on
loan.

It should be mentioned that, since the 1960s, the record manufacturers have generally become unhelpful, even to
libraries, when a single record in an album needs replacement.

It is now normal practice to refuse a request of this nature, so that the borrower responsible for damaging one disc badly may well have to pay the assessed value of the whole album if the individual record cannot be replaced. This unfortunate change of policy is apparently one of the less happy results of the companies' switching from manual to automated stock control.

Librarians and collectors may be offered package deals, such as forty-six Mozart symphonies (and that number is not a misprint), the complete piano works of Schubert, or the like. Such sets are issued in one or more albums and at an average cost per record that represents an attractive discount on normal prices. In most cases these offers are available for a limited period, after which individual records from the set may be reissued, but at normal rates and with different catalogue numbers. This is understandable enough. There are, however, cases in which individual records are issued separately over a period of months or even years, only to be collected together subsequently and issued as a set at a reduced price. One might instance, as examples, both the Boult and Previn versions of Vaughan Williams' symphonies. These reduced price offers, some of which require a fairly substantial financial outlay at one time, are probably less attractive to the librarian than to the individual, partly because the library may already have enough copies of X's symphonies to make the bulk purchase of a collected set of little interest, but mainly because of the handling problems involved. If the library's policy is to issue individual records from the set, the lack of outer sleeves and the manufacturer's supply of a single booklet or set of notes for the entire set will cause problems; this matter is considered more fully later in this chapter. If the library issues the album as a unit, it can still be a hurdle to good public relations. An intending borrower may find the sheer bulk of the album intimidating and impossible to play through in the normal loan period; on the other hand, he may wish to listen to one or two items only and find that, to do so, it is necessary to borrow a set of eight, ten or even more discs. One library supplier has called these sets a disaster for corporate purchase because of the difficulties caused by them. Where a library does buy sets of this nature, there may be justification of any duplication entailed if the works are popular in themselves or the single discs (in the case of a collection built up from previously issued recordings, such

as those of Vaughan Williams instanced above) have shown
that there is sufficient demand to warrant the extra coverage.

Composer as Interpreter

It has long been realized that the printed score can give
only an approximation of what the composer wishes to express. Since the introduction of recording, composers have
had the means to hand down to posterity a fairly clear demonstration of their intentions. They may play or conduct
the work; if that is not practical they may be willing to su-
pervise the musical side of a recording so that the resulting
performance ought to be satisfactory. The number of composers who have been executants of one type or another on
record has grown steadily over the years; one might cite Elgar, Rachmaninov, Richard Strauss, Samuel Barber and Benjamin Britten as a handful of examples. The [English] Decca
monophonic versions of the first six symphonies of Vaughan
Williams were all recorded in the presence of the composer,
who was there to be consulted by the conductor, Adrian
Boult, when any doubtful point of interpretation arose. It
was during this series that Vaughan Williams altered the solo
flute note at the end of the slow movement of the fourth
symphony and, on completion of the recording of his sixth
symphony, the composer made a short speech paying tribute
to the conductor and orchestra--an oral imprimatur. Although recorded performances sometimes indicate that composers do not necessarily follow their own tempi indications
and are not always the best performers of their own works,
recordings of this type deserve generous representation in a
library. It may be thought best to keep the first copies of
such records for reference use only, limiting home loans to
duplicate copies or alternative versions. This topic is fully
discussed in an article by Peter Griffiths [87].

Quite a number of coarsegroove recordings of this
authoritative type have been reissued subsequently in LP
format (Elgar has been generously treated in this way in
Britain). The present-day engineers have obviously had to
take the original discs or matrices (where they still exist
and are in reasonable condition) as a starting point, and the
skill with which some of the transfers have been made is often tremendous. The major disideratum of such discs has

been to eliminate as much of the surface noise as is possible
(even where the early disc or cylinder has been very scratch-
y) without impairing or distorting the musical sound [237]
and to make unobtrusive joins where one side of the original
ended and the next began. The best examples of these
transfers seems to be better than the originals, by adding
slightly to the ambience of the disc, (often by means of a
touch of reverberation to offset a constricted or "boxy"
sound) and a handful of recording engineers have gained
well-deserved reputations for their skills in this specialist
field. It may be of interest to mention that the British
Broadcasting Corporation has sometimes lent its copy of a
particular disc to the original manufacturer when the latter
has neither matrix nor a pressing in what are usually referred to as a company's vaults.

Of a different nature are the published recordings of
conductors at rehearsal; these are rather more variable in
value since they do not necessarily give an insight into the
individual alchemy that great exponents bring to music of
which they are noted interpreters. Beecham rehearsals, if
a particular record is taken at its face value, consisted mainly of witticisms (and it is said that the conductor was unaware that the recording was being made, and furious when it
was released). On the other hand, the recording of Mozart's
Linz symphony under Bruno Walter displays how this great
conductor tackled the problem of persuading an orchestra
that was strange to him to play as he wanted. The three
rehearsal sides (with the actual recorded performance taking
the fourth side) will never lose their historical and interpretative value.

For a long time, such performances seem to have been
better appreciated in Britain than in the USA where the
technical limitations of a recording of this type often caused
complaints, despite any explanatory sleeve note which made it
clear that this particular item was made available for its historical and interpretative values, and not for its aural ones.
However, mechanical limitations seem to matter much less with
enthusiasts of vocal music as microgroove reissues of operatic
excerpts, Lieder, etc., made by famous singers in the early
years of the century are still being reissued. Argument in
this specialist area tends to be limited to the matter of the
correct pitch of a recording, since early examples were made
to play at differing speeds by different manufacturers and

usually without clear indication on the label of what the playing speed should be. If vocalists had always sung the recorded items in the original key, there would be no problem, but it was common and understandable that transposition was often made so that the music was comfortably within the compass of the singer concerned.

Musical History

There are many recordings whose primary musical interest is probably historic rather than intrinsic. Some of the works will be played on instruments that are no longer in general use and many will use an harmonic language that may well seem harsh and rudimentary to ears long accustomed to listening to music of the eighteenth and nineteenth centuries. Such discs may include works by composers whose names can be found in musical histories but whose compositions have long since disappeared from the vocal or instrumental repertory, usually rightly. Posterity ruthlessly separates the wheat from the chaff, but not infallibly. Not least of the gramophone's virtues was (and is) the opportunity given to us to discover how much we had underrated certain composers. The outstanding example is perhaps Vivaldi whose return to popularity seems mainly due to the agency of the gramophone record. Other composers who have been discovered or rediscovered, to a greater or lesser degree, include Schütz, Telemann and Ives. If it was fair to say, less than twenty years ago, that works played on such instruments as the clavichord, viola da gamba and lute were regarded with some suspicion by many listeners, it is no longer true--and the gramophone can claim much of the credit for having opened the ears of many to the fact that works written for these, and other, obsolete instruments often sound better when played on original instruments or modern replicas than on the successors to these instruments. One would think this to be self-evident, but the truth took a long time to penetrate twentieth-century ears.

Music written before the time of J. S. Bach and his contemporaries may present almost as many harmonic problems as that of Bartók or Schoenberg to untutored music lovers. Music of this period, as well as earlier examples going back to the thirteenth century or even earlier, is now well represented in the recorded music catalogues, even

though it it still not often heard live in the church or concert hall. That public interest and acceptance has grown so
much in recent years is to the joint credit of the recording
and broadcasting companies.

There should be little need to recall and stress the
value of The History of Music in Sound series, but it must
be admitted that these recordings clearly show their age, not
least in the fact that the set is entirely monophonic; some of
the performances are also of a poorer standard than is desirable. The passing years have added yet another drawback, in that when the recordings were made, many of the
excerpts selected were not otherwise available in recorded
form; the metaphorical explosion of the recorded repertoire
since the introduction of stereophony has drastically altered
the situation. For example, there was no other version of
Haydn's Hornsignal symphony, in the British catalogues when
the "History" included the first and last movements of this
work. Now there are alternative performances of the complete work available; these do not have the artistry of horn-
ist Dennis Brain, but they do generally offer very much better recording. One could level other criticisms at the "History," which still has some value in a public library or college collection, although many librarians may regard it as
obsolete. One hopes that a replacement series of new recordings will soon be forthcoming to illustrate in sound The
New Oxford History of Music which is taking so many years
to reach completion.

The Archiv label, issued by Deutsche Grammophon
Gesellschaft, continues to provide its universally recognized
combination of scholarship, authentic instrumentation and
performance, and excellent recording. Few records in this
series can be regarded as failures. The basically uniform
sleeve cover, layout of the text and style of presentation
have combined to present a considerable deterrent to the
average borrower. The change of sleeve colour from pale
biscuit to light grey and the improvement in typography;
the addition, in many cases, of a suitable coloured vignette
in the middle of the front of a sleeve--all these factors together give, overall, a more attractive appearance, yet far
too many excellent works and recordings are liable to lan-
guish unborrowed on library shelves because the sleeve is
still too austere for many potential users. If the attractive
sleeve can persuade a potential borrower to take out an

inferior record, the reverse is equally true. The series'
terminal date of 1800 was extended during 1972 to allow for
the inclusion of some early nineteenth-century compositions.

Other companies have issued a variety of records illustrating, in particular, early music history up to the time of
J. S. Bach. Mention should be made of Telefunken's Das
alte Werk series which competes with Archiv for authenticity,
for detailed notes and, often, unattractive sleeves. When
one compares the position with that existing when the first
edition of this book was published, the librarian is now very
much better served, even though one may sometimes harbour
the unkind suspicion that some of the recorded performances
of mediaeval music have been far too raucous or garish in
their attempts to avoid any suggestion of dullness.

At the other end of the time scale, contemporary and
early twentieth-century music is also more fully represented
in the catalogues than it was in the early days of LP records,
and this music is not confined to top-price releases. The
thought may occur that the manufacturers seem to issue some
of these items from a sense of duty rather than according to
normal commercial considerations, since a high proportion of
such discs (for only a fraction have as yet appeared in cassette form) are deleted after an extremely brief life and before they have had adequate chance to establish themselves,
even when the recording has been subsidised by a body such
as the Gulbenkian Foundation or the Welsh Arts Council. It
behooves the librarian, therefore, to buy promptly any well-
reviewed recording of a contemporary work, since delay in
ordering may mean that the disc cannot then be supplied.

Mention must be made here of Composers Recordings
Incorporated, of New York, a company devoted exclusively
to producing performances of contemporary music. The catalogue comprises several hundred discs. For libraries and
educational institutions prepared to place standing orders
for all releases, the selling price of the discs is considerably reduced. The technical quality of recording and interpretation seems to have been generally good. Some of the
orchestras listed are not well-known internationally--one
might instance the Iceland Symphony Orchestra or the Im-
perial Philharmonic Orchestra of Tokyo. CRI's catalogue, it
should be noted, includes the name of the publisher of the
appropriate score, the duration of the work (where applicable)

and the instrumentation; all of these are points which add to the helpfulness of each entry.

Contemporary composers in other countries may also receive either government or semi-official help as with Donemus (Documentatie in Nederland voor Muzick) in Holland or CeBeDeM (Centre Belge de Documentation Musicale) in Belgium, both of which bodies issue recordings at regular intervals.

Rare and Early Recordings

It is unfortunate that few libraries (with the honourable exception of the national broadcasting companies) as yet seem to make any consistent attempt to build up archival collections of withdrawn discs; fewer still have any interest in the shellac examples of pre-LP days. There is an excuse for making no attempt to collect ancient rarities; some early vocal discs, in particular, are extremely expensive to buy. Although there may be only a small minority of dedicated enthusiasts really interested, the supply of these acoustic discs is generally well below the level to satisfy even a small market. The possession of collectors' items which have a scarcity value can be an embarrassment to the library, particularly if requests are received to make tape recordings of any of them. The majority of public and other libraries will, therefore, probably content themselves with the reissues in microgroove form of old acoustic recordings, rejoicing in the fact that the cost of a single reprint is almost certainly well below the price asked for one of the shellac originals, and equally pleased that problems of security and damage are no greater than with any other disc.

In general, university and college libraries have less interest in the archival aspect than the enlightened public library, but this is not universally true. A course of music history and appreciation, comparing different interpretations, or another course on the history and technique of sound recording would both have use for early recordings. Courses of both types are to be found in the USA.

For tracing old records and for some help in identifying the contents, there are a number of useful aids. Robert Bauer's New Catalogue of Historical Records, 1898-1908/9 has

been reprinted at least twice and remains valuable [15].
P. G. Hurst's The Golden Age Recorded, can also be recommended [100]. Voices of the Past, which consists of what
may best be described as sectional discographic lists, has
already been mentioned [16]. These volumes are of permanent reference value and worth adding to stock in any but
the smallest libraries.

Folk Music

Interest in folk music has grown at an amazing rate in the
period between the publication of the two editions of this
book. Its very popularity has been something of a mixed
blessing to public libraries, for reasons explained below.
The term "folk" (the word "music" is often omitted when
talking about the subject) covers at least three major categories with almost imperceptible shadings between each.
First, there is the genuine traditional song that would be
instantly recognized as such by collectors of the generation
of Cecil Sharp and Ralph Vaughan Williams, i.e., tunes and
words of varying antiquity, without a known author or composer, and often with regional variants in both words and
music. To this might be added the songs derived from the
Industrial Revolution, which frequently tell of poverty and
degradation or the struggles by the workers against tyran-
nical employers, which were clearly written as an outlet of
social protest and which have their counterparts today. Au-
thentically, these types of song are normally given without
accompaniment and often by singers of very limited vocal
range and technique. The result was that the appeal of
such recordings used to be restricted to a small band of
dedicated enthusiasts, social historians and the like. However, there seems to be a growing general tolerance of inadequate vocal attainment as authenticity has become more
fashionable.

   The second category is related to the first but here
the songs are fairly modern, are usually related to a particular industry or craft (such as cotton weaving or service
before the mast), and their authors/composers are occasionally known in Western Europe and the USA. Most often
these songs are sung to a fairly simple harmonic accompaniment of guitar, tin whistle, etc., and the singers are professional or semiprofessional; there has been a proliferation

both in Britain and the USA of both solo singers and small groups. The third type of folk song is synthetic and may be written in cowboy, hillbilly, West Indian or other style. In a few cases compositions of this nature are the result of conscious attempts to produce modern equivalents of the old-style folk songs, in that they deal with contemporary incidents, usually tragic, such as a mine disaster or a flood.

The problem is that this third, somewhat diffuse, category tails off into pop music and it is difficult, even for an expert, to draw a hard and fast line. Because of the pressures from borrowers to broaden still further the basis of selection if a library includes folk music, a number of librarians have deliberately refrained from providing any--however deplorable this decision might be considered by others.

No mention has been made of folk and national songs of countries other than one's own. Most East European countries, such as Bulgaria, Poland, and Romania, where record manufacturing is a state industry, have produced large numbers of discs of indigenous material, and this aspect of ethnomusicology seems generally acceptable in British collections. Similarly, there seems to be a better case for the provision of Scottish and Welsh folk songs than there is for English, even though Wales is now producing an increasing amount of pop music, an offshoot of the widening interest in that country's native language and culture. Synthetic Scottish folk songs have a much longer history, and a few examples of these may easily deceive the unwary into the belief that they are genuinely part of an undoubtedly rich heritage.

Pop Music

Language and music are constantly in a state of flux, and the popular music of our grandparents has little in common with that of today. Popular has been shortened to pop and, in that form, has acquired international acceptance. The same can be said for such records in library stocks. An increasing number of public libraries has extended coverage into this area over the past few years, and the introduction of cassettes into library stocks (with less likelihood of damage than is faced by the equivalent discs) has clearly provided an opportunity to think afresh on the matter, often

with positive results. As an American music librarian has
suggested: "If book collections had been developed with the
principles of selection used by today's record librarians, libraries would contain only incunabula and classic literature,"
and continues, "Record selection policies, however, generally
reflect the past rather than the present needs of the community" [91, p. 518].

Part of the difficulty is that the range of present-day
pop is very wide; another problem is that conservative music librarians are understandably biased in favour of standard classical music and have little knowledge of, and possibly as little sympathy with, pop. Many serious musicians
and music lovers aver that this is the area of music in which
most genuine advances are being made, and that too many
contemporary composers in the classical field, with their reliance upon aleatory music and/or atonality, and an apparent
unwillingness to write anything resembling a tune that can
be sung, are putting an ever-increasing distance between
themselves and their potential audiences. The border between what is often called progressive pop, jazz, and classical music is never stable, and the varied (and often imaginative) use of electronic sounds has made a great impact
upon composition.

Most libraries that stock pop restrict themselves to
12-inch discs, refusing to supply 45rpm singles for library
use, partly on the argument that the musical life of the
great majority of the items so available is extremely brief,
and partly on the assumption that adolescents (at whom this
market seems to be aimed) are often well able to buy such
discs for themselves. The ephemeral nature of the product
is perhaps best reflected in the flimsy paper sleeve provided
for protection. So selection in this area is as important as
in any other. To quote Hagist again, "Some aspects of popular music seem to hold the least justification for library expenditure. This is not to exclude the entire popular scene.
As in current fiction there is great variance in the quality
of composition. Much ephemeral material is produced which
does not meet the library's standards on grounds of composition and lasting value" [91, p. 520].

Jazz

This section of the equivalent chapter, in the original edi-

tion, began with the words: "This is a most controversial
field when considering provision." That is no longer true;
jazz is now widely accepted as an important part of our musical culture. It is an area (rather like folk music) in which
the demarcation between what might be called the permanent
and the ephemeral is not clear, yet which should not be impossible to discern by the conscientious music librarian.

The growing respectability of jazz is further indicated
by the increasing number of carefully researched reference
books which have been published on the subject. There is
clearly a large audience with an interest in the exact personnel of each item recorded by a band or other smaller jazz
group, and also in the lives and careers of the more famous
instrumentalists and singers. Such books as Leonard Feather's The Encyclopedia of Jazz [69] and its sequel, The Encyclopedia of Jazz in the Sixties [70], Brian Rust's Jazz Records, 1897-1942 [189], and Modern Jazz: The Essential Records, compiled by Max Harrison and others [93] are but a
few of the host of books that reflect this interest. Many
record sleeves are careful to include the dates of the recordings and the names of the various musicians on each
track. If this information is omitted (without explanation)
or is erroneous, the offending manufacturer is usually made
quickly aware of the heinous offence by a bevy of critics,
professional and amateur. One problem for the librarian,
particularly when using the lists of recommended records in
these and similar books as a purchasing guide, is that jazz
discs appear and are deleted, often to be issued again under a different number on a different label (perhaps with a
different omnibus title for the collection of items) with a ra-
pidity that makes the recommendations obsolete, at least as
far as the catalogue numbers are concerned, before the reference book appears from the printers.

There are various categories in this musical area, but
the basic division is between traditional and modern jazz.
Both styles, and their various categories, should be represented in the library collection, and the librarian may perhaps be accused by supporters of each type of unduly fa-
vouring the rival class. A decision about scope should be
made at the same time as the policy to buy. It may not always be possible at a later date to change or amend the
policy in respect of vocal jazz, or any other particular aspect of the field, in the light of different circumstances or
of experience. Expansion of the range covered is simple--

retrenchment may prove impossible without a major confrontation with aggrieved borrowers.

There was some hesitation in the planning stages as to whether jazz should be included in the Greater London Audio Specialization Scheme (GLASS) which began in 1972, but it was decided to make this coverage in the allocations to individual libraries, which was a particularly welcome decision for patrons of those libraries that previously had excluded this type of music. Various ways of giving allocation responsibilities to the individual libraries were considered--by period, by type of jazz, by instrument, etc., but in the end it was agreed that the simplest means was the arbitrary one of an alphabetical breakdown of performers' names into groups of initial letters that should produce roughly the same expenditure for each library taking part; responsibility for purchase is decided, when more than one featured artist is on a single disc, by the first-named person on the record sleeve.

Non-Western Music

There has been a tremendous upsurge in general interest in this area in the past twenty years; the major emphasis has been on Indian music. Executants of the calibre of Yehudi Menuhin have combined with Indian musicians in performance, and the sitar has joined the harpsichord and other unexpected instruments used by pop groups in their search for unusual musical sounds. It is instrumental music which has boomed; Indian vocal music usually remains very much less popular. Chinese and Japanese classical music (which frequently sounds oddly occidental to European ears) have so far had less impact, but their turn may well come. The exotic music of Bali has long been popular and has had its effect on western music for many years, as may be heard in some of Debussy's compositions, for example.

African music is as varied in its different forms as is Asiatic, but so far is little known; however, ethnomusicology is of increasing interest to many people and there is a growing realization that the spread of western civilisation is often inimical to native culture, so that attempts are being made to record as much as possible of both vocal and instrumental music.

Much of this extra-European material has proved of
interest to library borrowers in collections that have included
it; where the local authority has a sizeable immigrant population, there could be an expressed demand for music of
their respective countries. Such borrowers, however, may
be as difficult to satisfy as are those other residents who
are not prepared to borrow outside such areas as Gilbert &
Sullivan operas, brass band, or other equally restricted
field. The availability of new material in these very limited
areas is almost certainly to be an overriding factor, however
anxious the librarian may be to try to satisfy such requests.
It may be possible, in some cases, to strengthen representation by ordering records which have to be specially imported,
but this is usually an expensive process.

Educational

Comment here is limited to recordings concerned with music;
non-musical educational works are considered later. For the
keen instrumentalist or singer who (understandably) lacks
an orchestra, other instrumentalists or even an adequate accompanist, the American Music Minus One series is invaluable.
Each disc in the catalogue omits a single part in the recording
--the soloist in a concerto, one line in a chamber music work,
the vocal part in a song or aria. The user plays or sings the
unrecorded part in synchronisation with the recorded music.
The value of such discs should not need stressing; the drawbacks are also apparent. The performer accompanies the
record, rather than being accompanied by other players.
This limitation cannot be overcome, although it might be argued that a recording of this nature indicates to its prospective user what is a reasonable tempo for the piece of music
that is to be performed. The records really need a good reproducing machine to offer maximum benefit--not simply to
give the best possible sound in the accompaniment, but also
because it is usually only with comparatively expensive playing decks that one is able to make very small adjustments to
the turntable's playing speed which may be needed to bring
the recorded pitch into tune with the soloist's own instrument, particularly if the latter is a piano. The range of
available material is much wider than many British librarians
realize. Provision is made for such instruments as baritone
saxophone, recorder and vibraphone; there is also a Broadway

theater series of pit band accompaniments to popular musicals useful to amateur societies, and mention might be made
of the instruction records for different types of guitar playing.

The various series which illustrated musical chronology
have already received comment. The small (now apparently
defunct) Jupiter Recordings company issued a number of
7-inch EP discs under the series title Talking About Music;
these were recorded analytical outlines by Antony Hopkins
of standard classical works. These appreciations were given
with that lucidity and interesting approach that has made
this particular speaker so popular with many music lovers.
Unfortunately, the music illustrations to these recorded talks
were all played on a piano. It is regrettable that the issuing company apparently lacked a sufficiently close link with
the major firm that did the disc pressing for them to be able
to have access to orchestral recordings which would have
been so much more helpful to listeners.

In 1972, Discourses (a firm based at Tunbridge Wells
in Kent) inaugurated a series of discs with spoken commen-
taries by Denis Matthews dealing with Beethoven's sketch
books. This would seem to be highly suitable material for
purchase by public or academic library. Reference could
also be made to a number of records, issued by various
firms, which are designed to illustrate the instruments of
the orchestra. Any issue of this nature, unless very badly
reviewed, should find its way into a library stock unless the
department is considered to be entirely recreational and to
have no educational objective.

Poetry and Drama

Over the past twenty years substantial and easily available
additions in these related areas have widened the possible
scope considerably, although it must be said at the outset
that this type of recording is less likely to be borrowed than
any other, except in academic libraries. In public collections, loans are most likely to be made to teachers and to
students working for examinations in English or American
literature.

In drama, there are virtually two complete sets of

Shakespeare plays (on Argo and Caedmon), each with its own overall virtues and limitations. With the more popular titles, even the small collection should find both companies' recordings to be valuable and regularly borrowed. Although, presumably for reasons of commercial prudence, the available recorded dramatic repertoire tends to be fairly heavily weighted in favour of standard works, from Marlowe to Shaw, other playwrights are certainly not ignored. British domestic catalogues contain, at the time of writing, recordings of plays by Albee, Ibsen and Yeats (to select but three non-English dramatists).

There has been a large and heartening expansion in the number of poetry recordings issued; these should be useful to many colleges, schools and other educational institutions as well as to public libraries. Although many more contemporary poets have been recorded reading their own works than was the case a decade or less ago, some of these discs seem to have a short life in the current catalogues. This suggests poor sales and could well point to a sad lack of enterprise in selection and purchase by lecturers, teachers and librarians alike.

On the Argo label, The English Poets from Chaucer to Yeats (the latter is not English at all, but that may not be considered relevant) has covered a period of nearly 600 years, with varying adequacy from century to century, in about sixty discs. The problem of deciding which works to include and which to omit can easily be imagined and there will always be a measure of disagreement with any editor's choices. Generally, the series shows an understandable preference for the shorter, complete work but the manufacturers claim that "many of the important long poems [are] recorded either complete or slightly abridged." In 1971, the series was deleted from its top-price category and reissued on a midprice label with a different prefix and new serial catalogue numbers. This price reduction was clearly welcome; less welcome was the omission of leaflets giving the texts of the works on a disc.

Documentary

This is a wide field which requires only brief mention. Items will generally fall into one of two categories--the original and

the reconstructed. In the former class, one might cite
Churchill's wartime speeches taken from actual recordings
made at the time. The statesman's postwar rereadings of
some of his other earlier speeches probably fits the second
category. The BBC has made generally available a number
of items taken from its own recorded archives; one might
instance the disc entitled I Was There, which is a collection
of eye-witness descriptions including the British declaration
of war against Germany in 1914, of the Reichstag fire, and
of reminiscences by Lady Violet Bonham-Carter of her father
(Asquith), Lloyd George, and others. The second category
may be exemplified by a talk recorded by A. J. P. Taylor
on The Bolshevik revolution or by HMV's discs devoted to
such historical figures as Queen Elizabeth I, the Duke of
Wellington, and others in British history. These are a mixture of reportage, quotations from letter, etc., and may
help metaphorically to bring alive past history.

Railways

British enthusiasts have made something of a speciality in
this particular area. Unfortunately, steam traction was in
rapid decline by the time stereo recording was fully established, but the different sounds of a wide range of locomotives have been made available. The Argo label (through
its Transacord subsidiary) is the best known, but there are
a number of very small companies which have produced similar recordings, although such discs may be difficult both to
trace and to acquire. Having exhausted British possibilities
except for "preserved" locomotives running (rarely at speeds
higher than a comfortable amble) on privately owned tracks,
later recordings were made on the European continent where
steam traction was still to be found. A number of similar
recordings were also made in the USA by American companies.

Language Instruction

Not all librarians are yet prepared to stock language tuition
discs, although resistance to this form of provision is much
weaker than it was a decade or more ago. Where courses
are stocked and are available for home loan, it is still general practice to issue records singly rather than as sets.
When possible, extra instructional books that accompany each

set are purchased, so that a copy of the appropriate tutor
text can be issued with each record. To allow for the dilatory or recalcitrant borrower who fails to return a disc or
cassette on time, it has become common practice in larger
collections to buy extra sets of these courses, sometimes to
the extent of several copies for the languages most in demand. If it is possible to buy the first disc or cassette in
a set as a separate item, it is recommended that one or two
extra copies be added to stock, since there are sure to be
optimistic students who start a course with the best of intentions but whose fervour for another language fails to
survive beyond the first or second lessons.

Satisfaction with a particular course will vary from
student to student; since the teaching approach of a particular series is not necessarily the same as that of its competitors, there is much to be said for the provision of alternatives where this is possible. In Britain, choice is usually
between the BBC and Linguaphone sets. Comparisons are
not easily made. The British Broadcasting Corporation's
courses are appreciably the cheaper of the two, but coverage is limited to the major languages taught via radio or
television. Library users cannot take advantage of the
Linguaphone service which allows individual purchasers to
send to the company written work based upon the particular
course, for Linguaphone tutorial staff to mark and return
the scripts.

Public demand is usually concentrated upon a handful
of languages, reflecting commercial or holiday interests, so
that British libraries are normally strongest in the provision
of French, German, Italian, Russian, and Spanish. The possibilities, however, are very much wider than this. The
series offered by Spoken Language Services covers thirty
different languages. With one or two exceptions, each course
consists of six cassettes together with an accompanying book.
Some of the older courses are based upon those originated
for the use of American servicemen during the second world
war, so their credentials are good. Linguaphone, with
courses of about the same length, offer an even wider choice
with thirty-four languages--some on disc, some in cassette
form, and with a growing number available in both formats.

The Middle East is an area of growing commercial importance, so that there is likely to be increasing demand

for the courses originated by Osman Arabic Centre. There
are eight different sets, including Egyptian, Farsi (Persian)
and Omani. As for courses in the English language, one
has the impression that BBC courses are a little more idio-
matic than those of Linguaphone, but both are recommendable.

As has been indicated above, not all the same languages
are covered by each originator, so that the good librarian
will investigate the coverage of all the manufacturers mentioned above, as well as any others that are discovered.
Where the alternatives are available, both discs and cassettes should be bought, although the tape format is preferable here because it allows the regular replay of a section
without damage to the tape, whereas the regular lowering of
a stylus onto the same section of a disc can cause considerable harm over a brief period if the borrower is heavy handed and the reproducer does not incorporate a control to ensure the gentle lowering of the stylus into the groove. Many
of our users much prefer to borrow discs rather than cassettes, and one has a suspicion that this may well be because it is much easier to transfer the content of disc to
tape (quite illegally, or course) but more difficult to do
similar copying from a cassette original since a much smaller
proportion of the public has access to a second cassette
recorder. The matter of relative wear and damage, mentioned above in passing, is considered more fully towards
the end of the chapter.

The American issues of Conversaphone offer six courses
in cartridge form, but this format is not recommended, not
least because a very small percentage of potential borrowers
have a suitable domestic reproducing machine. Mention should
also be made of a number of basic courses for travellers issued by several manufacturers. Linguaphone sets include
flash cards that one can use to ask such things as the time
of a train departure if the enquirer's vocabulary or accent
proves an insoluble barrier to the person interrogated.
These courses are not usually stocked by libraries, and it
seems reasonable to expect individuals to buy their own package of cassette and handbook.

Miscellaneous Material

Available recordings deal with a multiplicity of subjects that are likely to contain some surprises for those who have not previously investigated this field. In general, companies in the USA have been very much more adventurous than British ones (possibly because the potential market is so very much larger), as an inspection of the Schwann catalogue will show. Most transatlantic discs can be imported into Britain through one or other of the various firms that offer this service; a number of these companies and individuals advertise regularly in Gramophone and similar periodicals. It would possibly be misplaced initiative for a British librarian to order a disc of bongo drum instruction or on How to be a disc jockey; similarly, only a highly specialist library is likely to find a public for the calls of North American frogs or Handwriting analysis--but the American manufacturers also provide a varied selection of potentially valuable material of more general appeal. There are, for example, instructional records on Tonal counterpoint of the eighteenth century, and "Teach Yourself Atonal Music."

Various companies have, at different times, issued readings from the Bible. The selected readers have ranged from the internationally famous (e.g., Lord Olivier) to the virtually unknown. There is a host of instructional records on commercial topics, such as shorthand, typing, writing business letters, and selling by telephone.

Libraries may find it useful to have in stock recordings which help to ensure that reproducing equipment is properly set up, with the left and right hand stereo channels properly separated and not reversed. Other recordings have been issued which allow one to check the range of frequencies reproduced by one's player, or the limitations of one's hearing, whichever is the narrower, since for older listeners the machine may well reproduce high frequencies which the ear can no longer discern. The firm of Discourses issued a record, in conjunction with Hi-Fi News and Record Review, entitled What is Good Recorded Sound? to illustrate some of the problems faced by recording engineers in matters of balance and microphone placing, and what can happen when correct solutions are not found.

It is in the educational and informational field that the librarian is likely to have most difficulty in discovering just what is available. A number of book publishers have branched out into the cassette market, and an appreciable proportion of the items issued by them (and by a wide variety of other

bodies of different kinds) is of potential interest to the
sound recordings librarian. One must discover one's own
sources to a very great extent, by looking at publishers'
catalogues, by reference to such lists of audiovisual media
as the Helpis [238] catalogue, and so on.

The difficulty in finding out just what has been produced underlines the need for a British National Discography
or, taking a wider view, a British Media Record. The Sound
Recordings Group of the Library Association, formed in 1964,
saw the need and collected what information it could; the
broadening interest, reflected in the change of designation
to the Audio-Visual Group in 1973, was also shown in members' pressing for a media bibliography rather than one limited to discs and cassettes. The basis of such a listing of
sound recordings has nearly always been envisaged as the
collection of the British Institute of Recorded Sound, (now
National Sound Archives) which is mainly funded from government sources and which currently receives a copy of each
disc published by the major companies, almost a form of copyright deposit. For a national agency to function effectively
in this way, legal deposit of all sound recordings would need
to be compulsory, as with books; a better system (because
of its probable greater effectiveness) would be the provision
of an annual grant which would permit the purchase every-
thing issued. If manufacturers knew that they would be
paid for every recording, even if it were at trade price,
there would be little point in trying to evade their responsibilities as could well happen if copies had to be donated.
The cost of such a programme would not be excessive. In
1973, it was reckoned to be "in the region of Ł15,000 to
purchase all UK LPs and singles during the current year
(roughly 5000 LPs and 3000 singles). This does not, however, take into account other carriers such as tape cassettes
and cartridges" [191, p. 50].

The article envisages a monthly publication (since this
coincides with the issue programme of the major disc manufacturers), with six- and twelve-month cumulations. The
latter could then be further cumulated into five or seven
year gatherings. This last figure, odd as it may first appear, is chosen because it is reckoned that this is the length
of time that it takes for a complete turnover of available
stock from any given date.

The most practical arrangement would seem to be in three sequences--by composer for classical music, by performer(s) for light and popular items, and in a classified sequence for non-musical material. DDC would be preferred for the last part since it would directly relate to BNB. As with BCM and the dividing line between books and scores, there would always be difficult cases that tended to slip between categories or to spill over into more than one but, as with that existing bibliography, a comprehensive index would overcome the problem. As for cataloguing, Saddington suggests the use of the LA/NCET rules; rather surprisingly, he "would not expect to find the names of a particular chamber ensemble cited on catalogue entries," but would relegate that information to the index. Additionally, he envisages a separate sequence of manufacturers' numbers which, at present, provide the nearest thing we have to an international system, since the habit is growing of issuing recordings under the same catalogue numbers in Britain, Germany, the USA, and elsewhere.

Mention might be made, on that point, that there have been attempts to agree on an international standard description for discs and tape cassettes and cartridges to match up with ISBD(M) for books and ISBD(S) for periodicals. Work has been going on for several years but not, so far, with any real success.

STOCK SELECTION

In the pages that follow, some types of sound recordings are noted together with points to consider when making selection, and with other aspects of provision. Although it results in a certain amount of repetition, readers may find it helpful to have a general review of the matter as a means of, metaphorically, getting their bearings. There are three major aspects of stock provision. First, the music librarian will require to know what performances of an individual work are currently available on disc or tape. Secondly, there will be need for recommendations of the most highly regarded version of a composition when there are several available competing recordings. The librarian's third requirement is to be able to keep up with new releases as they appear, month by month.

Only the first of these three complementary activities

is considered here. The other two are treated a little later
in this chapter. To discover what is currently available in
the area of classical music, be it on disc or tape, the standard British work is Gramophone Classical Catalogue [81],
published quarterly by the firm that publishes the monthly
periodical, Gramophone. The catalogue is nominally a listing
of current availability; one says "nominally" because many
dealers in records insist that the lists contain a proportion
(how large or small is apparently a matter of guesswork or
opinion) of items that are, in fact, no longer available. It
is quite possible, of course, that the record manufacturers
are the true culprits in some cases. On the other side of
the coin, coverage of records issued by some of the minor
companies is erratic. This is particularly regrettable in that
such issues are often of unusual items not otherwise available; however, a number of these releases cannot be obtained
through the normal trade channels. In total, when one considers the difficulties of compilation, the catalogue offers a
remarkably good service.

        The major part of each issue is a composer index; in
each case the year of birth and of death (where the latter
is applicable) and nationality of the person is given. If but
a handful of items is available, the arrangement of these is
alphabetical. Where the composer is better represented, then
works are classified under the headings orchestral, chamber,
instrumental, vocal and choral, and stage works. Where considered necessary, a heading will be subdivided. Under each
composition, recordings are usually listed in the chronological order of issue in the United Kingdom. If a work takes
more than one side, the number is given in italics, immediately preceding the name of the performer(s). Where there
is a second work on the disc, a brief reference indicates
what the other item is. If the disc or tape has three or
more works, the coupling will usually be shown as "Concert"
or "Recital" (the latter often abbreviated to "Rec"), indicating in light capital letters the name of the artist or group
under which the record is listed in the "Artist index" later
in the catalogue. By this means, one can quickly discover
brief details of all the items included in a particular disc or
tape. Opposite the name of the performer in the composer
section of the catalogue is given the record number (in bold,
for quick recognition) together with the date of the issue of
Gramophone in which the review can be found. The lists
include some records that have not been reviewed; in such

cases, obviously, no date is quoted. Occasionally, however, the omission is simply an oversight by the compiler. The symbol "(R)" adjoining a record number indicates that the disc has been previously reviewed under a different number. In certain cases, the date of the original review is also given, so that one might find, for example: (12/63)(11/74)(R). A reference to the issue of Gramophone for November 1974 would provide a brief review of the particular disc, but one would need to refer to December 1963 for a fuller appraisal.

A great virtue of this catalogue is that it provides individual entries for brief items used as "fill-ups" on discs and it also identifies excerpts from operas, etc., arranging them in the order in which each appears in the parent work. Thus, a work such as Sibelius' Finlandia, which is too short to have an LP record side to itself, is duly listed with details of the available recordings upon which the work is to be found. Similarly, if one wishes to obtain an operatic recital disc which includes "Voi che sapete" from Mozart's Figaro, entry under the opera shows that this aria is listed as no. 11. The enquirer then has simply to look at the recordings of excerpts, to find "11" in bold type and brief details of artist, review date, and record number provided for each appropriate soloist.

The artist index is arranged in alphabetical order. In the case of conductors, cross references are made to the orchestras they have conducted. One would suggest that public interest is usually much more in an individual conductor than in an orchestra (however much one may approve or disapprove of this), and that it would be better to give record details under the personal name rather than that of the orchestra. Part 3, "Opera," is in alphabetical order of composers and gives details of the casts in all complete recorded operas. Incidentally, it usually gives the date and place of first performance and the name of the librettist, which can be useful information.

The last part of each issue since March 1975 is devoted to listing, on the same lines as the main body of the catalogue, cartridges and cassettes. The major difference is that no review dates are given.

The same publishers also issue a quarterly Popular Record Catalogue, and an annual Spoken Word and Miscellaneous Catalogue.

A much more expensive aid is <u>Music Master</u>, published by John Humphries at Hastings, Sussex [149], which is bought on annual subscription that includes the appropriate <u>Music Master</u> main catalogue, plus monthly supplements which cumulate into a six month sequence, and are duly replaced by the annual volume. Basically, the coverage is of non-classical music, but a few items from the standard repertoire seem to stray by mistake into each volume. At the time of writing, in late 1983, contents begin with a singles series. Each entry quotes the artist or group, the record number, the label name, distributor, record size, and the month of release. This is followed by a rather similar section for artists, which contains the same information as the previous section, but arranged in a different order. The biggest section of the catalogue is the albums main section. Then comes "record company prices" which is, one suspects, something of a minefield. In some cases, the discography's publishers quote the dealer price, excluding Value Added Tax, and also the maximum selling price, including VAT.

In early days of the publication, it included many deleted discs, together with an indication of the month in which each was withdrawn by its manufacturer. Now, older records are kept in the lists for a maximum of three years in contrast with the earlier issues which retained details of such records indefinitely. As indicated above, the discography is not inexpensive but offers good value for the information supplied, and it is an important reference tool for any but the smallest reference library. It is not as useful for current selections as <u>Music Week</u>, simply because cumulation makes production less immediate. However, for retrospective selection and for general enquiry work, there is nothing to compare in the nonclassical music fields.

<u>Music Master</u> also publishes towards the end of each year, a "Labels list." This provides an alphabetical list of current British labels, record companies and distributors, and so gives access to a variety of information. For instance, a librarian can quickly check whether a label actually exists, who distributes a particular label, what labels an individual distributor supplies, which parent company owns a particular label, etc. Some of this information can be found in issues of <u>Music Master</u> itself, but is no real substitute for the labels list.

Reverting to the catalogues issued by Gramophone's producers, there is a third publication to complete the spectrum, the spoken word catalogue. Because of the much smaller number of records in this category, and possibly much smaller sales, this discography is limited to a single issue in the autumn of each year. Mention should perhaps be made of a compact disc catalogue, but past experience suggests that it will, sooner or later, be incorporated with Gramophone's other catalogues.

The American equivalent of these catalogues is The Schwann Record and Tape Guide [197]. This is also in three separate parts, but there are considerable differences between these and those described above. The major publication is identified as Schwann-1 and is published monthly. Since the publishing company (unlike Gramophone) has no connection with any reviewing periodical, only occasionally is the release date of a recording given to help one trace a review quickly. On the other hand, each issue contains a section of new listings for the month, under composers for classical music and under categories for the others. The lists also include new items for Schwann-2 (which is briefly described below), since the latter is not a monthly publication.

The coverage of this guide is wider than the classical catalogue of Gramophone, for there are sections devoted to musical shows, current popular music, and jazz, which the British publication lists in its popular volumes. Schwann notes electronic music in a separate sequence, under maker's label and catalogue number. However, this American publication is much less helpful if one is trying to trace a short, individual item, since it does not include analytical entries for those works which, because they are too brief to fill a whole side of an LP disc, are automatically relegated to become part of a disc with a major work, or with several other brief works.

It can be quickly seen that, whereas the British list uses a classified sequence of works for important composers, Schwann has the typical American preference for dictionary order, irrespective of whether the music is orchestral, instrumental or vocal. Schwann lists orchestral recordings under the name of the conductor concerned (which this writer

much prefers) in comparison with the British publication's
choice of entry under orchestra. Clearly, the recorded
repertoire available in the two countries will always be different, although there is a fair degree of overlap. Schwann
lists about 50,000 LP records, tapes and cassettes on more
than 1,000 labels each month. All three formats are in a
combined sequence, with cartridges identified by a small
black solid triangle before each appropriate number, and
cassettes similarly by a black circle--a method that is very
much easier on the eyes than the British catalogue's solution.

Schwann-2 covers popular music that is over two years
old, all jazz releases of a similar age, mono and electronically
reprocessed classical recordings, as well as poetry and drama.
The catalogue also lists religious, instructional, and miscellaneous records. It is issued twice each year in spring and
fall. The publishers also produce, occasionally and irregularly, an Artist Issue. And mention should also be made
here of Schwann Children's Records, issued in November of
each year. It lists discs, cassettes and cartridges "which
appeal to age groups from tiny tots to high schoolers."

For German discs of classical music, the guide is the
Bielefelder Katalog [18]; and this is probably the most useful to British librarians who wish to extend their potential
coverage beyond that listed domestically and in the USA.
This catalogue appears twice each year. For spoken word,
in a score of different languages, there is Poesie und Drama
auf Schallplatten und Cassetten, published in Düsseldorf by
the appropriately named Polyglotte.

ADMINISTRATION

Before dealing with day-to-day running of the gramophone
record library (tape recordings in their various forms have
a separate section devoted to them at the end of the chapter),
some preliminary factors will be considered. These are all of
importance and are dealt with in the following order: acces-
sibility; initial costs and coverage; running expenses; staff;
listening in the library; free provision v. subscription and/or
rental collections. The matter of record speeds no longer
concerns us, for this is a problem that has solved itself; the
historical aspects, for those sufficiently interested, can be
found in the first edition of this book, or elsewhere.

The foregoing must be considered before the service
begins; the remaining sections discuss, in turn: selection;
selection guides--books; selection guides--periodicals; acces-
sioning; classification; cataloguing rules; practical cataloguing.

Accessibility

In the past decade there has been a marked swing in British
library practice from what is usually known as closed access
(an obvious contradiction in terms, and subsequent references here will use the description "indirect access") to open
access.   This seems to have been caused by two factors.
First, libraries with open access seem generally to have suffered very small stock losses (a much lower percentage than
for books, it should be noted) and, second, the issue and
return of discs using this method is very much quicker than
is possible with any form of restricted access which requires
the use of some sort of indicator to show the availability of
records.

It would seem self-evident that it is much better to
shelve records so that the sleeves face the user.   Shelved
like books or scores, the narrow spines are difficult to read
(and not all sleeve edges print the information as to the
content of the record inside) and to arrange in correct order.   More important, if the records are kept tightly packed,
as they should be to prevent warping, they are not easily
extracted and constant handling is likely to make the sleeves
wear badly at this fore-edge, even in cases where there is
the added protection of a further transparent outer covering.
This "sideways-on" method of shelving is usual for domestic
use, but private collectors often know approximately where to
look for a particular disc in their own stock and are also
likely to be more careful in handling their own property than
is the case with many people using discs in communal ownership.   Records may be filed perfectly satisfactorily by this
method in an archive, reference, or indirect access collection.
It seems to be the most common method in both academic and
public library collections in the USA.   In some libraries there,
the borrower is assisted to find the appropriate section of the
classified stock by means of one or more colour coding strips
on the spine of each disc, and this also helps to prevent filing errors.

A number of libraries shelve records in tiered cases, with up to six steps from front to back. Each compartment is commonly about three inches (7.5 cm.) from front to back, and this depth would hold about twelve records in protective sleeves; the steps rise in stages of about two inches (5 cm.). This scheme has decided advantages; records are kept in small batches which are easily handled, and the top two or three inches, 5 cm. or 7.5 cm., (according to the height of each step) beyond the first batch will be visible to help in the correct filing of discs and possibly to attract the attention of a borrower. On the debit side is the fact that some space will be lost by the width of the material forming the dividers between tiers, and the back step may be too high to be within easy reach of short members of the public or staff. Construction is costly, which is a major reason for the system's lack of popularity.

Much more common and popular today is the so-called browser box; this is basically no more than a flat trough, so that all discs placed in it are on the same level. To aid the discovery of a wanted record, some libraries insert dividers at intervals of a few inches. These boards are usually of plywood, some fourteen inches (35.5 cm.) high and normally bear a catchword or class mark at the top, thus acting in a similar fashion to shelf guides for books, or guide tabs in catalogue trays, and breaking up the front-to-back sequence of sleeves in the same sort of manner as the tiered risers do in the other type. It had been thought originally that the weight of the front discs pressing on those behind them might warp the latter, but this seems to have been a baseless fear. The browser box should never be filled so tightly that one cannot flip through the discs in order to see what is available. The inside width of sections should be thirteen inches (32.75 cm.) to allow room for outer sleeves; thus a three-bay box would be forty inches (91.5 cm.) wide, including the partitions between sections. Either three or four sections in one case can be recommended; more than this could make the case cumbersome. From front to back, the suggested depth is twenty inches (50.8 cm.) and twenty-four inches (61 cm.) at base, or twenty to twenty-five inches at the top, to allow for the inward slopes referred to above. If the browser box is to stand in the middle of an area, rather than against a wall, it may be found an advantage to have it made double sided, since this allows a greater number of users to select discs at any one time.

At the front and sides of the cases, the retaining boards should be about seven to eight inches (17.75 to 20.25 cm.) high. The back board could be made several inches higher, with advantage, as with tiered cases. This space could be used to carry the equivalent of tier guides. For both tiered cases and browser boxes the height from the floor should be between twenty-eight and thirty inches (71 to 76 cm.). Both types can usefully be made to provide cupboard space or shelving beneath the display sections; the former may be used for discs transferred to reserve stock, the latter for filing back issues of appropriate magazines, or for discographies, etc. Finally, if the gramophone record section is only open on a part-time basis in a full-time department, or if the music library is used by local societies after normal library hours, browser boxes are preferable to tiered cases, as it is easier to have covers made for the former; hinged wooden lids fitted with locks are probably best.

One other fact should be mentioned, and that is that a browser box of twenty inches (50.8 cms.) from front to back would hold about eighty to a hundred discs protected by inner sleeves, manufacturer's outer (or liner) and a further protective cover provided by the library. Operatic and similar sets, particularly if filed with libretti and notes, will somewhat reduce this capacity figure.

Indirect access methods may be unavoidable where space for the gramophone record collection is very cramped and any sort of sleeve display is impossible. Where stored in this way, records are often shelved, preferably in a lockable cupboard, inside the staff enclosure. Because the public will not have access to the discs, space may be saved by providing shelves from ground level upwards to a height of four or five shelves. Since the borrowers cannot see the records, some type of indicator is useful to show which discs are available for loan when the potential borrower is there. A certain number of libraries have used the indicator as a catalogue also, but this must be deprecated because of its virtually unsurmountable inadequacies. A description of various types of indicator has been given elsewhere [97].

As a compromise between open and indirect access methods, one can display the sleeves in a tiered indicator or browser box to act as the indicator, retaining the discs

themselves behind the staff enclosure. This scheme has the
advantage that the borrowers can browse among the sleeves,
reading the notes on any that interest them or looking more
closely at those whose sleeve design attracts. The risk of
theft is minimal, since the discs are under staff control and
away from the public; there is little point in stealing an empty sleeve. The major drawback to this method is that it
necessarily results in a slow service. The borrower brings
the sleeve of the record of his choice to the counter, after
which the assistant has to find the appropriate record, give
it to the borrower to check for visible damage (if that is part
of the library's system), and then insert the disc into the
sleeve; the entire process has to be reversed when the disc
is returned, except that the checking for damage will be done
by the staff member. One small point that might be mentioned is an obvious one that could nevertheless be over-
looked--that the browser box will hold more empty sleeves
than would be possible if the records were in these protective covers rather than filed in the staff enclosure.

Initial Costs and Coverage

It is difficult to give clear guidance in these fields, partly
because no two libraries will have either exactly the same
resources or clientele, and also any prices quoted may seem
ludicrous to a reader of these pages a few years hence.
For this reason, numbers of recordings are generally quoted
in place of prices. Quite clearly, the larger the opening
stock, the better for staff and user but one cannot imagine
any library being given an unlimited budget, and governing
bodies will need to be given some guidance. Unfortunately,
there is considerable variation in the figures one finds in
different sources.

Although there are now no really small English library
authorities (in comparison with the situation before 1974),
such authorities still exist in such countries as Denmark, the
Netherlands and the USA, to quote but three examples, where
independent libraries serving populations of fewer than 10,000
are to be found, and in which the provision of a sound recordings collection is regarded as a highly desirable objective,
if it has not already been achieved.

A personal recommendation is that the absolute minimum

opening stock in a library serving up to 40,000 population
should be 400 discs (or discs and cassettes, or cassettes
alone, according to the chosen policy). This figure would
be increased in the proportion of one disc for every additional hundred of population. On such a basis, a city of
80,000 would need at least 800 discs for its opening stock;
one of 150,000 would need to budget for a figure of 1,500.
Lionel McColvin once told an audience that: "It is no use
starting a gramophone record library without sufficient funds
to start and maintain it for a substantial ready made public.
I speak from bitter experience. We started with 5,000 records. Within a week, there wasn't a record in the library.
People lined up to borrow what others returned.... I tell
you this solely to point a moral. The provision of gramophone records, like most other things, is only worth doing
when it can be done well" [128, p. 26]. Admittedly, Westminster is anything but an average library, and the 5,000
discs were all of the shellac 78rpm, variety, but the conflict
between the figures we have suggested and those of McColvin indicate the great need for the librarian to make prior
enquiries and diligent efforts to try to discover if more than
one percent of the local population is likely to enrol in the
sound recordings library. If it seems certain, or even likely, that this will be the case, then more generous provision
than our figures is required, or the service will be over-
whelmed.

We may cite three more statements on this matter of
the size of the opening stock. The first accepts the idea
of a modest collection in the fairly small authority, the second suggesting a very much greater initial requirement (five
times larger, in fact) and the third recommending a commit-
ment which seems to us to be far more idealistic than practical without very great financial resources. Mary D. Pearson
has suggested that, for a sum (which would need upward
revision to take into account the changed value of money),
sufficient for "Approximately 500 records could be purchased
by judicious selection from special sales as well as from normal channels. It would not be desirable to announce a smaller collection today for a community of 50,000" [176, p. 28].
Compare this figure with the recommendations submitted by
the Sound Recordings Group of the Library Association to the
Library Advisory Council's working party on new media, produced at the end of 1973, but regrettably never published.
Here the minimum figure quoted for an opening stock is 50

"issuable units" per 1,000 population. The phrase "issuable unit" was preferred to "disc" partly to take into account the different formats possible and also allow for the fact that an opera, whether it takes two, three or more records or cassettes must necessarily be loaned as a single set. With an initial stock of this size, it was envisaged that there would always be a fair selection of material in the library available for loan. Indeed, for spoken word, the suggestion was that there would be "three or four units on shelves for every one out on loan."

The third recommendation is from Holland [50]. Here, "The idea is to start with a minimum collection of 3,000 discs (applicable to small areas with 5,000 inhabitants), gradually increasing to facilities for the largest cities with 15,000 records." The tremendous discrepancies between these suggested figures cannot easily be reconciled. One can only say that circumstances may be such that, if a collection is to be initiated at all, it can only be done with a minimal stock. On the other hand, the advantages of starting with a comfortable margin over the likely demand do not need underlining. The problem, in such a situation, is the possibility that use of the collection proves to be very much less than originally estimated.

Branch libraries usually have an approximate figure of the population for their probable catchment area. If sound recordings are provided in these satellite service points (as should happen, if only on grounds of equity), the collection might be made on the basis of half of the figures we have recommended above, but with a minimum opening stock of 300 discs and/or cassettes. The assumption made here is that the keener music lovers will prefer to use the nearest regional, central or district headquarters library. As with bookstocks, branch collections may well be of a generally lighter, less specialist nature, according to local needs.

The bigger the initial stock, the greater the scope for a wider musical range or for better coverage and some duplication if the field is restricted until demand has been assessed by use. One major difference between British and American public libraries is that the former are highly unlikely to receive gifts of records from either private individuals or from commercial benefactors. In contrast, many American libraries have been presented with discs or have received monetary donations. The former is not an unmixed blessing; the gifts may be of older recordings replaced by the borrower, and some libraries put a large sticker on each sleeve with the word "Gift" on it, so that the donor can actually see the records available for loan, and may even boast about this to friends. At least, one trusts that the position now is rather better than that described in 1957: "... it is not surprising that many libraries have gladly accepted gifts and bequests as a source of supply. Until recently it was not unusual for music and record collections to consist solely of donations, and as is too often the case, the quality of the gift materials was frequently below the standard which the librarians would have imposed had they made the selection. Many collections still reflect the personal bias or haphazard selection of well-meaning donors" [10, p. 176].

Despite the risk of causing boredom, some points made earlier in the chapter deserve to be reiterated, in our view. A decision as to the breadth of coverage is highly desirable, if not an absolute necessity, well before the initial stock is chosen, thus taking into account the fact that it is almost certainly better to start with too limited rather than too wide a scope. It is simple enough to broaden, at some subsequent date, the types of material represented, but to restrict coverage after provision has been made in a particular musical or other field could well lead the librarian into considerable difficulties with borrowers. If the opening stock has no more than 1,000 recordings, a few alternative performances of popular works can be included if coverage is, in general, limited to standard music. On the other hand, a wide ranging collection of the same size will necessarily have to be very restricted in any one category if an acceptable balance between classical music, pop, jazz, spoken word, documentary, and various other classes is to be maintained.

As has already been suggested, buying performances published on budget and mid-price labels whenever possible will provide more recordings for a given sum of money, but at the risk of adverse public reaction to this policy. Some economies in selection may well be thought desirable but these should be reasonably defensible on both musical and aural grounds; such a plan needs to be operated with discretion and a keen awareness of the limitations that will be displayed in the chosen stock. There is a similar need for a careful balance between the familiar work and the unusual

or avant garde one, between the proportions of orchestral
music, chamber works, instrumental compositions and the
wide range of vocal items. No single category should be
favoured to the virtual exclusion of the others. The music
librarian should never allow personal predilections and dislikes to become all too clearly reflected in the library's holdings.

It is clear that musical tastes differ, not only from
one part of the country to another, but also between much
smaller areas that are geographically close. For this reason
alone, it is possibly unwise to suggest percentages of stock
for particular categories of music, although that risk is taken
later in this chapter. It is probably better at this point to
do no more than make such general comment as that orchestral music is usually several times more popular than instrumental items; in the latter categories, piano and organ lead
the field, with string music often coming third, and other
instrumental music decidedly less in demand. Chamber music has its devotees but it is generally ignored by the majority of our public. Those who do borrow are likely to
prefer the standard masters such as Haydn, Mozart, Beethoven, Schubert, Brahms, and the like, but there is almost sure to be a handful who are prepared to listen to
Webern, Bartók, Shostakovich, and other twentieth-century
composers. There is a public for opera, but the music librarian quickly learns that a lover of Italian opera is frequently quite uninterested in the Russian school; German
opera has its devotees but these usually have no time for
French stage compositions, and so on. The opera lover
who is interested in a number of different national fields
should be cherished.

Because of these imponderables, the wise librarian
will not spend all the initially available money at once, but
will keep perhaps a quarter of it in reserve, awaiting borrowers' comments and reactions, and checking to see which
records are most frequently borrowed, as well as those
areas of stock which are under-represented and which should
be quickly strengthened. Such gaps will surely be there to
be discovered, whatever the range of material provided to
inaugurate the collection.

After some fluctuations, the usual rate of discount
given by British suppliers to libraries is apparently 15

percent of the retail price. Since the disappearance of retail price maintenance, this figure is obviously open to ne-
gotiation, but only the larger spenders are likely to obtain
much better terms. On the other hand, the manufacturers
themselves realize the importance of the public library market, so that some library suppliers (with the full agreement
of the record companies) make special offers for limited
periods, with an increased discount given on all recordings
from the individual manufacturer concerned during that particular period. It is probably the smaller library that stands
to gain most from such offers--partly because these authorities are unlikely to receive more than the standard discount
in their month-to-month purchases, and also because budget
limitations mean that these libraries will not have been able
to afford as great a number of desirable records as would
be the case in a larger system. However, if a major collection has all well-reviewed releases in stock, it may still be
found that a special offer allows the chance for some judicious duplication (or more), and also the replacement of recordings that are nearing the end of their lives in the library stock.

There seem to be wider variations in discounts available to American libraries than to British. In 1966 it was
recommended that "A dealer should be selected who fills orders promptly from his stock or by prompt follow through
on items not in stock. His price policy should be competitive, which at this time of writing means a 30-40 percent
across the board discount on all list prices of $2.98 or more
--except certain imports--shipped postpaid. Prompt replacement should also be furnished in the case of any record
found to be defective upon receipt" [201, p. 67]. One or
two widely advertised firms offer discounts of this magnitude,
despite carriage charges, and many American librarians find
it well worth ordering from such companies, even if they are
two or three thousand miles away. In some areas, small libraries in the same part of the country have found it effective to buy cooperatively, thus increasing the total of the
overall order, reducing the unit carriage costs and possibly
increasing the discount because of the bulk of the joint order. The size of the markdown, be it in Britain or the USA,
is important, but it must never be overlooked that service is
equally important, if not more so.

Over the past decade or so, there has clearly been a

move towards a three-tier price structure in Britain, with the
categories usually referred to as top price, medium price and
bargain discs. In addition, there were the "premium price"
releases; these were comparatively few in number and justified their extra cost by the provision of an illustrated booklet with libretto (in the case of an opera or other vocal work)
or full notes about the composition, the major performers and,
possibly, the undertaking of the recording itself. Decca's
SET prefix series and EMI's Angel label are the most frequently met examples in this category, but prices of these
are now standard with top price discs.

The well-selected opening stock will try to contain a
judicious balance between all three (or four) categories.
Looking back, it seems surprising that during the early
days of LP when libretti and translations were not automatically included with most opera sets but often had to be
bought at the cost of a few pence each, few people (and by
no means all libraries) purchased them. The advantages of
having the words, with parallel English translation to allow
one to follow what is being sung and, at the same time, to
understand the situation and the emotions of the characters
in the opera need no stressing.

It might be argued that bargain category lists contain
a fair proportion of discs that are not up to the standards
that a library would really desire. On occasion, the comparatively poor quality of the sound may betray the age of
a recording. In theory, the year of publication shown on
the disc should be clear evidence; in fact, some companies
deliberately (or so one can only assume) attempt to mislead
by showing the year of reissue on the disc and not the true
date of original release. Reviews in Gramophone and entries
in that publication's quarterly catalogue almost invariably
quote the date of the original review, and also note the
earlier catalogue number, so that there is little problem in
seeing which of the month's releases have already been in
previous circulation in a different suit of clothes, as it were.
If a company issues a new disc on a mid price or bargain
price label, when its own lists already have a top price category, then it is probably true that the performer(s) has/
have yet to achieve true international status or else that,
the performance itself is not altogether satisfactory. Such a
decision is outside the province of some smaller companies
which have generally but a single price for all issues--
Lyrita is a British example.

The comment made in the first edition that although books were often reissued in cheap editions, records were not, is no longer true. Indeed, the situation now is that a record often seems to have a better chance of making a second appearance in the catalogues than do many books. The recording companies regularly prune their lists, and the version which sold well at full price for some years before demand fell away is a likely candidate for reissue, after a period of unavailability which may be as short as two or three months or as long as some years according, it would seem, to the manufacturer's whim. This second appearance will usually be on a different label (but from the same maker) and with a different prefix and number and at a cheaper price than before. A select few records have made not one but several reappearances over the years, for one or other of several possible reasons.

The recording that is withdrawn because sales were consistently bad throughout its period of availability is unlikely to be reissued. If the manufacturer or a wholesaler has any of these withdrawn discs still in stock after the due date of deletion, these copies may well be sold to dealers who specialise in this field and who will, in turn, offer the records to libraries and public at a reduced price. For the music librarian, here is the opportunity to buy unplayed records at a discount likely to be around 33 percent to 40 percent, but caution is advised until the buyer has acquired a reasonable knowledge of the recorded repertory, current catalogues, and the likely habits of particular manufacturers when it comes to reissue policy. What is needed is a metaphorical crystal ball so that one does not buy the deletion that is going to reappear quite quickly at an even lower price than that of the deleted disc, and also the willingness to buy the unusual or minor work that may well not be recorded again for many years and which the library could usefully have.

There are various shops, and also a number of private dealers who work from their own homes, in the secondhand market. The latter almost invariably deal solely through the post. Shops, a handful of which deal with 78rpm discs as well as microgroove, are usually open to visits by potential customers. Indeed, such establishments rarely issue lists but normally rely on callers to keep stocks moving. Secondhand discs can be useful as replacements for those worn out or damaged, or possibly as a means of filling a few gaps that

had been previously overlooked in the collection. Traders
of this type can also be a means of saving money on discs
which are still currently available. A librarian who uses
one or more of such retailers should establish the right to
return for credit any disc which proves, on playing over,
to be unsatisfactory. This proceeding assumes, of course,
that time can be found or spared to try part, if not all, of
each side.

A few dealers advertise their willingness to try to obtain out-of-print records, upon request. When successful in
tracing a copy, the seller may well ask a price that is noticeably higher than that of the record when it was new. Clearly, here is another buying area for the experienced librarian
rather than for the novice. There seems to be a number of
private collectors willing to pay high prices for discs which
they particularly wish to own; these items are often LP records of the early 1950s which had a short life in the manufacturers' lists and which usually sold comparatively few copies during the time that they were easily available (and so
have not been considered likely candidates for profitable reissue), but for which limited demand has subsequently increased. As with early shellac discs this microgroove market may interest few people, but that does not mean that it
is without any importance. Prices are understandably regu-
lated both by rarity and the ordinary economics of supply
and demand. Because, perhaps, in relative if not in absolute terms, the average price of discs in the USA is much
lower than in Britain, there is apparently only a small secondhand market on that side of the Atlantic.

Estimates of both initial costs and running expenses
will need to take into account stationery, such as application forms, borrowers' tickets, etc. Furniture, in general,
is an initial expense only. Consideration of these matters
is deferred until later in the chapter, since these particular costs are related to the administrative methods used in
running the service.

Acquisition Expenses

As with books, each year's expenditure may be divided between new items and the replacement of withdrawn items
considered worthy of this treatment. The proportion of the

latter category is likely to be lower with recordings than
with books, partly because the particular performances withdrawn are no longer generally available (which raises again
the matter of secondhand discs), partly because of basic differences between the two media. The library will naturally
have to have in stock at least one recording of each of Beethoven's symphonies, but however great the genius of any
particular conductor, the collection's emphasis is likely to be
on current performers. Before World War II, the series conducted by Weingartner was held in wide esteem. Half a century later, the sound of these will almost certainly be considered inadequate compared with that heard today on disc
or tape. In addition, styles in interpretation and playing
have changed since 1934. The "swooping" strings then
standard seem quite unacceptable to ears now used to an
almost clinical precision in the notes--although it is almost
certain that today's style will, in turn, be temporarily superseded by a different sort of performance again. Taste is
always altering, to a greater or lesser degree, like an aes-
thetic pendulum.

Unless, therefore, the recording is among those that
seem to stay perennially in the catalogues, such as the
Schubert Piano Trio, opus 99 (D893) in the 1926 recording
made by Thibaud, Cortot, and Casals; or Wanda Landowska's
performance of Bach's Goldberg variations; the general tendency will be to replace a withdrawn recording by a newer
performance of the same work. However, the longer a disc
or tape is retained in stock, the longer it is before it has
to be replaced, and the money "saved" can either be spent
on an alternative recording of the work or else in buying a
performance of a composition not currently included in stock.
From this, it is apparent that running costs are dependent
not only upon the number of records borrowed from the library (although that is usually the major factor) but also on
the lengths of their respective lives before withdrawal. This
latter figure, in turn, varies from library to library according to the rate of deterioration resulting from the average
standard of handling a recording receives at borrowers'
hands, and in differences in standards of what is considered
an acceptable physical condition for a recording to be retained for issue. The good music librarian, therefore, will
work consistently towards extending the useful lives of the
recordings in stock.

It ought to be possible, except perhaps in the busiest libraries, to reckon on an average life of sixty borrowings before withdrawal is needed. This is a matter which is discussed in more detail later. If this figure, or one near it, can be achieved then the proportion of the library's budget needed to maintain the size of the stock is easy to deduce after the first year's operations. Most librarians would hope and expect that the money allotted for the purchase of recordings would allow the collection to grow in size, even though that expansion might be slow.

Staff

The major cost in running a record library is the cost of staff salaries. In the library serving an area population below 80,000 (i.e., almost every district or branch library, and many central libraries outside Britain), the service may have to be provided without the appointment of a specialist member of staff; in such cases, the advantages that accrue from having one person with oversight of the service may not be entirely lost if the chief librarian or other nominated member of staff has sufficient knowledge in this particular area of service to take responsibility for the selection of stock and for general supervision. Clearly, it may not be financially possible to appoint even an unqualified but musically interested person to run the section; in any case, the use made of the service may be too small to justify either full-time opening or extra staff. Some libraries house the gramophone record stock in the adult lending department, with records borrowed from, and returned to, the same service point as books. This system seems undesirable, partly because if the recording is checked by borrower and staff the issue and discharge of gramophone records is a much slower process than that for books. It is also to be deprecated because the staff concerned will amost certainly be clerical assistants without the knowledge, experience (and, possibly, interest) required for the proper control of gramophone records, although cassettes simplify this problem considerably, as will be explained later. It is unfortunate, in the writer's eyes, that a lack of inspection is apparently customary in many large American public libraries and the condition of the gramophone record stocks provides a clear indictment of the false economy of such a method.

As suggested above, few branch libraries will be large enough or busy enough to warrant the provision of a specialist music librarian.   In Britain, such branch library posts are limited mainly to the thirty-two London Boroughs.   Where there is such an appointment, in a central or branch library, it is customary for the music librarian concerned to be responsible for both the gramophone record collection and for the stock of scores and, rather less generally, of books dealing with musical topics.   The assumption has been that a disc collection will consist mainly of musical items.   This being so, the collections of recordings and scores should show as much coordination as possible, particularly in the provision of miniature scores.   These should be available for loan with the appropriate recordings, if possible.   Such a scheme reinforces the claim that, for readers to gain the maximum benefit, the stocks of music and discs should be housed in a single department.   The point was made in Maureen Long's survey, "All ... readers required that a score of each recording should be available for issue concurrently with the record; they complained that either the miniature score collection bore no relation to the collection of records, or that if the score was stocked it was invariably impossible to procure both it and the recording at the same time.   The limited scope of gramophone record libraries was also criticised, and both professional and amateur musicians complained of the poor condition of many records in public libraries" [125, p. 84].

In passing, it should be repeated that if it is logical to keep scores and records of music in the same department, then there is equal force in the claim that recordings of poetry, prose and drama ought to be housed in the literature department or section.

The matter of qualification in librarianship, in music, and in foreign languages has already been covered in Chapter I.   Where a sound recordings collection is an additional responsibility for the music librarian, the person appointed should ideally also be technically minded, aware of the basics of sound recording and of high fidelity sound reproducing equipment, knowledgeable about the recorded repertoire and competent to discuss the relative merits of different recordings of the same work, if only to explain why the library has not added to stock the latest version of a popular classic which is already well represented there.

It is quite unrealistic to expect such diverse but necessary qualifications at the minimum rate for a qualified librarian, though an authority may be fortunate enough to
acquire a good assistant at this salary. The grade offered
should be at least one higher than the general minimum. If
the recordings library is open on a full-time basis, then an
assistant to the music librarian will be required together
with the services of a relief assistant to cover periods when
the other two are both off duty, as must sometimes happen.

The first assistant, if possible, should also be a qualified librarian, interested in music and ever willing to learn
more about the subject. Even the junior staff coming in for
relief duties should have some knowledge of both music and
of recordings. It is equally desirable that the number of
other staff who may be expected to work short spells in the
music library should be restricted to two or three who are
regularly seconded to work in this department. All of these
should undergo some subject training at the hands of the
music librarian, and, if possible, attend such one-day courses
as those organised in England by the Audio-Visual Group of
the Library Association dealing with the introduction to gramophone record librarianship or the handling and problems of
cassettes.

The sound recordings section seems to invite a rather
more personal approach to service than is common in most
other departments, except probably in small branch or mo-
bile libraries where close relationships between staff and
their public seem to flourish. This is another reason why
the same few members of staff should work regularly in the
department, if this be possible. The music librarian may
well, as users' tastes are noted and assessed, be able to
suggest and recommend works, for most listeners tend to
limit their selections to particular types of music, within a
restricted period.

We suggested, in the first edition of this book, that
150 transactions for an eight- or nine-hour day was a reasonably average workload for as assistant in a system using
an indicator, or 200 where open access was in operation. If
discs are properly checked on return, these figures are optimistic; if there is no checking, much higher averages are
possible. The chief or other senior librarian should have
little difficulty in assessing whether a member of staff is too

hard pressed or has a reasonable volume of work. Unfortunately, an average figure conceals the fact that there will
be periods when few borrowers will be using the library,
and other times during which an assistant will be under very
great pressure indeed. There will, however, always be a
number of routine tasks and listening checks to be done, so
that slack periods are likely to be welcome in providing necessary opportunities to keep abreast of what might be called
the library's housework. Relief staff should be supplied at
busy times for the benefit of the public service. Suitable
part-time staff may usually be recruited with little difficulty.

Listening Equipment

The so-called soundproof cubicles, once common in many
record retailing stores and also used in a few libraries, are
now rarely found. It is much more common today, in both
academic and public libraries, to provide one or more listening points. In some cases each point takes a single pair of
earphones; in other libraries provision is made for two or
more pairs of earphones to be used to listen to the one recording, if desired. Experience has shown that it is best
for disc or cassette to be separate from the listening points
and to be under direct staff control. Arrangements should
be made (but seem to be overlooked in some libraries) for
the sterilization of earphones after use by one listener and
before further use by another.

Where listening facilities are provided in public libraries, a decision may be needed as to the intention--are listeners expected to try brief excerpts from recordings that they
may wish to borrow, or to help them to decide which to take
home from several possible choices? Alternatively, are listeners to be allowed to use the earphones for a long period so
that they can play an entire symphony or similar major work?
There are arguments in favour of both policies, and it may
be possible to provide more than one listening point and to
divide the facilities between the two functions. Even so, it
may still be necessary to declare the maximum period that a
single user may be allowed to use this aspect of the service
if somebody else is waiting to do the same thing. In colleges
and other academic institutions where courses in music, practical or theoretical, are taken, it is natural that fairly long
periods of listening to recordings may be commonplace and

multiple turntables or cassette players, together with a large
number of listening outlets will be needed. The sound equipment itself does not usually need to be of more than modest
quality and so should not involve great expenditure. (This
is a good place to mention the useful annual guides to reviews of audio equipment, issued by the Music Library Association [101].) The more turntables, etc., available, the
greater the staff time likely to be needed for supervision,
for the changing of recordings and the issue and return of
headphones. These matters are therefore likely to be the
more economically accomplished in the large music department.
Care needs to be taken over the loan of earphones, particularly if they are of good quality. A reader's ticket or some
other form of acceptable deposit should be required when
earphones are borrowed; these adjuncts are easily concealed,
as a number of American libraries, both public and academic,
found to their cost when listening facilities were first made
available and headphone sets were stolen.

A few libraries have music played, usually fairly quiet-
ly, as a background to the department at work. This will
delight some users and infuriate others. If music is played,
therefore, fairly lengthy silences between items would seem
desirable and the selected music should be wide ranging both
in period and character rather than be limited to one or two
composers or genres which happen to be the particular favourites of the librarian in charge. This writer's view is
that, with so much piped music invading our privacy in a
host of public places, a library is wise to limit itself to headphone provision for the benefit of those wishing to hear particular items.

Playing records at well-prepared and musically balanced
recitals is a very different matter. If the library can arrange to present a series of concerts of recorded music on
disc or cassette, the librarian has a wonderful opportunity
to introduce listeners to music that might be well overlooked
in the normal way by the majority, and to persuade those
attending a recital to listen to items that would never be
given a hearing in the ordinary course of domestic listening.
Where public recitals are given, the library's equipment
should certainly be of very high quality, not least to show
off the records at their sonic best. This in itself will be an
inducement to some to come and listen, since performances in
a hall or small theatre should certainly sound better (partic-

ularly in the lower bass notes) than at home, because of the greater space and probably less absorbent acoustic conditions. This may not be true in a large hall, since records are cut with domestic listening conditions in mind and there is an optimum beyond which amplification is liable to distort and background noises that would be inaudible at a lower level to become obtrusive. Clearly the room, theatre or auditorium will need to be a separate unit, acoustically isolated (at least to a fairly high degree) from other public departments if the sound of music is not going to disturb other people in the building. Alternatively, recitals may be presented in the evenings after any adjoining public departments are closed. Where a library has suitable accommodation, and particularly where it also possesses playing equipment, it is desirable that either or both should be used as fully as possible, perhaps by allowing an existing local gramophone or recorded music society to use the library as its meeting place, or else by starting such a society for the benefit of local music lovers; this helps the library to play a greater part as a local cultural center.

Free Provision vs. Subscription

The Public Libraries and Museums Act 1964 specifically allows charges to be made for the loan of special materials, such as gramophone records (Section S, sub-section 5 of the Act). If a direct charge is levied for the use of the service, three choices are available--a subscription, a rental charge, or a combination of the two. The main advantage of the first alternative is its simplicity of administration. If the library charges on an annual basis, the borrower's contribution is collected but once a year and so uses minimal staff time to take in the appropriate sum and to supply a receipt for it. A number of libraries are prepared to accept subscriptions on a six-monthly basis or an even shorter period. The charges made may then be in exact proportion to the annual figure but will probably be slightly higher, partly to compensate for the administrative inconvenience and also to indicate to borrowers that it is a better bargain to join for a year at a time.

A rental charge has its proponents. Under this system, payment is directly related to the amount of use made of the service by an individual borrower. It is also to the advantage of the listener who wishes to take home library records infrequently or for whom the stock has but a handful of recordings that interest him. Logically, this scheme is fairer than that of subscription, but administratively it is slower since it necessitates a financial transaction each time a recording is borrowed.

The combination of subscription and rental, still to be found in a handful of British libraries at the time of writing, may be considered as one which makes the worst of both schemes, or to combine the advantages of each, according to one's viewpoint. It would probably be better to offer a choice, on the analogy that a season or contract ticket on public transport benefits the regular commuter but is useless to the occasional traveller. Thus, the frequent library user would almost certainly opt for a subscription, but the listener who only borrows now and again would save money by paying the individual rental fees. In passing, a library providing a rental system might consider the possibility of issuing a book of tickets or coupons (one to be used with each item borrowed), possibly sold at a discount below its nominal value. This would lessen the need to handle cash with every transaction and speed up the service to the public.

Whether the service is run as a free one, or whether payment is required for membership, a few libraries require a deposit from each new borrower. The sum varies from library to library, but it should be at least the price of a top-category disc if it is to be any sort of deterrent. It is asked as a form of guarantee of good behaviour and is repaid, less any outstanding charges for fines or damage, when the borrower ceases membership. At least, this is what should happen, but many users when they allow their tickets to lapse and make no further use of the service do not attempt to reclaim their money, which is an interest-free loan to the local authority. In the days when discs were, on average, more expensive than books the deposit probably was a useful safeguard. Today, it seems an anachronism and an unnecessary barrier between the potential user and the service, so that levying a deposit is not now recommended. A routine check on the new borrower's identity and address will probably be required as a precautionary measure.

The arguments in favour of what is euphemistically

called a free service have already been canvassed. All rate-
payers will have had to contribute towards the service (which
is highly unlikely to be self-financing if one takes into account staff time and accommodation in the equation) and there
seems no logical reason for insisting upon a second payment
from those who wish to borrow sound recordings. As a librarian in Ireland has written, "We see no justification for
making a distinction between a record and a book. They are
both provided with the same purpose and hope, namely that
they will please, stimulate and instruct the recipient and are
both subject to the same amount of abuse and are capable of
releasing the same amount of enjoyment, thereby adding to
the quality of life of the community in which they circulate"
[130, p. 26].

As has been mentioned above, gramophone records are
now, on average, cheaper than books. Cassettes are still
slightly more expensive than discs, but their use is continuing to grow, and their cost should become little, if any, different from that of records as time passes. Audiovisual materials are playing an increasing part in the lives of most
people today, and although one would certainly not subscribe
to the idea that the book is dead, its future use could well
show some relative decline. Even this is arguable, for this
same jeremiad was advanced as film, radio, then television
respectively entered our everyday lives. The number of
books published in Britain and in the USA each year has
generally continued to increase and the sale of paperbacks
is astronomical in total. There will clearly always be a place
both for books and periodicals, whatever other media may
exist now or in the future. Print and audiovisual materials
are complementary, so that each reinforces the other and it
is noteworthy that there is an increasing number of books
which have cassettes incorporated as a complementary part,
in a pocket in the binding, so that a good sound recording
can help to illustrate the written word.

One may sum up the foregoing paragraphs by suggesting that if a charge is made for membership of the sound recordings section, the library authority should understand
clearly that the fees charged are likely to produce no more
than a fraction of the total cost of the service; even at best
it is unlikely to be as much as the cost of new accessions.

Where charges are made, borrowers may mistakenly but

understandably feel that they are bearing the entire cost of
provision, and have greater expectations as a result. They
may be tempted to demand that the stock be in perfect condition (a worthy ideal but probably impossible to achieve except when the library first opens or unless a stringent withdrawal policy is operated); and that the records they want,
be they esoteric or hackneyed, should automatically be added
to stock. These and similar claims will be made on the
grounds that the particular user is "paying for the service."
It is nearly always difficult to make most people understand
that the monies they pay by way of fines and, where applicable, by subscription is, in fact, but a small proportion of
the actual cost of administering the service.

Selection

There is no ready-made answer to the question of how best
to make the original stock selection. The present writer (as
mentioned earlier in this chapter) has little faith in the idea
of working out set percentages for the purchase of different
genres of music, but admits that such a scheme could be a
means of checking that some sort of reasonable balance is
kept. If a librarian wishes to adopt a plan of this sort,
then our personal suggestion would be that about one-third
of the stock should consist of orchestral items--with concertos, symphonies, and other orchestral works in that order of
preference. Opera, including Gilbert & Sullivan, would need
about 25 percent of the original allocation unless the librarian
feels sure that the popularity of this species is sufficient
among the potential public to warrant more generous provision. As has also been indicated, one difficulty here is that
many self-styled opera lovers prove to be admirers of a particular national school and specific period rather than of opera in general.

    Although piano concertos are probably the most popu-
lar single type of music, solo piano works have considerably
less appeal. One would except from this verdict what might
be called the standard music diet, particularly compositions
by Beethoven and Chopin. Organ music, on the other hand,
has proved distinctly more popular in the writer's experience
than he would have expected. That this trend is general is
evidenced by the fact that the companies continue to issue
many records of this type, embracing a wide range of instru-

ments from different countries and by different builders.
The tonal merits of organs built in the eighteenth century
or earlier which are in their original condition or which have
been sympathetically restored and rebuilt have been clearly
demonstrated in a multitude of recordings. Unfortunately,
the recorded repertoire itself on disc and tape is usually
much less venturesome than the choice of instruments, so
that Rheinberger sonatas are still rarities in the catalogues,
while most librarians will have found themselves with far
more versions of the famous Bach Toccata and Fugue in D
Minor or of the last movement of Widor's Organ Symphony
No. 5 than might be felt to be necessary, or even desirable, with so many gaps in the instrument's repertory still
unfilled.

Chamber music is clearly a minority taste, as a glance
at the releases over a period of a few months will certainly
reveal; again, demand is likely to be mainly concentrated
upon the standard masters--Beethoven rather than Berg,
Schubert in preference to Shostakovich. Other instrumental
works are similarly of limited popularity, except those for the
guitar, whose small repertory of worthwhile compositions is
reflected in the high proportion of works duplicated in various recitals, as well as in the percentage of arrangements
for the instrument of music originally written for the piano,
other solo instruments, or even the orchestra. If one allows about 10 percent for piano, 8 percent for organ, 5 percent for chamber music and 4 percent for other instrumental
recordings, then 85 percent of the budget has been allocated.

A further 5 percent would be needed for religious and
secular choral works (from Messiah and Mozart's Requiem
Mass to Belshazzar's Feast) and including a tiny handful of
solo song recordings, for the British music lover generally
seems most unattracted to Lieder, however eminent the singer. The final 10 percent would then be taken up by spoken
word records, with a strong emphasis on Shakespeare. For
a very different scheme of stock allocation, based on experience in a London area, the reader is referred to John Morgan's recommendations [142]. Our suggestions detailed above
are for a classically based stock. If the library widens its
view to include jazz, brass bands, musicals, foreign-language
tuition, documentary, humour, folk songs, etc., then clearly
the suggested percentages for standard music will have to be
reduced, possibly drastically, even though the relative rela-

tionships between orchestral, instrumental and vocal music
may still be found valid or helpful.

How many records does one need for a start? There
can be no firm answer; it has already been proposed (on
p. 311) that the opening stock should be at least 400 records in a very small library authority such as still exists in
some countries, or one record for every 100 population in
the area served, whichever is the higher. A branch library
holding a subsidiary collection should have at least 300 recordings in stock.

The point has also been made that a public library is
not advised to buy too high a proportion of recordings in
the mid-price or bargain categories; in any case, there is a
limited number of what might be considered indispensable or
even highly desirable items in the two categories; so that
the bigger the opening stock, the higher the average unit
cost is likely to be. It has been indicated, a little earlier
in this chapter that (in 1984) one probably needs to work on
an average of Ł4.50 per recording. If this figure is accepted,
the 400 discs needed for the smallest starting collection would
cost approximately Ł1,800.

In nearly all British library authorities, one should be
able to assume that there is a qualified music or audiovisual
librarian, and that choice of stock will be left to that member of staff. For those authorities, in Britain or elsewhere,
where there is no such appointment, selection may well present problems. The chief librarian whose own knowledge of
music is small can still try to ensure that a fair balance is
achieved and that the collection if not overweighted by the
personal interests of the music librarian, or any other assistant deputed to oversee the collection by asking for a
breakdown of suggested stock on the lines indicated above.
If, to take an extreme example, this analysis showed seventy-
five percent of the recommended stock is operatic and only
10 percent orchestral, the imbalance would need to be rectified before any recordings were ordered.

The musically knowledgeable assistant is unlikely to be
expert in all categories. Particularly if there is no music
librarian on the staff, selection guides will amost certainly
be needed. Even the best qualified music librarian would
be well advised to use some works as a means of checking

that any major gaps in the collection are the result of deliberate exclusion, for financial or other reasons rather than
by oversight. The New Penguin Stereo Record and Cassette Guide [177] and its predecessors, including the nine
volumes of the Stereo Record Guide have the same team of
contributors. The first-named work is available in hard
cover form; this clothbound format is much more useful to
a library than Penguin's normal paperback binding because
of the constant handling that the work is likely to receive.

Both works have been published on a continuing basis
(the previous Penguin volumes were restricted in coverage
to cheaper issues) and the wise librarian will retain earlier
volumes to allow reference to older recordings, some of which
may reappear after an absence from the manufacturers' lists.
The guides provide an immediate rating of each disc by
means of a starring system, with three stars as the maximum
award (plus an occasional rosette as "a quite arbitrary com-
pliment by a member of the reviewing team"). Whatever the
grading, the accompanying text should always be read before reaching a decision for or against purchase. Discs containing the same music in different performances are listed
in descending order of recommendation. This guidance is
immediately helpful for a work such as the Symphonie fan-
tastique of Berlioz, which conveniently fills one disc, but
presents difficulties with a work such as Mozart's Symphony
41 (Jupiter), whose different recordings take one side and
so are issued with a variety of couplings. The careful se-
lector, therefore, will have to take into account not only the
Jupiter but the other item(s) on the record, the interpretations and the standards of recording. So, when using these
guides the librarian will have to try to check all entries relating to the Mozart symphony. It may happen, if a particular work is wanted, that one has to accept a "fill-up" that
is already well represented in the library's stock, or one
that is poorly performed or recorded, for the sake of the
item desired.

The great advantage of these books (whose regular
contributors are Edward Greenfield, Robert Layton, and
Ivan March) is that all entries are annotated. One may totally disagree with a particular comment but, as a general
rule, the guidance given is considered both reliable and un-
biased. The other once widely used guide, The Art of Record Buying [9] was an annual publication listing what its

parent periodical's critic(s) considered to be the best performances of individual works (although this must always be
a highly subjective field of judgment). Entries were arranged in composer order, subdivided into orchestral, instrumental and vocal music, although these subheadings are
not shown. There was an appendix for anthologies and recitals, roughly divided by genre. At one time, an attempt
was made to limit coverage to a single "best" version of any
work, but with the increasing variety of couplings for compositions that take only one complete side or less, allied with
the production of several highly recommendable versions in
the cases of a number of much-recorded standard works, it
became not uncommon for two or three different recordings
of such repertory pieces to be listed in The Art of Record
Buying. There were no annotations here, only the ratings
for performance and recording, together with a note of the
month in which the record was reviewed in The Monthly Letter. For maximum use, therefore, the librarian would need
to retain a file of the periodical in order to check back on
individual reviews of works that are of interest. Many dealers, as well as a number of librarians, used the publication
for an annual check to ensure that their current stock holdings were good and to note any obvious gaps and to fill
them. The cessation of publication of the magazine was a
very real blow, for there is no obvious replacement.

     With one exception, all the periodicals now to be con-
sidered are published monthly, since this is the normal basis upon which the major manufacturers issue recordings.
Coverage is limited to what may be considered the principal
reviewing magazines, taken in alphabetical order.

     FANFARE, 1977- . (Bimonthly) [65]

It is taken for granted in Britain that almost every newly
released, commercially-available recording of standard music
will be reviewed in at least one specialist periodical, and
probably more. This happy state, however, does not apply
in the USA where, it would seem, less than 40 percent of
classical releases are similarly treated. This is a handicap
for librarians on both sides of the Atlantic, particularly as
some of the minor American labels show considerable initiative in what they record, often selecting items that are not
available elsewhere.

A praiseworthy attempt to review a number of recordings from these lesser-known labels and of imports has been made by Fanfare, which naturally covers the releases of the major American companies also. The magazine first appeared in the autumn of 1977, and is published every two months, with monthly publication its goal if and when finances permit. There are no advertisements to help offset expenditure.

The bulk of each issue is arranged in a single alphabetical sequence of composers, with cross-references (e.g., BORODIN: In the Steppes of Central Asia. See GLAZOUNOV) for those discs containing works by two or three different composers; above that number there is a sequence of anthologies. A few selected items, considered to be important in their respective fields, are considered under the headings "Soundtracks and shows," "Jazz" and "Popcorn." Classical reviews are of adequate length (generally between 200 and 500 words) and are initialled. The reviewers are identified in each issue. There are a few illustrations, about two inches square, of photographs of sleeves or a montage imitation. It seems to have a well chosen panel of critics who write clearly, are musically knowledgeable and are aware of what has, and what has not, been recorded previously. Additionally, reviewers unhesitatingly criticize poor recordings or unsatisfactory pressings.

The greatest asset of the periodical, however, is probably its coverage. Lesser-known American labels such as Grenadilla, Louisville, Musical Heritage, and Pandora are to be found alongside imports from Britain, Germany, Hungary, Sweden, and elsewhere. The periodical is not inexpensive but represents a very good value for the sound recordings librarian.

GRAMOPHONE, 1923- . (Monthly) [80]

This is the oldest surviving periodical in its field in Britain, and is the best known. It began publication in 1923 with Compton Mackenzie as founder, editor, and major contributor. He was already well established as a novelist and critic, and he related (in the editorial to issue no. 200, published in January 1940) how he approached Edward Clark of HMV about his proposed new publication, and was encouraged to proceed. Mackenzie added, "I wonder if he remembers telling me that

there would be no objection to my using 'The Gramophone'
as a title, and when I looked rather surprised explaining to
me gently that it was still a proprietory title belonging to
His Master's Voice." The article in the title was omitted
from March 1974.

The major part of each issue is devoted to standard
music on disc. "Classical record reviews" is divided by
genre, with headings for Orchestral, Chamber music, Instrumental, Choral and song, and Opera. Other headings are
added when required, so that Spoken word, Documentary,
Gregorian chant, Instructional, and Children's records may
be found in some issues. Coverage is completed by "Nights
at the round table" (a pun that has lasted almost as long as
the periodical itself) for lighter classics, "Easy listening"
for a fairly small selection of pop, film, and show music,
etc., and "Jazz" (again with strictly limited coverage in
terms of the number of new releases and reissues reviewed).

Under each heading for classical music, the arrangement is alphabetical by composer, with composite releases
(recitals, collections, etc. by various composers) at the end
of each section. For many years there was a second and
separate section for reissues, but these are now inserted
into a single sequence with the new records. Reviews are
initialled, and as a list of panel members is given with each
issue, identification is simple. Comment is mainly concerned
with the performance, although lesser-known music is often
described or put into historical context. The sound quality
of a record is usually mentioned fairly briefly, but is rarely
given much prominence--a matter which receives criticism
from some readers, but presumably suits the majority. When
there are many versions available of a popular work, the reviewer may compare the issue under review with a selected
two or three rivals in the catalogue, particularly those in
the same price range. In other cases, when there are only
one or two alternative recordings in the lists, comparisons
may be made between them, but this feature is not as frequent as it used to be, which some regard as regrettable.

Reviews average around 200 words in length, but this
may be very much extended for a major new issue, particularly of an opera, or be noticeably shorter for a run-of-the-
mill performance of a hackneyed classic. The magazine also
includes a number of generally brief appraisals of newly issued

cassettes in the fields of classical, light classical, and "easy listening" popular music. If the equivalent disc has already been reviewed, comments often refer back to the views expressed at that time; in many cases, an individual writer does not deal with the same recording in both formats, and there is much to be said in favour of this plan which allows for some difference of opinion, in certain cases.

For four years, the magazine had a companion periodical, Cassettes and Cartridges, but it was merged into the parent magazine in October 1977. At the same time, the opportunity was taken to include a list of new record and cassette releases in classified arrangement. Classical composers are in alphabetical order, classical collections in artist order, followed by album titles when several artists are represented. Popular artists are in alphabetical order, after which are listed popular collections, films & TV, sound effects and spoken word.

Gramophone has, in recent years, strengthened its technical section with fuller coverage of technical matters, reviews of new equipment, etc., relating to both disc and cassette.

With three columns of text to a page and a few illustrations, the magazine is less attractive in appearance than its rivals--but the authority of its reviewing panel, its seniority, and its sustained reputation throughout its existence for impartial criticism have combined to make this the first choice for most librarians as well as for many gramophiles (an ugly, but useful word). The quarterly catalogues published by the same company are considered later in this chapter.

HIGH FIDELITY AND MUSICAL AMERICA, 1965- .
(Monthly) [95]

This is a most unusual periodical, in that it consists of two separate magazines, each with its own pagination, but appearing as a single publication. High Fidelity has been separately published since 1951.

Each issue carries a number of signed reviews, often running to several hundred words in length, of a high critical standard. British readers are likely to find reviews of

new American records and those of British origin, for which
they will already have seen reviews, of equal interest. Reviews of each year have been cumulated, since 1955, as
Records in Review. The 1975 edition is subtitled The Twentieth High Fidelity Annual and, following seven pages of preliminary material, runs to 553 pages. The general arrangement of the volume is alphabetical by composer, with subdivisions for those who are well represented in the year's releases. "Recitals and miscellany" covers the anthologies.
As with the original reviews, each piece carries the critic's
name. Coverage is limited to classical and semiclassical music only. Details are given, where applicable, both of discs
and tape issues (in whatever form). Finally a point of very
considerable value and unique in our experience, is the provision of an artists index of all performers reviewed during
the year, which has obvious value to the audio librarian.

> HI-FI NEWS & RECORD REVIEW, 1970- . (Monthly)
> [94]

This magazine, as its name suggests, is also a conflation of
what were two separate publications. Record Review, in fact
had undergone changes of title during its history, which
dates back to 1933 (when it began life as Gramophone Record Review). The first part of each issue is devoted to audio affairs, including stereo broadcasting and occasional do-
it-yourself guidance on the design and building of high quality equipment. Comments tend to be briefer than those found
in Gramophone but there are feature articles which may deal
with an individual composer, artist or set of records at considerable length. There is a strong reviewing panel, and
articles are signed. At the end of a review, opposite the
critic's name, is a shorthand overall rating, given in two
parts. The sound quality of the recording is shown as between "A" (very good) to "D" (poor). Performance is also
rated on a four-point scale, identified in descending order
from "1" to "4." If there are different works on each side
of a disc, the reviewer may well give a different rating for
each, e.g., B/C:3/4. For "superlative" examples in either
performance or recording, an asterisk may be added, so that
A*/1* would suggest a really outstanding if not virtually
perfect record. There is an additional classification, "H"
for historical and pre-LP recording; such records may be
given a performance grading, or can again be shown as
"H," as the reviewer feels is most appropriate.

Light music and pop are given fuller treatment than in Gramophone. The magazine is printed on art paper, is attractively produced and includes a fair number of photographs in each issue.

The periodicals receiving comment above are primarily devoted to sound recordings and to sound recording and reproducing equipment. A number of other periodicals dealing with particular categories and aspects of music also carry reviews of records and tapes; a number of them have been discussed in Chapter II (p. 136-50) and should certainly not be overlooked in selecting new stock. As an addendum, and possible corrective to the views expressed by this writer, the interested reader is referred to an article by Carol Lawrence Mekkawi [138]. There is a list of a dozen indexes and about twice that number of periodicals. For each item the compiler gives the frequency of publication, the cost and the publishing history (which includes changes of title and gaps in production). The average number of pages in each issue of individual periodicals is supplied but not, as would have been useful, a guide as to the proportion devoted to advertisements and that to text. At first sight, the listed items are in no obvious order; only in the course of the article is the explanation given that periodicals are grouped according to a rough classification.

The narrative annotations are generally admirable, indicating the coverage and approach of each index or serial, drawing attention to any special features. An indication of the average number of discs, etc. reviewed in each issue is quoted, as well as a note showing the indexes (such as Music Index or RILM Abstracts) through which major articles can be traced; similar information is given for the record reviews, with Notes as the most frequent source. Overall, Mekkawi's article provides valuable reading for any but the most experienced sound recordings librarian.

Another means of keeping abreast of most new issues is through the medium of the monthly lists published by the major manufacturers. Several of these companies (e.g., Decca, EMI, Phonogram and RCA) also publish detailed "in print" volumes. Although intended primarily for dealers, they can be useful to the librarian. However, they are comparatively expensive and it may be felt that the cost is not justified in terms of probable use. Unlike the usual

record shop, the library probably has a collection of discographical aids to reduce the need for company catalogues.

When considering comments in reviews, it must always
be remembered that the critics in these periodicals are usually men and women with musical qualifications who play their
test records on high quality equipment. Few of a public or
academic library's users will have more than an amateur musician's background, and only the minority will possess equipment that will, in doing full justice to the recording, also
bring to light the technical flaws.

Even if one relies upon a critical consensus as a guide
to purchase, the comment in the 1966 cumulated volume of
Record Ratings [158], collected from earlier issues of Notes,
is extremely apposite. "When eight or ten symbols are given
for the same recording, they generally establish a pattern of
approval, acceptance, or disapproval." To this unexceptional
comment is added the warning: "Indeed, anyone who rests
content with the symbols alone will miss half the fun, since
no system of symbols, no matter how elaborately designed or
judiciously assigned can possibly catch the full flavour of
the reviews themselves. The reasons a reviewer gives for
liking or disliking a particular release are more crucial than
his final decision, and often reveal that the decision should
be taken with a grain of salt."

However well a record is reviewed, some of our borrowers will probably find it disappointing; in contrast, even
the worst reviewed discs appear sure to find the occasional
satisfied listener. It is probably fortunate the judgment is
mainly subjective; if there should be a total agreement that
one performance and recording was "definitive" (a favourite
word with some reviewers), there would be no point in librarian or private purchaser buying any other, and aesthet-
ically we would surely all be the poorer. A great work can
usually survive a surprisingly wide variety of interpretations.

Radio, in Britain and elsewhere, usually includes a proportion of recent releases in broadcasts and such relays may
give the librarian a chance to assess the sound qualities of a
disc. Unfortunately, much musically attractive broadcasting
occurs when the librarian is working and cannot take advantage of the opportunity to assess the recording broadcast.

If the sound recordings librarian has to supply quickly a list of generally acceptable stock of standard music for
the initial collection in a branch library, for example, then
immediate guidance might be found in Recommended Recordings, published each spring and autumn by General Gramophone Publications, producers of Gramophone. An equally
quick means of checking that one has not, by oversight,
omitted a major work or has failed to select a balanced mixture from the available standard repertory, is to use Joan
Pemberton Smith's A Basic Stock List [205] which provides
400 recommended works but not, it will be noted, any suggested recordings, so that the list should not become outdated to any major degree. Another useful compilation is
the Basic Record Library, a booklet distributed by Schwann.

No two librarians are likely to have the same idea as
to what constitutes the perfect basic stock (even if such a
thing were possible), but one also feels that too few selec-
tors take really adequate thought over the matter of initial
choices. Earlier in this chapter (p. 328-9) we have offered
tentative suggestions for a breakdown of different categories of music, but this has been done with diffidence. There
are two reasons for this; first, such a breakdown by percentages tends to ignore the practicalities of the available
repertoire. With the constant flux of new recordings, reissues and withdrawals from the catalogues, the overall picture is never static, and one cannot tell if next year will,
for example, bring a bumper crop of new opera recordings
or if it will prove sterile and offer little but standard works
in performances and recordings that offer no advantages
over versions already in stock. One might add, as a rider,
that any theoretical balance is liable to be upset by the number of works added because of their fortuitous appearance
on the other side of a wanted item, or which are provided
as "fill-ups." The other point is even more basic. It
seems to us that the public who use the sound recordings
libraries in two (or one-hundred and two) different places
will not be, however superficially similar the areas may be,
the same mix of population. Each will have its particular
likes and dislikes and to supply exactly the same basic
opening stock in a number of branches, as happened with
one northern English county, is misguided at best, or lazy
and dishonest if one takes a less charitable view, for it
demonstrated that the staff responsible for selection had
made no effort to discover what the local borrowers wanted.

Even when the original stock is supplied and the library has been running for some time, the wise music librarian will consistently make a point of talking to users, getting their ideas and trying (within the limits of the budget, the fields of music that may be covered and the need to keep the collection in reasonable balance) to learn what it is that the public wants and, equally necessarily, what is unwanted and disliked--and why.

One would be extremely ill-advised to surrender all responsibility for the selection of new accessions to public demand (especially as some users will be very much more vociferous than others), but this could be little worse than the situation where the librarian makes all choices according to some abstract theory or personal tastes, and without any acknowledgement whatsoever to local borrowing patterns.

Accessioning

The local authority, or governing body of an academic institution, may insist that all sound recordings be bought from a local dealer or from a nominated supplier who has submitted the lowest tender (bid) for the supply of sound recordings for a specified period. Both restrictions may prove unsatisfactory. In the case of the latter, a maximum discount almost certainly means a minimum of service and the nominal savings may well be more than swallowed up by the additional staff time involved in checking inadequate invoices, supplying additional information for any disc not immediately traceable by the dealer and, because the supplier (in order to make a profit despite the abnormal discount) may well not check the condition of records, the library has to do the job and could well incur considerable expense in postage, returning unsatisfactory copies to the supplier. As for local dealers, these can also present problems, although some librarians are fortunate enough to have good and conscientious suppliers in their respective areas. In general, the major difficulty is likely to be that the local firm is probably concerned mainly, if not entirely, with the popular end of the market and has limited competence when dealing with classical music; and may be at something of a loss when asked to supply a recording issued by a small company on a little-known label or a disc which needs to be specially imported. There is much to be said in favour of the use of a library supplier

who is accustomed to tracing and obtaining records issued
by small and obscure firms, or to finding a source for, say,
Polish or Indian discs which the enterprising librarian feels
are necessary.

If it is decided to share the library business and use
both types of supplier, common fairness suggests that the
specialist is not used only for obtaining unusual or difficult-
to-obtain discs but is given a fair proportion of normal domestic issues. It should be mentioned that the specialist
supplier is likely to be very much more willing to do some,
if not all, of the processing necessary before a disc is ready
for public use than is the proprietor of the shop down the
street, and may also be able to provide accession and/or
catalogue cards for records bought. These additional services will amost certainly be charged for, which is to be expected, although the price may be below the cost actually
incurred by the dealer, and certainly less than it would
cost the library to do itself.

Although the supplier should already have examined
each record, it is as well for the library to do its own
checking as well. An inspection for pinholes, scuffs and
scratches (and a quick aural check on the latter to see if
these are marks that sound or only surface marks that are
unaffected by playing or make so little sound that they are
likely to disappear after one or two playings) may find
something that the dealer has overlooked. The record should
be placed on a turntable and the pickup lowered on to the
opening grooves to see that the plastic is neither badly
warped nor dished (i.e., warped so badly as to be concave/
convex). The absolutely flat record is now a real rarity
partly since inspection at the factory is much less rigorous
today than it was some years ago, one result of a constant
battle by the manufacturers to keep prices from rising more
than is absolutely necessary. Another potential cause of
trouble is that discs are very much thinner than in the early
days of LP. The various physical defects are almost all at-
tributable to the stresses and strains that the plastic from
which the record is made undergoes as it is quickly cooled.
The meticulous librarian who returns a disc because its condition is unsatisfactory is liable to find that the replacement
copy is in no better state, and one has to use discretion,
and realize also that the library supplier is not the culprit.
At the same time, the clearly defective pressing is sometimes

sent out by the manufacturer, and the librarian is right to
return such a defective example to the manufacturer or perhaps to the supplier for exchange.

Ideas on record protection have changed over the
years, although the problem of static electricity on the surfaces of discs is as acute as ever. In the late 1950s and
early 1960s, a number of libraries bought a Parastat machine
from Cecil Watts at Sunbury-on-Thames or asked their supplier to give all records this machine's antistatic treatment
before sending the discs to the library. The antistatic solution, thin as it is on the grooves, was found to cause problems with the ultralightweight tracking employed by machines
of really high fidelity, so that the Parastat process is no
longer recommended. Antistatic cloths, once a cause of
smears and other damage to the delicate grooves are now
much more satisfactory and the use (before playing each
side of a disc) of those produced by nationally recognized
firms is acceptable. One very experienced music librarian
recommends the use of a small sponge, slightly moistened
with distilled water.

Accession numbers will almost certainly be required by
the library, possibly for issue purposes, and possibly to act
as a register with details of the supplier, the date supplied
and the price paid, etc. The librarian has the choice between using the particular manufacturer's catalogue/label
number or of inventing a number; it is probably irrelevant
which method is used for purely office accounting purposes,
but it does matter if a number is needed for shelf arrangement or as the means of arranging an issue file. In some
local authorities, the audit department may insist upon the
allocation of unique accession numbers to all new stock.

The advantages of using the manufacturer's number
are that it is already shown, usually very clearly, on both
disc and sleeve, it is easily traced in record guides and in
trade catalogues and is easily recognized by a fair proportion of library users who are familiar with record names and
prefix numbers or letters, within their own individual fields
of interest. The maker's number is also the most important
item of information needed when ordering (or re-ordering) a
copy. On the other hand, it must be admitted that the commercial identification may be long, complex or both, often
dictated by the understandable desire of any company that

its discs or tapes should not be confused with the products
of another company because of use of the same or a very
similar catalogue prefix. The move in recent years, apparently dictated by the increasing use of computers in
stock control at the various main warehouses, towards an
all-figure identification--exemplified in Britain at the time
of writing by DGG, Philips, and Supraphon, rather than
the former preference for a letter prefix and a number--
is clearly more confusing for many people, and therefore
more likely to result in error in a manual system. This is
a major reason for the pressure for an international standard form of numbering. The advantages of a library-allotted
number for accession purposes are that it is generally short,
needs no modification if the library has more than one copy
of a particular disc, and may be used as a means of quick
identification of recently added stock.

Some mark of ownership should be placed on the
record, possibly by means of an electric stylus, by indian
or chinese white ink (according to the colour of the disc's
label), or by means of a self-adhesive label with the library's
name printed or rubber-stamped upon it. Similarly, the library stamp should be put on the back of each sleeve. Where
the library uses an embossing machine as an anti-theft device
for books, the same machine can be used to impress the library stamp on a gramophone record sleeve.

Classification

At first sight, it would seem axiomatic that discs should be
classified in the same way and by the same system as that
used for the library's scores, yet British and American practice is firmly against this. Liverpool is the only library in
this country known to the writer (although, clearly, there
may be others) to use the Dewey Decimal Classification for
arranging discs. A number of American libraries have
adopted the Library of Congress scheme for discs and found
it much more difficult to apply in this field than it is with
scores, and some American librarians have declared the
scheme to be unsatisfactory for use with recordings. A
Dutch librarian has noted, "It was interesting to find out
that users prefer records to be arranged alphabetically according to the name of the composer or performer instead
of a strict classification, which fewer than 10% wanted. A

marginal remark must be made here; most of the record libraries involved in the enquiry are using a strict classification scheme in arranging their records" [50]. Over the
years a considerable literature on recordings classification
has emerged [78].

There seems to be general agreement in Britain that a
detailed scheme is not needed, even with a large collection.
Where a classified arrangement is preferred, it is generally
under such broad headings as orchestral, chamber, instrumental, and vocal works, subdivided again as far as is considered necessary according to the size of the stock. Clearly, orchestral music will need special subsections for symphonies and concertos, and it may be thought advantageous
to separate ballet music and overtures from the general sequence. Vocal and choral music will also need a number of
subdivisions. Libraries following this approach usually include headings in some categories such as "Collections" or
"Recitals." If browser boxes are used, divider boards are
advantageous to mark the end of one section and the beginning of another. Where there are many records in a single
category, as is likely to be the case with general orchestral
records, or concertos, further guides (often giving the name
of a major composer on each) may be incorporated to break
up the alphabet and so facilitate the discovery of a wanted
work.

A plan for the arrangement of a gramophone record
library specifically prepared for that purpose, is ANSCR;
the Alpha-numeric System for Classification of Recordings
[194]. The compilers call their system ANSCR after the
initial letters of the title, and pronounce it "answer." The
way to apply the scheme is explained at length by its de-
visers who quote several examples in every section, which
proves to be a most useful aid towards better understanding. As Olga Buth has noted [34, p. 446], "ANSCR may
have been based on the scheme outlined in an article [136]
published several years earlier."

The basic plan in the field of classical music is that if
the first item on a disc occupies more than a third of the
side (as judged by a visual inspection rather than playing
and timing), the class mark is decided by that work. There
are exceptions as, for example, when a symphony has a fairly substantial fill-up which may take over a third of the

opening side but which is placed there to allow for a convenient turning-over point in the major work. The general
intention, however, seems to be to reduce to a minimum the
number of discs classified with anthologies. This general
rule is clearly unsuitable for pop music in which a record
is likely to contain anything from half-a-dozen tracks upward. Such discs, however, are usually all of the same
type or style of music, so that an overall classification
should normally be simple to provide.

The ANSCR class mark invariably comprises four
lines, arranged one above the other, which gives the scheme's
notation a superficial similarity to the Dickinson music classification, but it is no more than that. The first of the four
terms, quoted in the top line, shows the musical genre.
There are twenty-three main classes: orchestral music, solo
instrumental music, popular music, etc. This basic scheme
of arrangement could well be acceptable to many British librarians.

Criticisms could be made, but such points are often
subjective and do not offset the general merits of the scheme.
Interested readers can find a highly critical review of the
system in Notes [96a], and may prefer that assessment of
ANSCR to the one provided here. Reference will be found
in the section on cataloguing to the complete sets of ANSCR
cataloguing cards prepared for a selected number of discs
(mainly in the popular field) which can be purchased, without the scheme's classification mark if wished, from Bro-Dart.

If it is desired to subdivide a library of jazz discs,
the two schemes propounded by Derek Langridge [117] are
definitely worth consideration, since both plans are specifically devised for the purpose. One arrangement uses style
as its basis, with such headings as traditional, mainstream,
avant-garde, blues, and the like. The second scheme is
basically chronological. The former plan has some period
subdivisions, and the alternative classification breaks down
some periods into different types of music. Whichever is
chosen, the notation is alphabetical with either one or two
letter. The chapter which includes these suggested arrangements also considers other possible methods of sorting a collection of jazz discs, and of the various indexes needed to
allow for almost all approaches possible. The book as a
whole, in fact, can be very warmly recommended to any en-
thusiast in this area of music.

If any scheme of fairly broad classification is used for
a collection of discs and the records are filed on racks, side
on, so that only the spines are immediately visible, some
form of colour coding is highly desirable to assist in the
discovery of a wanted disc, and to draw immediate attention
to any item that has been filed in another musical or nonmusical sequence. All that is needed is a strip of coloured
adhesive linen, plastic or other tape which should be affixed
in a set position near top or bottom of the spine of the
sleeve. If more divisions are used than different colours
are easily available, then separation can be achieved by
varying the placing of the tape on the spine, so that a red
guide an inch from the top of the sleeve has a different de-
notation from a similar red guide halfway down the sleeve
which, in turn, is not the same as a red signal at the bottom of the sleeve. If thought necessary, extra subdivisions
can be introduced by means of a second colour. Thus, a
red slip at the top of a sleeve might indicate an instrumental
record, with different subsidiary colours to denote chamber
music (which could be further subdivided), piano works,
violin solos, clarinet recordings, etc. Correct placing is
vital to prevent mistaken interpretation of a signal's intent,
as well as to keep the sleeves looking tidy. Where indirect
access is in force, there seems no virtue in arranging the
discs themselves in classified order, but some sort of simple
shelving sequence will be required to enable staff to retrieve
particular recordings quickly. The usual choice is between
the manufacturers' catalogue numbers (a means commonly
used in shops that sell sound recordings) and the library's
own accession numbers.

Where the sleeves (with or without records in them,
according to practice) are on display to permit borrowers to
inspect them, it is not automatic that a classified order should
be used. It would be possible to arrange this display by
label or library accession number, but this idea seems to
have far less value for users than for staff, but the most
helpful alternative is to base the arrangement, in general,
upon the alphabetical sequence of composers' names. Under
such a scheme, virtually all records of Beethoven's music--
be they orchestral, chamber music, piano pieces or songs,
etc.--will be found together on the shelves, as will be most
works by other composers in their appropriate places. The
anthology type of disc which includes works by more than
one composer presents problems. One may file these mis-

cellanies under a heading such as "Collections"; it would seem decidedly more helpful, however, to file under what might be described the highest common factor. According to circumstances, this last may be the artist (particularly if a singer), the instrument (organ, guitar), the country from which the music originated (England, Germany) or even the title given to the collection by the issuing company.

Although this type of arrangement separates a collection's symphonies from one another, its operas, piano works, and other genres likewise, the plan may well suit the needs of a majority of users. It accepts as fact that many who borrow recordings make no use of the library's holdings of music scores, a matter that indicates that there is often disappointingly little overlap between those who listen to music and the minority who need scores to perform or to follow music, or who wish to read books about the subject and its practitioners. In short, it is mainly a different category of public library borrowers (and possibly in other types of library also) who borrow recordings, and one that is happy with any form of arrangement that is simple enough to be quickly understood, but with less interest in the music of a particular category or genre than in the composer or performers.

When the gramophone record collection was inaugurated in Widnes Public Library in 1959, it was felt that a composer-based method of arrangement of the sleeves would be most acceptable to users; at the same time, it was realized that such an approach--based on intuition--might completely misjudge demand, and would certainly be a handicap to the borrower whose interest was in specific types of music, and who is best served if a classified sequence is adopted. For the benefit of an approach via the medium, a coding system was introduced, using coloured adhesive tape along the top and left-hand edges of the outer sleeves. Under this plan, all discs of orchestral music had yellow tape affixed across the top of each sleeve. Symphonies were more precisely identified by the use of a red stripe down the spine, concertos by a vertical blue stripe and overtures by a green secondary guide. General orchestral works--serenades, suites, tone poems and the like--had a yellow tape on the spine to repeat that across the top. Similar types of colour pairings were used to show categories of instrumental, vocal and nonmusical recordings. No more than six colours were needed in all,

using different permutations. It was hoped that, with this
assistance, the borrower whose prime interest was in organ
music or in piano concertos had only to note the colour combinations involved (and their placing on a sleeve) to find the
appropriate music on the racks with little trouble. The plan
also allowed, had there been public resistance to the selected
method of filing, for the collection to be rearranged easily in
a broadly classified sequence.

In practice, the coding scheme seemed to be little used
--except for jazz, where the blue tape across the top of the
sleeve proved an invaluable identification to the patron who
had no interest in classical music. The vertical tape was
omitted on all accessions after a year or two's experience
had shown it to be unwanted. The horizontal tape (folded
over the top of the library-provided outer sleeve, to show
about one-half inch at the front) was retained, mainly to
provide a suitable surface and background for stencilling
(or, later, by means of a Dymotape machine) the composer's
name or other filing word(s). The advantages of providing
a basic indication of the type of music on the record, be it
orchestral, instrumental, vocal or nonmusical were now no
more than a bonus and not an important factor.

Although personal experience has shown that, in public libraries, the needs of people using music scores and
those using recordings of the same works are usually very
different (as has already been suggested), this judgement
is not necessarily true in all libraries of this type, and is
much less likely in an academic library. However, except
for students of music, it seems fair comment that only a
small percentage of those who borrow sound recordings are
active music makers, and few more can read a score. Listeners seem happy enough with a composer arrangement,
but it is accepted that while this was true of a particular
library with a stock of nearly 6,000 discs, it would not necessarily be equally acceptable in other collections in the public library field, especially if holdings exceed 10,000 records,
and it would almost certainly be untrue in a university or
other academic library.

A further aid to borrowers, unconnected with classification but mentioned here for convenience, was an attempt
to help borrowers in the appreciation of music which had
been selected for listening. A note was made on the outer

sleeves, where applicable, drawing attention to the fact that
the library stock included a score of the work recorded on
the disc, or the text of a play or poem.   References were
also provided to such works as Tovey's Essays in Musical
Analysis [213] to allow the interested patron to supplement
the information given on the sleeve, particularly where the
company's note was felt to be inadequate.   Perhaps a scheme
of this type would be welcomed and put to practical use in
some areas; in Widnes the lack of interest was sadly disappointing and the idea was discontinued after two or three
years, for it took a considerable amount of time in checking
scores and books for appropriate references.   To British
music lovers, American sleeve notes often seem to fall into
one of two categories--the highly technical which require a
wide knowledge of music to understand and appreciate the
commentator's information, or the personality approach which
makes minimal reference to the music on the disc but confines itself to publicity highly eulogistic of the performer(s).
Neither type is normally enjoyed on this side of the Atlantic;
it is possible that British sleeve notes may be equally unattractive to American readers.

Cataloguing Rules

The need for special cataloguing rules for dealing with sound
recordings has been recognized by practitioners in the field
for more than forty years.   The reasons for the desirability
of expert guidance are easily appreciated--recordings of musical items will demonstrate many of the problems to be found
when dealing with sheet music but, additionally, there are
the performing and technical aspects of the mechanical reproduction which need to be incorporated in the entry.   Different performers using the same musical text may produce con-
trasting interpretations.   Furthermore, the library users
should be able to discover immediately, from the catalogue
entry, whether the physical format of the recording is suitable for their own equipment; it is useless, for example, to
lend a gramophone record to someone who has only a cassette player.

     The Music Library Association's Code for Cataloging
Phonograph Records of 1942 is now probably of little more
than historical interest, but the Association deserves credit
for this pioneer effort which was later replaced by the Code

for Cataloging Music and Phonorecords, prepared by a joint
committee of the MLA and the American Library Association's
Division of Cataloging and Classification, and published by
the ALA in 1958 [147]. This work has already been considered in part in an earlier chapter. At this point, however,
we are solely concerned with Chapter III, devoted to "Phonorecords." The chapter is exactly similar, except for the layout and the numbering of the rules, to Chapter 9a of the
Library of Congress' Rules for Descriptive Cataloging [219].
The intention was that the chapter should be valid for all
types of sound recording then current--discs and cylinders,
wire and tape recordings, player-piano rolls, etc. Additionally, it was planned that entries formulated from these rules
would be compatible with those for books and scores, and so
allow for integration in a single catalogue, if so desired.
This is a fairly common practice in the USA, though rare in
Britain. The use of the prefix "phono" for each type of material was claimed to be economical and to be useful as an
aid to uniformity; it may be remarked here that the British
code of 1973 (see page 354) prefers the more customary word
"sound" in preference to "phono."

        Section A of the MLA code deals with "Main entry"
which is governed, in this case, by the 1949 A.L.A. Cataloging Rules for Author and Title Entries [2]. The text
points out that in popular music, the author/composers tend
to be listed without specifying the area for which each person named is responsible, but that it is customary for the
composer of the music to be quoted last, e.g., if a work is
identified as being by Brown, Jones, and Robinson, then
the composer is almost certain to be Robinson. With serious
music, however, the composer's name is usually clearly
stated.

        Recordings of more than one work are often to be
found embodied in a single disc or tape. If two works are
thus joined each work is catalogued separately; if there are
three or more works, no single solution is proposed. If all
the works are by the same composer (or author, in the case
of a spoken word recording), then the name of that writer
is chosen as the heading for the main entry. Should the
three or more works be by different composers, however,
then entry is made "under title"--which presumably means
the composite title of the disc or cassette, as indicated by
the manufacturer.

Section B of the chapter relates to the physical medium and this identification (phonodisc or the like) is added to the entry at the end of the conventional title, in order to warn any catalogue user that the remainder of this particular entry deals with a recording rather than with a score or other text in printed form. Section C is concerned with transcription of title, D with Imprint, while E and F give guidance on Collation and Notes respectively. From this brief outline it can be seen that the order of consideration is basically the same as that for books. The Code offers a comparatively long section on notes and a brief one dealing with "Issues and copies." Finally, H is the heading for guidance on secondary entries, which the code recommends should be made for performers, performing groups and, sparingly, for titles of works and for recordings issued as part of a series, in those cases that a note of the latter would have practical value.

The joint code of the MLA/ALA was clearly the basis of Chapter 14, "Phonorecords," in the Anglo-American Code Rules of 1967 [4]. An introductory note reminds users that the chapter might usefully be considered as an appendix to chapters 1 (Entry), 6 (Descriptive cataloguing of separately published monographs and other non-serial publications), and 13 (Music). By means of these references back to earlier sections of the code, considerable repetition has been avoided. At the same time, this separation emphasizes the fact that sound recordings were a section of an appendix (Non-book materials) that seemed only partly integrated into the code as a whole.

For single works in recorded form, or for excerpts from works, the entry "is the same as the entry for the same material in its visual form." If a disc or tape contains two or more works by as many different composers, and if the recording has been issued with a collective title (such as the BASF disc, Romantic horn concerts, which contains three works of this genre--by Schumann, Schoeck, and Weber) all of them with the same soloist, orchestra, and conductor, entry is made under the manufacturer's title. The only exception to this is for "a person or corporate body" prominently named as compiler, on the label or elsewhere; in such cases, this name is selected for the main entry. There would seem to be few examples of this type of publication.

The style of entry is based on that used for music,
but at the end of the uniform title is added a descriptive
word in italics to show the format, e.g., [Phonodisc]. For
imprint, the cataloguer has to decide whether the company
responsible for issuing the recording "is primarily a record
publisher." If it is adjudged that this is so, then "the imprint consists of the name of the publisher," followed by the
catalogue number that the publisher has allotted to the recording. If the exact year of release cannot be supplied,
an approximation should be given. If the issue of recordings is but a minor part of a publisher's business, then imprint follows the same form as for books. In short, the
rules provide two different types of imprint, according to a
publisher's main business, which may not be always easy to
decide, particularly if the balance of a company's output
should alter over a period. The inconsistency between the
two styles of imprint seems unnecessary.

Collation for discs (252D) includes the number of
sides. Fractions of a side are noted where applicable, but
the code gives no indication as to how precise the figure
should be; an example in the text quotes a work as taking
one-and-one-third sides. The addition of the word "Microgroove" presupposes that the library also stocks some coarsegroove discs, and unless described as stereophonic, the entry is assumed to relate to monophonic recording. For open
reel tapes, the spool diameter and the playing speed are to
be quoted, together with the number of tracks on the tape,
etc.

As for performers (in Notes, 252F3), the sequence of
details is one that has become well established through LC
usage on its printed cards. First is the name of the soloist,
followed by the function or activity--e.g., "Claudio Arrau,
piano" or "Cecil Day Lewis, reader." For orchestral works,
the name of the orchestra precedes that of its director, e.g.,
"London Symphony Orchestra: André Previn, conductor."
If there are vocal and instrumental soloists, their names
precede that of the orchestra. Voices are listed before
instruments and are shown in descending order of voice
range or in full score order as appropriate.

The limitations of this chapter in the code quickly
drew a mounting barrage of criticism from all quarters. In
the USA, the chapter was amended and revised to the extent

that a version of the North American text of chapter 14 was published separately in 1976. This, according to the cataloging-in-publication data on the reverse of the title page comprised "the currently valid revisions ... incorporated in the original 1967 version of the chapter to form a continuous text." One very obvious difference was the substitution of "sound recording" or "phonorecord" throughout the chapter. The physical extent of a work that took between one and two sides of a record was now described as "on sides 1-2 of 1 disc." In all, the chapter gave an impression of patchwork when fairly substantial amendment was needed.

From the title of Nonbook Materials: The Organization of Integrated Collections ..., by Jean Weihs, with Shirley Lewis and Janet Macdonald [229], it can be seen that the collaborators envisage a multimedia catalogue, which is still unusual in British academic and public libraries, although of growing importance in the increasing number of schools and colleges where multimedia resource centres are often well established. The code is divided into six parts, which are virtually chapters. The first deals with cataloguing policy for nonbook materials. It gives brief advice on such areas as description and headings; subject analysis; methods of indicating the type of material. There is some general information on the sample cards which abound throughout the text, and upon the three levels of description quoted in AACR 2. The second part covers cataloguing rules for nonbook materials. It begins with "General rules for entry and descriptive cataloguing." The basis is clearly chapter 1 of AACR, but the scope is wider in that it includes rules for main entry but not, be it noticed, added entries or other items. There follow sections on individual media, over twenty in all.

The rules cover description and choice of main and added entries. Headings are not considered in this code, but references are. This may be regarded as practical if a trifle illogical. For the preparation of uniform titles, readers are referred to chapter 25 of AACR 2. One minor curiosity about the uniform titles in the examples is that every one ends with the formula "Sound recording": but this is allowed, as an option in AACR at 25.5E. Marginal notes against the examples draw attention to the particular problems illustrated. Reference is occasionally made to parallel examples in the first edition in cases where the rules have been changed in the interim.

Part 3 concerns "Reference to materials not listed in the catalogue" and seems to have very little relevance here. Part 4 is a glossary and abbreviations. Part 5 considers storage; there is much comment on total or partial intershelving. It is clear that the authors are enthusiasts for collecting all material in a single sequence as far as this can be achieved. Brief notes are given on the conservation of materials. There are separate sections for magnetic tape (which includes video tape), for sound discs, and for such items as microscope slides, 3D materials, 2D opaque materials, and transparencies. The last part of the book is a series of appendices. There are three of these—on notes; list of general material designations (which is the same as in AACR 2), and a bibliography.

Considered as a whole, this may be regarded as an admirably clear and competent abridgement of the appropriate section of AACR 2. It must be remembered that there is nothing here relating to books or to printed music, nor does the Canadian code offer any guidance on headings (be they personal or corporate) nor on uniform titles. It is, as has been stated above, a "cut down" AACR, but it does not offer any form of simplified cataloguing beyond that permitted in AACR itself in its first and second descriptive levels. This code, in other words, accepts AACR 2 fully, whereas there were some disagreements between the two sets of rules in the Canadian volume. In one or two respects, Weihs and her collaborators go beyond AACR, in that the latter for example makes no mention of "sound pages," perhaps because they seem to be currently used solely in schools.

British dissatisfaction with chapter 11 onwards in AACR, i.e., that section concerned with non-book materials, resulted in the production of Non-book Materials Cataloguing Rules, prepared by the Library Association Media Cataloguing Rules Committee; it was published in 1973, jointly by the Association and the National Council for Educational Technology (which later dropped the "National" from its title) and so were often referred to as the LA/NCET or NCET rules [123]. This code recognized the increasing need to produce the maximum amount of uniformity between entries for various types of nonbook materials and to permit the setting-up of a machine-readable file. To this end, the code consisted of a chapter of general rules, followed by others dealing with graphics and three-dimensional representations, motion pic-

tures, and sound recordings. The code kept fairly close
links with AACR 1; indeed, its rules "show explicitly how
they can be slotted into the existing framework of AACR"
(p. 5). The organization of Part 1 (Description) of AACR 2
is apparently derived from LA/NCET.

The commercial recording which includes more than one
item--be it on disc, cassette, cartridge or open-reel tape--
is commonplace. Indeed, it is probable that, even in the
area of standard music where long works may form a major
part of the collection, the proportion of shorter pieces that
occupy only part of a composite recording is quite high.
Although the problem of the recording that contains more
than one work is common, it does not, unfortunately, lessen the cataloguer's difficulties. The NCET approach to
cataloguing such an anthology is similar to that of AACR,
i.e., if the material has been issued with a collective title
by the manufacturer, that title should be used as the main
entry heading. Individual items in the anthology will or
will not receive added entries in accordance with an individual library's practice. If it should happen that the publisher has not given a particular compilation an umbrella title, the rules make two different provisions--one for the
sound recording which contains two or three items, and the
other for the issue that has four or more works within its
compass.

For the former category, separate entries are made for
each of the works, linked by means of "with" notes. For
the anthology with four or more items, treatment depends
upon whether there is what the code calls a "unifying and
identical element" in the form of a single composer responsible for all the content or in the shape of a single artist or
group of performers. In either of these cases, it is clearly
best to use the name of the composer or performer(s) respectively for the major heading. Should the four or more works
be by different composers and without the same performers
throughout, so that there is no unifying element, the cataloguer is instructed (SR2b) to make the main entry under the
first work on the disc or tape, and to add "[and other
works]." The "other works" would then be identified in the
notes. In passing, attention should be drawn to the fact
that the Canadian code has an alternative rule for the main
entry under performers or performing group, for "collections
of works by more than one author or composer, with or

without a collective title applied by the publisher"--an approach which avoids NCET's heart searching as to whether
or not a collective title sufficiently identifies a work.

    This partly repeats a point forcefully made by Sey-
mour Lubetzky some years earlier, when he suggested that
"... not all men and media are treated alike. One category
of people tacitly excluded from provisions of authorship are
performers...." Thus, the recording of Leonard Pennario's
artistry on the piano will not be found under his name, but
under the title of the recording: The Best of Leonard Pennario in Stereo [phonodisc] [126, p. 29]. Lubetzky accepts
that a recording of Schumann's piano concerto with Pennario
as soloist would receive its primary entry under the name of
the composer, and used the analogy of "an edition or a
translation of the work of a certain author." But, "In the
absence of any particular composer, however, it would seem
that the recording could only be construed as exhibiting the
work--the artistry--of Pennario, as is also implicit in the title The Best of Leonard Pennario, and the main entry should
be under Pennario (analogous to the entry of translations of
works of various authors by a certain translator under the
name of the translator). Again, the denial to performers of
the status of authorship is ignoring realities." He suggests
that "the failure to recognize the work of performers is primarily due to an unconscious bias for 'the book'.... The
art and artistry of a singer, violinist, or pianist, cannot be
conveyed by the medium of the book; hence, their works are
orphans--they have no authors. They can be and are related in the catalog indirectly by means of added entries
under the performers' names, but the main entries are under the titles." Lubetzky draws attention to the unhappy
result: "They will be separated by their titles, as The Best
of Leonard Pennario, among the various entries under B,
and Pennario Plays Just for Fun, a distance away under the
letter P. This does not contribute to the systematic structure of the catalog or its effective use." Lubetzky, as
these quotations show, generally advocated main entry under
the "most sought" heading principle, whereas AACR 1 favours
"primary intellectual responsibility." There must be numerous occasions when the two methods produce quite different
answers, and it is significant that AACR 2 has changed its
approach and now takes what might be called the Lubetzky
line.

Reverting to the LA/NCET code, it recommends for imprint: "In general, give as imprint the brand or trademark name as found on the label of the recording and omit all other names," (SR 7C) which seems to be the best solution to a possibly difficult choice, and avoids the artificial differentiation in AACR 1 between those companies which are primarily manufacturers of records and the others for whom it is a secondary activity. For the rest, the code kept fairly close links with AACR 1.

With cataloguers in the USA, Canada and Britain (and, doubtless, elsewhere) making suggestions for the improvement of AACR 1, it should come as no surprise to learn that there is, we suggest, nothing revolutionary in the 1978 revision of AACR, but rather that Chapter 6 (Sound recordings) owes something to all these attempts to update and improve the 1967 rules. For instance, it will be noted that the "phono ..." prefix of AACR 1 has been changed, as the very title of this chapter indicates. A reminder may be needed that (as with music, Chapter 5), the rules here often amplify the general instructions provided in Chapter 1 of the code. For practical purposes, this specialist section deals with discs, open-reel tapes, tape cassettes and tape cartridges, piano (and other) rolls, and wound recordings on film. This last type is confined to its aural aspects; if the recording "is intended to accompany visual images," the user is referred to Chapter 7 of the code, concerned with "Motion pictures and video recordings."

Section 6.0B1 (the style and numbering of the rules is very different from that used for AACR 1) indicates the chief source of information to each type of material. The label affixed to the disc, cassette, etc. is preferred as the source to the container in which the item is placed, although it must be realized that the protective covering (particularly in the case of gramophone records) may well have much fuller information than is, or can be, shown on the label. This latter source, however, is firmly affixed to the vinyl of the gramophone record; the slip case can be mislaid, or the record may be misplaced in the wrong sleeve. So the label, be it on disc, cassette or cartridge housing becomes the first information choice. A recording's title is to be transcribed exactly as shown by the manufacturer (6.1B1), even though a very different form may be employed in the uniform title.

As with scores, the general material designator may be given
in brackets after the actual title. The North American view
appears to be that this identification will be necessary in a
multimedia catalogue; in contrast, British opinion is that
such identification can be adequately achieved by means, for
example, of a shelf-mark. The difference in prefix between,
say, G786.4 and C786.4 could adequately differentiate between a disc and a cassette recording of the same work.
Where the item covers more than one type of material, the
major aspect should be entered as the general material designator; if there is no predominant type, then "multimedia"
or "kit" should be added to the title proper.

Referring back to the matter of information sources
for sound recordings, it will be quickly discovered, after
handling a few items, that what might be called the title-
page principle does not exist. In the case of cassettes,
particularly, the information on the plastic housing which
contains the tape itself is often grossly inadequate, and may
well refer the listener to the printed card which acts as a
sort of much smaller (and generally much less adequate)
back of the sleeve which protects a disc. The code's principle here is that the label or disc or its equivalent on tape
is the first source of information. Only if that proves insufficient does the cataloguer go to the next source, the accompanying textual material. The third possibility is the
container and, if the information found is still inadequate,
then the cataloguer is advised to use any other available
source.

Where an item has no collective title, the choice is
given (6.1G) between describing the whole collection as a
unit, or making a separate description for each individually
titled work. The LA/NCET rules, it will be recalled, adopted
the latter approach if there were no more than three items
on a recording, but expected the cataloguer to look for what
it called a "unifying and identifying element" where there were
four or more items on a single disc or cassette.

The 1978 code offers the cataloguer a choice over what
is the equivalent of a book's imprint. Preference is given to
the conventional style, "as instructed in 1.4D," but the name
of the distributor may be added to that of the publisher
(6.4D1). It seems possible that the LA/NCET rule (SR7C)
was the source of the sensible decision to enter a commercial

recording under the name of the label, so that Ace of Diamonds, Vox, Turnabout, etc., will be shown under these
individual names rather than Decca, at one time the parent
company of all these labels in Britain. Unfortunately, as
will be shown, this decision becomes muddled a little later in
this chapter of AACR 2. Date of publication is to be listed
(6.4F), even though (as we have mentioned) that quoted on
the label may not always be accurate, and the cataloguer
could sometimes be aware of this. However, misleading dates
are comparatively few. If the actual recording date(s) is/are
known, this information is to be included in a note at the end
of the entry.

Physical description (6.5) expects the cataloguer to
give the playing time in minutes "to the next minute up," so
that a disc shown to play for twenty-six minutes and ten
seconds would be listed as lasting for twenty-seven minutes.
If the information is not provided by the publisher, the cataloguer is told to give an approximate time "if that can be
readily established." Short of playing over an item, even an
estimated time may be difficult to judge. Only larger libraries are likely to have such reference works as the British
Broadcasting Corporation's music catalogue, Aronowsky's
Performing Times of Orchestral Works [8], or the like to
hand. In this instance, the code does not supply any prescribed sources of information, as is done in some other
sections.

The requirement that the diameter of discs, in inches,
should be quoted (6.5D2) seems pedantic. Unless they are
"other than the standard dimensions," the cataloguer is not
expected to give measurements for either cartridges of cassettes. From this discrepancy, one is apparently expected
to believe that the twelve-inch disc is not standard. The
"pop single" is pressed on a seven-inch record but, whatever the situation in other countries, few British libraries
have such items--or others--in this format. In any case,
should a library have any seven- or ten-inch discs, the appropriate diameter could be quoted in each case. In passing, one might have expected a 1978 code to have adopted
metric measurements in line with the growing international
trend.

The description of the material, if one follows AACR,
may appear to be a little too precise at times. To quote an

example given in rule 6.5E1: "1 sound disc (50 min.);
33 1/3 rpm, stero.; 12 in. + 1 pamphlet (11p.:   col. ill.;
32 cm.)" is both fussy and apparently inconsistent in its
use of a full stop after "stereo" but with no similar separation for "rpm" (although this agrees with the punctuation
rules laid down in the code), while to show the exact playing speed instead of the generally accepted approximation
of "33" is a space-wasting refinement.   Similar comments
could be made about other examples.   To take but one of
them: 6.5D shows "1 sound cassette (85 min.); 3 3/4 ips.
mono.; 7 1/4 × 3 1/2 in. tape." Equally cumbersome, in
our view, is the method now suggested to show the length
of works that take part of a side, but it on disc or cassette, or those items which occupy more than one side but
which also contain another item or items.   The three examples quoted in the code read, respectively, "on 1 side of 1
sound disc (13 min.)," "on cassettes 3-4 of 4 sound cassettes (67 min.)," and "on one side of two sound discs (ca.
25 min.)." For the first and third examples, we would much
prefer (both on grounds of simplicity and time saving) the
area taken by the item to be shown as "part side." This is
the method adopted by LA/NCET.   In Weihs, all the gramophone records shown in the cataloguing examples relate to
complete sides; in cassettes are shown works which occupy
part of a side (shown as "1/3 side") but no guidance is
given as to how precise the fraction should be.   The use of
the description "part side" overcomes that difficulty for the
cataloguer.

No alteration is suggested by us in the case of the
second example quoted in the preceding paragraph, although
one might well be annoyed with an inconsiderate manufacturer
who spread a work over two cassettes that could easily have
been issued on one. As for the last item, the example given
suggests that the major work takes up rather more than three
sides, with a twenty-five minute "fill-up" on the fourth side.
In such a case, our personal preference would be to describe the major work item as occupying "3 1/2 sides (ca.
67 min.)." This should be easily understood by the catalogue user and, again, save both space and cataloguing time.

Having commented upon some points of physical description that might be considered unnecessarily precise, it is interesting to note that, almost before publication of AACR 2,
British audiovisual librarians and others were suggesting that

better searching facilities should be provided on UK MARC
records. At the beginning of 1979, by no means all audio
and related material were searchable on BLAISE (British Library Automated Information Service), and useful distinctions
are not always possible. For instance, it could be helpful
if one could trace all 7-inch gramophone records in the files;
at present, such a search is impossible. BLAISE offers this
facility on the Audiovisual MARC file; unfortunately, the
file is very incomplete.

Reverting for a moment to the description of a cassette quoted in a previous paragraph, it will be noted that
this example (6.5D) gives the playing speed, shown as
3 3/4 ips, since this is not the usual rate for the medium,
which is 1 7/8 ips. An "optional addition" mentioned in
6.5C8 is of reproduction characteristics, such as "Dolby
processed" (although that is now the norm and not the exception). This information, in the LA/NCET code, was
considered to be an "enrichment."

The series area (6.6) is likely to be of limited relevance in Britain where, unless its provision is clearly of
value to the prospective borrower, such a statement would
normally be omitted, particularly in public libraries. Thus,
to take a single example, Vanguard's Historical Anthology of
Music seems to be of peripheral interest as a series (excellent as many of the individual records are) to library users
on this side of the Atlantic, however important it might be
considered by a North American listener. There would appear to be two possible problems concerning recordings that
are parts of series, and the reader is referred to rule 1.1B9
for a work that is a section of a larger one, and to 1.6H for
series and subseries. Untangling such items can prove something of a problem with certain audiovisual materials.

There are several subheads under 6.7 (Note area),
and mention must be made of 6.7B6 (Statements of responsibility), since this (among its examples) includes the names
of a number of performers. Although this listing suggests
that the standard order in the field of music is: 1) vocalists, in descending voice order; 2) instrumentalists, in full
score order; 3) orchestra; and 4) conductor; the sequence
is not spelled out at any point in the code, unlike rule
252.F3 in AACR 1, to the potential confusion of the inexperienced cataloguer.

Unexpectedly, this section is where the publisher's catalogue number is to be quoted (rather than in the imprint), and is preceded by the label name. The two items are separated by a colon. This seems likely to give many cataloguers considerable puzzlement, since 6.4D2 (mentioned earlier) uses "Ace of diamonds"--the example given at that point--which is both label and trade name. It seems inconsistent with the rules for normal printed matter; for instance, "Pelican books" is merely a series, but the publisher on the catalogue entry would be shown as "Penguin." In cases of doubt with sound recordings, it would seem most practical to use the label name, if only because this is almost invariably clearly shown, whereas the publisher's name may not be so easily discovered. In extreme cases, such as "pirate" or "bootleg" records, the publisher's name is understandably missing. It must also be remembered that the right to use a particular label name in an individual country may change from one manufacturer to another as one licence agreement expires and a fresh one is negotiated with a different agent.

Most other points that apply both to music scores and to sound recordings have been covered in the previous chapter and generally need not be repeated here. However, it should be pointed out that the rules for analytical entries are to be found in Chapter 13, and will often be applied to sound recordings. Three methods of procedure are suggested, with decision left to the cataloguer as to which will be used. For consistency, once a choice has been made among the three, it should be applied to all examples. The first plan (13.4) is to make author-title added entries for all such items, and this is the simplest choice. The second possibility (13.5) is to make an "In ..." analytical entry, should it be felt that "more bibliographic description is needed for the part than can be obtained by displaying it in the note area...." The final proposal is supplied in 13.6, "Multilevel description," and this is intended for use by national bibliographies and major cataloguing agencies. In this plan, the descriptive information is divided into two or more levels, the first relating to the multipart item as a whole, and subsequent levels relating to groups of parts, and finally to the individual part. This method is most suitable in cases where the title of the individual part is in some way dependent upon the title of the comprehensive item; otherwise it is simpler to prepare a description of the part as a separate entity and relate it to the whole by means of a series statement (13.2).

Volume V of the International Code [102], concerned with the cataloguing of sound recordings, was compiled by Simone Wallon and Kurt Dorfmuller, with the collaboration of Yvette Federoff and Virginia Cunningham. It was published in 1983, in the standard three languages of French, German and English, but shows signs of its French origin, not least in the layout of the entries (fiches formulaires), apparently based on the practice of the French Bibliothèque Nationale, where the various areas of the description are conveniently named.

According to the Foreword, the text was completed "in the middle of the 1960s, but was substantially modified in 1971-2 in connection with the work of translation." It is claimed that this volume fits with the character of the first of the set "in presenting problems rather than giving solutions.... Although the three versions are identical in content, they show certain peculiarities of the various language and bibliographical traditions." Virginia Cunningham was responsible for the English translation. It is suggested that the standardization of sound recordings has still to be further thought through and refined before it can be accepted in terms of national bibliographies and discographies as well as libraries. As mentioned above, the volume is possibly unique in simply presenting problems, rather than setting out a code in the usual sense, which is why the examples are catalogued according to the French, Anglo-American, German and Russian cataloguing codes. The code offers suggestions for works that occupy part of a disc and also to other detailed problems, but a lot of space is allotted to problems of principle: the nature of the cataloguing unit; the principle of main entry, types of catalogue card (which seems quaint for a 1983 publication), and methods of making analytical entries. In the case of discs, the title is that of the label (4.21) "even though the sleeve may be fuller and more helpful to the cataloguer." Entry should be made in a standard sequence, which is not that of the label, "because the label does not yet have a uniformity of presentation ... as does the title page of a printed book." This seems to be a very dubious argument. The trade name of the record publisher is to be used in the record imprint (4.31). As for the collation, fractions of a side indicate the total number of works on that side, not their respective lengths. To describe a work as occupying a third of a side simply means that it is one of three works or movements on the side, whose respective lengths may be noticeably dissimilar. The code stresses the desirability of having a title catalogue, if only because there is a large number of records and tapes that contain several works "and because this means of approach is often used in research." One suspects that the authors are recommending title entries, to be entered in one catalogue with other entries.

Appendix I deals with arrangement on the shelves, and offers several alternative systems. The first is by trade name, then by record number. The suggested disadvantage for a small library is that a blank number may have several possible reasons; the disc may be on loan, it may never have been added to stock, or it may not even exist. For the library whose stock includes noncommercial recordings, the problem can be easily recognized.

The second suggestion is arrangement in alphabetical order by composer. The code's authors reckon that "It ends up creating enormous difficulties very quickly." No explanation is given of these alleged problems. The third suggestion is to follow normal practice in book libraries and to classify by subject, although it is felt that this method is only possible in small libraries, "where the listener has access to the shelves." None of the three methods is recommended, partly on the grounds that space should be left for future expansion. If discs are shelved in accession order, the result could be a variety of record sizes in a single sequence, and the code accepts that this would be undesirable, and then indicates its view that size should be the first criterion. If it is decided to shelve discs, the code apparently presupposes multiple catalogues, but (as mentioned above) may well mean multiple entry.

Appendix II is concerned with storage of sound recordings, and seems to be unexceptional. Appendix III is given over to record examples. There are nineteen of these, all dealt with according to the rules of the Bibliothèque Nationale in Paris, and also in accordance with AACR in Library of Congress practice, plus German and Russian codes. A separate appendix briefly explains catalogue of the Swedish Radio Gramophone Library, which is computer-produced. The code is completed by a separate pamphlet which gives a series of label facsimiles of ten discs, accompanied by a reproduction of part or parts of the sleeve that houses the disc. The pamphlet is printed on art paper, for it consists mainly of half-tone illustrations. Having these separately, the cataloguer can easily compare an example with the facsimiles without having the problem of turning pages over.

One can sum up by suggesting that the international code is well thought out, but it is very traditional in its principles. This is indicated by the fact that it appears to think entirely in terms of the card catalogue. The range of examples is very much restricted to classical music, with a pair of folk music items, and a solitary spoken word example (Finnegans Wake). There is no jazz, no pop. The compilers of this code seem to have no concept of the jazz musician who improvises. "Simple logic would oppose this method of cataloguing. The performer is actually not an author in either the strict or the broad sense." (3.510). There are very many people who would argue with that! The code seems intended to apply to major collections that are already well established and restricted in scope, but is likely to be of very much less use in the smaller library.

Practical Cataloguing

Many librarians agree that collections of sound recordings need to be properly catalogued for the benefit of both staff and users of the recordings, but it would be disingenuous to pretend that no contrary views are held. This is certainly the case in times of financial stringency, when a library may not be allowed to employ an adequate number of qualified staff, or other requirements of the service result in a chronic shortage of staff time to deal satisfactorily with the problems of cataloguing. Mary Pearson has suggested that, "A new item can usually be cataloged in a half hour by a cataloger of some experience.... Records requiring many analytics or extensive reference work to establish a correct entry might take an hour or more to complete" [176, p. 63]. This gives some idea of the likely cost of compiling such a catalogue unless the library is willing to make do with simpler entries than Pearson seems to have envisaged. It is sometimes argued that a catalogue of recordings is unlikely to be used sufficiently by borrowers to justify its existence, but this claim cannot be conclusively sustained unless a good catalogue has been provided and has been found, by constant observation, to be used very rarely. It has to be admitted that a cost-benefit analysis would, if properly done, need a long time to reach a firm conclusion.

Whatever the type of library, public or academic, the average borrower is likely to be primarily interested in seeing what is actually available at a given time; it is a very small minority whose first move is to consult the catalogue. When this does happen, the searcher is almost certainly trying to trace a particular item, or possibly the holdings relating to a specific composer or artist. These comments are true not only for recordings, but apply to book borrowers also. In a library without a catalogue, the patron may feel a real sense of loss or deprivation since there is no immediately apparent way of discovering just what is available; one always tends to assume that the most popular items are, by definition, almost always out and in the hands of another borrower. However, the absence of a catalogue is almost certainly going to result in greater reliance by borrowers on staff expertise, and this may be felt to be desirable, if only as a cause of increased contact between staff and their clientele.

If a quick look in the appropriate place (or what is thought to be the most likely location) for the desired recording is unrewarding, the average borrower may well seek for a suitable alternative that is likely to provide equally acceptable listening. It is also possible, however, that having failed to locate the desired work, the patron will ask for it to be reserved, or to suggest it as an addition to stock (assuming that the library accepts requests/recommendations for recordings which it does not possess). These two ways of trying to obtain the desired composition (or specific recording of it) may have meant that the catalogue has been completely ignored, even if the library has an excellent one, freely available for consultation by anyone.

With the small collection, turnover of recordings is likely to be more rapid than occurs with the large, more comprehensive stock. The librarian in charge of a comparatively limited collection (certainly up to two or three thousand discs/tapes, but possibly many more) will know with a fair degree of accuracy what is available, without the need to consult any file of holdings. Constant work with the stock helps to keep the memory fresh as to what its holdings are; difficulty is likely to arise with the occasional, or

part-time member of staff, or with a librarian whose interests are confined to books and scores and to whom recordings are, at best, a necessary evil. A simple stock register
for staff use (possibly arranged by manufacturers' catalogue
numbers, or by composer, etc.), supplemented by a good
range of back-up material in the form of printed catalogues
and discographies should make it possible to trace most of
the items required, and to do this at a fairly small fraction
of the cost of providing a comprehensive catalogue. However, if such a plan is put into practice, it must always be
both remembered and recognized that these guides cannot be
more than an imperfect substitute for a catalogue, and the
librarian should never pretend that such guides are more
than substitutes.

A card catalogue can be provided for most items of
standard music, at reasonable cost, by the use of entries
prepared by one or other agency that supplies them. In
the USA, the Library of Congress printed cards are generally accepted as models of their kind, albeit possibly rather
too detailed for the small library. Prepared on a dictionary
catalogue basis, the main entry indicates, in small type,
tracings for all added entries and references considered
necessary by LC's cataloguers. Any library can buy a complete set of entries for a single disc or album, if desired.
Although certainly not inexpensive, the cost of these cards
is still well below that which would be incurred if the library
prepared its own catalogue of sound recordings without any
reference to what has been done by LC. The physical quality of the stationery is excellent. For those libraries who
consider these cards too detailed and who are satisfied with
simpler cataloguing, the service available from such firms as
Bro-Dart, which offers entries for many popular items which
are outside the scope of LC, is clearly satisfactory. At the
other end of the spectrum, libraries that find the Library of
Congress entries insufficiently detailed at certain points or
entirely lacking in information thought to be indispensable
(such as the names of the individual members of a string
quartet, the playing time of each movement of a work, and
the like) have no apparent alternative but to prepare their
own catalogue entries.

In Britain, as has been lamented, there is still no national media bibliography nor national cataloguing service
(such as is provided in its own field by BNB) for recordings.

However, two or three commercial firms that sell recordings
to libraries also make available catalogue entries on cards,
at a price which, one imagines by no means represents the
true cost of the service. The financial loss is presumably
acceptable because of the value placed by the firms on their
business with libraries, with the cataloguing costs absorbed
by the more profitable aspects of the individual firm's activities.

An interesting method of duplication of cards is used
by the Long Playing Record Library of Blackpool, Lancashire.
The firm uses addressograph plates, which are practical although the lettering is not attractive. There are distinct
limitations to be faced with this method--a card of the usual
five inches by three inches will only allow a maximum depth
of nine lines, and the latter have a limit of forty-six characters each. Although these restrictions are generally of
little account when cataloguing the disc with but a single
work on it, or one on each side (a format that suits the majority of eighteenth and nineteenth century symphonies and
concertos), three or more items on a single disc or tape are
liable to result in a congested catalogue card or the need to
extend the entry on to a second card or, in a few cases (usually discs of the anthology type) to a third or more. Ideally, there should always be a blank line left between the details of the work(s) performed and the information about the
artists; this assists rapid visual comprehension, but the unused line may well be omitted if, by doing so, the necessary
information can be contained on a single card, saving contin-
uation to a second one.

Very similar limitations face the cataloguer in the library that has adopted a computerised format, with fixed
fields. This means that there is a limitation on the number
of characters possible for any entry. Indeed, an entry may
finish in the middle of a word, for this reason. In contrast,
MARC cataloguing uses variable length fields so that there
is no restriction on the length of any part of the entry.
The catalogues of libraries using BLCMP (Birmingham Libraries Co-operative Mechanisation Project) for music provides an excellent example of this. Cheshire's COM (Computer Output Microfilm) catalogue has fixed fields, so that
the cataloguer is allowed forty-eight or ninety-six characters, i.e., one or two lines, for the author/composer heading, with a further 300 or 240, in the respective cases, for

the title, imprint, collation, etc. In other words, the maximum for a single "card" is 348 characters.

How full should cataloguing be? There can be no
hard-and-fast rule on this hotly debated topic, if only because circumstances vary from library to library in so many
ways. In the first edition of this book, mention was made
of Fort Wayne, Indiana, whose library served a population of
some 140,000 and which needed three professional cataloguers,
one subprofessional, and two clerical assistants to deal with
its collection of discs which was catalogued with great thoroughness. In contrast, William Shank and Lloyd Engelbrecht
state that "Simplified cataloging is often used for circulating
records on the ground that they are essentially ephemeral
materials which will wear out quickly and, in many cases,
will not be replaced" [201, p. 67].

Lester Asheim and Arthur Byler take a more detailed
look at the problem [10, p. 186]. They quote An Anthology
of English Church Music from the 15th Century to the Present Day as a by-no-means extreme example. Full cataloguing
would need, it is pointed out, entries for fifteen composers,
twenty-one titles, three titles of parent works from which
excerpts are extracted, seven choirs, and seven conductors.
Additionally, entries could be justified for E. H. Fellowes,
the collection's compiler and editor, for the British Council
who sponsored this particular set of recordings, plus the
appropriate subject headings.

"The logical escape from such an overwhelming task,"
they continue, "is the utilization of printed sources which
already perform these services. In many libraries it is the
practice to eliminate analytics that would duplicate information already available elsewhere." Asheim admits that "the
printed sources appear late," but suggests that manufacturers' catalogues may help to fill the gap, and that "it seems
a wasteful duplication of effort in a busy and understaffed
library to duplicate all the cross references and analytics
...." Finally, he adds a most useful word of warning, "...
if the library does restrict the number of its own analytics
in favor of analytics in printed sources, it should make sure
that the public knows that this practice is followed, so that
the user of the card catalog will not miss those items which
the library owns but which are analyzed elsewhere."

For British users, as well as many in other countries, the standard guide for analytic entries is the Gramophone Classical Catalogue [81]. This is excellent in its guidance as to what is nominally currently available at the time of publication each quarter, but its limitations must be recognized and accepted. First, it is basically an in-print catalogue, though some items will appear that are no longer available and others are omitted for one reason or another. Any library is likely to have in stock a fair proportion (depending upon the use made of the collection and the standard of record checking) of discs that have been deleted at some earlier date. This is of some importance if the library retains older discs on an archival basis, rather than simply withdrawing them. Second, it is inevitable that every issue of the quarterly list will contain a small proportion of errors, the majority of these the result of inadequate or inaccurate labelling on the discs themselves, others a result of the haste that must occur when the compiler has to meet a printing deadline for each volume; third, discs that contain excerpts from longer works seem more prone to have these items omitted or overlooked.

The decision as to how full the library's catalogue of sound recordings should be is not one to be hastily made, for it is dependent upon a number of factors, and no two libraries will find the equation identical. The initial size of the stock is one factor, for it is much easier to catalogue fully a small collection than a large one, if only because the bigger stock is the more likely to include a higher proportion of difficult items. The rate of withdrawal must loom large (as quotations and comments in previous paragraphs have suggested), the availability of staff capable of doing this task properly, and what is perhaps the most important factor of all--the priority which the chief librarian, music librarian or other responsible person is prepared to allocate to this matter.

Different people will each have ideas as to what can be omitted, and what is essential information in the cataloguing of sound recordings. Two quotations from a lecture by Geoffrey Cuming (half of the team who compiled WERM) admirably illustrate this. He asked, "... do we provide the maximum or the minimum of information? Do we want a person who takes out a record of Gretchen am Spinnrade to be told straight away that the words are by Goethe, or do we leave him to go and get a book on Schubert and find out for himself?" [43, p. 117]. Later, he added:

> Now there are other things which I think ought to be on the ideal card, but you may not. Works exist in different versions. In the first volume of WERM we divided the recordings of Mozart's G minor symphony [i.e., no. 40] into those which used clarinets and those which didn't.... In the case of Mozart's concertos and some of Beethoven's, I think the author of the cadenza played should be stated. The companies are very bad about this and it isn't easy to find out. But it seems to us the height of injustice that any fiddler who writes out the vocal part of a Schubert song on a separate piece of paper and adds an extra twiddle in the second verse, becomes immortalised; from then onwards his name is inseparably linked with Schubert's. The man who puts three minutes of his own composition into the middle of a Mozart concerto can get away without mentioning his name at all; nobody seems to mind.

The speaker also mentioned the matter of repeats, quoting the famous example of Mendelssohn's Italian Symphony. Most performances omit the exposition repeat in the first movement, and so fail to play the twenty-three bars, written out by the composer, which lead the music back to the beginning again.

Despite what has been said, very few library catalogues will make any mention of whether recordings of the Mozart symphony include just two oboes in the orchestra or add the two clarinets introduced in Mozart's revision, nor will catalogue entries draw attention to whether a particular recording of the Italian has, or has not, the exposition repeat. The cataloguers may be partly at fault, but (as Cuming has indicated) the companies rarely give the information. Even in cases where it is provided, it may well be virtually hidden in the middle of a sleeve note, and one cannot really blame the cataloguer who does not read the text on the back of every slip case. Indeed, if this were done, complaints might be made about alleged time-wasting.

So, in suggesting what an entry should contain, widespread agreement among cataloguers is unlikely. It is possible to make out a case (a weak one, in our view) for the

provision of a catalogue listing the works in recorded form
that the library holds, and giving no other details of performers, label name, etc., whatsoever. It would not be difficult to keep uo to date, for catalogue alterations for replacements would be reduced to a minimum. The library
stock would surely always include at least one version of all
the Beethoven symphonies, and a single entry for each would
be permanent. Such a plan would ignore the individual orchestras and conductors--names that often receive greater
prominence on the front of a record sleeve than that of the
composer.

        The entry for standard music naturally begins with
the name of the composer: how full does this have to be?
For practical purposes, there is only one composer named
Beethoven, and one could agree that this heading, unadorned,
is quite enough. Mention was made, in the previous chapter,
of such headings as "Dukas, Paul Abraham" and "Borodin,
Alexksandr Porfir'evich" suggested in the Canadian code for
nonbook materials (5,75) but only multimedia catalogues may
require such detailed listing. Only with such composers as
the Gabrielis, the Scarlattis and the Stamitzes should an added initial (not full forenames) be required for differentiating
in a purely sound recordings catalogue. It may be noticed
that we have failed to mention the Bachs, Mozarts and Haydns;
in such cases the world-famous representative could be entered under surname only, while Johann Christian and Carl
Philipp Emanuel Bach, like Leopold Mozart and Michael Haydn,
could have the appropriate initial(s) added to differentiate
them from the towering figure whose surname these talented
musicians also bear.

        Although we now strongly favour the idea of the use
of conventional title, there seems to be little point in including it if the transcription of the title of the recording is exactly the same. Again, the cataloguer may like to follow BCM
practice rather than that of AACR in quoting conventional title, where one is needed, on the same line as the title transcription. The added information will, as is customary, need
to be in square brackets to make it perfectly clear that this
is added information. The choice between one's home language and that used on the recording being catalogued is
exactly the same as that needed with sheet music; this matter has already been briefly discussed in the previous
chapter.

The suggestions above should present little difficulty for a recording with but a single item on the disc or tape; as the number of works increase, so matters are likely to become more difficult for the cataloguer. With two items, one can follow LC procedure and enter the second work, preceded by the word "With" at the end of the details of the first work. The Canadian code, when two works are by the same composer, suggests that the one title should follow the other before the imprint. Such a plan saves one entry, but at the cost of the second item being overlooked by a user of the catalogue who, looking under the title of the second work and not finding it, assumes that it is not in stock. Even if one uses unit entry, the separation of the two works on one card is, a useful aid to clarity.

For the many discs and tapes which contain more than two items by different composers, the librarian will need to have a settled procedure. If there are three or more items, preference for the main entry is likely to be for the overall title given to the disc or tape by the manufacturer; if there is no such title, then it is best to make entry under the first work, providing a contents note at the end of the details of that work, and providing additional entries for each of the other items, simply noting in these cases that the recording is included with the first work, and adding "etc." to show that there is a disc of collected items.

It is customary, when publishing such recordings, for the manufacturers to provide an overall title; it is quite often unsuitable or misleading, but that is of limited importance. One might cite a Philips disc issued as <u>Famous Oboe Concertos</u>, where "famous" could be regarded as hyperbole, even though one admits the musical stature of Vivaldi and Telemann, two of the composers represented. For all such recordings with more than two works, the use of the unit card method, simply adding the appropriate composer's name as the heading and, if thought helpful, underlining the relevant section of the body of the card, keeps cataloguing costs to a minimum.

When one disc contains more than two items by different composers, but performed by the same artist(s), we feel that entry under the name of the performer(s), a "highest common factor" approach, is best--providing the work is a vocal or instrumental one. It is less justifiable with orches-

tral items, not least because we do not recommend entries
under orchestras or conductors (a result of experience
which might not necessarily be true in all libraries) whereas added entries for solo performers have been fully justified. Entry under the name of the artist satisfies Lubetzky's point concerning the separation of recordings by the
same performer. If the manufacturer's title for the collection includes the name of the singer or instrumentalist (as
with Lubetzky's examples), there seems little reason for entering under the disc's title. With a compilation of orchestral works, it is quite likely that the general title of the
recording may be better remembered than the name of the
orchestra or conductor, or even--dare we suggest--possibly
the names of any composers represented. One thinks of such
anthologies as Musica Americana!, Christmas Concertos or
Popular Overtures. It may be that with the works entered
under the name of the artist, an entry under the general
title given by the manufacturer (if this is likely to be mem-
orable) will be of potential value in tracing the recording.

     The foregoing comments relate primarily to serious mu-
sic; for popular music in its diverse forms, entry under the
name of the performer or group seems inescapable, with a
more likely need to make an added entry under the general
title of the disc, if that title does not include the name of
the artist(s). In this musical area, the performers may well
have written their own music; where others have been the
composers, only in a restricted number of cases are their
names likely to be known to more than a tiny minority of
listeners. Additionally, as has been mentioned earlier, the
composer is but one of a team preparing the work for recording, and the musician who makes the arrangement that
is to be performed may well be of far greater import.

     So, in general, treatment of classical and popular mu-
sic will follow different patterns, the former mainly concerned
with the composer, the latter with the performer. There are
always going to be examples that could well fit into either
category and, when this happens, it seems simplest to expect the cataloguer to find a solution rather than provide a
string of rules that attempt to provide for every possible alternative.

     There is a fairly important matter upon which British
and North American practices differ, if one is following either

LA/NCET or the Canadian rules. Weihs recommends that the
"generic designation, given in parenthesis following the title,
will be amplified if necessary in the collation and notes." In
other words, the indication that the work to which the catalogue entry relates is presented in the form of a disc or tape
is made clear. At the end of the filing title is added such
a designation as 'Phonodisc' to alert the potential borrower
to the format. As the Canadian code explains, "The medium
designation is given early on the card to inform the user
succinctly and immediately about the type of material listed."
This, as already shown, is the AACR approach. With LA/
NCET this identification is shown far later in the entry, as
part of the collation, on the assumption that it is far more
likely to be noticed in that spot as the borrower looks to
see the details of the recording. One could argue that,
with little time and effort, the information could helpfully
be given in both places, for it is of vital importance.

If a catalogue is limited to one medium only, i.e.,
separate listings are provided for discs and cassettes (on
the grounds that the majority of users will not have both
turntable and cassette deck, although this may well
change in the next few years), then no designator will be
needed on an entry; the catalogue itself indicates its coverage. If, however, the two formats are included in a
combined catalogue, the note about the generic designation
might still be ignored by many users. The two forms could
be distinguished by differently coloured catalogue cards,
but such an answer adds to the expense, will not appeal to
all librarians, and will not be possible in a computer-produced
listing that does not use cards.

Turning now to imprint, it is not usual to include the
place of publication, and in limited cataloguing of the type
considered here, the label name and the manufacturer's catalogue number should be adequate, to be followed by the year
of publication, where this is given on disc or cassette label,
or on their containers. This date is now almost invariably
provided with British issues, much less so for those emanating from the European continent or the USA. Even if the
cataloguer is aware that the recording has been previously
issued, we doubt if there is any great value in stating this.
The publication date ought to indicate whether the disc is a
recent issue or not; that some manufacturers appear to mislead by showing the year of reissue rather than that of the

original release is objectionable, but still (in our view) does
not justify the expenditure of time checking back in earlier
catalogues in the hope of discovering just when the recording first appeared.

As to collation, the designation "part side" seems adequate, and can prove a very useful time-saving convention.
To show that a work takes seven-twelfths of a side, or some
similar unusual fraction is unlikely to be of any interest to
most users, while a visual or aural check to provide this
figure is another brake upon the cataloguer's progress. For
a work that takes more than a single side, but which has
one or more fill-ups on the last side, a slightly different
convention illustrates this fact. If, for example, a work extends to a fourth side but, because the last section is too
short to be regarded as filling the side, the manufacturer
has added another fairly brief item, then we suggest that
this last side is shown as "$\frac{1}{2}$," whether in fact the proportion is smaller or greater; "$3\frac{1}{2}$ sides" will inform staff and
borrowers that the major work runs on to a fourth side, but
that there is at least one additional, if fairly short, work to
complete the disc.

Since cassettes show "Side 1" and "Side 2" on their
labels, the same convention of "part side" and "$\frac{1}{2}$ side" is
applicable. There is (unless the collection includes Elcas-
settes) only one playing speed for cassettes, so there is no
point in showing this in the entry. Similarly, there is no
need to indicate that a disc is to be played at 33rpm if the
collection has no records except these normal LPs. Indeed,
even if there are some 16, 45 or 78rpm items available, it
will save considerable time if the assumption is made that all
discs are to be played at 33rpm unless the entry indicates
differently. In the same way, there should be no need to
indicate that longer works are coupled in manual sequence;
only automatic sequences need be noted. However, unless
the collection eschews such recordings, it will be necessary
to show whether a record is mono or quad (and such abbreviations are perfectly acceptable); the assumption being that,
unless otherwise shown, the recording is stereo. With quad-
raphonic recordings, the format used will need to be shown,
since most machines will produce the desired results with but
one type of recording; the decoder that can be switched to
accept any of the three normally-available modes is expensive
and uncommon.

The cassette tape which has not been subject to the Dolby process to reduce tape hiss and background noise is now rarely found among current issues. Dolbyised tapes are less attractive to the owner of a reproducer without in-built Dolby circuitry because some reduction of the treble is really needed, and this control is not to be found on most cheap machines. However, even without this tone limiter, the sound should certainly be no more than a trifle over-emphatic at the top of the frequency range. Since the per-centage of untreated tapes is already small and continues to shrink, the cataloguer may rightly decide to omit all mention of Dolby except when that process has not been used. There is no difficulty in discovering this, for any tape which has been subject to Ray Dolby's patented process carries a little symbol, based on a capital "D" facing forwards and back-wards, on both the cassette housing and on the spine of the container's housing.

Notes can be full or minimal, and it is difficult to offer guidance except to say that an entry must contain the name of the performer(s). The standard method is that long used by the Library of Congress; this shows the name of any solo-ist followed, in parentheses, by a brief indication of role, e.g., John McCabe (piano), Ian Partridge (tenor). Some li-brarians may prefer "pianist," but this is a minor point. For orchestras and choral groups with a conductor, the rule is for the latter's name to come last. Any soloist can then be named before details of the choir or orchestra are supplied and, in this way, clearly indicate the respective roles of the named artists, e.g., John Mitchinson (tenor), Chorale Ste-phane Gaillat, Orchestre de Paris, con. Baudo. If, as is a growing practice today, the soloist in a concerto by Mozart or a contemporary of his, also directs the orchestra in a re-version to the common practice of the time, it is probably most consistent to retain the normal layout and so quote the soloist as such, and repeat the name as that of conductor.

Some further simplification and saving of both space and time can be achieved in two ways. First, instruments can be shown in normal abbreviated form, as "Gervase de Peyer (cl)," and orchestral names can be similarly shortened: LSO should be immediately recognizable to any British read-er, as should NYPSO (although gramophone records now al-ways seem to refer to the orchestra as the New York Phil-harmonic, and to omit Symphony Orchestra). Second, identi-fying designations can be omitted when there is no reasonable

chance of misunderstanding, so that for a violin concerto
entry the listing of performers as Suk/LPO/Boult should
cause no problems and, as already claimed, be economical
as well.

With more than one soloist, it is usual to list vocalists
before instrumentalists (when both are taking part) and to
include the persons in descending pitch order for voices,
e.g., soprano before tenor, and in full score order for instruments, e.g., violin after bassoon.

There is certainly enough interest in performers to
justify entries under their names if these are not used for
the main entry. One need only look at a selection of record
sleeves to see how highly the companies who issue commercial recordings rate their star performers. Although the
general plan is simple enough to apply, there are difficulties.
How far is a library justified in making an entry for a soloist in a work that takes only a small part of one side? There
is no infallible rule, and if the result is an instinctive decision in such cases, it should not be without consistency.
From personal experience, we cannot recommend that entries
should be made for accompanists, however distinguished; nor
even for members of chamber groups, such as string quartets.
The probable value of such entries does not seem to justify
the time and trouble taken. Again, if no entries are made
under the names of conductors or orchestras, the bulk of
the catalogue is likely to be considerably reduced. On the
other hand, we have mentioned elsewhere the possibility of
making brief references under instruments (perhaps excluding the most popular ones), so that the listener who wishes
to borrow records of the double bass or clarinet can, by
looking under the name of the instrument, be referred to
entries listed by performer-solos, sonatas and concertos, etc.

After these suggestions for what might be considered
to be minimal cataloguing--or perhaps not even that--it may
seem surprising to recommend the generous provision of title
references. There are two reasons for this; first, many
users will ask for a work by name, without necessarily knowing the composer. Tracing the item, if it is a major work,
may be fairly simple; what is difficult, as has been mentioned
earlier, is the excerpt that may be performed on its own.
For example, a request for information about a Bach work
that has had various translations into English, but which is

usually rendered as <u>Mortify Us with Thy Goodness</u> (Ertöte uns durch deine Gnade) would be difficult to track down without a title entry to show that it is an excerpt from Cantata No. 22. So, title entries can be invaluable to save possibly fruitless searches. Secondly, when a record is withdrawn and a different performance of the same work is bought as a replacement, the title reference can be retained in the catalogue. It needs no amendment.

We complete this section with some sample entries and comments to illustrate some of the points made, and must stress again that these examples are intended to illustrate what (in our view) is minimum cataloguing yet is adequate enough to answer the majority of borrower enquiries.

Haydn, Joseph, 1732–1809.
Concerto. violoncello, H. vɪɪb, 2, D major₁ *Phonodisc.*

Concerto in D major, op. 101. Angel S 36580. ₁1969₁
1 s. 12 in. 33⅓ rpm. microgroove. stereophonic.

Jacqueline Du Pré, violoncello; London Symphony Orchestra; Sir John Barbirolli, conductor.
Duration: 29 min., 50 sec.
Playable also on monaural equipment.
Program notes by Robin Golding on slipcase.
With: Monn, G. M. Concerto, violoncello & string orchestra, G minor.

1. Concertos (Violoncello)—To 1800.   ɪ. Du Pré, Jacqueline,
1945–   ɪɪ. Barbirolli, Sir John, 1899–   ɪɪɪ. London Symphony
Orchestra.

79–750016

Library of Congress   69 ₁2₁   R

The Library of Congress catalogue card illustrated here demonstrates a fairly full main entry. The composer is given all Christian names and dates, followed by the uniform title for the work recorded. The description "<u>Phonodisc</u>" permits the card to be interfiled with others for books and scores, should this be the particular library's practice. Notice that the diameter of the record, its playing speed, the

fact that it is not a coarsegroove example, and that it is a
twin-channel recording are all listed, whereas we have suggested earlier that these are all points which could be omitted, since they now represent the norm. The performers
are also listed at length, with the timing of the side to an
exact second. To how many potential borrowers is it likely
to be vital to know that the stereo disc can be played on
"monaural" (the current preference for the much more accurate term "monophonic" has not persuaded LC to change
its terminology) equipment? Very few indeed, we would
guess. Robin Golding is a respected writer and critic, but
the borrower who selects his records because of admiration
for individual musical annotators must be very uncommon.
In short, nearly all the points mentioned may be regarded
as expendable with very little loss to the average listener.
The work performed on the other side of the disc is quoted,
and the card is completed by indicating tracings which show
that there is (in the complete LC set for this disc) a subject
entry and three performer cards for the Haydn concerto.

Having suggested that there is far more information
than the average listener is likely to need or use, our own
recommendations follow. If one limits the catalogue to composer entries (and this would be the bedrock of any listing),
the following "code" would be equally basic:

   HEADING. Give composers' surnames only, adding
   initials simply to distinguish between different composers of the same name. For performers, give
   surname and forename, followed by a designation of
   function, in parentheses (as illustrated on the LC
   card and Du Pré).

   DESCRIPTION. Give the following elements: Composer, if not in heading. The name of the work,
   as found (and title in English, or appropriate language, if considered necessary. Manufacturer (i.e.,
   the name shown on the record label). Date. Extent.
   Performer(s) note, where applicable.

Let us try to show how this would work out in practice, taking a number of different cases to illustrate particular points. The simplest case is that of a single work which
takes an entire disc to itself:

ELGAR

> Symphony no. 1, in A flat, op. 55 Decca SXL 6569.
> 2 sides LPO/Solti

A cataloguer might well decide that "no." was unnecessary,
and simply show "Symphony 1," and that "two sides" could
be more quickly shown by abbreviating to "2s." For a disc
or cassette containing a complete work on each side, the
presentation is almost as simple:

HUMMEL

> Sonata for piano, in f sharp, op. 81. Oiseau Lyre
> DSLO 530. 1977. 1 side. <u>With</u>: Hummel--Sonata
> for piano, op. 106. Binns, pf.

The cataloguer might prefer to show the artist as "Malcolm
Binns," but there should be a consistent policy for details
of performers. With the example shown above, a good case
could be advanced for making a single entry only, quoting
the two sonatas one after the other as what could be regarded as a joint title; this would be done on the grounds
that the library was unlikely to have other Hummel piano
sonatas, so that if two entries were made, they would be
adjacent in the catalogue. A preference might be exercised
for the form "Piano sonata ...," a matter discussed earlier
in this part of the chapter. It will be noticed that there is
no suggestion that either the key or the opus number should
be omitted, since we would regard both as important parts
of correct identification. The label name has been quoted in
full; time and space could be saved by abbreviating to
"Oiseau L." or even "OL," but such shortening should not
be made for generally available and well-known label names.
In the same way it may be felt better to include the artist's
forename, and a library may prefer to use "piano" ("pianoforte" would certainly be too fussy).

As it happens, the works recorded here are played on
two early nineteenth-century grand pianos, roughly dating
from the period when the music was composed. A personal
preference would be for the inclusion of the fact in a note,
since the choice of instruments certainly affects both the
soloist's technique and the actual sounds produced. However,
we would not argue very strongly with the cataloguer who
felt that to provide such information is far from basic.

The third example, like the second, is of a disc that
contains two works--but they are not evenly distributed
over the two sides; there are other differences also, it will
be noted:

RIMSKY-KORSAKOV

Le coq d'or (The golden cockerel):   opera--orches-
tral suite.   Fontana KFR 4000 (195-) 1½s.   10 in.
mono.
RPO/Beecham
With: Franck- Le chasseur maudit

The second entry would be similar:

FRANCK

Le chasseur maudit (The accursed huntsman):   symphonic poem.   Fontana KFR 4000 (195-).   Part side.
10 in.   mono.
RPO/Beecham
With Rimsky-Korsakov--Le coq d'or: orchestral suite

For the keen-eyed reader who has noticed that we have used
"s" instead of the earlier "sides," the variation is deliberate,
as an illustration of the different appearance of the entry
and a means of making a personal choice as to which is the
more acceptable.   The particular recording and coupling listed
in the example above were originally issued in Britain at the
beginning of 1954 on the (British) Columbia label, later to be
reissued in 10-inch format (compared with the 12-inch of
Columbia) when contract rights were transferred from EMI
to Philips.   However, the cataloguer could be completely unaware of this small item of gramophonic history, and there
seems no good reason for suggesting that time should be
wasted in trying to discover the age of the recording.   It
will also be seen that the record size and the fact that it
is a monophonic recording are shown, since neither is now
the norm.

Having stressed the view that title entries are vital,
even in a skeleton catalogue, we suggest that the works here
deserve two title references apiece (in French and in English)
since enquiries could well be made for either form.   As has
been indicated earlier in this section, the title entries might
well be regarded as permanent ones, on the grounds that
both works deserve representation in a library stock.

The next disc has four items on it, but the manufacturer has not given the anthology a collective title. According to AACR, analytical entries are not compulsory for collections containing more than three works, yet to omit them,
particularly in our example, would seem to be an extremely
shortsighted procedure. All the works here are by contemporary English composers, and all are played by the London
Philharmonic Orchestra. However, ignoring our own suggested "highest common factor" approach, on the grounds
that there is very little likelihood of an enquiry for works
performed by this (or any other) orchestra, we would treat
the first work on side one as the main one.

MACONCHY

Proud Thames overture. Lyrita SRCS 57. 1972.
Part side.
LPO/Handley
With: G. Bush--Music for orchestra; Berkeley--
Symphony 3; Alwyn--Four Elizabethan dances

Both sleeve and label show the first work as "Overture,
Proud Thames," but the altered form seems better to us,
and would certainly be preferred for the title reference.
"G. Bush" is so identified because both Geoffrey and Alan
Bush are represented in the current lists, and the library
might well have in stock compositions by both men. For
the other three items on the disc, the entries would generally follow the same lines as that for Maconchy, except that
the contents note would simply show: "With: Maconchy--
Proud Thames overture, etc." There should be no need to
list all the other three works on the disc. The really interested enquirer should not find it too time consuming to refer
to the entry under Maconchy to discover what exactly are
the other works on the disc, and the cataloguer will have
been saved some time with all three subsidiary entries.

A somewhat different problem is faced with another
anthology, again of British music. This shows, both on face
and back of the outer sleeve (or liner) "The sound of the
Georgian piano: English keyboard music, 1760-1860." The
second line of type is appreciably larger than the first
(quoted here before the colon), while a much smaller face
is used for the third line, "John Field, Sterndale Bennett,
John Burton, George Frederick Pinto." Although there are
again four composers involved, there is at least one important

difference between this anthology and that of the Lyrita disc
considered above, in the provision of a collective title by the
manufacturer. Indeed, there are two such titles, and the
cataloguer must decide (if following AACR) whether "Sound"
or "English" is the initial word. The former appears first,
the second is shown in appreciably larger type. From the
layout, we would suggest that the upper line might well be
regarded as a subtitle, and so enter under "English." Of
the four composers represented, John Field is well known,
Sterndale Bennett may be recognized by a minority of music
lovers, but Burton and Pinto are very minor figures. The
temptation, therefore, is to ignore analytical entries in these
cases. We have argued above that such a decision would be
a mistake; each composer is represented by a complete work
or a fairly substantial movement. Without individual entries,
how are staff and library users to know that these men are
represented in the collection, unless one is already aware of
the existence of the record, of its collective title, and that
the library possesses a copy?

By coincidence, as the title or subtitle suggests, the
RCA disc used early pianos (1794-1825), as did the Oiseau
Lyre recording considered earlier. To draw attention to the
fact may be regarded as unnecessary because "The sound of
the Georgian piano" provides the implication. It might well
be argued that there would be some value in keeping a separate file with brief details of recordings which feature forte-
pianos, early upright and grand pianos, and other early instruments. The Hummel disc could well prompt an enquiry
as to whether the library had other records which use early
pianos--and the RCA disc would be an excellent recommendation. A request for discs illustrating the sounds of pianos
of Mozart's or Beethoven's time is both understandable and
deserving of satisfaction. In fact, the bare bones of a catalogue may well prove too restrictive, even if one still eschews
cataloguing with the amount of detail provided on the Library
of Congress cards.

An Anthology of English Song (one of the earliest recordings made by Janet Baker, on Saga XID 5213) is another
example that offers alternative choice for the major entry.
It could be entered under Anthology, which is hardly helpful, or English which seems rather more attractive; but the
really unifying agent here is the singer. Entry under her
name would be very useful and the most likely sought heading.

BAKER, Janet (contralto)

An anthology of English song. Saga XID 5213.
1963. 2 sides. Mono.
with Martin Isepp (piano)
<u>Contents</u>: Vaughan Williams ...

The first song is Vaughan Williams' <u>The Call</u>, and the sleeve
note indicates that this "is the fourth of a set of <u>Five mysti-</u>
<u>cal songs</u>." This should mean that the cataloguer makes the
entry under Vaughan Williams (as well as the contents note)
in an adaptation of <u>AACR</u> and LC: "Vaughan Williams—5
mystical songs; no. 4, The call." There seems no need to
enter the filing title on a separate line or in brackets. Following our previous recommendations, we suggest that title
entries are needed for the song itself and also for the set;
indeed, title references under both "Five" and "mystical"
could be helpful to users. Another point of interest here
is that the singer is described as contralto, whereas on most
other discs she will be shown as mezzo soprano or soprano.
This may appear contradictory or even a little untidy to the
meticulous cataloguer, but it simply reflects changes in the
singer's voice over the years. It should cause no more concern than ought the fact that, to take another example,
Yehudi Menuhin has appeared as a violist and also as a conductor on some records, to complement his more familiar role
as a violinist.

Yet another anthology, <u>Monteverdi's Contemporaries</u>
(disc ASD 3393; cassette TC-ASD 3393—the obvious relationship between the two numbers is, we feel, helpful to librarians and their public) contains music by nine Italians, all
minor and very obscure indeed. Monteverdi himself is not
represented, yet this is the word under which the recording
should be entered. Since, to take one example, the composer Mainerio (who has two sets of five dances recorded here)
seems virtually unidentifiable, with neither forenames nor
dates known, analytical entries for the composer seem value-
less. This is admittedly inconsistent, but as only one or two
of the composers represented are to be found mentioned in an
ordinary music dictionary, it seems justified treatment.

HMV'S <u>Treasury</u> series includes (HLM 7110) a disc
whose contents are described on both sleeve and labels as
"Elgar Cello Concerto" and "Brahms Cello Sonata"; the

cataloguer will need to decide at an early stage in listing
the collection whether to use "cello" or "violoncello," and
use the preferred form consistently thereafter. The former
saves six letters every time it is written or typed, but is
less accurate. Additionally, the choice will affect the filing
order for entries with most major composers. A further
point arises; there is a strong case for making an additional
entry under Mieczyslaw Horszowski, the cellist's partner in
the Brahms work. This reflects the classification problem of
whether chamber music requires a minimum of two or three
performers. With two players, one of them a pianist, the
decision to justify or ignore a separate entry for the keyboard player should depend upon whether the two players
have been treated as equals by the composer, or whether
the pianist is simply an accompanist to the soloist. The latter can be ignored for an individual catalogue entry and, in
cases of doubt, we would recommend entry under the other
player's name only. If the cataloguer is not sure of the
pianist's status in a work, the recording's presentation will
often help, for an accompanist usually rates a much smaller
type face than the soloist, but this form of guidance is not
infallible.

How many soloists should be listed when noting the
performers in an operatic recording? The only really consistent policy is to make entries for all of them, or for none,
but neither answer is likely to make an outright appeal to
the music librarian, to cataloguer or to the user. With a
recording such as Turnabout TV 34435, which contains excerpts from Rameau's Zoroastre, the soloists are excellent,
but they are apparently all young Americans who are (so
far, at least) little known to the average opera lover, so
that one could reasonably describe the performers as:
Soloists/Hamburg Ch.O./Kapp.

In contrast, Haydn's La vera costanza lists five soloists on the front of the container, which is perhaps too
many to include on a single entry. As with advertisements
for feature films, the major stars are usually clearly indicated by the relative size in which their names are displayed.
Important singers may be shown less prominently when it happens that they are taking minor roles. So the simplest solution would seem to be, if one does not wish to list all, to
limit the number to a maximum of two or three and, if more
than that number are displayed on the box in the same sized

type, to treat them in the order in which they are listed there. If one followed that procedure with the Haydn opera mentioned here, and quoted only two names, these would be Jessye Norman and Helen Donath of the five singers shown on the container. In this set, the records have individual numbers (9500 336-338) which fit into Philips' top-price sequence, while the set also has its own number (6703 077). Here, for certain identification, we would suggest that both numbers are quoted, the series of single disc numbers being shown in brackets after the set identification.

Now we look at two examples or more popular material. The Rick Nelson Singles Album (Coral CDL 8053) would be entered under "Rick" if one followed AACR 1. but it seems much more sensible and attractive to make "Nelson" the main heading, as one recalls Lubetzky's strictures on this matter with Pennario. Because the music is pop, and the life of the disc possibly much shorter than those already considered in this section, there seems no reason nevertheless for omitting a contents note. But title entries for each item seem to us to have a much weaker claim and would take a deal of time for possibly little benefit, since one would not normally make composer entries with this type of material. However, the decision again must be made by the librarian or cataloguer. A composer main entry would be fully justified for Keith Ingham Plays Jerome Kern (World Record Club WRC 1003), since he is the writer of all the songs on the disc and is, moreover, a well-known name.

The two examples immediately above show, we feel, logical decisions in choice of entry--but it could be argued that it would be more practical and sensible to enter all recordings in the field of pop under the names of the performing artist(s). In the case of the Ingham/Kern disc, the only satisfactory solution would seem to be double entry, since both the name of the composer and that of the musician are likely to be sought terms. A similar answer may be best for some recordings of the sound tracks from films and for musicals. South Pacific (RCA VCS 67259) has the score written by Richard Rodgers, and so is allied to the Kern example, whereas A Star is Born (CBS 40-86021) is a film with music written by several composers and therefore more nearly related to the Rick Nelson example. To aid consistency, the simplest ruling would be to make entry for all such items under the title of the film or show, but to make an additional

entry under the composer of the music when the same person has been responsible for writing all (or nearly all) of
the tunes. A less satisfactory alternative would be to make
a blanket reference under such outstanding writers as Ham-
merstein, Kern, Rodgers and similar librettists and composers, instructing the catalogue user to look under the appropriate titles of the films/plays--but unless one listed individually the titles, the inexpert enquirer could well wonder how
many there were and how they were to be traced.

Some pop singers and groups can prove to be a cataloguer's nightmare. If a group's title starts with the name
of an individual (genuine or assumed) should one enter under the forename or the surname? The only safe decision is
to use both, simply referring from the unused form to that
felt to be the more correct. The constant changes in group
personnel may mean, in some cases, that an apparent, named
leader may not be performing on the sound recording that is
being catalogued, and indeed may no longer be a member of
the group concerned. So music by Steve Harley and Cockney rebel (The Best Years of Our Lives, on HMV TC-EMC
3068) is satisfactorily entered, in our view, under "Steve,"
but with approaches from "Harley" and "Cockney rebel" as
well as via the cassette title (Best ...). This forename entry admittedly conflicts with our Rick Nelson recommendation,
but one hopes that readers can see why. In any case, if
the cataloguer makes references from unused forms, collection titles, etc., the potential borrower of a recording is
served.

A cassette entitled The Sensational Alex Harvey Band
(Vertigo 7138071) could well have its main entry under "Sensational" since this was part of the group's title. Following
the recommendations we have made, links would be needed
from "Alex" and "Harvey." More difficult for the cataloguer
are those groups who have taken a name that is apparently
that of an individual, such as Jethro Tull. In this particular example, if the library interfiled entries for recordings
with the main catalogue, regardless of format, there could be
some potential confusion between the pop group and the
eighteenth-century writer on agriculture in England whose
name has been used in this very different context. Yet another duplicated name, that of Engelbert Humperdinck (the
German composer who wrote Hänsel und Gretel) whose present-
day namesake is an individual and was certainly not christened

by his current pseudonym, suggests that most enquirers
would look under "Humperdinck" rather than "Engelbert."
A more bizarre example is "Alice Cooper"--at different times
the name adopted by a group and by a single male singer in
the group.

If classical music is full of traps for the unwary, inexpert cataloguer, so it is equally simple to make comparable
howlers in the field of pop, and one could hardly blame the
cataloguer who immediately recognized Alkan as a pseudonym
but failed to appreciate that Alice Cooper was equally misleading. We would suggest entry under "Alice" with a reference from the other half of the name but, providing both
words appear in the catalogue, it seems of little consequence
which is given priority.

A completely different category of stock is that of
foreign language tuition sets. Some borrowers will have a
strong preference for a particular method of approach; others
will be much more willing to take what is immediately available in the language they wish to learn. So, once again,
double entry seems desirable. The first would be under the
name of the manufacturer, such as BBC, Conversaphone,
Linguaphone, etc., and the other under the English form of
the name of the language. It might also be felt that a reference might be helpful from the native form of the name, if
this seems a possible term of enquiry, so that the entry for
"Deutsch" would refer the catalogue user to "German."

If the suggestions we have made are followed, a catalogue of recordings listing a varied stock will be basically an
author (i.e., composer) one, with what might possibly be regarded as a plethora of title entries and almost as many for
pop artists, as with Nelson and other examples quoted above.
But what about Keith Ingham, Jessye Norman, Helen Donath,
Malcolm Binns, and the rest? Even though it would increase
the bulk of the catalogue considerably, there is little doubt
that even a moderate number of artist entries would be frequently consulted and would certainly be welcomed by users.
If the music librarian decides that such entries are not really needed because use can be made of the Gramophone quarterly catalogue and similar tools such as Music Master, this
solution is only effective for currently available discs in the
classical and pop fields, as well as for a limited number of
older records in the area of pop. Deleted records which the

library still retains after they have been removed from the
manufacturers' lists may well become virtually untraceable.
In short, we would strongly recommend that entries be made
for soloists and for pop groups; there seems much less need
and demand for entries under the names of orchestras, conductors, chamber music combinations and the like. Looking
back over the entries we have used in this section, the recommendations made would mean that there would be no entries
under LPO or Solti, but they would be found for Casals.

At this stage, if not before, the reader may well feel
that the description of "minimal" cataloguing described here
is very far from being skeletal, the more so when one considers the stress on ample title entries. The defence of our
position can be partly seen if one looks back at the LC card
at the start of this section. The information given there in
the body of the entry is far more detailed than that we have
suggested; additionally, we have made no mention of subject
entries and, if our proposals are followed, there would be
but a single artist entry--that for Jacqueline De Pré. Our
suggestions are for brevity in the entries, but not in the
number of references and the like. Analytical entries are
ignored by most libraries, in our experience, yet these are
surely vital, if neglected, parts of basic cataloguing. Without such entries, the enquirer (and it could also be true of
the librarian) cannot be sure if the collection includes a recording of a particular work and, if so, by whom it is performed. This comment applies particularly to the multitude
of overtures and other fairly brief works that never fill a
complete record side on their own.

Finally, as yet another addition to the cataloguer's
burden, if only a slight one, is our suggestion (assuming
that separate entries are made for soloists) that references
should be made under any instrument outside the most common ones. By listing the names of performers as appropriate, the borrower who is keen to hear as many trumpet recordings as possible has a simple means of discovering which
solo trumpeters are represented in the stock, and by following up the entries under their names, which works for trumpet the library possesses. That would seem to us to be a
genuinely helpful pointer.

To sum up, if the ideas propounded here are followed,
the catalogue ought to be of considerable value, but the

proposed slimming down processes have occurred solely in
the amount of information given in any individual entry,
whereas the total number of entries is almost certainly very
much higher than would be found in many other libraries
with collections of roughly the same size. The wise librarian will ponder these ideas for some little time and not accept or reject the plan proposed out of hand.

Readers are reminded that the recommendations in this
section of the chapter are specifically based on the idea of a
separate, independent, sound recordings catalogue. If entries are intended to be integrated with those for books and
scores, or if there is a possibility that, in the foreseeable
future, the catalog will need to be converted into a mechanised form, then compatibility with existing catalogues becomes very much more important in order to avoid, when the
time comes for change of format, a fairly substantial amount
of editing of the existing entries.

The Department in Action

This section is intended to give practical advice, usually
supplementary to (but sometimes duplicating) that already
provided in earlier pages.

At each service point, the staff should have a number
of items of equipment to assist them in their duties. A
stereo record player and a cassette player, not necessarily
of more than modest sound quality, will be needed to check
the condition of suspect discs and tapes and to assess any
damage caused by a borrower to a recording. If such checking is to be done in the public area and the library does not
permit background music, then the machine should be capable
of operation with headphones instead of the normal loudspeakers. The headphones themselves should be of the type that
allows the user to hear some external sounds. It is one thing
to be cut off from extraneous noises in one's own home, but
a very different matter if a member of staff is nominally
available to deal with library users but, with earphones in
use, is completely oblivious to what is going on except for
the recording being played.

If borrowers are required or encouraged to bring in
their styli for inspection and checking, a microscope must

be to hand in the library. A model specially built or adapted
for this purpose does not seem to exist. What is needed is
one with a magnification of at least 150 times, and preferably
300 to 400 times, and which has room to put a stylus (and,
if not detachable, the cartridge) under it. This apparently
simple need is surprisingly difficult to fill. For British
readers, there is currently available a Czech instrument (the
Miopta); a cheaper, less effective model can be bought in
some branches of Boots the Chemists.

Staff will also need a small supply of plasticine in
which to set the stylus while it is being inspected. Concentrated light for the inspection of a stylus, or a disc if
one is checking it closely, is probably best supplied by an
anglepoise lamp, although some people prefer the natural or
artificial light at the counter and find a strong spotlight
more of a hindrance than a help. There should be to hand
a supply of cleaning sponges and cloths; as previously indicated, there is no uniform recommendation as to the best
means of keeping discs clean. Again, staff should have by
them as wide a variety of catalogues and lists of recommended
records as they find necessary to answer likely queries. The
usual range of stationery--application forms for membership,
reservation and overdue postcards, tickets, date labels (if
these are used), and the like, will be wanted.

One important, yet often overlooked adjunct, is a well
produced and clearly written guide to the service, which
also includes a section on the care of discs and tapes. The
text should be clear and unambiguous, the size should be
convenient for handbag or pocket without having to be folded, and an appealing pictorial cover may help to persuade
the public to read it; much library publicity misses its tar-
get completely because it is insufficiently attractive to invite
perusal.

The library may have recordings to aid the correct
setting-up of stereo equipment and may also provide on loan
a stylus pressure gauge to allow an enquirer to check the
playing weight of the cartridge and arm on the stylus itself.
If the department also issues cassettes, the staff will require
cleaning tapes to keep the library's own cassette deck in
good condition and perhaps to lend to users, both as a helpful gesture and (more importantly) to show its effect on
sound quality and, one hopes, persuade the users to buy

their own tapes. A supply of cassette boxes will also be
wanted to replace damaged ones. When dropped or roughly
handled, the housing often breaks at the hinge and repair,
even if possible, is almost certainly uneconomic. The librarian would be well advised to seek quotations from more than
one source for replacement cases.

Two other points that do not really belong here, but
which are equally difficult to fit in elsewhere, need to be
mentioned. First, if a library lends both discs and cassettes
and uses the Plessey light pen method of recording loans,
the pen will read through a plastic record transleeve, but is
unable to pick up the equivalent information through the much
thicker cassette case, so that the issue system will have to
allow for this fact. The other matter concerns disabled users. If the outer sleeve or cassette case can be given an
embossed tape (such as Dynotape) with composer's, etc.,
name together with some indication, however abbreviated, of
the content, this can be of immense help to the blind or par-
tially sighted. If the department is not on the ground floor,
a small permanent display or notice directing attention to the
location of the collection of recordings can be a useful indication to the physically handicapped for whom, if they cannot
easily get to the department, special arrangements should be
made so that they can borrow cassettes (which are much
easier for such users to cope with than are discs) if they
so wish.

Although the provision of shelving for the collection
has been considered, no mention has been previously made
of the desk or counter from which discs are issued to users
and to which they are returned after borrowing. Within general limits the size of the desk will depend upon the amount
of room that can be spared in the department, the possible
adaptation of existing furniture, etc. The issue and return
of records at the same enclosure used for book loans is not
recommended. The two things are very dissimilar in format
and it is much more difficult to discover damage to a gramophone record than to a book; thus slowing down the whole
process. For preference the gramophone desk, counter or
enclosure should be constructed to that the assistant on duty
can sit comfortably and not have to stand. A height of
thirty-six inches (91.4 cm.) is convenient both for standing
and sitting on a stool of normal height. Secondly, it is desirable to have both good natural and artificial lighting (and

the latter is doubly important if the former is poor) to allow
the careful examination of the surface of each record as it is
borrowed and again when it is returned to the library. This
separation of books and records should also mean that only
trained staff handle the discs; if the general issue desk has
to be used for both books and records, music-lovers may be
horrified to see inexpert handling of discs by members of
the library staff. This is one of the points to which music
library staff should educate by example. It can be most
useful in the struggle to see that discs are always handled
with care and respect.

If records are checked by borrowers before they are
taken from the department and are checked again by staff
when they are returned (as we continue to advocate, if it is
at all possible), then ample space is going to be required.
A clear desk top some five feet (1.5 m.) in width and three
feet (1 m.) in depth would seem desirable.

In accordance with suggestions already made, each
record after receipt from the supplier will have been acces-
sioned, marked with some indication of library ownership,
classified (if this is required) and catalogued. There are
further steps needed to prepare the disc for loan. Gramophone records should never be kept on the shelves or allowed out of the library without the immediate protection of
an inner sleeve, although this highly desirable practice is
certainly not followed by all libraries. Such a lack of care
is a sure forerunner of surface scuffs or worse, and must
result in comparatively rapid deterioration in a disc's physical condition. When records are supplied by the manufacturer with all-polythene or cheap, unlined paper inner sleeves,
these should (in our view) be replaced immediately by
polythene-lined paper sleeves, preferably with the centre
circle cut out of the paper so that the record label can be
read with the disc in the inner sleeve. Most specialist suppliers will have these for sale. If a polythene-lined card or
paper inner-sleeve is used by the library, there is ample
room for an accessions/process stamp if desired, for a date
label, or for a small sheet giving guidance about the correct
handling of records.

It is possible to issue records in the manufacturers'
outer covers without any additional protection, but such a
policy must be deprecated since constant handling will quickly

produce a very noticeable deterioration in the appearance of the stock on the shelves, only slightly mitigated if the sleeve edges are protected to some extent by the use of transparent adhesive tape. The two most used types of additional outer covers in Britain are the entirely transparent one and the cover which has a transparent front panel welded to manila or stout kraft paper for the back section. The clear cover is usually made of a fairly heavy-gauge polythene and may be heat-welded or otherwise affixed to the manufacturer's sleeve so that the two are permanently joined. The great advantage of this type of protection is that one can read any notes on the back of the sleeve as easily as before. With the second type, the manufacturer's sleeve has to be removed from the library cover should the borrower wish to read the printed remarks on the maker's cover. In passing, experience suggests that a disappointingly high proportion of British library users are not sufficiently interested to do this. On the other hand, the manila backing of the library protection provides ample space for a date label, for a note of any damage to the record, etc., and this type of cover is appreciably cheaper than the all-transparent version. In general, public libraries seem to be moving towards the all-transparent cover, but the cheaper type remains popular, especially with colleges where a certain amount of rather rough handling of the sleeve is apparently normal.

Sets in boxes present difficulties. If it is decided to display the boxes as supplied (using the inside top for date label, etc.), it will amost certainly happen that the boxes break at the corners, which looks untidy and makes handling and safety for the discs in the box a matter of increasing concern. The solution successfully used at Widnes was to remove the top from the box and use it in the same way as the front of a manufacturer's sleeve, i.e., to put in it a transleeve with the accompanying discs behind it. This was adequate for an album of two, three or four discs. If the box had more than that, then two sleeves were needed, and the enclosed libretto or booklet was used as the second item for display. The two outside sleeves were clearly marked to indicate that they were part of the same set, not least to ensure that a borrower did not borrow only half of a set by mistake.

To stick a pocket, label, or other item of stationery to a manufacturer's sleeve, at either front or back, suggests

an alarming philistinism to this writer. Where an all-clear
sleeve is used for additional protection, it may have a small
open-ended pocket welded on to it. When the record is on
the shelves, the pocket contains the book (i.e., record)
card; when the record is on loan and the bookcard is retained in the issue file, the pocket may be used for the insertion of another card showing the due date. There are
advantages in the provision of a permanent date label, not
least that it allows the librarian to see immediately how often, and at what intervals, a disc has been borrowed. With
a clear plastic "outer," the date label could be affixed to an
inner sleeve of the polythene-lined cardboard type. If this
method is followed, staff must always remember to remove the
record from the inner sleeve before the date label is stamped.
If the system used expects the borrower to check the condition of a record for visible damage before it is borrowed,
this period gives the opportunity for the date stamping.

Fragility and damage as such are considered later in
this section. Here we are concerned with methods of recording visible marks on discs. Some libraries use a special inner sleeve, with a twelve-inch circle printed on each side.
In the centre circle is an indication to show whether it represents side one or side two and, not infrequently, a reminder of the need for proper handling. Any scratches, etc.,
can be depicted, life size, on this inner, in the appropriate
places, i.e., a scratch or surface scuff which starts at the
outer edge of a disc at seven o'clock (the clock-face method
of reference is general and easily understood; one could perhaps refer to compass points, but this would surely be more
difficult to comprehend quickly except in a nautical community and runs for half-an-inch towards the centre of the disc
is shown in the same place, full size, on the printed circle.

If the inner sleeve is used for affixing library stationery, it is possible to order separately printed thin card circles. The librarian will have to pay for the blocks with the
original order, but they should then last for years without
need for replacement. This life-size chart is then fixed by
adhesive tape to the inner sleeve and hinged at the left-hand
side. This is both time consuming and a little cumbersome,
so seems generally less satisfactory than the alternative
methods. A third, and most generally used, possibility is
to use reduced facsimile circles; printed on single slips of
gummed paper, they can be affixed to show one circle above

the other, or else placed side by side, as is thought best or more convenient. Inside the centre of each circle is marked the appropriate side number. With an opera or similar multi-record set, a quick glance will always be required first to see that the borrower has returned the correct disc to each sleeve. If this elementary precaution is neglected, difficulties between staff and borrowers are unavoidable until the mistake is cleared.

In all three types of diagram, the chart travels with the record and so is in the hands of the borrower while the disc is on loan. It is sometimes claimed, therefore, that there is nothing to stop the dishonest patron from adding the appropriate mark(s) to the damage chart if there is an accident with a disc. This is possible, although British library users in general do not seem to stoop to this particular form of trickery. If the risk is felt to be at all serious, the easiest answer is to mark all damage with ink of a colour not easily copied. This may be done by mixing the contents of two bottles of ink of quite different colours, such as purple and orange. It may also help if one notes, against each mark on the chart, the date on which the damage was recorded, not least because superficial "scratches" marked on a chart may well disappear again after a few playings and the date of the mark may show that it was entered some time previously.

A fourth plan is to have the two circles for marking damage printed on the record card, so that any marks are noted on the card; the latter is retained by the library while the appropriate disc is on loan. Other schemes, such as the use of chinagraph pencils to note damage on the "run-out" between the end of the recording and the centre label, or a written note on the inner sleeve or elsewhere listing damage and where it is to be found, do not seem satisfactory, if only because they are less precise than the earlier suggestions and are less quickly comprehended.

Where any system of noting damage is in operation, the appropriate chart may give the appearance, after only a few borrowings, that the disc is covered with scratches and is, therefore, in poor condition. This might easily be a deterrent to a borrower, although if the system is open access, one can check the actual surface condition of the record on the spot and may well find that it does not deserve to be

rejected out of hand. As already suggested, many so-called
scratches are no such thing, but simply hairline surface
scuffs which later disappear and which never sound. New
users of the service, in particular, are often anxious to
have every tiny mark entered on the chart in the unchari-
table belief that, unless this is done, they will be charged
large sums for damage when the record is returned. If we
have staff of the right calibre, nervous borrowers of this
type will quickly learn that their fears are groundless and
that the library is not trying to secure the maximum financial income with every record returned from loan. It may
well be easier, in many cases, simply to make a note to the
effect that there are numerous hairlines, and to try to
point out the differences between the soundless marks and
the click-producing scratch.

Somewhere on the sleeve or protective cover, a note
should be made of the classification or its equivalent, both
to help the discovery of a wanted record and to try to ensure that it is put back on the shelves in its correct sequence. This link between catalogue and disc may require
a little thought. In Widnes, a one-inch strip of linen tape
was fixed across the top of the protective cover, folded over
to show about a half-inch at the top front of the cover. On
this was stencilled the necessary information. In this particular library, since the arrangement was basically by composer, the appropriate heading was stencilled on the left hand
side of the tape, and in the middle was the manufacturer's
catalogue number. If the library has used its own accession
numbers, the appropriate one would have been used instead.
As the catalogue entry gave both the filing word and the
number of the record, discovery of a wanted disc (or a
check that it was not on racks in the correct place) should
be made in a matter of seconds.

A note should be made in some prominent place that is
not easily overlooked, such as by the date label, to indicate
where additional material is issued as part of a record or set
--libretto, booklet, miniature score, or other item. This is
a precautionary measure, but personal experience suggests
that checking the presence of such items is not automatic--
with the result that some of these loose items tend to disappear without trace, which must be due to some degree to
careless checking by staff. At least one library fixes the
libretto, when supplied, by adhesive tape, to the inside

cover of the box. This makes it awkward to use the text, but has proved very successful as a means of ensuring that the booklet does not become mislaid.

If each user is limited to one or two tickets, as is the case in most British libraries at present, the Browne issue system is probably the simplest to use. If an individual number is allotted to each patron and this is shown on the front of each ticket, it should be little trouble to stamp the record card as the disc is issued to show the due date for return and to write the borrower's number by the side of the stamp. If the library staff is pressed for time when the records are borrowed, the identification can still be added to the card later in the day or at the beginning of the next day, before the department is opened. By this means, one can check the identities of previous borrowers of a disc or set--a useful facility when trying to trace the person who has lost a libretto or damaged a disc. Where token, photo- or computer-charging methods are used, or tickets for borrowing books and discs are interchangeable, it may be difficult to limit the number of discs borrowed, except by a ruling that not more than a certain figure can be taken out at any one time--an embargo that is often circumvented by the determined user by means of repeated visits to the department. With Browne style tickets, borrowing is limited to the number of tickets that a user holds, and some computer systems are programmed to limit the total borrowings of each person, but without this it is almost impossible to keep a close check upon the number of recordings borrowed by an individual.

It is strongly recommended that all library patrons use carrying cases to transport gramophone records to and from the library, for protective purposes. Indeed, such use may be written into the department's rules which the borrower undertakes to observe. These containers should be provided by the local authority, preferably free of charge, but at no more than the cost price (with a small percentage added to cover administrative expenses, if thought necessary) should users have to buy cases. There are various types of carriers although, in Britain at least, there is general agreement that the plastic bag which incorporates handles (basically, the type supplied by a shop when one purchase a disc) is currently the best value for money. The reinforced cardboard carrier continued to hold its own in many places because its combination of cheapness and of length of life

made it, for some years, the most economical solution. Its
susceptibility to wet weather was much less than might be
expected from a material that is likely to go soggy in water.
In 1972, for an order of 1,000 cases or more, the cost was
around 5p each. Rapidly rising board costs increased the
price of carriers to what is, for the moment at least, too
high a price in Britain. This type may well continue to
hold its own elsewhere.

The best, and most expensive, type of plastic carrying
case is that made from a heavy-gauge plastic, with a metal
zip fastener to seal the opening when the case is in use, and
incorporating a reinforced handle for carrying purposes.
Again, in 1972, the cost of an order for 200 cases worked
out at a little more than 50p each; a much larger order reduced the average price very little. A cheaper form, using
an equally strong plastic but without a handle and with a
plastic zip instead of a metal one, was about one-third cheaper. The lack of a handle was a distinct handicap for some
users, and the zip was damaged fairly easily. With both
types the library's name could be printed by silk screen
process on one or both sides of the body of the carrier.
Given reasonable care in handling, and ensuring that they
were not regularly filled so full that the welds at the sides
were split, these carriers had a useful potential life extending to several years.

The plastic carrying cases used by shops are generally
very flimsy; they are understandably the least expensive that
are still strong enough for the purchaser to get the record
home. The dealer makes no charge for them, and their theoretical life is simply the single journey. This is not likely
to be regarded as a suitable type for library use, even if
the case is expected to last for two or three journeys, as
may well happen. The cost of these very flimsy bags used
to be but a small fraction of a penny; the alarming rise
in oil prices during the 1970s raised that figure considerably.

Libraries could probably keep costs down by means of
a combined order which would bring the total required to a
substantial figure, with subsequent economies of scale. On
the other hand, such a plan would probably preclude the
possibility of having the library's name printed in large lettering on the bag; if the public had to buy these cases, it
could be argued that the library's name should be omitted.

A popular design, to be seen on library carriers in several different countries, is one based on an early table model gramophone, complete with a large external horn--a modern hi-fi set does not have a fraction of the same visual impact.

Because of the considerable rise in postal charges in recent years it has become decidedly expensive to send gramophone records through the post, yet for individual borrowers who live in remote and isolated areas there may be no cheaper method. If discs have to be sent by post, adequate protection is needed for them. Cardboard boxes, of the type used both by manufacturers and retailers who send out large numbers of discs, are probably more cost-effective than the much longer lasting vulcanised fibre case; the latter is many times dearer in cost. It is also much heavier, a factor likely to increase transport costs. So, despite the better protection that it gives, the fibre case has generally been supplanted by its lighter and cheaper cardboard rival, with librarians accepting the appreciably shorter life of the box as reasonable.

This is one area in which cassettes have a very considerable advantage over discs. The cassette needs less protection against damage in transit, is easier to pack, and can be sent at a postal charge that is usually little, if any, higher than that for a letter, as the average weight is only about 75 grammes.

It may be helpful to go through the procedures for borrowing recordings in a library that follows the recommendations listed on the previous pages. There will be some repetitions here, and apologies for them are offered in advance. The intending borrower looks through the sleeves on display (whether or not they contain discs) or, wanting a particular work or artist and being unsure if the library has it in stock, checks the catalogue and, assuming a successful search, moves to the browser boxes or cases, etc., to find the desired recording. The patron takes the discs to the staff desk and inspects the playing surfaces of the records to see that any scratches or other visible damage are already noted on the defects sheet or equivalent. If necessary, the staff member will add a note of any newly discovered marks to the sheet, or will reassure the borrower, as is most appropriate under the circumstances. Before the disc is returned to its sleeve, the date of

return is stamped on the date label. If date cards are used,
one of these (taken from a pile prestamped before the beginning of the day) is slipped into the pocket on the sleeve, to
replace the book card which has been removed and, in turn,
placed in the borrower's ticket. The date of return is
stamped on the book card and the borrower's number noted
by that date. The disc, with its three protective covers
(inner sleeve, manufacturer's sleeve, transleeve) is then
placed in a carrying case and is ready to be taken away.
The inner sleeve opening should always be at the top to
help keep out dust.

When the recording is returned, the processes are reversed as far as is necessary. The librarian checks the
date of due return and requests any fine that has been incurred, after which the disc is inspected and any marks on
it are compared with those already noted on the damage
sheet. This should normally take no more than a few seconds, once the librarian is experienced in the operation.
Any apparent damage found that is not marked on the chart
should be pointed out to the borrower and the record put
aside. The person returning the disc may then be told that
if the new damage is found to be audible, a request for compensation will be sent within a limited period--a week to ten
days seems to give reasonable time for proper checks to be
made.

But what if the music librarian is too busy issuing
records on the one hand and taking them in on the other, to
have time to make any checks? Returned discs may be put
aside, to be inspected as soon as time allows, but this almost certainly means that any offender will have taken out
other discs and left the building. If damage should be found,
the disc in question must be put aside for the borrower who
returned it to have the chance to inspect it another time,
with a chance to explain or argue. Librarians become scepti-
cal about those borrowers who claim that, for one reason or
another, they did not play the side that is damaged; indeed,
they may aver that the record was never taken out of its
sleeve. This may possibly be true, but does not alter the
fact that the same borrower should have checked the disc
before it was borrowed.

On occasion, a record may be accepted back by the
music librarian and a fault pointed out when the disc is

returned by the next borrower. It is easy, for example, to
miss a fairly slight warp or internal groove damage caused
by a worn stylus. Bad warping should be quickly seen; the
cause is usually that a disc has been left inside a car in
warm weather, or too near a fire or radiator on a cold day.
In extreme cases, the heat will have melted some of the
grooves--an occurrence that ought to be impossible to miss
on inspection.

Where a library has no system of visual checking or
has started with one but had to abandon it, members of the
public should be encouraged to report on any record, as it
is returned, which is considered by the borrower to be no
longer fit for retention in stock. Standards among users
will vary enormously, but the music librarian will relate comments to the person making them, learning from experience
which members of the public tend to be ultracritical. There
may also be the opportunity, when not too busy, to exchange
a few words about returned records, to find the particular
borrower's reactions to the music, the performance and the
recording, and perhaps to recommend other discs or tapes
that might be enjoyed.

A typical set of rules is given at the end of the chapter. It is not suggested that these be adopted en bloc by
any library; they are provided for guidance and as a working basis for those who need help in this area. A few comments on individual rules may be found helpful.

It is customary in Britain to have a minimum age limit.
Regrettably, there seems no practical means whereby this
arbitrary figure could be replaced by what might be called
a "responsibility" lower limit, which would be infinitely more
desirable, although doubtless a possible cause of heated argument on occasion.

Libraries may wish to add one or two points that are
not included in the specimen set under "Care of records."
Some libraries insist that a user must have a diamond stylus
fitted to the pickup head, and so hope to avoid damage to
discs through the use of a blunt stylus. This problem is
much more likely to occur when a sapphire stylus is used,
because of its very limited life. The second matter is to
insist that the cartridge or stylus be brought to the library
for inspection before membership is allowed. The stylus is

checked under a microscope by the librarian to ensure that
the point is in good shape and has not been blunted by
wear. Even the novice librarian should learn quickly to notice the difference. The major difficulty, using an ordinary
microscope, is to place the stylus in the correct end-on position for viewing. If the stylus is detached from its head,
it is advisable to embed it temporarily in a small piece of
plasticine for ease of inspection.

The objection may be made that the user does not know
how to remove the pickup head, but this cannot be accepted
as an adequate argument against inspection since, sooner or
later, the stylus will have to be replaced and the removal of
the worn-out one will clearly be part of the operation. It
may also be argued that stylus inspection is psychologically
valuable in impressing the borrower that the library is far
from indifferent to the conditions in which its records are
played. If the validity of each user's ticket is one year,
then a stylus inspection will be required annually. At least
one authority known to the writer made a check every six
months, sending a postcard to the borrower when this semi-
annual check was due. The administration of such a plan
requires no more than a simple register of names, addresses
and dates, but whether the staff time, stationery and postal
charges involved in making these checks can be justified is
open to argument.

Different experts do not have a standard figure for
the potential life of a sapphire stylus, but the most generally
accepted seems to be a hundred sides for mono, fifty for
stereo. From these figures, it is apparent that even a six-
monthly check is too infrequent for borrowers who have styli
with sapphire tips. The problem was tackled in Widnes by
an admittedly arbitrary and imperfect plan, but one which
seemed to work satisfactorily. A library user with a sapphire stylus had a small "S" written at the bottom left-hand
corner of the ticket and a stroke was made on the back of
the ticket for each disc borrowed. In the case of dual membership (such as with husband and wife), a note is made on
the tickets of the one set warning the staff to make the mark-
ings on the back of the other. Strokes were made on the
"five-bar gate" system (four vertical strokes with a horizontal cross one for the fifth) and when twenty records had
been borrowed, the patron was reminded that it was time to
replace the stylus. It is based on the arbitrary and unprov-

able premise that, if each record has been played twice, it
represents eighty sides--an estimate that can be considerably wrong on either side. If the library checks styli, it
is advisable to ask the borrower to bring in a new sapphire
before it is actually used, since manufacturing defects occasionally occur and can cause havoc if overlooked; diamonds
are exempt from this unreliability. When a new stylus is
fitted, a fresh series of strokes is begun on the ticket.

Unless the same tickets are valid for either books or
sound recordings, those for borrowing discs should be of a
different colour or have some immediately recognizable over-
printing for the purposes of identification. A library must,
in commonsense and fairness and irrespective of the number
of tickets issued, allow a complete work which occupies more
than one disc (operas are the most obvious examples) to be
borrowed on a single ticket. Library practice varies in the
treatment of albums which consist of two or more musically
self-contained records, such as a complete set of Beethoven
symphonies or piano sonatas, where the music on each disc
is arranged, if found necessary, out of chronological order
but in such a fashion that no single work spills over from
one record to the next in the set. It is easiest for the library to treat the album as a single unit, but there are disadvantages. If the library is lending records on a rental
basis, the pressures to issue each disc as an individual unit
to increase income may be strong. From the borrower's viewpoint, if a complete set has to be taken out on a pro rata basis, the cost is liable to be considerable--and this could cause
annoyance if the patron wishes to play but one or two records in a larger set. From the librarian's side, there are at
least two handicaps to splitting up the boxed set into single
units. One is that the records may have to be issued in
plain sleeves, and possibly without the set of notes which
should be available to every listener, since only one set will
be supplied with the album. It may be possible, of course,
to obtain extra copies of notes, or to photocopy the relevant
page or pages. The second problem is that, if one or two
records are borrowed much more frequently than the others,
they are likely to prove impossible to replace separately when
they are worn out.

Every potential borrower will be expected to complete
an application form in most libraries, and the text would do
well, in the writer's view, to require the applicants to indicate

whether their equipment has a monophonic or stereophonic
head (the former type, although almost certainly quite elderly, is taking a surprisingly long time to vanish from the
scene). It is also valuable to include a space in which to
show how many sides the user's stylus has played, or when
a new one was last fitted. Few people keep a note of the
use made of a machine, but may be able to recall with fair
accuracy when a stylus was replaced.

     The form should also ask the applicants whether their
machines are fitted with diamond or sapphire styli (although,
as has been made clear earlier in this chapter, a strong case
can be made out for insistence upon a diamond). In cases
where the person is unsure, the probabilities are fairly
strongly in favour of a sapphire. Since a diamond can cost
as little as three or four times the price of a comparable
sapphire, yet have a life expectancy of at least ten times
that of its cheaper rival (and probably a much higher ratio),
it is decidedly more economical to fit a diamond. There will
also be the added advantage that the reproduction will almost
certainly be audibly superior. Yet many people seem unwilling to expend the extra money, and there are some pickups
(such as that on a once popular Soviet record player sold in
Britain) for which no diamond stylus is available. Some
high-fidelity heads need to be sent back to the manufacturer
for stylus replacement, but the owners of such equipment
will probably be among the most careful users (and, perhaps,
the strongest critics of the general condition of the stock).
A number of firms advertise replacement styli, listing the
most popular head models and showing the price of each
type.

     It has previously been mentioned that people with mono
equipment need not be automatically debarred from borrowing
and playing stereo records, subject to certain conditions. It
may be possible for some machines to be adapted by replacing
the mono head with a suitable stereophonic one. The stylus
in the latter has the ability to move in both a vertical and a
lateral plane; the mono pickup head permits the stylus to
move only from side to side as it follows the groove; there
is no vertical compliance. However, the playing weight of
the stylus is often too great to be acceptable with stereo
records, since such use may degrade the stereo image and so,
in effect, make the record almost monophonic; if the playing
weight is over five grammes, the borrower should not be

allowed to borrow stereo discs until both arm and head have
been changed. The alteration may be considered uneconomic
in many cases, and the listener would find it little dearer
and certainly very much more satisfactory to replace the entire playing deck, if not the amplifier and loudspeakers at
the same time, i.e., the complete outfit. The library ought,
therefore, to have a stylus pressure gauge which could be
available for short-term loan. If there is any doubt about
the matter, it may be necessary to send a member of staff
to check that the potential borrower's machine is acceptable.
Fortunate is the town that has at least one good and reliable
high-fidelity equipment dealer who is willing to advise the
public with a fair degree of altruism.

It is patent that a number of library users borrow
discs to copy the recordings on to cassette or open reel tape.
However widespread the practice, it is entirely illegal in the
United Kingdom as an infringement of the Copyright Act of
1956, although in some other countries such copying is within the law. British borrowers who boast about their activities (as a few tend to do) should be reminded of the appropriate library rule and the fact that, when joining the gramophone record library, every borrower agrees to abide by
these rules.

There is some merit in the argument that, particularly
when a collection is small and until its rate of use can be
properly assessed, the borrowing period should be brief. A
week should be ample time to play a single disc through the
two or three times that one might expect to be the average
use. There is clearly a wide variation between individual
borrowers; even a single user may find it difficult to quote
an average, since use naturally depends upon the relative
attractiveness of a particular disc when it is first played
and on the varying opportunities for listening. The only
available statistics on this matter known to the writer were
published in 1975, and relate to a London borough. From
the 350-odd forms returned, it appeared that: "Thirty-nine
percent played items four times or more, 27 percent three
times, 25 percent twice, 8 percent once only" [144, p. 88].
The fact that every respondent claimed to have played through
the last record borrowed at least once might be regarded as
a little too good to be true, but the conclusion is drawn that
(because of the repetitive playings) copying library discs on
to tape "was not as prevalent as imagined."

If these figures, suggesting an average of three playings per disc per loan, are reasonably correct, one may still feel that a week's loan is not unreasonable except for the proper hearing of a Wagner opera or other large album. The best loan period, in the writer's view, is the same as that allowed for book borrowing. The user who visits the library to exchange books, scores and recordings will know that, if the different types of material were borrowed at the same time, they are also due for return together.

Libraries usually allow renewal by any one of four methods--by bringing in the discs for reissue, by bringing to the library a note of the record numbers and the date(s) due for return, or supplying this same information by telephone, or by post. A number of libraries limit renewals to a single occasion on the assumption that this should allow reasonable opportunity to hear a work more than once with intervals of a few days between playings, and possibly a fear that continued renewal may indicate excessive playing. We should perhaps be pleased that a recording is receiving regular use, but clearly we might well also have reservations. Fines for overdue loans may well be at the same rate as for books, although a higher charge is not unusual. A decision will be needed as to whether the charges are made on a per disc or per loan basis. If the library is prepared to lend a two- or three-volume work on a single ticket and charge fines as though a single item had been borrowed, then equity suggests that the same procedure should be adopted for discs.

Special loan conditions may be invoked for language tuition sets. It is still general practice to issue these discs singly rather than as a complete course at one time. At least one company (Linguaphone) is prepared to sell multiple copies of the accompanying course texts to public libraries, so that each record can be issued individually but still have a booklet with it. The advantages of buying extra copies of the first one or two lessons on disc, and of having duplicate, triplicate or more copies of a complete course (according to demand) have already been mentioned earlier in this chapter.

Although the plastic material from which LP discs are manufactured permits the dropping of a record with an extremely good chance that no damage will occur, in marked contrast to the reaction of a 78rpm shellac disc, the newer material is very susceptible to surface imperfections. The plastic has a superb capacity for storing static electricity. Over the years, a host of anti-static devices have been produced; it seems fair to say, however, that none has been or is entirely successful--and some do appreciable harm. So good advice would be to ignore all commercial aids and to limit treatment to wiping the disc just before playing with a slightly dampened (not wet) cotton cloth or with a sponge holding a few drops of distilled water. The record surface should be lightly wiped, following the grooves in clockwise fashion (certainly not with radial movements from centre hole to record edge) and this should temporarily discharge the static electricity held in the disc. A disc made of static-resistant material should play better, if only because it would not attract dust. It is understood that such a material is available, and has been used in Japan, but that the cost of production is considered prohibitive.

All staff should handle records correctly as a matter of course, restricting fingers to contact with the centre label and the outer edge. Example is an invaluable help towards ensuring that borrowers learn how to hold records and are always careful. Those who join the service should be told of the need for correct handling and be given the simple explanation as to why it is necessary--that even the cleanest hands leave traces of grease on the playing surface if the record is touched on the grooves. Grease retains dust, and the latter is abrasive and ruinous to the sound.

Damage to records is one of the most controversial aspects of a library service. As a general rule, the more carefully records are inspected on their return from loan, the less likelihood there is of damage, which perhaps only reflects the attitude that too many people have towards public property.

The ideal is to have a system which permits careful scrutiny of every record, but such a method is likely to be impossible in the great majority of libraries. The busier the service point, the less chance there will be of either adequate time or staff to undertake this duty. The choice that any librarian must make probably lies somewhere between the two extremes of detailed checking of every record or of making no check whatsoever. The former plan should greatly prolong the life of any disc, and so reduce the sum required for replacements, but this admirable objective is achieved at

a very high cost in staff time. If no checking is done, staff
costs are kept down and the service is speeded up, but the
average life of a disc will be much lessened. It may be argued that the price of new records is very much less than
the cost of extra staff; this is true, but a poorly maintained
collection is not only a bad advertisement for the service but
will tend to drive away the best borrowers, leaving the less
desirable ones.

If the sheer volume of borrowing precludes more than
cursory inspection, a quick glance should still be given to
each disc if it can possibly be managed, to look for the obvious scratch or bad case of warping. In addition, a member
of staff should try to check, by listening for a minute or two
(particularly where the surface clearly shows that the recording is at high volume) at three or four different places on
each side after a disc has been borrowed a certain number of
times. Twenty-five loans may be considered as a convenient
checking figure. If the disc's condition is considered acceptable, a further check should be made after each additional twenty-five loans until such time as a decision is made
to withdraw the disc or transfer it to the reference or archive collection. In addition, users of the service should be
encouraged to draw the attention of the staff to records
which, when played, were considered to be unsatisfactory
or defective. This will reveal different standards among library users, but the majority of comments are likely to display a reasonable attitude.

Although charging for damage is difficult, the problem
should be squarely faced. Unless it is immediately apparent
that the returned disc will have to be withdrawn, it is advisable to make no charge until checking is possible by the
staff. In a number of cases it will be found that surface
scuffs which look as though they would seriously affect the
sound quality prove, upon test, to be noiseless; on the other
hand, an innocuous looking mark may produce a resounding
click at each revolution. The music librarian will have to
decide whether the damage is so obtrusive or affects the
sound for so many revolutions as to spoil the average listener's pleasure. If this happens, the disc will normally be
withdrawn from stock and the appropriate payment requested
from the offender, who will be given the withdrawn disc when
the debt is cleared. It could happen, however, that this particular recording is no longer in the manufacturer's catalogue

and that, because of the content or the interpretation, the librarian is unwilling to discard the record. Even though damaged, it may be thought desirable to retain the record in stock; if this is the case, the guilty borrower can only be charged the assessed cost of damage, even though this may be a little less than the charge asked if the record had to be withdrawn from stock.

Before leaving the subject of damage, it is worth considering the consensus of opinion expressed by five experienced music librarians who, as a subcommittee of the Sound Recordings Group of the Library Association, prepared a report on the matter [190]. The following paraphrases some of the points that are made. It was considered desirable that a record should be checked for damage at least once with each transaction, be it on issue or return. As for the assessment of the damage itself, it was suggested that the full purchase price be required if a record had been lent out less than ten times. Above that figure, a percentage reduction should be made, based upon the number of issues achieved and the average life expectancy of a disc in the library concerned. If, as has been suggested earlier in this chapter, sixty loans is a fair average (but one hopes that individual librarians will set an honest figure for this, worked out from stock discarded as in too poor condition to be left in circulation) and the record had been borrowed forty times, then the user who returned the damaged disc would be charged one-third of the cost. But what is the cost? The subcommittee agreed that it should be the original charge paid by the library. This is clearly open to contention; there would be occasions when the record was, at the time of replacement, available on a cheaper label as a reissue. Much more common would be the cases when the current cost of a new copy would be very much more than the library had originally paid. A library ought, therefore, to have a standard policy on this matter, whether it agrees or disagrees with the recommendation just quoted. For discs that had reached their life expectancy (i.e., had already been borrowed sixty times or more, to take the figure quoted in the previous paragraph), then a standard minimum price would be asked. Additionally, in all cases, the library might reasonably add a small administrative charge, to take into account the cost of re-ordering the disc, and the other routine work involved. Minor damage was to be assessed by the music librarian, after playing the record over, and should not exceed one quarter of the original cost. If this was felt to be inadequate, then the disc would presumably be counted as badly damaged and withdrawn. If a single disc in a set was damaged, but individual records were not available, then the borrower would be charged as though the whole set had been damaged. Finally, if a record was irreplaceable and considered sufficiently valuable, it was to be retained in stock whatever its condition, on the assumption that a bad copy was better than no copy at all, and the offending borrower charged as for minor damage.

A complaint that is not uncommon is that of groove jumping. The fault in these cases is almost always that of the playing equipment and not of the record. To prove this, the library would need to have good quality equipment and, presumably, play the queried section of the disc with the borrower present. In general, the subcommittee felt that the number of cases of damage could be taken as a yardstick to the standard of service provided by the library. If new borrowers were properly briefed about handling discs and playing them as part of a routine introduction to the sound recordings service, then damage should be a rare occurrence.

Cassettes present some particular administrative problems. The library's mark of ownership and/or accession number is not easily affixed, and it may be necessary to use a transfer tape and electric stylus or otherwise engrave the necessary information on the cassette's housing. Classification and cataloguing will follow the system already adopted for discs, with the catalogue showing quite clearly the difference in format. Because cassettes are so easy to handle and conceal, few librarians are willing to use open access methods, yet it seems to us that it produces a barrier between the listener and the product if any form of indirect access is used. It is noteworthy that some of the largest shops that sell cassettes have taken the risk (perhaps because of the obvious economies of operation) of exposing them, face on, for buyers to pick off the shelves, take to the counter and pay for in a simple operational sequence.

One can buy special display units which have a grille on the side of the case facing the public; this allows a clear view of the cassettes available, but they cannot be removed by a borrower. Withdrawal from the case is effected by a staff member who has free access at the rear of the case. Because of their size, browser boxes for cassettes are quite impractical so that a different form of indirect access is necessary. The case, with its colourful miniature "title page" can be made immediately available to the borrower but, as with the equivalent procedure with discs when the user brings the empty sleeve to the counter for the staff to find the appropriate gramophone record, so with cassettes the outer casing will be handed over for the member of staff to find the correct cassette for issue and to insert it into the container.

The majority of librarians dealing with cassettes have now apparently reached the conclusion that the best display method is to use a number of carousels. These are available in a variety of sizes to house from around fifty cassette containers to four hundred. Those supplied to retail outlets seem generally to be better made and more robust than similar items sold by library furnishers. Such units are not cheap, but they are effective. Available colour schemes may appear a little garish in the eyes of the conservative librarian, but that is a minor drawback.

A different display idea was used at Newcastle-under-Lyme public library, where details of each available cassette were put into the same style and sized transleeves as were used for records, and both sets were filed in a single sequence. Thus, a borrower who had facilities for playing both cassettes and discs had only a single series of sleeves (or magnified photographs of the cassette equivalents) to inspect. If the same recording was available in both formats, one would expect the listeners to prefer cassette because of its smaller bulk; there was also the likelihood that it would be in better playing condition.

With cassettes, a "bookcard" can be placed in the outer housing while that is on display, to be replaced by a date due card as it is charged out to the borrower. We have seen cassette housings with a small date label gummed to the back of the case, but this method seems unnecessarily clumsy, even though it does allow an immediate indication of the popularity and frequency with which the cassette has been borrowed.

Operas that take more than one cassette are usually

issued in boxed set form. Unfortunately, the companies
have not used a standard format for the presentation of
these lengthy works, so that the containers come in a variety of shapes and sizes, and so have to be displayed
apart from the other cassettes. There is, however, at least
one advantage with these boxes--space is allowed for the
inclusion of a libretto, in a reasonably-sized type face and
also for other notes. With single cassettes, the programme
notes included with the recording are usually extremely
sketchy, if not non-existent, and are far inferior to those
usually supplied on the back of the outer sleeve holding a
disc. The manufacturers could very easily improve the situation; perhaps they need convincing that it matters.

One way in which tapes are following in the steps of
discs is in the appearance of "bargain classics," while some
old recordings of historic interest are again becoming available but in this newer format. Most prerecorded cassettes
contain the same amount of musical material as the equivalent
gramophone record, but the turnover spot on a long work is
not necessarily the same as on disc. With a gramophone
record it is not important if, for example, there is twenty-
eight minutes' music on one side and only eighteen on the
other. If such timings allow, say, two complete movements
of a symphony on one side of the disc and the last two on
the second, or if the turnover point is in the middle of a
movement but makes musical sense to break at the chosen
bar, the difference in playing time between the two sides is
perfectly acceptable and may not even be immediately apparent to the listener. With a cassette, a break in the same
place would mean that there would be a ten minute silence
at one end or the other of the second side. Faced with this
problem, the manufacturer may well make the break at a different point to help even up the playing time. If a convenient break cannot be found, then an extra item compared
with the content of the equivalent disc may be added at the
end of the second side to fill that ten minute space. If the
difference between the length of the two sides is not too
long, the manufacturer may include a note on the casing:
"As the playing times of the two sides is unequal, it is advisable to wind the tape on to the end before turning it
over."

There were a few "double-play" cassettes when the
tape market began to expand, and these contained as much

music on each tape as two gramophone records. Philips produced these, but there was a gap before subsequent additions were made to the catalogue, which suggests that there
were technical problems but that they have been overcome.
The advantages of this format, using extra thin tape, are
particularly noticeable with opera, where a break in the middle of an act can be annoyingly obtrusive. For example,
the Philips recording of Berlioz' Benvenuto Cellini is on four
discs, but on two cassettes. So the advantages of this particular piece of technology are appreciable, if not quite as
dramatic as that changeover from 78rpm discs to LP.

     With the quality of normal iron oxide coated tapes im-
proving and with the use of certain chromium dioxide tapes
for outstanding results, the audible differences between disc
and tape should continue to narrow, although disc recording
itself is not marking time but making continuing improvements.
Cassette hardware (the playing decks, etc.) is making its own
advances as are the techniques for bulk copying of tapes,
while the physical improvement in the quality of the materials used makes the future for this format look rosy.

     From the librarian's viewpoint, the cassette tape has
an outstanding advantage over disc. With both types of material, there are a number of things that can go wrong, but
with the tape there is a fair chance of restoring the damage
with moderate do-it-yourself expertise; but discs must suffer
a deterioration in sound quality, however good the equipment
and however carefully the disc is handled.

     One of the most encouraging things that has happened
in many libraries is that younger listeners--those aged between fourteen and twenty-one, or thereabouts--have been
attracted to the library by the provision of cassettes. This
is an age group that libraries have, in general, failed to attract and hold. It is a development that gives the music librarian a good chance of making and (one hopes) keeping a
new public.

     If the repertoire on tape is rapidly outgrowing its
earlier limitations, some problems remain. In a number of
cases, the high and low frequencies are not as good as on
disc, or there may be a possible lack of body in the middle
range--but few borrowers will worry about that. Manufacturers have suggested that the life of one of their products,

given reasonable handling, should be several hundred playings. Actual library use suggests that the figure is wildly
optimistic and that, in practice, the life of a cassette tape
is not very much more than that of a disc. Tapes suffer
occasional mishaps, although these ought not to occur. The
tape may spill out of the cassette; should this happen, it
can be patiently wound back by turning one or the other
spool with a pencil or similar object, but it may be found
that when the cassette is played again, there is a little wav-
ering in pitch at the rewound section as the tape has stretched
slightly there. If the tape has been wound back carelessly,
it may well have become twisted. When this occurs, the tape
is probably useless and will have to be withdrawn from stock.
It may be possible, particularly if it has a screwed top, to
open the casing and straighten the tape. With a welded casing, the tape will almost certainly have to be transferred to
a new housing. This is a fiddling job, and one is likely to
be festooned with yards of loose tape unless very deft-
fingered.

Like discs, tapes are susceptible to heat and should
not be left inside the body of a motorcar in hot weather; if
discs or tape must be left, the boot (trunk) is usually much
safer. In winter, tapes and discs should be kept well away
from a fire, radiator, or other direct heat source. Tapes
should also be kept clear of any loudspeaker cabinet that
contains a drive unit with a strong magnet incorporated in
it, or the tape may become demagnetized and the recording
ruined. Another possible source of trouble, fortunately
very rare, is for the tape to become detached from its spool
at one end.

Although cassette tapes are free from the problems of
scratches and sound deterioration caused to discs by careless handling or the use of a blunt stylus, the reproducer
(like the disc's playing deck) needs to be kept in good order, and the tape head on the machine cleaned regularly by
means of a special tape generally available from most specialist dealers. Without such a precaution, the sound quality
will slowly deteriorate as tiny particles from a tape become
detached and adhere to the head, and the reproducer will
lose some of the top and bottom frequencies of the tape until the head is cleaned.

When one balances the pros and cons, it seems quite

clear that there are extremely strong arguments in favour
of the inclusion of cassettes in music library stocks. Whether
the price of these items will reduce to the same level as those
of comparable gramophone records, particularly in the bargain
category, remains to be seen. On the face of the situation,
the market for discs is threatened as cassette sales rise, but
it would seem that the sales of gramophone records are also
increasing. In short, there is growing up a double market
--a public for tapes to supplement that for discs. At present, comparatively few collectors add both types of recording
to their personal libraries. From this, it would seem a fairly
safe prediction that it will be many years before a public library will be able to regard its collection of gramophone records as no more than museum items of historical interest only,
as would be the case with a batch of Edison cylinders, or
even 78rpm discs.

Suggested Rules and Regulations for the
Loan of Sound Recordings

The following rules cover most of the points to be found in
a British public library. They should be fairly easily adapted
for use elsewhere (ignoring any that are considered irrelevant) or in a different sort of library. After the suggested
rules some comments and annotations are provided in the hope
that this will clarify any difficulties.

1) Who may join? The simplest rule is probably this:
Persons of ____ years of age and over, who reside, study,
or are employed in the Borough (or appropriate authority).

2) Application forms. The appropriate application form
must be completed by the applicant personally. If accepted,
tickets will be issued for use with the collection, valid for
twelve months.

3) Period of loan/fines. Recordings may be borrowed
for ____ days excluding the day of issue. If the record/
cassette has not been reserved by another it may be renewed once by personal call, postcard or telephone providing that the record/cassette number(s) and date due for
return are quoted. Borrowers keeping recordings after the
date due for return, unless renewed, shall be fined such
sum as is fixed from time to time by the appropriate Committee of the Council.

4) <u>Reservations</u>. Any record or work in the stock of
the sound recordings library may be reserved for a borrower
on prepayment of such sum as is fixed from time to time by
the appropriate Committee of the Council.

5) <u>Hours of opening</u>. The sound recordings library
shall be open at such hours fixed from time to time by the
appropriate Committee of the Council.

6) <u>Care of records</u>. (See "Annotations" below.)

7) <u>Borrowing procedure</u>. All records must be examined
by the borrower before acceptance, and the assistant-in-charge
notified of any damage not already recorded on the defects
sheet. If possible, records will be examined in the presence
of the borrower or his representative on return. If this
cannot be done, borrowers will be notified by post of any
damage at the earliest opportunity.

8) <u>Loss or damage</u>. The amount payable in respect of
a record/cassette or set which is not returned, or is returned
so damaged as to be unfit for future use, shall be assessed
by the Librarian at the full replacement cost or such lesser
sum as the Librarian may determine having regard to the
previous use and condition of the recording. Payment of replacement charges shall entitle the borrower to retain the
damaged recording(s). If any missing or damaged record
forms part of a work on more than one record/cassette and
the missing or damaged recording cannot be replaced without
purchasing the whole work, the borrower shall, if so required, pay the cost of purchasing the whole work or set.
The borrower at whose cost a damaged record is replaced
shall be entitled to retain the damaged record. Where a set
of records has to be purchased at cost to a borrower, in
order to replace records damaged or not returned by the
borrower, then the borrower shall be entitled to retain the
old set of records, but the Librarian has discretion to reduce the sum to be paid for replacement by an appropriate
amount in respect of wear of the old set.

If a replacement of a record/cassette not returned or
returned so damaged in the opinion of the Librarian as to be
unfit for further use cannot be obtained at the time in the
normal markets, the borrower shall pay such sum as will, in
the opinion of the Librarian, adequately compensate for the
loss sustained thereby.

9) <u>Copyright or public performance</u>. Records will be
issued to borrowers on the express understanding that the
loan does not confer on the borrower any right or licence
in respect of copyright or public performance and that the
borrower shall indemnify the Authority against all costs,
claims, demands, and liability resulting from any infringement of copyright committed in respect of the recordings
while they are on loan.

10) <u>Suspension or cancellation of tickets</u>. Failure to
comply with these rules shall be deemed sufficient reason to
cause the suspension or cancellation of sound recordings
tickets.

11) <u>Right of appeal</u>. Any borrower whose tickets have
been suspended or cancelled shall have the right of appeal to
the appropriate committee whose decision shall be final.

Annotations

<u>Rule 1</u>.   Proof of identity and residence may well be
required. British public libraries usually accept a driving
licence, a bank's cheque card, a rent book, or similar docu-
ment. At least one British library requires non-residents,
in addition to proving their home addresses, to have "the
official stamp of their place of employment" on the application form to prove their eligibility for membership.

Those would-be users who have no claim upon the
Authority may still be allowed to use the library (if tickets
issued by other Authorities are accepted) or to join by
means of a subscription. If the library makes a subscription or rental charge on all users of the service, then out-
siders will usually be expected to pay a higher rate.

<u>Rule 2</u>.   Some British libraries (as well as those in
other countries) allow the use of the same ticket(s) for borrowing all materials, including sound recordings; this is
particularly likely with an automated issue system. The majority of libraries, however, still seem to require potential
users of the sound recordings collection to complete a special
application form and to use tickets specifically limited to use
in the department. If gramophone records are to be borrowed, the library may require some details of the potential
borrower's equipment, particularly the stylus. In some cases,

libraries will not accept machines with a sapphire stylus as
suitable but insist that the potential borrower's equipment
has a diamond stylus. In a number of Authorities, the borrower has to bring the machine's stylus to the library for
inspection before membership is accepted, or before a renewal of membership is permitted.

The form will not normally show the number of tickets
to be issued, nor the period of validity, but these points
should be covered in the rules as well as any subscription
and/or rental fees required of users.

Rule 3. The normal loan period together with a further one upon renewal may be regarded as adequate time for
any user to play through a work on a number of occasions.
This is why a single renewal may be the maximum allowed by
post or telephone, although extended renewal is usual if the
recordings are brought back. This permits inspection and
may show that one section of a disc is being played and so
causing uneven wear. With cassettes, similar inspection is
not possible. In theory, with its longer active life, the cassette could be treated this way without harm.

The rule should be explicit about the rate charged for
fines on overdue loans. Is it on a per disc/cassette basis,
or is a complete set (such as a long opera) counted as one
item? The difference in fines incurred can be quite considerable between the two methods. Since a set is loaned on a
single ticket one might argue that the fine should also be as
a single unit.

Rule 4. The reservation fee usually covers the cost
of postage, plus a sum for the cost of stationery involved.
To charge an economic fee would be a major deterrent. It
is recommended that no restrictions upon the type of material reserved are made, although it may be thought desirable to limit the number of items reserved at any one time.

Rule 5. If the opening hours are the same as in other
departments, no special rule is needed. Some libraries include a sentence to the effect that "Records must be returned at least fifteen minutes before closing time." The intention here is to give the staff time to check any returned
record, and also to allow the borrower adequate time to select and borrow another recording, if so desired.

Rule 6. Insofar as rules are needed and are enforceable, these may be concerned with the nominal banning of automatic record-changers when playing library records (although it is obviously virtually impossible to enforce); the transport of records to and from the library in carrying cases/bags can only be a recommendation unless the library supplies suitable containers. Other points that need to be made are best confined to a separate leaflet dealing solely with the correct handling and treatment of recordings. For discs, mention should be made of the dangers of finger-marking the playing surfaces, a warning against proprietory (commercial) cleaning fluids, the limited life of a stylus (particularly if the library allows borrowing by those whose equipment has sapphires), an even stronger warning about the effects of heat--with mention of the likely disaster if a disc is left in a car in sunny weather) and the need to store records in an upright position, packed fairly tightly. Borrowers should also be asked to take records from the turntable as soon as playing is finished and to return them to the inner sleeve immediately. That, in turn, should be replaced in the outer sleeve in an upright position, i.e., so that the opening is at the top as a further deterrent to dust.

For cassettes, similar warnings against heat and excessive humidity are needed. Warnings are usually given against placing the cassette within close range of a magnetic field, such as the top of a loudspeaker, or even in a metal file. As an aside, we may express doubt as to the need for this latter warning; it is an alleged danger that has yet to materialize for us in an admittedly limited experience. The need to keep the cassette player regularly serviced with a cleaning tape deserves stress. The idea that a gramophone stylus is permanent took much effort to defeat, and a similar battle with the equivalent fallacy for cassette players is also needed.

Borrowers should be asked to return cassettes with the tape wound to the end. Not only does this reduce the possibility of dirt and dust affecting the tape, but helps the staff to see that the tape is in good condition; one stopped halfway through is an immediate signal that damage may have occurred. The usual faults of tape slippage, tape twisting, tape breakage and tape jamming are very often the result of bad maintenance of the playing equipment. Borrowers should be warned, if any of these accidents should occur, to leave

the tape as it is and return it to the library. Outline instructions in the repair of cassettes can be found in George
B. Saddington and Eric Cooper's <u>Audiocassettes as Library</u>
<u>Materials</u> (Leicester Central Library: The Audiovisual Li-
brarian, 1976; 2nd ed., 1984).

Rule 7. If the library checks the condition of records
on issue and return (as we strongly feel should be done if
at all practical), the matter should be incorporated in the
rules. It is admittedly unsatisfactory if damage is discovered
after the borrower has gone, but one would deprecate even
more a lack of checking under these circumstances. If the
borrower has to be told, in a letter, that a charge for damage is being levied, the disc or set should be retained at the
counter until the borrower comes in, even though this may
well increase the likelihood of argument. It is noteworthy
that, when challenged in this way, a large number of users
will claim that the damage was already there (but no explanation as to why no request was made to make a note of it), or
that this particular record or side was not even played during the time the work was on loan.

Rule 8. One can only take into account the age of the
record and the number of times it has been borrowed, together with the actual damage. The London librarians' recommendation that the charge should always be based on the
original cost (see p. 411) must sometimes result in an apparent injustice.

Rule 9. This applies, as suggested, to Britain. For
other countries, suitable wording would need to take into
account the matter of copyright as affected by national legislation.

Rules 10 and 11. The former is a safeguard to prevent use of the collection if monies for fines or replacements
are not made. It is also a means of penalising the persistent
offender. However, the recalcitrant user may feel that the
librarian is making a personal vendetta of the matter, hence
the right of appeal to allow further consideration of the situation.

BIBLIOGRAPHY AND KEY TO REFERENCES

1 Abraham, Gerald. The Concise Oxford History of Music. London, New York: Oxford University Press, 1979.

2 American Library Association. A.L.A. Cataloging Rules for Author and Title Entries. Chicago: The Association, 1949.

3 Andersen, Elizabeth Louisa. "A Study of Recordings in 60 Municipal Libraries Serving Populations of 75,000 and Over as of 1948." M.A. thesis, University of Chicago, 1950.

4 Anglo-American Cataloging Rules. Prepared by the American Library Association, the Library of Congress, the Library Association, and the Canadian Library Association. North American text. Ed. C. Sumner Spalding. Chicago: American Library Association, 1967. Supplement of additions and changes, 1970.

5 Anglo-American Cataloguing Rules. 2nd ed. Prepared by the American Library Association, British Library, Canadian Committee on Cataloguing, the Library Association, and the Library of Congress. Ed. Michael Gorman and Paul W. Winkler. Chicago: American Library Association; Ottawa: Canadian Library Association; London: Library Association, 1978.

6 Apel. Willi. Harvard Dictionary of Music. 2nd ed. Cambridge: Belknap Press of Harvard University Press, 1969; London: Heinemann, 1970.

7 _____, and Daniel, Ralph T. The Harvard Brief Dictionary of Music. Cambridge: Harvard University Press, 1960.

8 Aronowsky, Salomon. Performing Times of Orchestral Works. London: Benn, 1959. (Durations are subjectively derived, and not based on actual recordings.)

9 The Art of Record Buying: A List of Recommended Microgroove Recordings. London: EMG, 1955-1980.

10 Asheim, Lester, and associates. The Humanities and the Library. Chicago: American Library Association, 1957.

11 Baker's Biographical Dictionary of Musicians. 6th ed. Ed. Nicolas Slonimsky. New York: Schirmer, 1978.

12 Barksdale, A. Beverly. "On the Planning and Arranging of
    Music Exhibitions." Notes 10 (Sept. 1953):565-569. (Re-
    printed in ref. 24.)

13 Barlow, Harold, and Morgenstern, Sam. A Dictionary of Musi-
    cal Themes. New York: Crown, 1948; London: Williams
    and Norgate, 1949. (A 1975 revised edition showed only
    minor changes.)

14 _____. A Dictionary of Opera and Song Themes, Including
    Cantatas, Oratorios, Lieder, and Art Songs. New York:
    Crown, 1966; London: Benn, 1976. (An unaltered reprint
    of A Dictionary of Vocal Themes, 1950.)

15 Bauer, Robert. The New Catalogue of Historical Records. 2nd
    ed. London: Sidgwick and Jackson, 1947.

16 Bennett, John Reginald. Voices of the Past: Vocal Record-
    ings, 1898-1925. Lingfield, Surrey: Oakwood, 1956- .
    (For descriptions of 14 volumes published to date, see Marco
    [132], numbers 0471, 2054, 2215, 3265, 3573.)

17 Bibliography of Discographies. Vol. I, Classical Music, 1925-
    1975. By Michael Gray and Gerald D. Gibson. Vol. II, Jazz.
    By Daniel Allen. New York: Bowker, 1977-1981. (Planned
    as a 5-vol. set. The first two volumes include more than
    7,000 entries with considerable detail on the recordings and
    extensive indexing.)

18 Bielefelder Katalog. Bielefeld, Germany: Bielefelder Verlagan-
    stalt, 1953- . Semiannual. (Title varies.)

19 Blom, Eric, ed. Everyman's Dictionary of Music. 5th ed.
    London: Dent; New York: St. Martin's, 1971.

20 BMG. 1- . 1903- . London: Clifford Essex Music Co.,
    1903- . Monthly.

20a Boston. Public Library. Dictionary Catalog of the Music Col-
    lection. Boston: G. K. Hall, 1972. 20 vols. Supplement,
    1976. 4 vols.

21 Bowen, Jean, and Jackson, Paul T. "A Study of Periodicals
    Indexed in Notes Index of Record Reviews." Notes 22-2
    (Winter 1965):945-955.

22 Bradley, Carol June. The Dickinson Classification; a Catalogu-
    ing and Classification Manual for Music. Carlisle, Pa.: Car-
    lisle Books, 1968.

23 _____, ed. Manual of Music Librarianship. Ann Arbor,
    Mich.: Music Library Association, 1966.

24 _____, ed. Reader in Music Librarianship. Washington,
   D.C.: Microcard Editions Books, 1973.

25 Brio. 1- . Spring 1964- . London: UK Branch of IAML,
   1964- . 2 per year.

26 British Catalogue of Music. London: British Library, 1957- .

27 British Library. The Catalogue of Printed Music in the British
   Library to 1980. New York, Munich: Saur, 1980. Distributed
   by Gale, Detroit. (Replaces earlier catalogs of the library's
   music holdings.)

27a British Library Yearbook, 1900-1901; A Record of Library Progress and Work. Ed. Thomas Greenwood. London: Scott,
   Greenwood, 1900.

28 British Union-Catalogue of Early Music Printed before the Year
   1801; A Record of Holdings of Over One Hundred Libraries
   Throughout the British Isles. Ed. Edith B. Schnapper. London: Butterworths, 1957. 2 vols.

29 Brody, Elaine. Review of A Short History of Opera, by
   Donald J. Grout. Notes 22-3 (March 1966): 1029.

30 Brook, Barry S. Thematic Catalogues in Music: An Annotated
   Bibliography. Hillsdale, N.Y.: Pendragon Press, 1972.

31 Brown, James Duff. Guide to the Formation of a Music Library.
   London: Simpkin, Marshall, Hamilton Kent, 1893. The Library Association Series, 4.

32 Bryan, Alice I. The Public Librarian. New York: Columbia
   University Press, 1952.

33 Bryant, Eric Thomas. Music Librarianship: A Practical Guide.
   London: Clarke; New York: Hafner, 1959.

34 Bryon, J. F. W. "Subject Enquiries." Librarian and Book
   World 43-1 (Jan. 1954):1-4.

35 Buth, Olga. "Scores and Recordings." Library Trends 23-3
   (Jan. 1975):427-450.

36 Callander, T. E. "Mobilising Stock in Municipal Branch Libraries." Library Association Record 40 (June 1938):256-257.

37 Cataloguing Rules, Author and Title Entries.... London: Library Association; Chicago: American Library Association,
   1908.

38 Chesterian. 1-41. 1915-1939, 1947-1961. London: Chester, 1915-1960. Quarterly.

39 Clough, Francis F., and Cuming. G. J. The World's Encyclopedia of Recorded Music. London: Sidgwick and Jackson, 1952. First supplement bound in; Second supplement (1951-1952), 1952; Third supplement (1953-1955), 1955. (Reprinted --Westport, Conn.: Greenwood, 1970.)

40 Coates, Eric J. The British Catalogue of Music Classification. London: Council of the British National Bibliography, 1960.

41 Cobbett, Walter Willson. Cyclopedic Survey of Chamber Music ... with supplementary material ed. by Colin Mason. 2nd ed. New York: Oxford University Press, 1963. 3 vols.

42 Coover, James B. "Selection Policies for a University Music Library." In ref. 24, pp. 236-246.

43 Cuming, Geoffrey. "Problems of Record Cataloguing." Recorded Sound 1-4 (Autumn 1961):116-122.

44 Currall, Henry F. J. Gramophone Record Libraries. 2nd ed. London: Crosby Lockwood, 1970.

45 Cushing, Helen Grant. Children's Song Index. New York: Wilson, 1936.

46 Cutter, Charles Ammi. Rules for a Dictionary Catalogue. 4th ed. Washington: Government Printing Office, 1904. (Reprint --London: Library Association, 1935.)

47 Cylke, Frank Kurt, and Hagle, Alfred D. "Handicapped, Service to." Pp. 230-234, ALA World Encyclopedia of Library and Information Services. Chicago: American Library Association, 1980. (This is a world summary of library programs for the blind, deaf, physically handicapped, and mentally retarded users, with emphasis on developments in the United States.)

48 Dane, William J. "Organizational Patterns in Public Libraries." Library Trends 23-3 (Jan. 1975):329-348.

49 De Charms, Désirée, and Breed, Paul. Songs in Collections: An Index. Detroit: Information Services, 1966.

50 Deetman, Huib. "Public Record Libraries in the Netherlands." Fontes artis musicae 21-3 (Sept.-Dec. 1974):111-115.

51 _____, and Roberts, Don L. "Statement on Qualifications for Music Librarians." Fontes artis musicae 29-1/2 (Jan.-

June 1982):66-67. (Official statement of the IAML Commission on Education and Training.)

52   De Lerma, Dominique-René. "Music Periodicals." 133, pp. 464-472.

53   Dewey Decimal Classification and Relative Index. 19th ed. Albany, N.Y.: Forest Press, 1979.

54   Diamond, Harold J. Music Criticism; An Annotated Guide to the Literature. Metuchen, N.J.: Scarecrow Press, 1979.

55   "Discophily." Editorial [by W. B. Stevenson]. Library Association Record 51-7 (July 1949):203.

56   Drone, Jeanette Marie. Index to Opera, Operetta and Musical Comedy Synopses in Collections and Periodicals. Metuchen, N.J.: Scarecrow Press, 1978.

57   Down Beat. 1- . 1934- . Chicago: Maher, 1934- . 20 per year.

58   Duckles, Vincent. Music Reference and Research Materials. 3rd ed. New York: Free Press; London: Collier-Macmillan, 1974.

59   Early Music. 1- . 1973- . London: Oxford University Press, 1973- . Quarterly.

60   Editorial. Recorded Sound 68 (Oct. 1977):717.

61   Elmer, Minnie A. "Music Cataloguing...." M.A. thesis, Columbia University, 1946.

62   Enciclopedia della musica. Ed. Claudio Sartori. Milano: Ricordi, 1963-1964. 4 vols. (New edition announced.)

63   Encyclopédie de la musique. Ed. François Michel. Paris: Fasquelle, 1958-1961. 3 vols.

64   Escreet, P. K. Introduction to the Anglo-American Cataloguing Rules. London: Deutsch, 1971.

65   Fanfare: The Magazine for Serious Record Collectors. 1- . 1977- . Tenafly, N.J., London: Flegler, 1977- . Bimonthly.

66   Farish, Margaret K. Orchestral Music in Print. Philadelphia: Musicdata, 1979. Music-in-Print, 5.

67   _____. String Music in Print. 2nd ed. New York: Bowker, 1973.

68 Farkas, Andrew. Opera and Concert Singers; An Annotated
    International Bibliography of Books. New York: Garland,
    1984.

69 Feather, Leonard. Encyclopedia of Jazz. New York: Horizon;
    London: Barker, 1960.

70 _____. Encyclopedia of Jazz in the Sixties. New York:
    Horizon; London: Barker, 1966.

71 Fellinger, Imogen. "Periodicals." 164, pp. 407-535.

72 Fling, Michael. Shelving Capacity in the Music Library. Phil-
    adelphia: Music Library Association, 1981. MLA Technical
    Reports, 7.

73 Fontes artis musicae. 1- . 1954- . Kassel: Bärenreiter,
    1954- . Quarterly.

74 Forbes Library, Northampton, Mass. Report for 1896. By
    Charles Ammi Cutter. Northampton: The Library, 1896.

75 Forsyth, Ella Marie. Building a Chamber Music Collection; A
    Descriptive Guide to Published Scores. Metuchen, N.J.:
    Scarecrow Press, 1979.

76 Freitag, Wolfgang M. "On Planning a Music Library." Fontes
    artis musicae 11 (Jan. April 1964):35-49. (Reprinted in ref.
    24.) Gives recommendations on all aspects of housing and
    equipment, concentrating on the needs of academic and re-
    search libraries. A useful guide to other literature is ap-
    pended.)

77 Fuszek, Rita M. Piano Music in Collections: An Index. De-
    troit: Information Coordinators, 1982.

78 Gaeddert, Knisely. The Classification and Cataloging of Sound
    Recordings. Rev. ed. Philadelphia: Music Library Associa-
    tion, 1981. MLA Technical Reports, 4.

79 Goodkind, Herbert K. Cumulative Index to the Musical Quar-
    terly, 1915-59. New York: Goodkind Indexes, 1960. Sup-
    plement, 1960-62, 1963.

80 Gramophone. 1- . 1923- . London: General Gramophone
    Publications, 1923- . Monthly.

81 Gramophone Classical Catalogue. 1- . 1953- . Harrow:
    General Gramophone Publications, 1953- . Quarterly. Title
    varies.

82 Great Britain. Board of Education. Public Libraries Committee.
    Report on Public Libraries in England and Wales. Presented
    by the President of the Board of Education to the Parliament
    by command of His Majesty, May, 1927. Cmd 2868. London:
    H.M.S.O., 1927. Sir Frederic G. Kenyon, Chairman.

83 _____. Library Advisory Councils for England and Wales.
    Public Libraries and Cultural Activities: A Joint Report.
    London: H.M.S.O., 1975. Department of Education and
    Science. Library Information Series, 5.

84 _____. Ministry of Education. Standards of Public Library
    Service in England and Wales. Report of the Working Party
    appointed by the Minister of Education in March, 1961. Lon-
    don: H.M.S.O., 1962. H. T. Bourdillon, Chairman.

85 _____. Ministry of Education. The Structure of the Public
    Library Service in England. Report of the Committee ap-
    pointed by the Minister of Education in September, 1957.
    London: H.M.S.O., 1959. Cmmd. 660. Sir Sydney Roberts,
    Chairman.

86 _____. Parliament. Public Libraries and Museums Act.
    London: H.M.S.O., 1964.

87 Griffiths, Peter H. "Composers' Recordings of Their Own Mu-
    sic." Audiovisual Librarian 3-2 (Autumn 1976):48-55.

88 Grout, Donald Jay. A History of Western Music. Rev. ed.
    New York: Norton, 1973.

89 Guitar Review. 1- . 1946- . New York: Society of the
    Classic Guitar, 1946- . 3 per year.

90 Guitar: The Magazine for All Guitarists. 1- . 1972- .
    London: Musical New Services, 1972- . Monthly.

91 Hagist, Barbara. "Resistance and Reluctance in Record Selec-
    tion." Library Journal 93 (Feb. 1968):518-520.

92 Harman, Alex, and Mellers, Wilfrid. Man and His Music: The
    Story of Musical Experience in the West. London: Barrie &
    Jenkins; New York: Oxford University Press, 1957-1959. 4
    vols. (Reissue in 1 vol., 1962.)

93 Harrison, Max, et al. Modern Jazz: The Essential Records.
    New York: Aquarius, 1975.

93a Heyer, Anna Harriet, compiler. Historical Sets, Collected Edi-
    tions, and Monuments of Music: A Guide to Their Contents.
    3rd ed. Chicago: American Library Association, 1980. 2
    vols.

94 Hi-Fi News and Record Review. 1- . 1956- . Croydon:
    Link House, 1956- . (From 1956-1969 title was Hi-Fi News.)

95 High Fidelity and Musical America. 1- . 1951- . Great
    Barrington, Mass.: Wyeth, 1951- . Monthly. (Title from
    1951-1964 was High Fidelity.)

96 Hill, George R., and Boonin, Joseph M. "Music Price Indexes:
    1982 Update." Notes 39-3 (March 1983):580-584. (This is
    the most recent number seen, in a series that began in
    1978/79.)

96a Hilton, Ruth. "Review of ANSCR...." Notes 27 (Sept. 1970):
    52-54. (Refers to the scheme as "ill-conceived, ill-advised,
    badly written and edited....")

97 Hitchon, Jean C. "Indicators." In ref. 44, pp. 80-83.

98 Horner, John. Special Cataloguing; with Particular Reference
    to Music.... London: Bingley, 1973.

99 Howes, Frank. The English Musical Renaissance. London:
    Secker & Warburg, 1966.

100 Hurst, P. G. The Golden Age Recorded. 2nd ed. Lingfield,
    Surrey: Oakwood, 1963.

101 Index to Audio Equipment Reviews. Comp. by Arne Jon
    Arneson and Stuart Milligan. Philadelphia: Music Library
    Association, 1979- . Annual. MLA Technical Reports.

102 International Association of Music Libraries. International
    Cataloging Code Commission. Code international de cata-
    logage de la musique. Frankfurt: Peters, 1957-83. Sched-
    uled for 5 vols. All have appeared [given here in their
    English titles]: 1. The Author Catalog of Published Music;
    2. Limited Code....; 3. Rules for Full Cataloging; 4. Rules
    for Cataloging Music Manuscripts; 5. Rules for Cataloging
    Sound Recordings.

103 _____. Public Libraries Commission. International Basic
    List of Literature on Music. The Hague, IAML, 1975.

103a International Catalogue of Music Publications in Braille. New
    York: American Foundation for Overseas Blind, 1956.

104 International Conference on Cataloguing Principles, Paris, 9-18
    October 1961. Report. Ed. A. H. Chaplin and Dorothy
    Anderson. London: Bingley, 1963. (Reprinted 1969.)

105 International Cyclopaedia of Music and Musicians. 10th ed.

Ed. Bruce Bohle. New York: Dodd, Mead; London: Dent, 1975.

106 International Standard Bibliographic Description for Printed Music. London: International Federation of Library Associations, Office for Universal Bibliographic Control, 1980.

107 Jazz Journal International. 1- . 1948- . London: Billboard, 1948- . Monthly. (Incorporates Jazz Journal and Jazz and Blues.)

108 Katz, William A. Introduction to Reference Work. 2nd ed. New York: McGraw-Hill, 1974. 2 vols. (The comment is from Vol. 1, p. 143. In the latest edition [4th, 1982], there is no reference at all to the work.)

109 Kaufman, Judith. Library of Congress Subject Headings for Recordings of Western Non-classical Music. Philadelphia: Music Library Association, 1983.

110 Kennard, Daphne J. "Music for One-handed Pianists." Brio 13-2 (Autumn 1976):39-43. Revision, same title, in Fontes artis musicae 30-3 (July-Sept. 1983):117-131.

111 _____. "Music Services for Handicapped People." Fontes artis musicae 27-2:(April-June 1980):77-84.

112 Kinkeldey, Otto. "Training for Music Librarianship: Aims and Opportunities." ALA Bulletin 31 (August 1937):459-463. (Reprinted in ref. 24.)

113 Kobbé, Gustave. The New Kobbé's Complete Opera Book. Ed. and rev. by the Earl of Harewood. 9th ed. New York: Putnam, 1976.

114 Krummel, Donald W. "Twenty Years of Notes--a Retrospect." Notes 21-1/2 (Winter-Spring 1963/64):56-82. (For those who do not know the Stockhausen piece, it should be explained that it is printed on a single sheet measuring 54 × 93 cm., supplied with its own music stand. The score itself consists of a series of brief music phrases, each printed separately. The performer may choose between different permissible tempi, dynamics, and type of touch, and may also start at any one of these snatches of music; and, having reached the end of it, should follow the instructions there to discover which is the next section to be played. This is perhaps reminiscent of a treasure hunt or point-to-point race, but not all listeners are likely to feel that the chase is worth pursuing.)

115 La Montagne, Leo E. American Library Classification.... Hamden, Conn.: Shoe String Press, 1961.

116 Landau, Thomas, ed. Who's Who in Librarianship. Cambridge,
     Eng.: Bowes, 1953. (Unfortunately the second edition,
     1972, does not collate the special interests of the respond-
     ents.)

117 Langridge, Derek. Your Jazz Collection. London: Bingley,
     1970.

118 Larousse de la musique. Ed. Norbert Dufourcq. Paris:
     Larousse, 1957. 2 vols.

119 Larrabee, Bernice B. "The Music Department of the Free Li-
     brary of Philadelphia." Library Trends 8-4 (April 1960):
     574-586.

120 Larsen, John C. "Education of Fine Arts/Music Librarians.:
     Library Trends 23-3 (Jan. 1975):533-40.

121 Lenneberg, Hans. "Early Circulating Libraries and the Dis-
     semination of Music." Library Quarterly 52-2 (April 1982):
     122-130.

122 Library Association. Memorandum of Evidence to Be Laid Be-
     fore the Committee Appointed by the Minister of Education
     to Consider the Structure of the Public Library Service in
     England and Wales. London: The Association, 1958.

123 _____. Media Cataloguing Rules Committee. Non-book Ma-
     terial Cataloguing Rules. London: The Association and the
     National Council for Educational Technology, 1973.

124 Line, Maurice B. "A Classification for Music Scores on His-
     torical Principles." Libri 12-4 (1963):352-363.

124a Loewenberg, Alfred. Annals of Opera, 1597-1940. Compiled
     from the original sources. 2nd ed., rev. and corr. by
     Frank Walker. Genève: Societas Bibliographica, 1955. 2
     vols. (Reprint, as "3rd edition, revised and corrected,"
     Totowa, N.J.: Rowman and Littlefield; London: Calder,
     1978.

125 Long, Maureen W. Musicians and Libraries in the United
     Kingdom. London: Library Association, 1972.

126 Lubetzky, Seymour. Principles of Cataloging. Final Report,
     Phase I: Descriptive Cataloging. Los Angeles: Institute
     of Library Research, University of California at Los Angeles,
     1969.

127 Luening, Otto. Music Materials and the Public Library. New
     York: Columbia University Press, 1949.

128 McColvin, Lionel R. "Gramophone Records in Public Librar-
     ies." Recorded Sound 1 (May 1961):22-27. (At that time
     the resident population of the City of Westminster was about
     95,000; but the daytime figure was estimated at 500,000 be-
     cause of the very large number of offices in the area.)

129 _____, and Reeves, Harold. Music Libraries, Including a
     Comprehensive Bibliography of Music Literature and a Select
     Bibliography of Music Scores Published Since 1957. Rev.
     and ed. Jack Dove. London: Deutsch, 1965. 2 vols.

130 McCoubrey, W. K. "Gramophone Record Service." An
     Leabharlann, new series, 1 (June 1972):19-23.

131 Marco, Guy A. "Historical Survey." 133, pp. 340-358. (This
     concise review seems to be the only history of music librar-
     ies from ancient times to the twentieth century. The bibli-
     ography cites the important secondary literature.)

132 _____. Information on Music; a Handbook of Reference
     Sources in European Languages. Vol. I, with the assistance
     of Sharon Paugh Ferris, Basic and Universal Sources, 1975.
     Vol. II, with Ann M. Garfield and Sharon Paugh Ferris, The
     Americas, 1977. Vol. III, with the assistance of Sharon
     Paugh Ferris and Ann G. Olszewski, Europe, 1984. Little-
     ton, Colo.: Libraries Unlimited, 1975- .

133 _____, ed. "Music Libraries and Collections." Encyclo-
     pedia of Library and Information Science 18 (1976):328-493.
     (See refs. 52, 131.)

134 _____. Opera: A Research and Information Guide. New
     York: Garland, 1984.

135 _____, and Freitag, Wolfgang M. "Training the Librarian
     for Rapport with the Collection." Library Trends 23-3 (Jan.
     1975):541-546.

136 _____, and Roziewski, Walter M. "Shelving Plans for Long-
     playing Records." Library Journal 84 (15 May 1959):1568-
     1569.

137 Maynard, Harry E. "Report from America." Gramophone
     54-645 (Feb. 1977):1340. (Refers to the National Associa-
     tion of Record Manufacturers who commissioned the Baruch
     School of Administration "to assist them in a massive survey
     of the adult market." The relevant point here was that
     college graduates buy three times as many recordings as
     the less educated. Classical music and hard rock lovers
     buy the greatest number, averaging twenty-one per year.)

138 Mekkawi, Carol Lawrence. "Music Periodicals: Popular and
     Classical Record Reviews and Indexes." Notes 34-1 (Sept.
     1977):92-107.

139 Melody Maker. 1- . 1926- . London, 1926- . Weekly.

140 Monthly Musical Record. 1-90. 1871-1960. London: Augener,
     1871-1960. Monthly.

141 Moran, W. R. "Discography: Rules and Goals." Recorded
     Sound 66-67 (April-July 1977):677-681.

142 Morgan, John. "Gramophone Record Selection, Withdrawal
     and Replacement--General." 44, pp. 179-182.

143 Motherwell Times, 24 April 1953.

144 Munro, D. J. "Bromley Audio Survey." Library Association
     Record 77-4 (April 1975):88.

145 Music and Letters. 1- . 1920- . London: Oxford Univer-
     sity Press, 1920- . Quarterly.

146 The Music Index. Detroit: Information Coordinators, 1949- .
     Monthly: annual cumulations.

147 Music Library Association. Code for Cataloguing Music and
     Phonorecords.... Chicago: American Library Association
     and Music Library Association, 1958.

148 _____. Committee on Professional Education. "Qualifica-
     tions of a Music Librarian." Journal of Education for Li-
     brarianship 15-1 (Summer 1974):53-59. Also printed in
     Fontes artis musicae 21 (1974):139-143; and in College Mu-
     sic Symposium 15 (1975):87-93.

149 Music Master. London: John Humphries, 1974- . Annual.

150 Music Review. 1- . 1940- . London: Heffer, 1940- .
     Quarterly.

151 La musica: enciclopedia storica. Ed. Guido M. Gatti.
     Torino: Unione Tipografico-Editrice Torinese, 1966-1968.
     6 vols.

152 Musical Opinion. 1- . 1877- . Melton Mowbray, Eng.:
     Musical Opinion, 1877- .

153 Musical Quarterly. 1- . 1915- . New York: Schirmer,
     1915- . Quarterly.

154 Musical Times. 1- . 1844- . Sevenoaks, Eng.: Novello,
     1844- . Monthly.

155 Die Musik in Geschichte und Gegenwart. Ed. Friedrich Blume.
     Kassel: Bärenreiter, 1949- . (16 vols. published through
     1979, including a 2-vol. supplement; index to be published.)

156 Myers, Kurtz. Personal letter to the author. (At the time of
     writing, Myers was Chief of the Music and Drama Dept., De-
     troit Public Library.)

157 _____ . Index to Record Reviews. Boston: G. K. Hall,
     1978. 5 vols.

158 _____ . Record Ratings: The Music Library Association's
     Index of Record Reviews. Ed. Richard S. Hill. New York:
     Crown, 1956.

159 Nardone, Thomas R., et al. Choral Music in Print. Philadel-
     phia: Musicdata, 1974. 2 vols. Supplement, 1976. Music-
     in-Print, 1-2. (Other items in the series are refs. 66, 160,
     161. Combined annual supplements have been issued since
     1979.)

160 _____ . Classical Vocal Music in Print. Philadelphia:
     Musicdata, 1976. Music-in-Print, 4. See note at ref. 159.

161 _____ . Organ Music in Print. Philadelphia: Musicdata,
     1975. Music-in-Print, 3. See note at ref. 159.

162 National Library for the Blind (London). Catalogue of Braille
     Music. Bredbury, Cheshire: The Library, 1969-1975. 3
     vols.

163 National Union Catalog: Pre-1956 Imprints. London: Mansell,
     1968-1980. 685 vols. Supplement, 1980- .

164 The New Grove Dictionary of Music and Musicians. Ed. Stanley
     Sadie. London: Macmillan; distributed in USA by Grove's
     Dictionaries of Music, Washington, 1980. 20 vols.

165 New Musical Express. 1- . 1952- . London: IPC, 1952- .
     Weekly.

166 New Oxford History of Music. Ed. Jack A. Westrup, et al.
     London: Oxford University Press, 1954- .

167 New York (City). Public Library. The Research Libraries.
     Second Edition of the Dictionary Catalog of the Music Col-
     lection. Boston: G. K. Hall, 1982. 45 vols. (The first

edition appeared in 1964-1965, in 33 vols., with supplements
in 1966 and 1973. The new edition is supplemented annually
by the Bibliographic Guide to Music [Boston: G. K. Hall,
1975-], which includes also items catalogued in the Library
of Congress.)

168 Norton History of Music. New York: Norton, 1940-1966.
     8 vols.

169 Notes. 1-15. July 1934-Dec. 1942. Series 2, 1- . Dec.
     1943- . Washington: Music Library Association, 1934- .
     Quarterly.

170 Ochs, Michael. "A Taxonomy of Qualifications for Music Li-
     brarianship: The Cognitive Domain." Notes 33-1 (Sept.
     1976):27-44.

171 Opera. 1- . 1950- . London: Seymour, 1950- . Monthly.

172 Opera News. 1- . 1936/1937- . New York: Metropolitan
     Opera Guild, 1936- . Frequency varies; weekly during
     season.

173 The Organ; A Quarterly Review for Its Makers, Its Players
     and Its Lovers. 1- . 1921- . Melton Mowbray, Eng.:
     Musical Opinion, 1921- . Quarterly.

174 Oxford Companion to Music, by Percy A. Scholes. 10th ed.
     Ed. John Owen Ward. London, New York: Oxford Univer-
     sity Press, 1970.

175 Parsons, Denys. The Directory of Tunes and Musical Themes.
     Cambridge, Eng.: Spencer Brown, 1975.

176 Pearson, Mary D. Recordings in the Public Library. Chicago:
     American Library Association, 1965.

177 Penguin Stereo Record and Cassette Guide. New ed. Ed.
     Edward Greenfield, et al. Harmondsworth: Penguin, 1984.

178 Pickett, A. G., and Lemcoe, M. M. Preservation and Storage
     of Sound Recordings. Washington: Library of Congress,
     1959. (This study shows that vertical storage is preferable
     to horizontal storage.)

179 Randel, Don Michael. Harvard Concise Dictionary of Music.
     Cambridge: Belknap Press of Harvard University Press,
     1978.

180 Recorder and Music Magazine. 1- . 1963- . London:
     Recorder, 1963- . Quarterly.

181 Redfern, Brian. Organizing Music in Libraries. 2nd ed.
     London: Bingley; Hamden, Conn.: Linnet, 1978-1979.
     2 vols.

182 _____. "Public Lending Right: A New Law in the United
     Kingdom." Fontes artis musicae 27-3/4 (July-Dec. 1980):
     202-204.

183 Répertoire international de littérature musicale. RILM Abstracts.
     Ed. Barry S. Brook. New York: International RILM Center,
     1967- . 4 per year.

184 Répertoire internationale des sources musicales. International
     Inventory of Musical Sources. Published for the Interna-
     tional Musicological Society and the International Association
     of Music Libraries. Munich: Henle; Kassel: Bärenreiter,
     1960- .

185 Rezits, Joseph, and Deatsman, Gerald. The Pianist's Resource
     Guide. 2nd ed. Park Ridge, Ill.; San Diego, Calif.: Pall-
     ma Music Co., 1978. (A list by composer and title of more
     than 70,000 works, from the catalogs of about 1,000 publish-
     ers.)

186 Riemann, Hugo. Riemann Musik Lexikon. 12th ed. Ed.
     Willibald Gurlitt. Mainz, N.Y.: Schott, 1959-1969. 3 vols.
     Supplement (Ergänzungsbände) 1972-1975. 2 vols.

187 Rovelstad, Betsy. "Condensation of the Library of Congress
     M Classification Schedule." Notes: Supplement for Members,
     no. 34 (June 1963). (Quoted in ref. 115, pp. 340-341.)

188 Rules for Compiling the Catalogues of Printed Books, Maps and
     Music in the British Museum. Rev. ed. London: The Mu-
     seum, 1936.

189 Rust, Brian. Jazz Records, 1897-1942. Chigwell, Essex:
     Storyville, 1970. 2 vols.

190 Saddington, George H., et al. "Record Checking and Record-
     ing Damage Charging." Prepared for the Association of Lon-
     don Chief Librarians. Private document of the Association.
     London, 1967.

191 _____. "Some Personal Thoughts on a British National
     Discography." Audiovisual Librarian 1-2 (Autumn 1973):
     49-51.

192 _____, and Cooper, Eric. Audiocassettes as Library Ma-
     terials, 2nd ed. Hatfield, Polytechnic Library, P.O. Box 110,
     Hatfield, Herts. AL10 9AD.

193 Sadie, Stanley. "The New Grove." Notes 32-2 (Dec. 1976):
     259-268.

194 Saheb-Ettaba, Caroline, and McFarland, Roger B. ANSCR;
     The Alpha-numeric System for Classification of Recordings.
     Williamsport, Pa.: Bro-Dart, 1960.

195 Savage, Ernest A. "One Way to Form a Music Library."
     Library Association Record, series 4, 2 (March 1935):100-
     107. (Reprinted in ref. 196.)

196 _____. Special Librarianship. London: Grafton, 1939.

197 Schwann Record and Tape Guide. Boston: W. Schwann,
     1949- . Monthly. (Title varies.)

198 Sears, Minnie Earl, and Crawford, Phyllis. Song Index: An
     Index to More than 12,000 Songs in 177 Song Collections
     Comprising 262 Volumes. New York: Wilson, 1926. Song
     Index Supplement: An Index to More than 7,000 Songs in
     104 Collections Comprising 124 Volumes. 1934.

199 Sears List of Subject Headings. 12th ed. Ed. Barbara M.
     Westby. New York: Wilson, 1982.

200 Seibert, Donald. The MARC Music Format: From Inception to
     Publication. Philadelphia: Music Library Association, 1982.
     MLA Technical Reports, 13.

201 Shank, William, and Engelbrecht, Lloyd. "Records and
     Tapes." In ref. 23.

202 Sheehy, Eugene P. Guide to Reference Books. 9th ed.
     Chicago: American Library Association, 1976. Supplement,
     1980. Second Supplement, 1982.

203 Slonimsky, Nicolas. Music Since 1900. 4th ed. New York:
     Scribner, 1971; London: Cassell, 1972.

204 Smiraglia, Richard P., and Papkhian, Arsen R. "Music in
     the OCLC Online Union Catalog: A Review." Notes 38-2
     (Dec. 1981):257-274.

205 Smith, Joan Pemberton. "A Basic Stock List." In ref. 44,
     pp. 162-175.

206 Sounds. 1- . 1970- . London: Spotlight, 1970- .
     Weekly.

207 Spivacke, Harold. Review of Music Librarianship, by Eric
     Thomas Bryant. Library Quarterly 31-3 (July 1961):283-284.

208 Stevenson, Gordon. "Discography: Scientific, Analytical,
     Historical and Systematic." Library Trends 21-1 (July 1972):
     101-135.

209 Stevenson, Robert Murrell. "The Americans in European Music
     Encyclopedias: Part I." Inter-American Music Review 3-2
     (Spring-Summer 1981):159-207.

210 The Strad. 1- . 1890- . Sevenoaks, Eng.: Novello,
     1890- . Monthly.

211 Tempo. 1- . 1939- . London: Boosey and Hawkes,
     1939- . Quarterly.

212 Thorin, Suzanne, and Vidali, Carole Franklin. The Acquisition
     and Cataloging of Music and Sound Recordings: A Glossary.
     Philadelphia: Music Library Association, 1984. MLA Techni-
     cal Reports, 11.

213 Tovey, Donald Francis. Essays in Musical Analysis. London:
     Oxford University Press, 1935-1944. 7 vols.

214 Turner, Malcolm. "Conservation in Music Libraries." Fontes
     artis musicae 27-3/4 (July-Dec. 1980):183-201.

215 Ulrich's International Periodical Directory. 22nd ed. New
     York: Bowker, 1983. (There are about 800 entries for
     current periodicals under "Music." One authoritative esti-
     mate of the grand total of music journals published to date
     is 20,000 [ref. 52, p. 466].)

216 United Nations Educational, Scientific, and Cultural Organiza-
     tion (Unesco). Public Library Manifesto. Published in
     Unesco Bulletin for Libraries 26-3 (May-June 1972):130.

217 United States. Copyright Office. Catalog of Copyright En-
     tries, 1891-1946. Washington, D.C.: Government Printing
     Office, 1891-1947. Series 3, 1947- . (Published music is
     in a separate section. Format changes and complexities of
     this work are well described in Sheehy, ref. 202, at BH 52.)

218 United States. Library of Congress. Catalog Publication Di-
     vision. Music, Books on Music, and Sound Recordings.
     Washington, D.C.: The Library, 1953- . 2 per year.
     (From 1953-1972 titled Music and Phonorecords.)

219 _____. _____. Processing Department. Rules for De-
     scriptive Cataloging in the Library of Congress. Washing-
     ton, D.C.: The Library, 1949.

220 _____. _____. Subject Cataloging Division. Classifica-

tion, Class M. Music and Books on Music. 3rd ed. Washington, D.C.: The Library, 1978.

221 _____. _____. _____. Library of Congress Subject
Headings. 8th ed. Washington, D.C.: The Library, 1975.
2 vols. Supplements published quarterly.

222 Vaughan Williams, Ralph. "The Centenary Credo: Responsibility to Music." Library Assistant 43 (Aug.-Sept. 1950):111.

223 Voorhees, Anna Tipton. Index to Symphonic Program Notes in
Books. Kent, Ohio: Kent State University, School of Library Science, 1970. Keys to Music Bibliography, 1. Distributed by Libraries Unlimited, Littleton, Colo.

224 Walford, Albert John. Walford's Guide to Reference Material.
4th ed. London: Library Association; Distributed in North
America by American Library Association, Chicago, 1980-   .
(In progress. Coverage of music has not yet been reached
in the 4th edition; the 3rd edition, quoted here, included
entries for about 350 works on music.)

225 Walters, Irwyn R. Music and the Physically Handicapped.
London: Disabled Living Foundation, 1969.

226 Warrington Library and Museum. A Catalogue of Standard
Music Deposited in the Warrington Library and Museum by
Mr. Marsh. Appendix to the Library's book catalogue, 1850.
Warrington: Printed for the committee by Haddock & Son,
1850.

227 Watanabe, Ruth. "American Music Libraries and Music Librarianship: An Overview in the Eighties." Notes 38-2
(Dec. 1981):239-256.

227a _____. "Current Periodicals for Music Libraries." Notes
23-2 (Dec. 1966):223-235. (A more detailed survey of the
subject can be found in Watanabe's Introduction to Music
Research [ref. 228], Chapter 10. That chapter is strongly
recommended for an expert assessment of a far wider selection of periodicals than we have considered here.)

228 _____. Introduction to Music Research. Englewood Cliffs,
N.J.: Prentice-Hall, 1967. (New edition in preparation.)

228a Waters, Edward N. Personal letter to the author.

229 Weihs, Jean Riddle, et al. Nonbook Materials: The Organization of Integrated Collections. 2nd ed. Ottawa: Canadian
Library Association, 1979.

230 Wheeler, Joseph L., and Goldhor, Herbert. Practical Administration of Public Libraries. New York: Harper & Row, 1962.

230a Willemsen, Annie. "The Music Library for the Blind at the Amsterdam Public Library." Fontes artis musicae, 21-3 (Sept.-Dec. 1974):130-133.

231 Williams, Richard G. "A Service to Music." Graduate paper, College of Librarianship Wales, 1972.

232 Wohlford, Mary Kathryn. "A Study of Record Collections in Public Libraries of the United States and Canada." M.A. thesis, Kent State University, [Kent, Ohio] 1950.

233 Wright, A. Shaw. Herefordshire County Librarian. Personal letter, 1973.

234 Wright, Richard. Personal letter, 1972.

235 Cobbett, ref. 41, p. 284. This somewhat tantalising reference intrigued us sufficiently to do a little investigation. Cobbett himself apparently filed two applications for patents. The first, No. 4038 (12 Oct 1878) was for "Woven driving belts or bands" and the second, No. 8791 (21 July 1885) for "Strap forks or belt guides, faced with glazed porcelain." A third application in the name of W. W. Cobbett Ltd., No. 10128 (26 April 1912) concerned a design for "Cable suspending sling." This last would date after his retirement from Scandinavia Belting Ltd., and it would seem a reasonable surmise that the first patent (or possibly another patent in this same field whose rights he bought) produced his wealth. This was the period when factory machinery was changing from gear driven models, which lost a high proportion of the driving power in the process, to belt driven, which had a much greater efficiency.

236 I have not been able to find any statistical evidence for this, but all librarians consulted have agreed with the view expressed. At Romford Central Library, in the London Borough of Havering, a week's count of the number of users (April 1978) showed 426 male and 192 female. Some librarians have suggested that the disproportion in favour of male users increases with age.

237 A development dating from the mid 1970s, with techniques still advancing, is the method of turning the original program signal into digital form (i.e., computer language). The computer is programmed to recognize the main aberrations inherent in acoustic recording, such as resonances in the horn used. These distortions are removed as the music

is played. The method is reminiscent of that used on the
television pictures from the moon, which were similarly
"cleaned up" to remove extraneous and unwanted noise.

238   This is the Higher Education Learning Programme Information
      Service, 3 Devonshire St., London W1N 2BA, Council for
      Educational Technology in the United Kingdom.

239   Information supplied by St. Paul Public Library, Minn., in a
      letter dated 23 October 1968.

INDEX

This is a practical index, in which the entries are intended to anticipate likely approaches by the reader.
In general, passing references to persons, organizations,
or works are not indexed. Works that receive more sub-
stantive comment are indexed by title (the Bibliography
gives full information on all works cited, under author
or main entry). Certain topics have been clustered under a few principal headings in the index: Cataloging,
Classification, Music Libraries, and Sound Recordings.
Alphabetization is word-by-word. Acronyms and initial-
isms are filed like words.